AF806394

Local and Urban Governance

Series Editor

Carlos Nunes Silva, LISBOA, Portugal

This series contains research studies with policy relevance in the field of sub-national territorial governance, at the micro, local and regional levels, as well as on its connections with national and supranational tiers. The series is multidisciplinary and brings together innovative research from different areas within the Social Sciences and Humanities. The series is open for theoretical, methodological and empirical ground breaking contributions. Books included in this series explore the new modes of territorial governance, new perspectives and new research methodologies. The aim is to present advances in Governance Studies to scholars and researchers in universities and research organizations, and to policy makers worldwide. The series includes monographs, edited volumes and textbooks. Book proposals and final manuscripts are peer-reviewed.

The areas covered in the series include but are not limited to the following subjects:

- Local and regional government
- Urban and metropolitan governance
- Multi-level territorial governance
- Post-colonial local governance
- Municipal merger reforms
- Inter-municipal cooperation
- Decentralized cooperation
- Governance of spatial planning
- Strategic spatial planning
- Citizen participation in local policies
- Local governance, spatial justice and the right to the city
- Local public services
- Local economic development policies
- Entrepreneurialism and municipal public enterprises
- Local government finance
- Local government and sustainable development
- Anthropocene and green local governance
- Climate change and local governance
- Smart local governance

The series is intended for geographers, planners, political scientists, sociologists, lawyers, historians, urban anthropologists and economists.

Local and Urban Governance—now indexed in Scopus

Karl Kössler • Eva Maria Belser
Editors

Local Government Structure and Intergovernmental Relations

An Urban-Rural Perspective

Springer

Editors
Karl Kössler
Institute for Comparative Federalism
Eurac Research
Bolzano, Italy

Eva Maria Belser
University of Fribourg
Fribourg, Fribourg, Switzerland

ISSN 2524-5449 ISSN 2524-5457 (electronic)
Local and Urban Governance
ISBN 978-3-031-99819-5 ISBN 978-3-031-99820-1 (eBook)
https://doi.org/10.1007/978-3-031-99820-1

© The Editor(s) (if applicable) and The Author(s) 2026. This book is an open access publication.
Open Access This book is licensed under the terms of the Creative Commons Attribution 4.0 International License (http://creativecommons.org/licenses/by/4.0/), which permits use, sharing, adaptation, distribution and reproduction in any medium or format, as long as you give appropriate credit to the original author(s) and the source, provide a link to the Creative Commons license and indicate if changes were made.
The images or other third party material in this book are included in the book's Creative Commons license, unless indicated otherwise in a credit line to the material. If material is not included in the book's Creative Commons license and your intended use is not permitted by statutory regulation or exceeds the permitted use, you will need to obtain permission directly from the copyright holder.
The use of general descriptive names, registered names, trademarks, service marks, etc. in this publication does not imply, even in the absence of a specific statement, that such names are exempt from the relevant protective laws and regulations and therefore free for general use.
The publisher, the authors and the editors are safe to assume that the advice and information in this book are believed to be true and accurate at the date of publication. Neither the publisher nor the authors or the editors give a warranty, expressed or implied, with respect to the material contained herein or for any errors or omissions that may have been made. The publisher remains neutral with regard to jurisdictional claims in published maps and institutional affiliations.

This Springer imprint is published by the registered company Springer Nature Switzerland AG
The registered company address is: Gewerbestrasse 11, 6330 Cham, Switzerland

If disposing of this product, please recycle the paper.

Acknowledgement

This project has received funding from the European Union's Horizon 2020 research and innovation programme under grant agreement No. 823961.

Contents

Chapter 1
Local Government Structure and Intergovernmental Relations: Four Issues in Focus

Karl Kössler

Abstract This edited book assembles chapters that deal with issues regarding the structure of local government and the role municipalities play in intergovernmental relations. Within these broad thematic areas, research within a Horizon 2020 project on "Local Government and the Changing Urban-Rural Interplay—LoGov," which brought together the expertise of 18 partner institutions from six continents, has revealed several issues as particularly salient and under-researched from a global comparative perspective, namely decentralization within metropolitan areas, mergers and inter-municipal cooperation as tools to tackle structural challenges in rural areas, the role of local authorities in vertical intergovernmental conferences, and the representation of urban and rural interests through local government associations. This chapter provides short introductions to these four issues and presents the guiding questions for the case studies included in this volume.

Keywords Metropolitan governance · Decentralization · Mergers · Inter-municipal cooperation · Intergovernmental conferences, · Local government associations

This edited book assembles chapters that deal with issues regarding the structure of local government and the role municipalities play in intergovernmental relations. Within these broad thematic areas, research within a Horizon 2020 project on "Local Government and the Changing Urban-Rural Interplay—LoGov," which brought together the expertise of 18 partner institutions from six continents, has revealed several issues as particularly salient and under-researched from a global comparative perspective. These issues are decentralization within metropolitan areas, mergers, and inter-municipal cooperation as tools to tackle structural challenges in rural areas, the role of local authorities in vertical intergovernmental

K. Kössler (✉)
Institute for Comparative Federalism, Eurac Research, Bolzano, Italy
e-mail: karl.koessler@eurac.edu

© The Author(s) 2026

K. Kössler, E. M. Belser (eds.), *Local Government Structure and Intergovernmental Relations*, Local and Urban Governance,
https://doi.org/10.1007/978-3-031-99820-1_1

conferences, and the representation of urban and rural interests[1] through local government associations.

The case studies included in this volume, conducted across multiple countries, underscore the extensive geographical breadth of the LoGov project. While some of the core themes explored have been previously addressed in scholarly literature, the distinct contribution of this edited collection lies in its global comparative scope. To expand the analytical horizon, it includes lesser-known cases which have so far been understudied in relation to classical European cases. Anchored in a comparative framework, the volume adopts a multiple case study design (Yin, 2003, p. 56). This enables a systematic cross-case analysis while preserving the integrity of intra-case specificity. The aim is to identify convergences and divergences in how comparable governance challenges are addressed across different institutional, legal, and socio-political contexts, and to assess the potential for policy transfer and contextual adaptation.

Methodologically, the chapters enhance the credibility and robustness of their findings by using, to the extent possible in each case, multiple data sources (Patton, 2002, p. 38). Each case study endeavors to integrate multiple sources of evidence, contingent upon contextual feasibility and data accessibility. The interdisciplinary character of the volume—drawing upon the expertise of scholars specialized in public law, political science, and public administration—facilitates a methodologically pluralistic approach. Data sources include but are not limited to statutory and constitutional texts, judicial decisions, statistical data, reports issued by governmental and non-governmental organizations, and peer-reviewed publications from the three above-mentioned disciplinary fields.

While desk research has played a key role, our authors have, to varying degrees, also engaged in original field research. This includes, in particular, semi-structured interviews with local government stakeholders, conducted within the framework of the LoGov project's country reports,[2] which are referenced in the chapters where analytically pertinent. The synthesis of data from these diverse sources enables each case study to deliver a multidimensional analysis, enhancing descriptive richness, mitigating single-source bias, and producing robust, triangulated findings concerning the four salient issues identified above. These four overarching topics and their respective research questions structure the chapters assembled in this edited book.

1.1 Decentralized Governance Within Metropolitan Areas

Metropolitan areas, which can be defined as coherent territories with a large urban core and a socially and economically integrated periphery, have recently received increasing attention in research and beyond (Stren & Cameron, 2005, p. 275).

[1] This dualism is, of course, a simplification. Instead of a binary distinction implied by the thinking of an urban-rural divide, our point of departure is the recognition that it is more appropriate to speak of an urban-rural continuum and that local governments are located at different points of this continuum.

[2] https://www.logov-rise.eu/country-map/.

Academics predicted that the twenty-first century will be metropolitan because "[i]n the ongoing globalisation of economic, social and cultural processes, metropolitan areas play the role of nodal points where human activities concentrate" (Heinelt & Kübler, 2005a, p. 1). Policy papers of international organizations similarly started to speak of a metropolitan century, with some of them coupling this outlook with a warning that for such an age "the world has neither prepared nor adjusted" (Clark & Moonen, 2006; OECD, 2006; Stahl, 2011, p. 3–5). At the national level, the increasing relevance of metropolitan areas became reflected in law and/or policies. In Switzerland, for example, Article 50(2–3) of the Constitution obliges the national government since 1999 to consider the impact of all its activities on municipalities, especially "the special position of the cities and urban areas". In addition, the Tripartite Agglomeration Conference established 2 years later has enhanced collaboration between the three levels of government, not least regarding the country's five officially designated metropolitan areas. Section 155(1a) of South Africa's Constitution even goes as far as to define *metropolitan* municipalities as a distinct category. Currently, there are eight urban areas defined as such municipalities, each with populations of nearly one million inhabitants or more.

It seems crucial to recognize that this obvious increase in importance in research, law, and policy is linked to both the specific assets and specific challenges of metropolitan areas. As for their assets, certain economic and demographic dynamics are relevant. As the argument goes, economic globalization entailed a "metropolitan revolution" through which metro areas became part of a global mosaic (Katz & Bradley, 2013). Within this mosaic, metro areas would have interdependent commercial relationships with each other as both strong partners and competitors and enjoy the ideal scale to facilitate innovation (Sassen, 2001). The latter has been attributed, in particular, to the ability of metropolises to attract the "creative class" as a crucial driver of economic development (Florida, 2002). More generally, as huge agglomerations, these cities may exploit economies of scale and benefits of proximity due to a critical mass of territorially concentrated people and companies. These benefits are particularly significant in high value-added services and research-intensive sectors because they require a large, highly educated workforce (Odendahl et al., 2019, p. 14–18). In contrast to manufacturing, which tends to spread out over space in search of cheaper land and labor, these sectors cluster closely together in metropolitan areas and thus set in motion a virtuous circle: "Having a large labour pool of accountants attracts accountancy firms, for example, and the benefits of proximity trump the high cost of office space in rich cities" (Odendahl et al., 2019, p. 8). On the other hand, small cities are forced to find a unique niche because otherwise they would face "a relatively high likelihood of experiencing gambler's ruin" (Krugman, 2017).

Besides the assets that have made metropolitan areas so important, they also share specific challenges. Indeed, awareness of these challenges should put any rosy portrayal of a "triumph of the city" into perspective (Glaeser, 2011). Among them are congestion, environmental degradation, sharp inequalities, and problems linked to the use of urban space like gentrification, segregation, and unaffordable housing (Sellers & Hoffmann-Martinot, 2009; Florida, 2017). Importantly, deindustrialization exacerbated the coexistence of extreme wealth and extreme destitution.

Especially in North America, poverty became during the 1970s and 1980s a more concentrated and urban phenomenon (Hajnal, 1995). On the other hand, economic expansion has also had certain negative side effects on metropolitan areas, as sharp increases in housing prices due to population growth and speculation force people on lower salaries to move to peripheries ever further away from the city center (e.g., Dublin) (Pratschke & Morlicchio, 2023, p. 273).

Given the growing importance of metropolitan areas as places with quite specific assets and challenges, it hardly comes as a surprise that their governance has become a main subject of local government studies. For example, a classical comparative study from the early 2000s concentrated on issues like policy networks, state-society relations, and democracy in metropolitan areas (Heinelt & Kübler, 2005b). Another book observed that the fragmentation of metropolitan areas into many small local authorities makes it easier for subnational governments to dominate governance in these areas (e.g., Australia). By contrast, in the rarer cases of unified metropolitan governments, mayors are strengthened to a point that they may compete with higher government levels for power (Steytler, 2009, p. 404). Still, another volume pointed out that political boundaries rarely match the boundaries of metropolitan areas as economic and social spaces, which inevitably creates issues of coordinating public services and cost-sharing (Slack & Chattopadhyay, 2013). It identified several possible metropolitan governance structures (e.g., one-tier fragmented, one-tier consolidated, and two-tier structures, as well as voluntary cooperation, inter-municipal agreements, and special purpose districts). The volume concluded that institutional fragmentation is the rule and a one-tier metropolitan government the exception.

Against this background, our book focuses on a very specific aspect of the governance of metropolitan areas, namely decentralization within such areas by means of sub-municipal units (SMUs). Such units are characterized by having territorial jurisdiction over a part of the municipal territory, are multipurpose entities with responsibilities in different policy areas, and have democratic legitimacy through direct or indirect elections. However, SMUs are not a completely separate level of local government because their territorial jurisdiction over local affairs is not exclusive but shared with municipal institutions whose decisions are applicable without sub-municipal implementation (Hlepas et al., 2018a, p. 4). While SMUs have started to be explored by comparative research in some parts of the world, this phenomenon still requires analysis from a broader global perspective (Hlepas et al., 2018b, p. 256–257). We provide precisely such a perspective with insights from countries on different continents, that is, Canada, Mexico, Spain, and India. To focus on this issue seems timely because SMUs have been introduced or reformed in recent decades in several countries and because decentralization strategies in the context of ongoing urbanization are very likely to depend increasingly on these entities, if its promises of subsidiarity, efficiency, and accountability are to be realized (Swianiewicz, 2015, p. 173–174). In our case studies, we also explore other forms of decentralization within metropolitan areas, such as self-governing neighbourhoods, administrative city districts, and other forms of sub-municipal autonomy.

The reason why this book focuses on SMUs in metropolitan areas and disregards such entities in rural areas is because SMUs in these two contexts face very different conditions, tasks and challenges. First, they differ regarding their objectives. Being often established in rural areas in the wake of mergers, SMUs aim to preserve the historically grown identity of former municipalities and provide "compensation" for their loss of autonomy. Other objectives related to service delivery and participation seem to play a lesser role, except for territorially vast local governments covering several distinct villages. By contrast, the latter two rationales are at the very heart of SMUs in metropolitan areas. Such large and heterogeneous areas crucially depend on bringing governance closer to the people. Neighborhoods often have very different needs, which must be considered, if public services are to be tailored and efficient. Importantly, SMUs are key for participation, as they give a voice not only to *institutions* from various parts of a metropolis but also to their *citizens* (Hlepas et al., 2018a, p. 5–6). To achieve these aims of better service delivery and more participation, SMUs in metropolitan areas are typically much stronger in terms of organizational capacity, political clout, and financial resources than their counterparts in more rural areas (Hlepas et al., 2018b, p. 253–254).

If countries opt for metropolitan decentralization, they are confronted with several crucial questions. They must determine the status, reach, and the borders of SMUs while considering the need for flexibility and adaptability. They must divide power between the municipality and its units and establish mechanisms for metro-wide strategic planning and effective coordination. They must ensure that SMUs are empowered and staffed, that decision-making processes are inclusive, and decisions are implemented. They must finally ensure the financial viability of SMUs and, at the same time, prevent or overcome increasing inequality within urban spaces. To enable a comprehensive and comparative analysis of the insights on decentralization within metropolitan areas from our four case study countries (Canada, India, Mexico and Spain), all chapters assembled in section one of this volume respond to the same set of guiding questions:

1. Is the issue of local government being too big/too far away from the people relevant in metropolitan areas of your country? Have you experienced the division of local governments into SMUs? Have amalgamations been rejected with the argument that the new unit would be too big to govern legitimately and effectively?
2. What are the origins and rationales of SMUs? Are they, for instance, based on formerly independent and amalgamated units or the result of planning and design?
3. What is the legal status of SMUs? Are they based on constitutional or statutory law or on practice? Do all the metropolitan areas which are decentralized in your country follow the same regime or is there asymmetry in urban decentralization? Do all SMUs within the same city have the same legal status or is there a diversity of status?
4. What are the institutions and structures of SMUs? How do they make decisions and implement them? What are the competences, tasks, as well as financial and staff resources of SMUs?
5. What institutions and forums guarantee coordination across SMUs?
6. How can the legitimacy and efficiency of SMUs be assessed? What is their relevance in urban life? What future developments would you expect or recommend?

1.2 Mergers and Inter-Municipal Cooperation in Rural Areas

What has been called "the problem of smallness in rural local bodies" (Steytler, 2024, p. 584) is a pressing global issue which has gradually emerged because of the interconnected processes of industrialization and urbanization, first in Europe and during the twentieth century also in other parts of the world. Two widespread strategies to tackle the structural challenges faced by small rural municipalities are to merge local governments and to facilitate inter-municipal cooperation (IMC). While the two strategies are sometimes portrayed as alternatives due to their different pros and cons, the literature indicates that they are not mutually exclusive (Ostrom, 1972, p. 474). In fact, they often co-exist and complement each other in the same country and IMC has also been used in several cases as a transition phase towards amalgamation.

As far as mergers are concerned, it is key to recognize that they are not merely technical processes to scale up local governments to some (alleged) optimal size, whatever that might be, but inherently political and highly politicized processes (Reingewertz & Serritzlew, 2019, p. 607; Swianiewicz et al., 2022, p. 2). As such, these processes are dominated by countervailing arguments for and against amalgamations. The former typically revolve around considerations of efficiency. Small and sparsely populated municipalities in rural areas suffer from higher unit costs for the provision of services and infrastructure, making them unattractive for private investors. Rural local governments hence often struggle to implement (expensive) tasks, which are nevertheless crucial for their demographic and economic survival. This is because adequate services and infrastructure are decisive factors for the attractivity and accessibility of a place for (mobile) locals and for newcomers, which—through a virtuous circle—again reinforce accessibility (just as inaccessibility reinforces inaccessibility) (Farrington, 2007, p. 325). In this light, it is not difficult to see why the pursuit of more efficiency often leads policymakers to propose mergers for rural areas. Arguments are then about "production efficiency" in terms of services and infrastructure through economies of scale, but also about other things, such as increased administrative efficiency as a result of more specialized civil servants (Steiner et al., 2016, p. 35). The question, however, to what extent amalgamations really entail scale effects and thus allow municipalities to reduce costs is still far from being solved, as empirical research has provided mixed results (Reingewertz & Serritzlew, 2019, p. 604 and 607). As some studies suggest that economies of scale exhaust themselves with population size in larger local governments exceeding a certain threshold, there seems to be greater potential for such effects in the small rural municipalities that our book focuses on (Roesel, 2017, p. 22–36). The continuing uncertainty about scale effects is part of the bigger issue that ex post evaluations of mergers are, at least in European countries, not a standard practice and mostly carried out only in case of comprehensive one-off reforms but not for incremental reforms (Swianiewicz et al., 2022, p. 152–168).

Whereas efficiency arguments are used by advocates of mergers, their opponents typically bring forward various points related to identity. This is because local institutions are, especially in smaller rural municipalities, often the very centers of social and political life (Swianiewicz, 2010, p. 192). Following this rationale, smallness is therefore not always a problem, but can also be a virtue. For example, historically grown procedures of direct democracy like the town halls in the United States and the Swiss *Landsgemeinden* (assembly of all people entitled to vote) thrive upon a manageable population size of municipalities. In addition, voters in representative democracies may feel more connected with elected politicians in smaller jurisdictions (Lassen & Serritzlew, 2011). Yet, empirical research in this regard is inconclusive and suggests that in the case of mergers, an expected decrease of the local voter turnout (because of people feeling less connected) is only identifiable in the long run and to a limited degree (Reingewertz & Serritzlew, 2019, p. 605–607). There is some evidence that participation in local decision-making is enhanced by municipalities of limited territorial scale (the "small-is-beautiful" view). But the argument that it is, on the contrary, the greater scope of political issues in bigger municipalities that will engender a feeling of democratic ownership (the "large-is-lively" view) cannot be totally discarded. Therefore, much about the link between population size and participation remains unclear (McDonnell, 2019, p. 2).

As for the processes of amalgamations, a key factor to consider is whether small rural municipalities are actually in a position to oppose it. In fact, the intergovernmental dynamics of mergers are often top-down rather than bottom-up, with the national and/or subnational government being the driving force. In these cases, different degrees of coercion are typically involved. In several countries, amalgamations can easily be enforced either by subnational governments (e.g., Canada and Australia) or by an independent body (e.g., South Africa's Municipal Demarcation Board) without the approval of the local governments concerned. In other cases, there is an obligation of prior consultation of municipalities (e.g., Austria), but rarely a veto right. In this regard, most Swiss cantons are outliers, as their constitutions require a positive referendum vote and thus make mergers entirely "voluntary marriages" (Belser & Setz, 2013, p. 18). In Europe, the Charter of Local Self-Government provides that changes in local authority boundaries "shall not be made without prior consultation of the local communities concerned, possibly by means of a referendum" (Article 5). The evolving European consensus hence suggests that amalgamations cannot be made without, at least, consulting the local communities involved (and not just the local governments). If local governments or communities are involved, whether by having some input or the final say, they are often swayed by financial incentives for mergers. Given their widespread financial vulnerability and their difficulty in attracting capable local administrators, small rural municipalities can hardly refuse such "marriage bonuses" which frequently come as part of a "carrot-and-stick" strategy enforced by national and/or subnational governments (Ebinger et al., 2019, p. 8; Steiner et al., 2016, p. 31). In sum, even if processes have varied considerably, amalgamations have been implemented over the past five decades in a number of countries. Evidently, this has had the corollary of increasing the jurisdiction size of local governments (Blom-Hansen et al., 2016). When mergers have been optional, they have at times increased the (demographic) inequality of rural local governments, with some opting for amalgamations and others against them. Accepting smallness for identity (or other) reasons thus raises the question of whether asymmetric regimes must apply to rural communities.

Instead of creating larger municipalities through mergers, inter-municipal cooperation (IMC) has been another strategy to deal with the structural challenges that small rural local governments are confronted with. In fact, IMC has been touted as a "soft" alternative to amalgamation (Swianiewicz & Teles, 2018b, p. 4). After all, it similarly aims to benefit from economies of scale regarding public services, but allows for more flexibility, a variety of partners, and a selected set of joint services. At the same time, IMC preserves local autonomy because the legal status of the municipality is not changed. Moreover, local governments decide for themselves which services they provide *jointly* with other local governments or private suppliers and which ones they provide *directly on their own*. Given their greater knowledge about specific local circumstances, this seems to be an assessment that they are best suited to make themselves (Bish, 2000). Non-amalgamated municipalities also preserve the power to autonomously choose their cooperation partners and can sometimes produce a competitive environment for service delivery. While cooperation between municipalities was proposed as a tool to optimize public services as early as the 1960s, it has experienced a steep rise since the turn of the millennium around the world, especially in Europe (Ostrom et al., 1961; Swianiewicz & Teles, 2018a, p. 335–337). Two factors have been seen as key for this sharp increase in popularity (Bel & Sebő, 2023, p. 393). One is growing disillusionment with the cost-saving potential of forced amalgamation, and another one is a trend in many countries over the last decade of re-municipalization, which is linked to decreasing enthusiasm about efficiency gains through privatization of local services. While the efficiency of public services resulting from economies of scale has certainly been the main objective of IMC from the beginning, other objectives are also relevant. Among such aims are better quality, availability and equity of local services, joint policies regarding issues that transcend the boundaries of one single municipality, the coordination of public services in case of a fragmented local governments structure, the sharing of risks, and the pooling of expertise (Hertzog, 2010; Bel & Warner, 2015).

But how is IMC, which shall achieve all these goals, defined? There is a broad conception of it which encompasses "all arrangements where local governments co-operate with each other, with other public authorities or with private institutions". By contrast, a narrow understanding regards IMC as "purely inter-municipal co-operation" involving only local authorities (Hulst & van Montfort, 2012). For our edited volume, we rely on the latter—quite basic—working definition. Any more sophisticated conceptual frameworks would need to overcome the challenge that "diversity is the best word to describe IMC institutional landscape," and it is certainly not within the scope of this book to take on this challenge (Swianiewicz & Teles, 2018b, p. 9). Such diversity, which is reflected in the constant re-invention of IMC in pioneering countries like France, arguably also entails that any typology tends to water down the substantial differences in IMC arrangements between and within countries (Swianiewicz & Teles, 2018a, p. 338). Yet, typologies seem useful to some extent because they provide orientation. Quite common is the differentiation of four types of IMC, that is, quasi-regional governments, planning forums, service delivery organizations, and service delivery agreements, to which ad hoc project cooperation has recently been added as a fifth type (Hulst & van Montfort, 2012, p. 129–138; Franzke et al., 2016, p. 85). By contrast, those in favor of a "'post-typology' approach" prefer to limit themselves to listing several dimensions to distinguish IMC arrangements, such as their level of formalization (from quite informal cooperation typical of the United States, to inter-municipal associations as stand-alone organizations in other countries), the degree of voluntariness, their purposes, scope of functions, number of partners, nature of partners (e.g., other government levels and private actors), as well as their areas of cooperation (Swianiewicz & Teles, 2018b, p. 6–7). As for these areas, an important distinction is between policy coordination and joint service provision. The former is about "the regulation of externalities of local policies and the distribution of scarce resources in a way that is rational from a supra-local perspective" (Hulst & van Montfort, 2012, p. 125). The latter most often occurs in areas with considerable scale effects like school transport, water collection and waste management, tourism, and economic development more generally (Swianiewicz & Teles, 2018a, p. 341).

Expected economies of scale in these areas and resulting cost savings are the main motivations for local governments to engage in IMC. Yet, empirical research regarding financial effects has produced mixed results. Further studies are needed, for example, concerning the extra cost of more complex governance which results from the externalization of certain decisions and collective action problems in case of municipalities with heterogenous interests (Bel et al., 2023, p. 423–425). What appears to be clear, however, are savings in two cases, that is, for services with great potential for economies of scale and, importantly for our purposes, in case of IMC between small municipalities simply because they have a relatively greater potential for reducing the average cost of service delivery (Bel & Sebő, 2021; Franzke et al., 2016, p. 85).

Surprisingly, however, research suggests that in some countries (e.g., Spain and Poland), small local governments are actually less involved in cooperation than larger ones, perhaps due to insufficient organizational capacities to engage in IMC (Swianiewicz & Teles, 2018a, p. 340). Besides such capacities and an organizational culture that favors cooperation, other factors regarded as key for successful IMC, are, at least for metropolitan areas, strong leadership and external incentives (e.g., additional finances or more powers) (Heinelt & Kübler, 2005b). Whether that is similar or different in the case of cooperation in rural areas remains unclear. This is in line with the assessment that comparative studies regarding IMC have so far been focused on its drivers and cost reduction effects rather than on its functioning and the big question of what actually makes it work (or fail) (Swianiewicz & Teles, 2018b, p. 7; Bel & Sebő, 2023, p. 393).

Countries with large rural areas which struggle to efficiently deliver services are confronted with several crucial questions. They must either design a top-down territorial reform and impose amalgamations, incentivize bottom-up initiatives and encourage voluntary mergers, or find ways to improve service delivery without decreasing the number of (small) municipalities. As an alternative or—more frequently—complementary strategy, they must deal with IMC, possibly also by deciding not to interfere and allow local governments to autonomously determine if and how they cooperate with neighboring local governments or regional actors. More generally, they must ensure that constitutional values, such as democracy, equality, and transparency, are respected, and not hindered by unaccountable bodies and untransparent inter-municipal decision-making processes. Against this backdrop, the chapters in this book's second section aim to contribute to comparative research by exploring how our case study countries (Australia, Ethiopia, Italy and Poland) differ regarding their strategies to tackle the structural challenges of local governments in rural areas. To ensure coherence, the case studies address the following questions:

1. Do rural municipalities deliver on the promises of local government most relevant in the country concerned (providing public services, allowing for local development, etc.)?
2. What are the main strategies for dealing with the structural challenges of rural areas? Is there a top-down strategy, a variety of bottom-up approaches, or a combination of the two?
3. How does the country deal with amalgamations in rural areas? Is there a constitutional or statutory framework? Are there obligations or incentives to merge? How are amalgamations decided and implemented in political practice?
4. Once an amalgamation has happened, how does the country deal with the challenge that local government is now no longer as close to (all) the people as before? Do amalgamated units preserve local identities, institutions, and some public services?
5. How does the country deal with IMC? Is there a constitutional or statutory framework? Are there obligations or incentives to cooperate? Who decides about IMC and how does it work in practice? Is cooperation horizontal (only) or also vertical? Is it limited to subnational entities, or does it operate across subnational boundaries?
6. How does the country deal with the challenges linked to cooperation arrangements? Is there public participation and transparency, as well as democratic legitimacy and accountability (e.g., through elected or nominated officials in IMC structures)?
7. How do you assess the country's strategies for dealing with the structural challenges of rural areas? What future developments would you expect or recommend?

1.3 The Role of Local Authorities in Intergovernmental Conferences

Intergovernmental relations (IGR) are the "lifeblood" of any state premised on formal rules introducing a vertical distribution of responsibilities (Poirier, 2023, p. 79). Thus, they are of vital importance not only for federal systems with three levels of government, including subnational entities such as provinces, cantons, etc., but also for countries featuring merely national and local authorities. This generally holds true even if intergovernmental dynamics evidently differ depending on the number of government levels involved and the scope of functions that they perform.

The importance of looking beyond formal rules has been emphasized, in particular, by neo-institutionalist literature on local governance with an increasing focus not only on rules as "hardware" but also on the "institutional software" such as "skills, symbols and relationships" (Lowndes, 2005, p. 303). Whereas "old" institutionalism was very much about "formal organizations that set the rules and create the context for collective decision-making", its "new" variety looks at governance "through a complex interplay between formal and informal institutional forces" (Stoker, 2006, p. 495–496). This shift in research perspective went hand in hand, of course, with a noticeable trend towards local *governance*, involving private actors next to actors from local *government* proper. Such public-private collaboration came into fashion during the 1990s especially in the United Kingdom (Denters, 2011; Leach & Percy-Smith, 2001). The result is polycentric local decision-making with relatively autonomous players coming not only from different sectors, that is, public and private, but also from different levels of government. As some observers have put it, local government had traditionally been "conceived of as being based on geography (i.e., territory)" and is now much more "based on multilevel, intermunicipal, and multigovernment relationships" (Bergström et al., 2021, p. 278). A necessary corollary is that IGR of local governments are increasingly taking center stage.

As for the implications of this new mode of governance, views tend to differ. While some accounts paint a rather pessimistic picture of local governments becoming increasingly marginalized by other government levels or even by private actors (in line with the slogan of "governance without government"), others claim that they still play a pivotal role (Stoker, 2011). As a pioneer in studies on IGR of local governments pointed out, these relations may play out differently in federal and unitary countries because in the former the subnational level of government is traditionally the main point of reference for municipalities, which would often result in a weaker role of the national government (Goldsmith, 2005, p. 230). More recently, however, direct relations between the national and local levels have been identified as an emerging trend in a number of federal systems, especially regarding national legislation and financial issues that affect municipalities (Steytler, 2024, p. 575). But what does this increasing importance of the national government mean for the role of municipalities in intergovernmental relations? In most cases it does not give rise to a genuinely three-tiered system in which national, subnational, and local governments are on an equal footing. Indeed, the characterization of municipalities as "policy takers, not policymakers" seems to have a certain relevance because their focus is all too often on the implementation of policies "whose character has been determined by national or even international processes over which they have little control" (Leuprecht & Lazar, 2007, p. 2). In this regard, there is an enormous difference between urban and rural municipalities, as the world's big metropolitan cities play a clearly increasing role in policymaking in both the national and international arenas (Steytler, 2024, p. 585–86). Whereas at least smaller municipalities indeed often have a junior role within federal systems involving "two and a half partners", the increased importance of the national level regarding local government has sometimes also entailed a diminished role of *subnational* governments (Palermo & Kössler, 2017, p. 315). Indeed, it was at their expense that the central government in countries like South Africa, Brazil, and India has empowered municipalities, bypassing the level in between (Dickovick, 2007, p. 133; Watts, 1999, p. 133; Steytler, 2024, p. 540). Thus, it is not without any reason that subnational entities are sometimes deeply suspicious of a stronger role of local governments, especially of larger cities, in IGR. After all, the scenario of what has been called "hourglass federalism," in which subnational governments are squeezed out between the national and local government, has become a reality in some countries and fear of it is therefore not totally unfounded (Courchene, 2004, p. 12; Steytler, 2017, p. 362).

When assessing the role of municipalities in IGR, it is key to be aware of the distinction between informal and formal interactions with other levels of government. A case in point for formalized IGR is the participation of the South African Local Government Association (SALGA) as a non-voting member in sessions of the country's second chamber of parliament, the National Council of Provinces (NCOP), and in meetings of the President's Coordinating Council together with the provincial premiers (Powell & Ntliziywana, 2015, p. 299–305). In sharp contrast to South Africa, IGR of local governments in the United States stand out through a particularly low extent of formalization. Whatever that extent is in a single country, it is important to note that formal mechanisms are not the only means of IGR and sometimes not even the most relevant ones because, in reality, they sometimes "carry little weight in the multilevel policy decision process" (Leuprecht & Lazar, 2007, p. 18). Indeed, this process is also shaped, in some countries more than in others, by informal networks. Therefore, as pointed out regarding Spain, "personal knowledge and party politics really matter" regarding IGR (Agranoff, 2010, p. 177). In some countries like South Africa and Ethiopia, relations between governments can even be said to operate "under the cover of political parties" (Steytler, 2024, p. 575). As such, informal interactions can overshadow formal institutions or fill the void resulting from the absence of such institutions.

Against this background, our book seeks to explore the role that organized local government plays in intergovernmental conferences. For this book we define intergovernmental conferences broadly as all forums that bring together members of cabinet or senior civil servants from different levels of government irrespective of how these institutions of vertical IGR are called (conferences, councils, committees, etc.). Even if vertical intergovernmental conferences in a few countries also exist between legislators (e.g., India and South Africa), those bringing together actors from the executive branch (cabinet members and senior civil servants) seem for several reasons more relevant, especially for the purposes of our book (Poirier & Saunders, 2015; Palermo & Kössler, 2017, p. 253–254). First, conferences that assemble legislators typically involve only the national and subnational government levels, thus excluding municipalities. Secondly, institutions of IGR are generally characterized by a predominance of the executive branch (Palermo & Kössler, 2017, p. 253–256). This is also reflected in the fact that the work of such institutions is, especially in parliamentary systems with multiple government levels like Canada and Australia, sometimes equated with what has been termed "executive federalism" (Smiley, 1987, p. 83). Thirdly, executive-based intergovernmental conferences also appear to be particularly relevant because of a recent trend in local government. While strong executive leadership, especially through directly elected mayors, has been a longstanding phenomenon in, for example, US cities, this has become a more general trend worldwide (Denters & Rose, 2005, p. 255).

Previous research has demonstrated that vertical intergovernmental conferences exist in manifold forms and can be differentiated along various lines. Their dynamics can be top-down or bottom-up depending on what government level is induced to perform a certain action or refrain from it. Another distinguishing factor is the degree to which participation is voluntary. One would expect that actors are willing to participate when they expect certain advantages from joint decision-making. In this regard, four basic motivations for governmental actors have recently been identified: to influence other such actors, to protect their autonomy from external interference, to coordinate joint action, and to exchange information (Behnke & Mueller, 2017, p. 514). Another key factor is the extent to which vertical intergovernmental conferences are institutionalized. In fact, this may range from more or less regular meetings to a permanent infrastructure and the continuous publication of meeting protocols and other documentation (Behnke & Mueller, 2017, p. 510; Bolleyer, 2009, p. 18).

As for the importance of such conferences, they arguably play a greater role for smaller local governments because big cities often have other channels of access. The chapters in section three of our book explore the wide variety of vertical intergovernmental conferences in four case study countries (Italy, Poland, South Africa, and Spain). More precisely, they aim to shed light on the role that both urban and rural municipalities play (mostly mediated by local government associations) in such conferences. For the sake of coherence, the case studies are guided by the following questions:

1. What intergovernmental conferences exist that bring together actors from two levels (local-subnational and/or local-national) and three levels of government?
2. What is the real impact of these conferences on policymaking? Do they serve as venues for co-determining policies or only for communicating decisions already made by other government levels in a top-down manner?
3. What is the formal role and real impact of local government associations (LGAs) within these conferences? Can they count on regular meetings or call a meeting when they deem it necessary? Do LGAs have influence on the agenda-setting of conferences?
4. Does the greater political and economic power of large urban local governments result in a more influential role in intergovernmental conferences and/or do they make themselves heard through other (informal) channels?
5. Does a spirit of cooperation prevail in intergovernmental relations with higher levels of government?

1.4 Local Government Associations and the Representation of Urban and Rural Interests

There can be little doubt that the role and workings of local government associations (LGAs) which bring together municipalities is a rather under-researched topic, especially regarding comparative work. This continues to be the case in spite of several publications on this particular issue over the last two decades (Entwistle, 2002; Entwistle & Laffin, 2003; Callanan, 2012) and notwithstanding these assocations' arguably "growing importance" (Goldsmith & Page, 2010, p. 259). A lack of studies is even more evident concerning the delicate role in which organized local government often finds itself where it is expected to represent and promote differing urban and rural interests.

What can be said with certainty about LGAs is that they are quite unique hybrid organizations. To be sure, they have some characteristics of an interest group, as their core business is to lobby national and, where they exist, subnational governments. Yet, it has been rightly emphasized that LGAs are, due to their hybrid nature, not just another special interest group but obviously have—as umbrella organizations of local authorities—specific governmental features (Cigler, 2011; de Widt & Laffin, 2018, p. 1586). First, the benefits pursued are not exclusive to their members but of wider public interest. Secondly, LGAs are, due to informal contacts, typically closer to the policy makers they lobby, which can give them insider information and privileged access. Thirdly, they have been described as "topocratic," as their focus is on territorial interests as opposed to the functional interests of "technocratic" interest groups (Rhodes, 1986, p. 12).

The hybrid nature of LGAs also entails that they are often confronted with unique challenges when playing their role within IGR. First, the central task of organized local government as topocratic interest group is to "represent local concerns nationally," which is quite a challenge given the diversity of interests and priorities (Rhodes, 1986, p. 404). Moreover, the view from a national government and, possibly, subnational government is usually different, as their broader perspective pushes them, for example, to seek country-wide unification, harmonization, and coordination of local public services. In comparison, local governments tend to insist on diversity and autonomous service delivery.

Secondly, LGAs may struggle to find common ground due to the diversity of specific situations their members are in, which has several implications. First, the need to generalize may give rise to collective action problems. For example, the benefits which LGAs achieve in negotiations with other governmental actors may also be enjoyed by non-member municipalities, which could result in a free-rider issue. A question is then to what extent an LGA needs to provide particular services to its members (e.g., training events, policy reports, advice) to avoid their leaving of the association. Keeping a substantial share of all municipalities as their members is obviously a vital issue for LGAs because this lends credibility to their claim for comprehensive representation. Such representation is key for being recognized by higher government levels as a serious partner which can aggregate a maximum number of local views in the policy adoption phase and ensure that municipalities are involved in the co-creation of policies, thus facilitating compliance with decisions in the implementation phase. Other challenges resulting from the need to generalize in the face of local diversity are related to asymmetries in terms of the capacities of member municipalities, as their size, wealth, staff resources, etc., evidently vary enormously (Leuprecht & Lazar, 2007, p. 10). This situation is recognized, for instance, in South Africa's Municipal Finance Management Act, which speaks of local governments with high, medium, and low capacities and holds them, at least for a transitional period, to different standards (Steytler, 2007, p. 252). Besides the capacities of municipalities, their interests are another issue regarding which immense diversity prevails in many countries. This is because local governments differ significantly in terms of wealth, territorial size, population and, importantly for our book, their more urban or more rural character. Indeed, there seems to be much truth in the statement that "the divergence of interests makes organized local government speak in muted tones" (Steytler, 2024, p. 546). One might add that in other cases this divergence leads to a cacophony which is similarly detrimental to an effective representation of local interests.

Two strategies are common for the balancing act of reconciling diverse interests. The first is fragmentation into more than one LGA, with each representing specific interests so that a balance between urban and rural interests can be found *between* these associations. Many countries have two organizations, one for cities and one for other municipalities. Poland even features four associations of municipalities along the urban-rural continuum: the Union of Polish Metropolises, the Association of Polish Cities, the Association of Small Polish Towns, and the Association of Rural Communes. The second strategy is to have one single LGA with a broad membership base, including both urban and rural local governments which must attempt to balance diverse interests *within* the association.

Given that LGAs are still an under-researched topic, both regarding their representation of urban and rural interests and in a more general sense, we are only beginning to understand what factors really make them effective and successful actors in intergovernmental relations. For one, they certainly need to have a great ability to navigate a political arena in which the interests of parties and the bureaucracy of higher government levels often run contrary to the territorial interests of LGAs. This implies that they must have access to relevant policymakers, even if such access is not the same as influence (de Widt & Laffin, 2018, p. 1586). A question is then whether this access (and perhaps influence) increases when LGAs get close to party politics. In fact, partisan tendencies of associations are quite common and typically go hand in hand with an urban-rural divide on the ideological spectrum. In line with the preferences of their respective electorates, LGAs representing rural municipalities have more sympathies for conservative parties than those representing cities. However, it is evident that the potential benefits of party-political alignment may quickly become disadvantages in case of a change of government. While the ability to navigate the political arena can thus be seen as the political resource *par excellence* of LGAs, several other resources have been identified as crucial for their effectiveness: legal resources such as their recognition under public law (e.g., SALGA, as well as Austria's Association of Cities and Towns and Association of Municipalities) or their formal inclusion in procedures of intergovernmental decision-making[3]; financial resources because they determine power and independence; organizational resources like overall staff capacities, the degree of specialization, and facilities; and informational resources such as access to professional advice (Rhodes, 1986).

The aim of section four of our book is to contribute to a nascent literature on LGAs, especially regarding their representation of urban and rural interests. To achieve this goal, all chapters on our case study countries (Austria, Germany, and Switzerland) respond to the following guiding questions:

1. What is the formal position of LGAs in intergovernmental relations between the local level and the national and subnational levels of government?
2. What are the matters covered by these relations and do these matters differ for urban local governments (ULGs) and rural local governments (RLGs)?
3. How do national or subnational LGAs with a *general* membership base, i.e., those representing all types of local governments, deal with the challenge of representing the different interests of urban local governments (ULGs), on the one hand, and rural local governments (RLGs), on the other? How do LGAs with a *special* membership base, i.e., those promoting the specific interests of ULGs (e.g., associations of cities) or of RLGs, cooperate so that all interests are considered in policy-making?
4. What are the legal and political factors that make LGAs effective and successful actors in intergovernmental relations?

References

Agranoff, R. (2010). *Local governments and their intergovernmental networks in federalizing Spain*. McGill-Queen's University Press.

Behnke, N., & Mueller, S. (2017). The purpose of intergovernmental councils: A framework for analysis and comparison. *Regional & Federal Studies, 27*(5), 507–527. https://doi.org/10.1080/13597566.2017.1367668

Bel, G., Bischoff, I., Blåka, S., Casula, M., Lysek, J., Swianiewicz, P., Tavares, A. F., & Voorn, B. (2023). Styles of inter-municipal cooperation and the multiple principal problem: A comparative analysis of European Economic Area countries. *Local Government Studies, 49*(2), 422–445. https://doi.org/10.1080/03003930.2022.2041416

Bel, G., & Sebő, M. (2021). Does inter-municipal cooperation really reduce delivery costs? An empirical evaluation of the role of scale economies, transaction costs, and governance arrangements. *Urban Affairs Review, 57*(1), 153–188. https://doi.org/10.1177/1078087419839492

Bel, G., & Sebő, M. (2023). Intermunicipal cooperation: An assessment of drivers and effects. In F. Teles (Ed.), *Handbook on local and regional governance* (pp. 393–406). Edward Elgar.

Bel, G., & Warner, M. E. (2015). Inter-municipal cooperation and costs: Expectations and evidence. *Public Administration, 93*(1), 52–67. https://doi.org/10.1111/padm.12104

[3] See Sect. 1.3 above.

Belser, E. M., & Setz, R. (2013). The territorial structure of Federal Switzerland revisited—About the difficulty of being small. In S. Mangiameli (Ed.), *Federalism, regionalism and territory* (pp. 1–30). Giuffrè.

Bergström, T., Franzke, J., Kuhlmann, S., & Wayenberg, E. (2021). Future outlook and scenarios. In T. Bergström, J. Franzke, S. Kuhlmann, & E. Wayenberg (Eds.), *The future of local self-government: European trends in autonomy, innovations and central-local relations* (pp. 277–286). Palgrave Macmillan.

Bish, R. (2000). *Local government amalgamations: 19th century ideas for the 21st century*. Howe Institute.

Blom-Hansen, J., Houlberg, K., Serritzlew, S., & Treisman, D. (2016). Jurisdiction size and local government policy expenditure: Assessing the effect of municipal amalgamation. *American Political Science Review, 110*(4), 812–831. https://doi.org/10.1017/S0003055416000320

Bolleyer, N. (2009). *Intergovernmental cooperation: Rational choices in federal systems and beyond*. Oxford University Press.

Callanan, M. (2012). Subnational collective action: The varied patterns of mobilisation of local government associations. *Local Government Studies, 38*(6), 753–775. https://doi.org/10.1080/03003930.2012.683863

Cigler, A. (2011). Not just another special interest. In A. Cigler & B. Loomis (Eds.), *Interest group politics* (pp. 264–296). CQ Press.

Clark, G., & Moonen, T. (2006). *The role of metropolitan areas in the global agenda of local and regional governments for the 21st century*. https://www.gold.uclg.org/sites/default/files/LAVUE_EN.pdf

Courchene, T. (2004, April 1). Hourglass federalism. *Policy Options*, 12–17. http://irpp.org/wp-content/uploads/assets/po/budget-2004/courchene.pdf

de Widt, D., & Laffin, M. (2018). Representing territorial diversity: The role of local government associations. *Regional Studies, 52*(11), 1585–1594. https://doi.org/10.1080/00343404.2018.1462488

Denters, B. (2011). Local governance. In M. Bevir (Ed.), *The SAGE handbook of governance* (pp. 252–270). SAGE Publications.

Denters, B., & Rose, L. E. (2005). Toward local governance? In B. Denters & L. E. Rose (Eds.), *Comparing local governance: Trends and developments* (pp. 246–262). Palgrave Macmillan.

Dickovick, J. T. (2007). Municipalization as central government strategy: Central–regional–local politics in Peru, Brazil, and South Africa. *Publius, 37*(1), 1–20. https://www.jstor.org/stable/4624779

Ebinger, F., Kuhlmann, S., & Bogumil, J. (2019). Territorial reforms in Europe: Effects on administrative performance and democratic participation. *Local Government Studies, 45*(1), 1–23. https://doi.org/10.1080/03003930.2018.1530660

Entwistle, T. (2002). Explaining the birth of the Local Government Association. *Local Government Studies, 28*(1), 91–102. https://doi.org/10.1080/714004132

Entwistle, T., & Laffin, M. (2003). The multiple strategies of the Local Government Association: Partner, player or think-tank? *Policy and Politics, 31*(1), 37–50. https://doi.org/10.1332/030557303321095798

Farrington, J. H. (2007). The new narrative of accessibility: Its potential contribution to discourses in (transport) geography. *Journal of Transport Geography, 15*(5), 319–330. https://doi.org/10.1016/j.jtrangeo.2006.11.007

Florida, R. (2002). *The rise of the creative class*. Basic Books.

Florida, R. (2017). *The new urban crisis: How our cities are increasing inequality, deepening segregation, and failing the middle class, and what we can do about it*. Basic Books.

Franzke, J., Klimovský, D., & Pinterič, U. (2016). Does inter-municipal cooperation lead to territorial consolidation? A comparative analysis of selected European cases in times of crisis. In S. Kuhlmann & G. Bouckaert (Eds.), *Local public sector reforms in times of crisis: National trajectories and international comparisons* (pp. 81–98). Palgrave Macmillan.

Glaeser, E. (2011). *Triumph of the city: How urban spaces make us human*. Palgrave Macmillan.

Goldsmith, M. J. (2005). A new intergovernmentalism? In B. Denters & L. E. Rose (Eds.), *Comparing local governance: Trends and developments, government beyond the centre* (pp. 228–240). Palgrave Macmillan.
Goldsmith, M. J., & Page, E. C. (Eds.). (2010). *Changing government relations in Europe: From localism to intergovernmentalism*. Routledge.
Hajnal, Z. L. (1995). The nature of concentrated urban poverty in Canada and the United States. *Canadian Journal of Sociology, 20*(4), 497–528. https://doi.org/10.2307/3341855
Heinelt, H., & Kübler, D. (2005a). Introduction. In H. Heinelt & D. Kübler (Eds.), *Metropolitan governance in the 21st century: Capacity, democracy and the dynamics of place* (pp. 1–7). Routledge.
Heinelt, H., & Kübler, D. (Eds.). (2005b). *Metropolitan governance in the 21st century: Capacity, democracy and the dynamics of place*. Routledge.
Hertzog, R. (2010). Inter-municipal co-operation: A viable alternative to territorial amalgamation? In P. Swianiewicz (Ed.), *Territorial consolidation reforms in Europe* (pp. 289–312). OSI/LGI.
Hlepas, N.-K., Kersting, N., Kuhlmann, S., Swianiewicz, P., & Teles, F. (2018a). Introduction: Decentralization beyond the municipal tier. In N.-K. Hlepas, N. Kersting, S. Kuhlmann, P. Swianiewicz, & F. Teles (Eds.), *Sub-municipal governance in Europe: Decentralization beyond the municipal tier* (pp. 1–24). Palgrave Macmillan.
Hlepas, N.-K., Kersting, N., Kuhlmann, S., Swianiewicz, P., & Teles, F. (2018b). Conclusions. In N.-K. Hlepas, N. Kersting, S. Kuhlmann, P. Swianiewicz, & F. Teles (Eds.), *Sub-municipal governance in Europe: Decentralization beyond the municipal tier* (pp. 247–260). Palgrave Macmillan.
Hulst, J. R., & van Montfort, A. J. G. M. (2012). Institutional features of inter-municipal cooperation: Cooperative arrangements and their national contexts. *Public Policy and Administration, 27*(2), 121–144. https://doi.org/10.1177/0952076711403026
Katz, B., & Bradley, J. (2013). *The metropolitan revolution: How cities and metros are fixing our broken politics and fragile economy*. Brookings Institution Press.
Krugman, P. (2017, December 30). *The gambler's ruin of small cities (Wonkish)*. The New York Times. https://www.nytimes.com/2017/12/30/opinion/the-gamblers-ruin-of-small-cities-wonkish.html
Lassen, D. D., & Serritzlew, S. (2011). Jurisdiction size and local democracy: Evidence on internal political efficacy from large-scale municipal reform. *American Political Science Review, 105*(2), 238–258. https://doi.org/10.1017/S000305541100013X
Leach, R., & Percy-Smith, J. (2001). *Local governance in Britain*. Palgrave.
Leuprecht, C., & Lazar, H. (2007). From multilevel to 'multi-order' governance? In H. Lazar & C. Leuprecht (Eds.), *Spheres of governance: Comparative studies of cities in multilevel governance systems* (pp. 1–21). McGill–Queen's University Press.
Lowndes, V. (2005). Something old, something new, something borrowed: How institutions change (and stay the same) in local governance. *Policy Studies, 26*(3/4), 291–309.
McDonnell, J. (2019). Municipality size, political efficacy and political participation: A systematic review. *Local Government Studies, 46*(3), 331–350. https://doi.org/10.1080/03003930.2019.1600510
Odendahl, C., Springford, J., Johnson, S., & Murray, J. (2019, May). *The big European sort? The diverging fortunes of Europe's regions* (pp. 1–18). Centre for European Reform. https://www.cer.eu/sites/default/files/pbrief_eusort_2030_21.5.2019.pdf#:~:text=Fewer%20have%20considered%20how%20structural%20economic%20changes%20have,fortunes%20among%20its%20rural%20regions%2C%20towns%20and%20cities
OECD. (2006). *Competitive cities in the global economy*. OECD. https://read.oecd-ilibrary.org/urban-rural-and-regional-development/competitive-cities-in-the-global-economy_9789264027091-en
Ostrom, E. (1972). Metropolitan reform: Propositions derived from two traditions. *Social Science Quarterly, 53*(3), 474–493. https://www.jstor.org/stable/42860228

Ostrom, V., Tiebout, C. M., & Warren, R. (1961). The organization of government in metropolitan areas: A theoretical inquiry. *American Political Science Review, 55*(4), 831–842. https://doi.org/10.2307/1952530

Palermo, F., & Kössler, K. (2017). *Comparative federalism: Constitutional arrangements and case law*. Hart Publishing.

Patton, M. Q. (2002). *Qualitative evaluation and research methods*. Thousand Oaks.

Poirier, J. (2023). Intergovernmental relations: The lifeblood of federalism. In J. Kincaid & J. Wesley Leckrone (Eds.), *Teaching federalism: Multidimensional approaches* (pp. 79–90). Edward Elgar.

Poirier, J., & Saunders, C. (2015). Conclusion: Comparative experience of intergovernmental relations in federal systems. In J. Poirier et al. (Eds.), *Intergovernmental relations in federal systems: Comparative structures and dynamics* (pp. 451–455). Oxford University Press.

Powell, D., & Ntliziywana, P. (2015). 'South Africa Inc.': The rise of the developmental state and the corporatization of intergovernmental relations. In F. Palermo & E. Alber (Eds.), *Federalism as decision-making: Changes in structures, procedures and policies* (pp. 292–314). Brill–Nijhoff.

Pratschke, J., & Morlicchio, E. (2023). Poverty and social cohesion in metropolitan areas. In F. Teles (Ed.), *Handbook on local and regional governance* (pp. 267–281). Edward Elgar.

Reingewertz, Y., & Serritzlew, S. (2019). Special issue on municipal amalgamations: Guest editors' introduction. *Local Government Studies, 45*(5), 603–610. https://doi.org/10.1080/03003930.2019.1615465

Rhodes, R. A. W. (1986). *The national world of local government*. Allen and Unwin.

Roesel, F. (2017). Do mergers of large local governments reduce expenditures? Evidence from Germany using the synthetic control method. *European Journal of Political Economy, 50*, 22–36. https://doi.org/10.1016/j.ejpoleco.2017.10.002

Sassen, S. (2001). *The Global City: New York, London, Tokyo*. Princeton University Press.

Sellers, J. M., & Hoffmann-Martinot, V. (2009). Metropolitan governance. In UCLG (Ed.), *World report on decentralization and local democracy* (pp. 255–279). UCLG.

Slack, E., & Chattopadhyay, R. (Eds.). (2013). *Governance and finance of metropolitan areas in federal systems*. Oxford University Press.

Smiley, D. (1987). *The federal condition in Canada*. McGraw-Hill Ryerson.

Stahl, G. (2011). Foreword. In G. Stahl & R. Chattopadhyay (Eds.), *Governance of metropolitan regions—European and global experiences*. Forum of Federations; Committee of the Regions.

Steiner, R., Kaiser, C., & Eythórsson, T. G. (2016). A comparative analysis of amalgamation reforms in selected European countries. In S. Kuhlmann & G. Bouckaert (Eds.), *Local public sector reforms in times of crisis: National trajectories and international comparisons* (pp. 23–42). Palgrave Macmillan.

Steytler, N. (2007). National, provincial, and local relations: An uncomfortable menage a trois. In H. Lazar & C. Leuprecht (Eds.), *Spheres of governance: Comparative studies of cities in multilevel governance systems* (pp. 229–256). McGill–Queen's University Press.

Steytler, N. (2009). Comparative conclusions. In N. Steytler (Ed.), *Local government and metropolitan regions in federal systems*. McGill–Queens University Press.

Steytler, N. (2017). The Constitutional Court of South Africa: Reinforcing South Africa's hourglass system of multilevel government. In N. Aroney & J. Kincaid (Eds.), *Courts in federal countries: Federalists or unitarists?* University of Toronto Press.

Steytler, N. (2024). Comparative conclusions. In N. Steytler (Ed.), *The Forum of Federations handbook on local government in federal systems*. Palgrave Macmillan.

Stoker, G. (2006). Comparative local governance. In R. Rhodes, S. Binder, & B. Rockman (Eds.), *The Oxford handbook of political institutions* (pp. 497–515). Oxford University Press.

Stoker, G. (2011). Was local governance really such a good idea? A global comparative perspective. *Public Administration, 89*(1), 15–31. https://doi.org/10.1111/j.1467-9299.2011.01900.x

Stren, R., & Cameron, R. (2005). Guest editor's preface metropolitan governance reform: An introduction. *Public Administration and Development, 25*(4), 275–284. https://doi.org/10.1002/pad.381

Swianiewicz, P. (2010). If territorial fragmentation is a problem, is amalgamation a solution? An East European perspective. *Local Government Studies, 36*(2), 183–203. https://doi.org/10.1080/03003930903560547

Swianiewicz, P. (2015). Intra-municipal units in urban political systems in Poland: Vicious roundabout of marginalization or dead-end street? *Journal of Public Administration and Policy, 7*(2), 173–198. https://doi.org/10.2478/nispa-2014-0008

Swianiewicz, P., Gendźwiłł, A., Houlberg, K., & Klausen, J. E. (2022). *Municipal territorial reforms of the 21st century in Europe* (1st ed.). Routledge.

Swianiewicz, P., & Teles, F. (2018a). Inter-municipal cooperation diversity, evolution and future research agenda. In F. Teles & P. Swianiewicz (Eds.), *Inter-municipal cooperation in Europe: Institutions and governance* (pp. 335–350). Palgrave Macmillan.

Swianiewicz, P., & Teles, F. (2018b). Motives for revisiting inter-municipal cooperation. In F. Teles & P. Swianiewicz (Eds.), *Inter-municipal cooperation in Europe: Institutions and governance* (pp. 1–13). Palgrave Macmillan.

Watts, R. L. (1999). *Comparing federal systems* (2nd ed.). McGill–Queen's University Press.

Yin, R. K. (2003). *Case study research: Design and methods*. Thousand Oaks.

Open Access This chapter is licensed under the terms of the Creative Commons Attribution 4.0 International License (http://creativecommons.org/licenses/by/4.0/), which permits use, sharing, adaptation, distribution and reproduction in any medium or format, as long as you give appropriate credit to the original author(s) and the source, provide a link to the Creative Commons license and indicate if changes were made.

The images or other third party material in this chapter are included in the chapter's Creative Commons license, unless indicated otherwise in a credit line to the material. If material is not included in the chapter's Creative Commons license and your intended use is not permitted by statutory regulation or exceeds the permitted use, you will need to obtain permission directly from the copyright holder.

Part I
Decentralized Governance Within Metropolitan Areas

Chapter 2
Strange Multiplicity: Diverse Patterns of Governance for Canadian Metropolitan Areas

Zack Taylor

Abstract This chapter relates two scales of governance and political representation that are inextricable, but which are rarely considered together: the metropolitan and the municipal. The contemporary effectiveness and legitimacy of local governance, and the capacity of local institutions to articulate conflict, depends in large part on how these inherited institutions are "wired up", and how contemporary actors use them. This chapter provides a window on the wide variation in institutional arrangements found in Canada, which has been enabled by federalism (provincial jurisdiction over local government), fiscal decentralization, and the non-integration of local politics with provincial and federal party systems. Canada's decentralized federalism and dispersed urban system have enabled considerable institutional experimentation since World War II, especially over the past 25 years. The result is a differentiated patchwork of institutional structures and models. This variation is illustrated first through descriptive analyses of the relative institutional consolidation of local governance and intensity of political representation in Canada's 41 metropolitan areas, and then through a comparison of Toronto and Montréal's very different coordinating and representational structures. Convergence on a single model is unlikely to occur; rather, experimentation will continue in ways that defy easy generalization.

Keywords Political representation · Metropolitan governance · Local governance · Multilevel governance · Institutional change · Canada

Z. Taylor (✉)
Department of Political Science, Western University, London, ON, Canada
e-mail: zack.taylor@uwo.ca

© The Author(s) 2026

K. Kössler, E. M. Belser (eds.), *Local Government Structure and Intergovernmental Relations*, Local and Urban Governance,
https://doi.org/10.1007/978-3-031-99820-1_2

2.1 Introduction

Canada is a curious case. One the one hand, it is a country whose population is highly urbanized and concentrated in a limited number of mostly geographically isolated urban regions. On the other hand, it appears to have weaker metropolitan governance, as evidenced by the paucity and modest role of metropolitan institutions, than is warranted given the numerosity of municipal governments, and associated coordination problems. Closer inspection reveals that this apparent institutional underdevelopment is the product of a conjuncture of factors. *Federalism* is the most obvious institutional factor. As the Canadian Constitution assigns jurisdiction over local government to the provinces, each province has its own legislative framework for the establishment and legal authorization of local governments, including general-purpose municipalities and special-purpose bodies of various kinds, and has erected elaborate administrative machinery to manage "municipal affairs" (Taylor & Dobson, 2019). Provinces set the rules of the local game through laws, regulations, institution-building, and fiscal arrangements. These include conditional grants and rules governing municipal borrowing. They also define authority related to land-use planning and the internal processes and structures of local government administration. Some provinces, including New Brunswick, Nova Scotia, Ontario, and Québec, have used their constitutional powers to unilaterally amalgamate smaller municipalities into larger ones, while others have taken a more laissez-faire approach. The federal government acts primarily as a funder of capital projects and human-services programs in its areas of jurisdiction. Canada's decentralized federalism has produced considerable interprovincial variation in the organizational structure and responsibilities of local and metropolitan governance, producing a wide range of models across the country.

A second and less visible factor is *fiscal decentralization*. Unlike in some other countries, where grants from national governments fund a substantial proportion of local budgets, Canadian municipal budgets for operating purposes are mostly funded by local property taxes and user fees, and a considerable proportion of capital spending is financed through local development exactions and borrowing. Heavy reliance on the local property tax intensifies intermunicipal competition for investment, both within and between metropolitan areas. Under such conditions, voluntary intermunicipal collaboration on important policy initiatives is disincentivized. No municipality's leaders or voters are likely to accept localized losses in pursuit of aggregate benefits—a dynamic that Scharpf (1988, 2006) calls the "joint-decision trap" (see also Taylor, 2019a). While provincial governments have absolute constitutional authority over local government, provinces have largely expected municipalities to finance their own operations and manage service delivery within their territorial jurisdiction as they see fit.

The final factor is *political autonomy*. Local elections are officially nonpartisan in all provinces save British Columbia and Québec. (The Alberta government recently changed the law to permit local political parties to register to compete in the Calgary and Edmonton general elections in 2026.) There, municipal-level political parties or electoral slates are purely local affairs and often constructed around mayoral candidates, rather than extensions of provincial or federal parties. While many local politicians are personally affiliated with provincial or federal political parties, party linkages do not function as an alternative conduit of vertical policy influence (upwards or downwards), nor do they coordinate horizontal political relationships across municipal boundaries within metropolitan areas.

These factors complicate generalization about the governance and politics of Canadian cities. Where local government is fragmented—that is, the metropolitan area contains numerous local governments, of which the central municipality is one actor among many—political conflicts are more likely to play out *between* rather than *within* municipalities. In such institutional environments, provincial governments have sometimes chosen to promote policy coordination and limit destructive competition by creating metropolitan institutions and policy frameworks. Where local government is highly consolidated—that is, the metropolitan area contains few and larger local governments, and/or the central municipality is dominant—important political conflicts are more likely to play out *within* rather than *between* municipalities. The internal structures of representation and decision-making likely matter a great deal within large, more heterogeneous municipalities. We therefore see a multiplicity of governance forms across Canada, with significant variation in local political representation and horizontal and vertical intergovernmental relationships (Hamilton et al., 2004).

Building on these insights, this chapter describes and explores the relationship between supra- or inter-municipal institutions at the metropolitan scale, on the one hand, and municipal or infra-municipal governance arrangements, on the other. In so doing I illustrate that provincial governments have, through the cumulation of institutional design choices, established governance systems that channel political conflict among place-based interests (urban, rural, and suburban) into different institutional venues at a variety of scales.

To illustrate this variation, this chapter first provides an overview of urbanization and metropolitan concentration in Canada, as well as the degree to which local jurisdiction and political representation are fragmented within metropolitan areas. This enables interrogation of the quality of local democratic responsiveness in relation to institutional organization (i.e., whether government is too large or distant). The following section briefly describes the legal, institutional, and political characteristics of metropolitan and local governance in Canada's two largest city-regions, Toronto and Montréal. The chapter concludes with a discussion of potential future developments.

2.2 Metropolitan and Local Governance: An Overview

2.2.1 Local Government Consolidation in Metropolitan Areas

Almost three-quarters of the Canadian population lives in 41 Census Metropolitan Areas (CMAs), defined by Statistics Canada as commuter zones with populations of greater than 100,000 (see Table 2.1).[1] While statistical authorities do not do so, we may consider contiguous CMAs in greater Toronto and Vancouver to be single

[1] Whether the CMA construct meaningfully represents metropolitan spheres of influence beyond commuting patterns, for example with respect to housing markets, economic linkages, and ecosys-

"megaregions". The population of the nine CMAs that comprise the Toronto megaregion is almost 8.6 million people, or 24% of the national population.[2] A further 12% live in the Montréal CMA, and 7% in the Vancouver-centred Lower Mainland megaregion. An additional 27.1% live in the other, smaller CMAs. The remainder live in smaller cities, towns, and rural areas. Excepting the less urbanized Atlantic Canadian provinces (New Brunswick, Nova Scotia, Prince Edward Island, and Newfoundland and Labrador), most provinces have metropolitan majorities. The largest CMA or megaregion comprises more than half the provincial population in British Columbia, Manitoba, Ontario, and Québec, and Alberta's CMAs together comprise a majority in that province.

As Table 2.1 shows, most metropolitan areas are divided into multiple municipalities. The central municipality is often, but not always, the most populous municipality in the metropolitan area. Figure 2.1 visualizes two indicators of local government consolidation. The horizontal axis indicates central-city dominance—the proportion of the metropolitan population that lives in the core municipality. The vertical axis indicates institutional fragmentation outside the central city—the number of suburban governments per 10,000 suburban residents. The distribution pattern is intriguing. There is considerable variation in the relative dominance of central cities within their metropolitan areas. At one extreme are core-dominant metropolitan areas such as Red Deer, Halifax, Greater Sudbury, Winnipeg, and Calgary; at the other extreme are polycentric regions such as Vancouver and Victoria, where the central city is but one node of settlement among many, and by no means the one with the largest population in the metropolitan area.

There is also some variation in suburban government fragmentation, although intriguingly it occurs entirely in smaller core-dominant metropolitan areas. Polycentric metropolitan areas tend to have fewer suburban local governments than core-dominant ones in proportion to population. Why this is the case depends on each region's idiosyncratic history of municipal incorporation, urban growth, and provincially imposed institutional change. For example, municipal mergers imposed by the Ontario provincial government in larger metropolitan areas (e.g., Toronto, St. Catherines-Niagara, and Ottawa) re-organized suburban areas into fewer, more populous municipalities. This stands in contrast to "unreformed," mostly smaller, metropolitan areas in British Columbia (e.g., Kamloops and Nanaimo) and Québec (e.g., Drummondville and Saguenay) where the central city is surrounded by numerous suburban municipalities with relatively small populations.

---

tem services, is debatable. As Sancton (2008) notes, urbanization is inherently unbounded, any particular definition of a region will soon be obsolete.

[2]The 58-municipality Toronto megaregion defined here corresponds imperfectly to the Ontario government's "Greater Golden Horseshoe" policy area, which contains 101 lower- and single-tier municipalities. The additional 43 municipalities are non-metropolitan, mostly rural jurisdictions.

Table 2.1 Canadian metropolitan areas

CMAs grouped where appropriate into contiguous "mega-regions"	Population in municipalities	Number of municipal governments	Central city population	Central city as % of CMA population	CMA/ Region as % of national population	Cumulative share of national population
Greater Golden Horseshoe (Ontario)	**9,061,585**	**58**			**24.5%**	**24.5%**
Toronto (Ontario)	6,201,994	23	2,794,356	45.1%	16.8%	
Hamilton (Ontario)	785,184	3	569,353	72.5%	2.1%	
Kitchener—Cambridge—Waterloo (Ontario)	575,847	6	256,885	44.6%	1.6%	
St. Catharines—Niagara (Ontario)	433,604	10	136,803	31.6%	1.2%	
Oshawa (Ontario)	415,311	3	175,383	42.2%	1.1%	
Barrie (Ontario)	212,856	3	147,829	69.5%	0.6%	
Guelph (Ontario)	165,588	3	143,740	86.8%	0.4%	
Brantford (Ontario)	144,162	2	104,688	72.6%	0.4%	
Peterborough (Ontario)	127,039	5	83,651	65.8%	0.3%	
Montréal (Quebec)	4,291,732	91	1,762,949	41.1%	11.6%	36.1%
Lower Mainland (British Columbia)	**2,934,583**	**26**			**7.9%**	**44.0%**
Vancouver (British Columbia)	2,632,013	21	662,248	25.2%	7.1%	
Abbotsford—Mission (British Columbia)	195,043	2	153,524	78.7%	0.5%	

(continued)

Table 2.1 (continued)

CMAs grouped where appropriate into contiguous "mega-regions"	Population in municipalities	Number of municipal governments	Central city population	Central city as % of CMA population	CMA/ Region as % of national population	Cumulative share of national population
Chilliwack (British Columbia)	107,527	3	93,203	86.7%	0.3%	
Ottawa—Gatineau (Ontario-Québec)	1,488,307	25	1,017,449	68.4%	4.0%	48.1%
Calgary (Alberta)	1,481,806	8	1,306,784	88.2%	4.0%	52.1%
Edmonton (Alberta)	1,414,215	30	1,010,899	71.5%	3.8%	55.9%
Québec (Quebec)	837,111	29	549,459	65.6%	2.3%	58.1%
Winnipeg (Manitoba)	834,244	12	749,607	89.9%	2.3%	60.4%
London (Ontario)	543,551	8	422,324	77.7%	1.5%	61.9%
Halifax (Nova Scotia)	462,711	2	439,819	95.1%	1.3%	63.1%
Windsor (Ontario)	422,630	8	229,660	54.3%	1.1%	64.3%
Victoria (British Columbia)	391,950	13	91,867	23.4%	1.1%	65.3%
Saskatoon (Saskatchewan)	316,969	24	266,141	84.0%	0.9%	66.2%
Regina (Saskatchewan)	249,217	19	226,404	90.8%	0.7%	66.9%
Sherbrooke (Quebec)	227,398	11	172,950	76.1%	0.6%	67.5%
St. John's (Newfoundland and Labrador)	212,579	14	110,525	52.0%	0.6%	68.0%
Kelowna (British Columbia)	209,415	4	144,576	69.0%	0.6%	68.6%
Kingston (Ontario)	172,546	4	132,485	76.8%	0.5%	69.1%
Greater Sudbury/Grand Sudbury (Ontario)	170,069	3	166,004	97.6%	0.5%	69.5%

Table 2.1 (continued)

CMAs grouped where appropriate into contiguous "mega-regions"	Population in municipalities	Number of municipal governments	Central city population	Central city as % of CMA population	CMA/ Region as % of national population	Cumulative share of national population
Saguenay (Quebec)	161,567	10	144,723	89.6%	0.4%	70.0%
Trois-Rivières (Quebec)	161,295	6	139,163	86.3%	0.4%	70.4%
Moncton (New Brunswick)	157,681	7	79,470	50.4%	0.4%	70.8%
Saint John (New Brunswick)	130,613	6	69,895	53.5%	0.4%	71.2%
Lethbridge (Alberta)	123,847	7	98,406	79.5%	0.3%	71.5%
Thunder Bay (Ontario)	122,294	7	108,843	89.0%	0.3%	71.9%
Nanaimo (British Columbia)	114,505	2	99,863	87.2%	0.3%	72.2%
Belleville—Quinte West (Ontario)	111,184	4	55,071	49.5%	0.3%	72.5%
Kamloops (British Columbia)	109,854	4	97,902	89.1%	0.3%	72.8%
Fredericton (New Brunswick)	107,022	5	63,116	59.0%	0.3%	73.0%
Drummondville (Quebec)	101,610	12	79,258	78.0%	0.3%	73.3%
Red Deer (Alberta)	100,844	1	100,844	100.0%	0.3%	73.6%
Census metropolitan areas	**27,224,934**	**460**			**73.6%**	
Non-metropolitan areas (Canada)	9,388,945	3077			25.4%	100.00%
Indigenous authorities	378,102					
Canada	36,991,981	3537			100.0%	

Source: Statistics Canada, Census of Population 2021. Indigenous authorities include Indian Reserves and other Indigenous unincorporated or special-purpose authorities. CMA population totals do not include Indigenous jurisdictions or unincorporated areas. Municipal government counts do not include upper-tier governments in two-tier systems

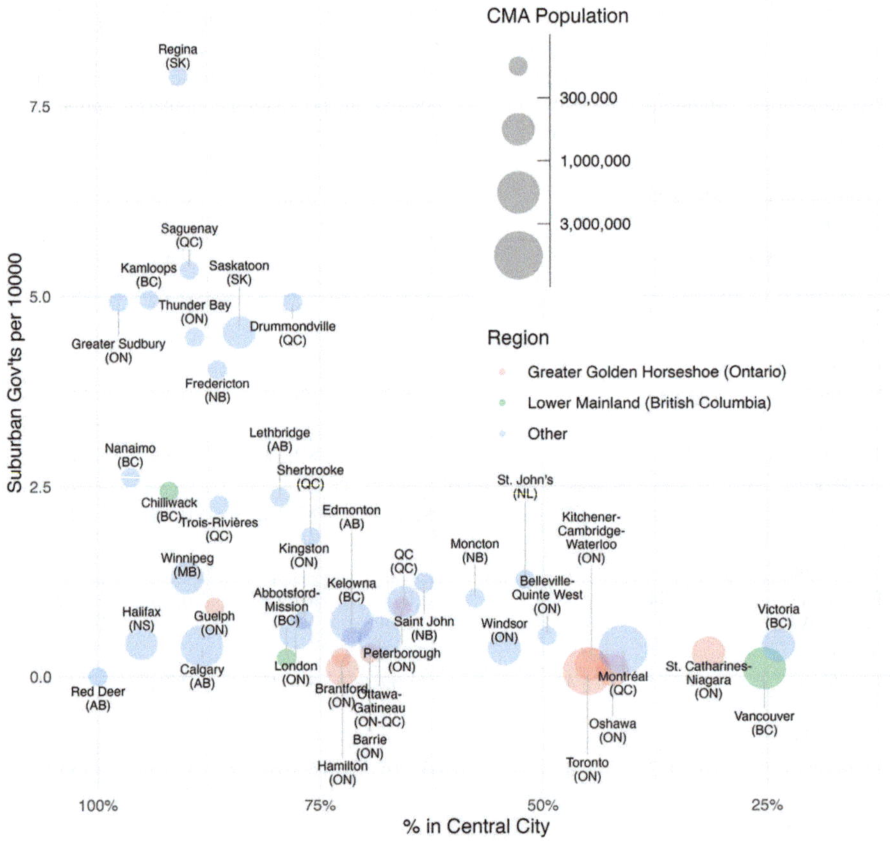

Fig. 2.1 Local government consolidation and central-city dominance, 2021. The further to the left a metropolitan area is, the more dominant is the central municipality. The closer to the bottom a metropolitan area is, the fewer the number of suburban governments there are relative to the suburban population; the closer to the top, the more institutionally fragmented suburban government is. Taken together, we may argue that metropolitan areas located closer to the bottom left are more consolidated, while those located toward the top right are more fragmented

2.2.2 Metropolitan Institutions and Policy Frameworks

As noted above, there is little consistency within or between provinces in the existence and organization of metropolitan institutions. Adapting Taylor's (2020, 2022) typology of Canadian metropolitan governance types, Table 2.2 assigns the 41 CMAs to four categories. The first is the *multi-purpose regional intergovernmental organization*. While these entities, which exist in five provinces, perform different functions in different provinces, and indeed in different regions of the same province, and have reached different levels of political and institutional maturity, they

Table 2.2 The existence of formal metropolitan institutions and policies

Multi-purpose regional intergovernmental organizations	Metropolitan single-purpose bodies	Direct intervention	No formal institutions
British Columbia—Regional Districts	Lower Mainland, BC—Translink (transit)	Greater Golden Horseshoe, ON—Provincial planning policies and Metrolinx transit agency	London (ON)
Abbotsford/Chilliwack (Fraser Valley RD)	Montréal, QC—Montréal International (ec dev)	Ottawa, ON-Gatineau, QC—National Capital Commission (Federal Planning Agency)	Halifax (NS)
Kamloops (Thompson-Nicola RD)	Montréal, QC—Autorité régionale de transport métropolitain (transit)		Kingston (ON)
Kelowna (RD of Central Okanagan)	Toronto, ON—Toronto Global (ec dev)		Greater Sudbury (ON)
Nanaimo (RD of Nanaimo)	**Saskatchewan—Regional Economic Development Authorities**		Lethbridge (AB)
Vancouver (Metro Vancouver RD)	Saskatoon—Saskatoon REDA		Belleville–Quinte West (ON)
Victoria (Capital RD)	Regina—Economic Development Regina		Red Deer (AB)
Alberta—Metropolitan Region Boards			Sherbrooke (QC)
Calgary (Calgary MRB)			St. John's (NL)
Edmonton (Edmonton MRPB)			Saguenay (QC)
Manitoba			Trois-Rivières (QC)
Winnipeg (Capital Region Board)			Thunder Bay (ON)
Québec—Metropolitan Communities			Windsor (ON)
Montréal (Montréal MC)			Drummondville (QC)
Québec (Québec MC)			
New Brunswick—Regional Service Commissions			
Moncton, (Southeast RSC)			
Saint John (Fundy RSC)			
Fredericton (Capital RSC)			

share key commonalities. Municipalities are represented on their governing boards. In addition, voting rights on the board and cost sharing are stipulated by provincially determined formulae. They are authorized to assume additional functions with the consent of member municipalities. Importantly, their existence, membership, and core responsibilities are, in each case, mandated by provincial law. The preeminent examples are British Columbia's regional districts, which function as metropolitan-scale authorities in that province's six CMAs, and the Montréal and Québec Metropolitan Communities. Analogous bodies exist in Alberta, Manitoba, and New Brunswick.

The second, less prevalent, model is the standalone *metropolitan single-purpose body* whose board is completely or predominantly appointed by municipal governments. The best-known examples of such bodies coordinate and/or operate transit service or economic development services, the latter including place promotion, branding, investment attraction, and site selection services.

Whether multi- or single-purpose, these entities are creatures of provincial governments, established by provincial law.

The third model, which does not entail the existence of metropolitan-scale institutions, is the *direct intervention* by the provincial or federal government. This may take the form of a *policy overlay*—a prescriptive policy framework adopted by provincial governments and given the force of law that binds local government activities within a defined urban-centred regional geographical area. The leading example is an integrated collection of policy frameworks adopted and periodically revised by the Ontario provincial government pertaining to a broad definition of the Toronto region, the Greater Golden Horseshoe. No metropolitan area–specific provincial plans such as this exist elsewhere in the country, although British Columbia and Québec have province-wide agricultural land protection plans. This model also includes provincial or federal agencies with no or non-voting municipal representation. For example, the federal National Capital Commission is a major public landowner and planner for the Ottawa-Gatineau region, and the Ontario government agency Metrolinx is a transit planner and operator in the Greater Toronto region, coexisting with municipal transit operators.

The fourth category comprises CMAs in which no formal metropolitan institutions or policies exist. These constitute a minority of the 41 CMAs, and mostly the smaller and more core-dominated ones.

The definition of metropolitan institutions and policies employed here is restrictive. Sub-metropolitan entities such as counties and equivalent local governments are not included, although it should be noted that relative isolation from other settlements in conjunction with central-city dominance means that some local governments are de facto metropolitan authorities—Halifax and Red Deer, for example. This overview also does not capture the wide array of informal or less-institutionalized mechanisms, including intermunicipal agreements and contracts (Spicer, 2016).

2.2.3 Local Representative Institutions

There is also considerable variation in the character of political representation on municipal councils within and between Canada's provinces. Unlike in the United Kingdom, for example, there is no central prescription of ward sizes and boundaries (Norman et al., 2007). Provincial legislation sets out general rules. For example, provincial laws specify that municipalities must have directly elected councils, including a directly elected head of council, and specifies roles and procedures for the conduct of council's business. Some provincial laws specify that the council must have a minimum number of seats. Whether or not councils are elected at-large (that is, all members of the council are elected from a municipality-wide electorate) or by districts called wards, is at the discretion of municipalities in most provinces, as is the number of wards and their boundaries. Wards are not a level of government, but territorial units of representation on the municipal council. As discussed further below, the City of Montréal and several other urban municipalities in Québec are subdivided into "boroughs" with councils composed of city-level councillors and separately elected borough councillors who do not sit on the city council. This is an anomaly not found elsewhere in Canada.

The head of council, called the mayor in cities and towns and the reeve in rural townships, is directly elected by all eligible municipal residents in all 460 municipalities found in Canada's CMAs, and indeed in almost every municipality in the country. While the powers available to the head of council vary somewhat within and across provinces, in all cases, the mayor is a voting member of council. Across the 41 CMAs, most large or urban municipalities (31% of municipalities representing 19.2 million people) are divided into wards, while most small or rural municipalities (65% of municipalities representing 6.4 million people) hold elections at-large—that is, to a single, multi-member municipality-wide district. A further 1.5 million people live in the small number of municipalities with mixed systems. Ward elections are understood to facilitate the representation of geographically concentrated groups (Trounstine & Valdini, 2008).

The size of councils in relation to the municipal population varies considerably. This may have implications for democratic representation, responsiveness, and decision-making (Dahl & Tufte, 1973; Muzzio & Tompkins, 1989; Meloche & Kilfoil, 2017). Smaller districts are more likely to facilitate group representation. Councillors who represent very populous wards (or larger municipalities elected at large) may be less accessible to their constituents than those elected from small wards (or smaller municipalities at large) (Fissell, 2023). At the same time, coordination and timely decision-making may be more difficult on large councils than small ones. However, the small literature on council size has found little evidence that it affects, for example, municipal expenditure levels (Meloche & Kilfoil, 2017; see also Gardner & Foster, 2009).

To get a sense of variation in the *intensity of political representation* within CMAs and between provinces, we calculate the number of representatives per 10,000 residents, including heads of council, for each ward or at-large electoral district.[3] Figure 2.2 summarizes this information across the population of all CMAs. The plot divides the population by the representation intensity index score of the district in which they live. Of the 27 million CMA residents, approximately one-third live in jurisdictions with less than two representatives per 10,000. A further 36% live in jurisdictions with five or more representatives per 10,000 residents. Distinguishing between suburban and central-city residents, we see that a larger proportion of the former live in low-intensity jurisdictions than the latter.

Figure 2.3 shows the distribution of representation index values for six of the larger, more fragmented CMAs. At the low-intensity extreme is the Vancouver CMA, where over 80% of residents are represented by less than one representative per 10,000. At the other extreme is the Montréal CMA, where over half of residents, including those in the City of Montréal, are represented by 15 or more elected officials per 10,000. The Toronto and Edmonton CMAs are relatively low-intensity, while the Saint John CMA is closer to Montréal. These distributions are patterned by province and region of the country. CMAs in British Columbia and Alberta have relatively low intensity of representation. Québec CMAs are exceptional for having high-intensity representation. The CMAs in the other provinces occupy the middle ground.

This panoptic view indicates that there is no identifiable norm when it comes to the intensity of political representation. In fact, it can vary considerably within metropolitan areas and even within the suburban zones of metropolitan areas. Some

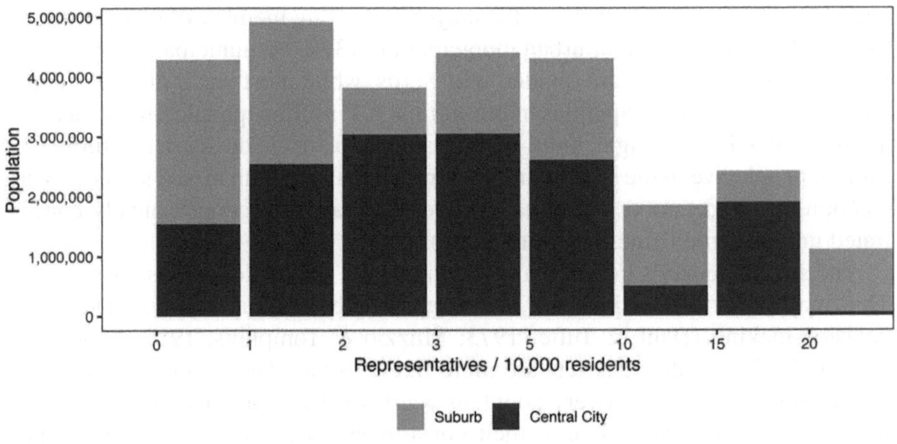

Fig. 2.2 Intensity of representation by total population resident in CMAs. The further left the peak of the population distribution, the fewer representatives per population; the further right, the more representatives per population

[3] Ward populations vary within the same municipality. Since the national census bureau does not disseminate population counts for wards, we approximate ward populations by dividing the municipal population by the number of wards. For the purposes of this analysis we exclude sub-municipal borough councillors in the Québec municipalities of Longueuil, Montréal, Québec, Saguenay, and Sherbrooke. Including borough elected representatives would increase the intensity of political representation in those parts of those CMAs.

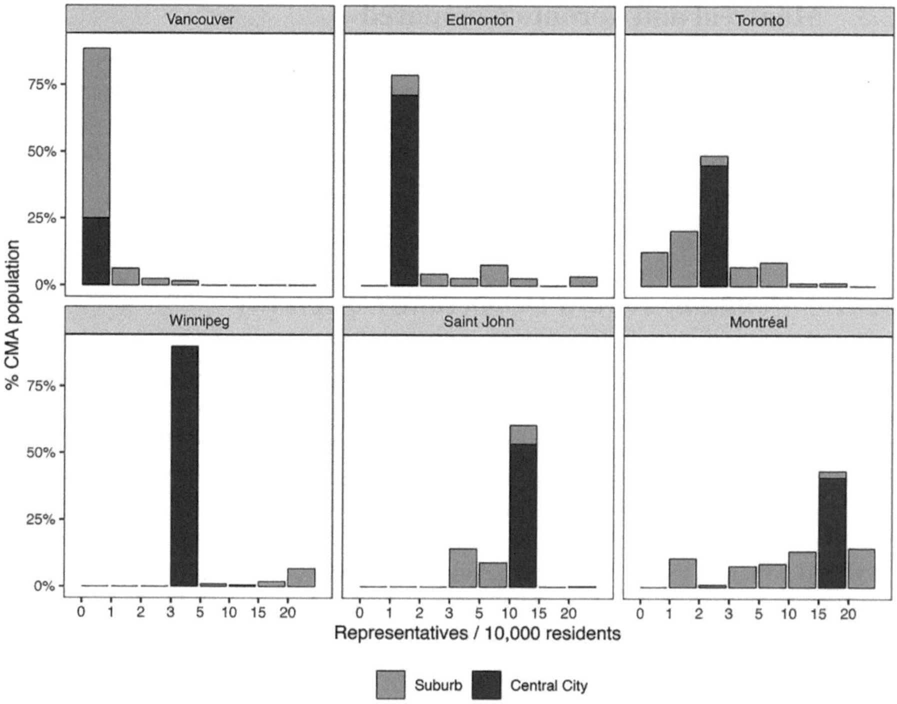

Fig. 2.3 Intensity of representation by % of CMA population, selected CMAs. The further left the peak of the population distribution, the fewer representatives per population; the further right, the more representatives per population

elected officials may represent many residents, while others represent relatively few. Having more representatives per capita may give residents greater access to elected officials and may encourage representatives to be more democratically responsive. Nevertheless, we can imagine how these relationships may be moderated by a variety of factors, not least the geographic size and density of electoral districts, the demographic profile of the population, and the character of institutional arrangements for public participation. For example, territorially expansive districts with dispersed populations may afford less frequent access to elected representatives than dense and compact ones, and different jurisdictions have different requirements and norms for citizen involvement in decision-making. Moreover, residents' engagement in local politics correlates with age, income, and educational attainment (Breux et al., 2017; Geys, 2006).

2.3 Montréal and Toronto Compared

To gain a more detailed perspective on how metropolitan and local governance may function and interact differently, I will now describe and contrast two very different city regions: Montréal and Toronto. Both are large metropolitan areas that have experienced disruptive institutional changes in recent years.

2.3.1 Montréal: Toward Democratic Complexity

The governance of the City of Montréal and its region has been reshaped several times since the 1970s, when the historical county system was replaced by a new system of upper-tier units called regional county municipalities (RCMs) and, on Montréal Island, a two-tier arrangement called the Montréal Urban Community (MUC) (Sancton, 1985). Lower-tier municipalities were represented on the decision-making bodies of the RCMs and the MUC. The governance of the MUC, which provided policing, transit, and other services for the 31 municipalities on the island, was however stacked in favour of the City of Montréal, which had a permanent majority on its decision-making board (Collin & Bherer, 2018). Within the City of Montréal, politics was dominated by the mayor, who could exercise considerable control over the local policy agenda through institutional prerogatives and control of his political vehicle, the Civic Party (McKenna & Purcell, 1980). Reformers and activists criticized the mayor's autocratic decision-making style.

Two institutional changes occurred between 2002 and 2006, the effect of which was to reshape Montréal's governance at all scales. By the turn of the century, the regional housing and labour market had come to spread far beyond the MUC's jurisdiction—indeed, the population of the off-island suburbs rivaled that of the island itself. In response, the provincial government dissolved the MUC and established a new entity, the Montréal Metropolitan Community (MMC), with boundaries similar, but not identical, to those of the Montréal CMA.[4] Its council is composed of 28 delegates from constituent local governments. It is chaired by the mayor of the City of Montréal and 13 of its members are appointed by the Montréal agglomeration council, assuring the central city's control of the institution. The remaining members are appointed by north and south shore local governments, ensuring representation from the various sub-regions. The MMC has significant land-use planning powers. It also appoints and partially funds a regional transit planning and coordinating agency, the Autorité régionale de transport métropolitain (ARTM), and provides some direction to Montréal International, an economic development and investment attraction agency structured as a public-private partnership.

[4] Of the 91 municipalities in the Montréal CMA, 79 are completely within the MMC's jurisdiction. The MMC also includes three municipalities that are not part of the CMA. The MMC's jurisdiction overlaps with that of 10 RCMs, two urban agglomerations, and two single-tier municipalities.

More controversially, the then 28 municipalities on Montréal Island were amalgamated into a single-tier City of Montréal, and other mergers occurred off-island as well (Collin et al., 2003, 18). The imposed mergers were hotly debated during the 2003 provincial election, with the victorious Liberal Party promising to allow communities to return to separate municipal government if approved by local referendum. The key issue from the perspective of the smaller suburban municipalities amalgamated into the City of Montréal was the preservation of their distinct identities and service norms. The identity question was especially salient in suburbs with English-speaking majorities, who opposed being submerged into a francophone majority city (Sancton, 2000).

In 2006, 15 municipalities were re-created on the island, and an additional 17 demerged elsewhere in the province, including four in the Montréal suburb of Longueuil. To maintain policy coordination on the island and in Longueuil, the provincial government established upper-tier "agglomeration councils" for each. While the demerged municipalities maintained their political identities, they were closely bound to the City of Montréal through the agglomeration council, which contributed half of the budgets, and was effectively controlled by the City.

Equally important was the creation of a new tier of "borough" government within the City of Montréal. These mostly corresponded to pre-existing municipalities, although the former City of Montréal was also subdivided into boroughs of comparable size, which created a new venue for representation. Each of the 19 boroughs has a directly elected mayor and councillors elected from between two and five borough districts. Thus, both the city council *and* the borough councils have district-based representation. Ward councillors sit on both the city and borough councils, as do directly elected borough mayors. The boroughs have become an important part of Montréal's political life, assuming powers over local planning, culture, recreation, roads, and the public realm. In total, Montréal's council comprises 65 members, including the mayor, who also serves as the mayor of the downtown Ville-Marie borough; 46 city councillors elected by ward; and 18 borough mayors. An additional 38 borough councillors are elected to the borough councils. A similar system exists in demerged Longueuil. However, the presidents of its three boroughs are not directly elected but selected by the borough councils from among their own membership.

2.3.2 *Toronto: Toward Centralization*

The broadest definition of Toronto is the Greater Golden Horseshoe (GGH), a semicircular zone spanning over 300 km from west to east containing almost ten million people and 112 municipalities. This area roughly corresponds to the nine contiguous CMAs centred on Toronto, plus additional rural areas. A more circumscribed definition is the inner ring of the GGH, the Greater Toronto and Hamilton Area (GTHA), which contains 24 lower-tier and six single-tier municipalities. This geography contains almost eight million people and generally corresponds to the area encompassed by the Toronto, Hamilton, and Oshawa CMAs.

With some exceptions, local government in the GGH is organized into two-tier systems. Historically, the upper-tier governments were counties. Established in the nineteenth century, counties possess a variety of functions, including land-use planning, major roads, and sometimes also administer public health and housing services. The lower-tier municipalities within counties are generally rural townships and small towns, each of which delegates representatives to the county council. Following nineteenth-century British practice, cities are separated from their counties and have no representation on county councils. County government persists in the outer ring of the GGH.

Following a provincially orchestrated reorganization of local government in the 1970s, the inner ring counties were transformed into "regional municipalities" that integrated separated cities and expanded their authority over planning, water and sewer infrastructure, transportation, and social services.

Waves of local government restructuring in Ontario produced large and sophisticated local governments, especially in the more urbanized GTHA, that possess the fiscal and administrative capacity to make and implement policy within their jurisdictions. At the same time, no metropolitan institution has existed since the late 1960s, when significant urbanization spilled beyond Metro Toronto's jurisdiction (for an overview, see Taylor, 2019b). The provincial government commissioned a Greater Toronto Area Task Force to study the problem in the early 1990s (Ontario, 1996). While it recommended replacing the existing patchwork of upper-tier local governments in the inner ring (but not including Hamilton) with a single, general-purpose regional body, a newly elected conservative government chose instead to maintain the existing suburban regional municipalities but amalgamate Toronto and Hamilton into single-tier cities. The government's reasoning has been debated. Some argue that it was a politically motivated action by a conservative government to dilute progressive voters and politicians, while others propose that it was a neoliberal project of streamlining government (Sancton, 2006). A brief experiment with a metropolitan Greater Toronto Services Board, which would have had roles in region-scale planning and transit coordination, was quickly abandoned.

After 2000, the Ontario Government incrementally took on the metropolitan governance role for itself, first by issuing or updating a series of legally binding regional and subregional land-use plans. These include the Growth Plan for the Greater Golden Horseshoe (2006; consolidated into a general Provincial Policy Statement in 2024), which assigns subregional population and employment growth targets, sets thresholds for the urbanization of rural land, and defines transit-oriented activity nodes; the Greenbelt Plan (2005), which protects agricultural land and ecologically and hydrologically significant features in a broad rural area surrounding the core contiguous urban zone centred on Toronto; and the Niagara Escarpment Conservation Plan (1985), the Oak Ridges Moraine Protection Plan (2002), and the Lake Simcoe Protection Plan (2009), which restrict urban development and protect ecologically significant natural features. While other provinces, namely British Columbia and Québec, have adopted binding land-use plans that protect agricultural land, Ontario's plans are unique in Canada in that they pertain to a specific urban region and are highly detailed and prescriptive. The province also created Metrolinx, a provincial agency to plan and construct major transit projects and operate regional rail and bus transit as well as a regional fare medium. In the same period, the province also supported the creation of Toronto Global, a regional investment attraction agency with municipal involvement. These policies and institutions exist today, although not without a high degree of intergovernmental conflict, implementation friction, and politicization. For example, the prioritization and design of new subway and light rail routes, as well as fare coordination, which involve both Metrolinx and municipal transit operators, have proven difficult to achieve as politicians at both levels jockey for electoral advantage. While Metrolinx's board initially had municipal representatives on it, the entire board is now appointed by the provincial government; as such, Metrolinx should not be seen as a local body (Horak, 2025).

While it can be said that the lengthy process of municipalities coming into conformity with the provincial plans has produced greater consistency in land-use and transportation outcomes than might have existed without them, the top-down, hierarchical nature of the province's role has created limited room for multilateral, horizontal municipal collaborations, although informal networks among municipal politicians and senior public administrators in the fields of housing and homelessness and COVID response have emerged (Eidelman & Nelles, 2025).

Since the City of Toronto's amalgamation into a single-tier municipality in 1998, there has been an ongoing search for a more responsive and effective governance model within the city. As initially constituted, the city was divided into 28 two-member wards, mirroring those of the pre-amalgamation upper-tier Metro Toronto, with an average of almost 100,000 residents in each. In its early years, the city lurched from one crisis to the next as it sought to merge the unionized workforces and harmonize the practices and procedures of the seven pre-amalgamation local administrations. The city appeared to be both too big and too small—too big because its large population (almost three million today), geographically large and populous wards, and painful merging of the six pre-amalgamation administrations limited public participation and neighbourhood influence; too small because the governance of the broader region remained uncoordinated. The council was redesigned to have 44 single-member wards in 2000. Moreover, in a gesture toward representation of the pre-amalgamation municipal areas, the city was divided into first six, then four, "community councils". In contrast to Montréal's highly institutionalized boroughs, which have elected councils, budgets, and administrators, these are no more than city council committees, composed of ward councillors, that handle minor planning matters. The prospect of devolving to the community councils final authority over important issues was never contemplated, for to do so would undermine the logic of amalgamation.

Toronto's "weak mayor", nonpartisan system enabled ward politicians to pursue their own agendas, militating against more strategic citywide policy agenda-setting. For many observers, the answer to this fragmentary policy environment is to reinforce the centre. In 2006, the mayor was given the authority to appoint an executive committee composed of standing committee chairs, through which all committee business must pass before coming to the council floor. In 2018, a conservative provincial government unilaterally, without any advance notice or consultation, passed legislation that reduced the size of Toronto's council to 25 single-member wards. In 2022, the same government, again without consultation or public notice, unilaterally strengthened mayoral powers, giving the mayor the ability to veto bylaws adopted by council and, in extraordinary cases, override council opposition to mayoral proposals (Taylor et al., 2023).

2.3.3 Montréal and Toronto Compared

Montréal and Toronto are territorially expansive city regions with large and growing populations. The cities have a long history of interventions seeking to improve policy capacity and coordination at both the provincial and local scales. Nevertheless, this brief sketch indicates that their governance has evolved along very different paths.

While initially far more centralized, Montréal's governance has developed in a direction of increasing governance complexity that has sought to balance strategic capacity with democratic access and accountability. The result is an elaborate vertical and horizontal governance network, characterized by Klein and Tremblay (2010, 569) as an "administrative archipelago," in which numerous layers with overlapping competences and interlinked representational systems are in constant interaction with one another. A typical municipal politician in the Montréal region serves far fewer residents than their counterparts in almost any other region of the country. Each Toronto city councillor represents about 120,000 people; Montréal city councillors represent about 40,000 people. Add the representation afforded by the borough councils and the intensity of representation is even higher. The multiplicity of elected offices and venues for participation enables a high level of democratic access and responsiveness, although sometimes at the cost of considerable friction among policy actors with diverse interests (Bherer & Collin, 2018; Sanger, 2021).

In Toronto, by contrast, the trend over the past 25 years has been toward the centralization of authority. Within the City of Toronto, "making amalgamation work" has meant strengthening mayoral authority and reducing the size of councils in the hope that more coherent policymaking oriented toward the citywide interest, rather than neighbourhood or ward interests, would result. Outside the central city, municipal councils are generally small. Authority is vertically integrated within two-tier local governments, but no institution incorporates local interests across metropolitan space. Instead, a distant provincial government routinely imposes its own policy priorities on localities. While a visual representation of institutional and representational relationships would be considerably "cleaner" in Toronto than in Montréal, the latter city's institutional "messiness" may enable a more lively local democracy and greater policy innovation in the long run (Bherer & Collin, 2018).

2.4 Conclusions: Metropolitan and Local Governance Futures

In this chapter I have sought to relate two scales of governance and political representation: the metropolitan and the municipal. These are rarely considered together, yet they are inextricable from one another. Together, they constitute the architecture of local government in city-regions. The territorial boundaries of local administrative units and political representation are path-dependent artifacts of idiosyncratic state formation processes and historical power relations. The contemporary effectiveness and legitimacy of local governance, and the capacity of local institutions to articulate conflict, depends in large part on how these inherited institutions are "wired up", and how contemporary actors use them. This chapter provides a window on the wide variation in institutional arrangements found in Canada, which has been enabled by federalism (provincial jurisdiction over local government), fiscal decentralization, and the dis-integration of local politics from provincial and federal party systems. Canada's decentralized federalism and dispersed urban system have enabled considerable institutional experimentation since World War II, especially over the past 25 years. The result is a differentiated patchwork of institutional structures and models.

Canada is among the fastest growing OECD countries, and virtually all of this growth occurs in the country's urban centres, and especially in its larger metropolitan areas. Rapid metropolitan population growth and territorial expansion have put pressure on local governance systems. In response, provincial governments across the country have intervened, often unilaterally, to address policy coordination gaps at the metropolitan scale and to overcome municipalities' perceived failure to engage in strategic and innovative governance.

As a result of these interventions, some metropolitan areas are highly consolidated (often as a result of amalgamations imposed by provincial governments), with most of the regional population living in a single large municipality and surrounded by relatively few suburban municipalities. Other metropolitan areas are fragmented into multiple local governments. In some parts of the country, two-tier, county-style local government is the norm; in others, single-tier local government prevails. In some regions, provinces have created multi-purpose or single-purpose metropolitan-scale institutions to integrate and broker local interests. In contrast, in others, the province has taken on the role of regional governor for itself.

There is also considerable variation in the structure of political representation in municipal governments. Some jurisdictions may prioritize local democratic access and accountability and appear to be undisturbed by having large numbers of very small municipalities and institutional complexity in the form of multi-tiered local government, large councils, and ward representation. The case of Montréal, for example, reveals an extraordinary four-tier structure featuring complex networks of resources and authority and numerous venues for public participation and political expression. Others valorize efficient and strategic decision-making, often at the expense of civic engagement. Thus, Ontario for Toronto and urbanized areas, but also, at different times, Manitoba, New Brunswick, Nova Scotia, and Québec, have implemented a range of institutional reforms intended to streamline local government, including strengthening executive authority, reducing the size of councils (thereby creating larger wards), and consolidating municipalities into larger units. The acceptability of different institutional models may be rooted in different provincial and local political cultures.

In sum, Canadian metropolitan and local governance is complex and ever changing. The considerable institutional change experienced by Montréal, Toronto, and other municipalities and regions in recent decades illustrates the ongoing search by local and provincial actors for better local governance, however construed. Canada's metropolitan and local governance future does not, therefore, point toward convergence on, or the imposition of, a single model. Rather, experimentation will continue in ways that defy easy generalization.

References

Bherer, L., & Collin, J.-P. (2018). Urban issues and political mobilization: From subsidiarity to institutionalized governance. In D. Fougères & R. MacLeod (Eds.), *Montreal: The history of a North American city* (pp. 379–415). McGill-Queen's University Press.

Breux, S., Couture, J., & Koop, R. (2017). Turnout in local elections: Evidence from Canadian cities, 2004–2014. *Canadian Journal of Political Science, 50*(3), 699–722. https://doi.org/10.1017/S000842391700018X

Collin, J.-P., & Bherer, L. (2018). One island, several cities: Montreal and its immediate suburbs. In D. Fougères & R. MacLeod (Eds.), *Montreal: The history of a North American city* (pp. 132–163). McGill-Queen's University Press.

Collin, J.-P., Dagenais, M., & Poitras, C. (2003). From city to city-region: Historical perspective on the contentious definitions of the Montréal metropolitan area. *Canadian Journal of Urban Research, 12*(1), 16–34.

Dahl, R., & Tufte, E. R. (1973). *Size and democracy, the politics of the smaller European democracies*. Stanford University Press.

Eidelman, E., & Nelles, J. (2025). A Fleeting Metropolitan Moment: Regional governance and municipal collaboration in Greater Toronto during the COVID-19 pandemic. *IMFG Papers on Municipal Finance and Governance*.

Fissell, B. M. (2023). Rightsizing local legislatures. *Utah Law Review, 2023*(2), 393–445.

Gardner, J. A., & Foster, K. A. (2009). *Sizing up local legislatures*. School of Law, University of Buffalo.

Geys, B. (2006). Explaining voter turnout: A review of aggregate-level research. *Electoral Studies, 25*, 637–663.

Hamilton, D. K., Miller, D. Y., & Paytas, J. (2004). Exploring the horizontal and vertical dimensions of the governing of metropolitan regions. *Urban Affairs Review, 40*(2), 147–182.

Horak, M. (2025). *Governing public transit in Canada: A primer.* Research Report 7. Centre for Urban Policy and Local Governance, Western University.

Klein, J.-L., & Tremblay, D.-G. (2010). Social actors and their role in metropolitan governance in Montréal: Toward an inclusive coalition? *GeoJournal, 75*, 567–579. https://doi.org/10.1007/s10708-009-9270-0

McKenna, B., & Purcell, S. (1980). *Drapeau*. Clarke Irwin.

Meloche, J.-P., & Kilfoil, P. (2017). A sizeable effect? Municipal council size and the cost of local government in Canada. *Canadian Public Administration, 60*(2), 241–267. https://doi.org/10.1111/capa.12211

Muzzio, D., & Tompkins, T. (1989). On the size of the city council: Finding the mean. *Proceedings of the Academy of Political Science, 37*(3), 83–96. https://doi.org/10.2307/1173754

Norman, P., Purdam, K., Tajar, A., & Simpson, L. (2007). Representation and local democracy: Geographical variations in elector to councillor ratios. *Political Geography, 26*(1), 57–77. https://doi.org/10.1016/j.polgeo.2006.10.013

Ontario. (1996). *Report of the GTA Task Force*. GTA Task Force.

Sancton, A. (1985). *Governing the Island of Montreal: Language differences and metropolitan politics, lane studies in regional government*. University of California Press.

Sancton, A. (2000). *Merger mania: The assault on local government*. McGill-Queen's University Press.

Sancton, A. (2006). Why municipal amalgamations? Halifax, Toronto, Montreal. In R. Young & C. Leuprecht (Eds.), *Municipal-federal-provincial relations in Canada—Canada: State of the Federation 2004* (pp. 119–137). Institute of Intergovernmental Relations.

Sancton, A. (2008). *The limits of boundaries: Why city-regions cannot be self-governing*. McGill-Queen's University Press.

Sanger, D. (2021). *Saving the city: The challenge of transforming a modern metropolis*. Véhicule Press.

Scharpf, F. W. (1988). The joint-decision trap: Lessons from German federalism and European integration. *Public Administration, 66*, 239–278.

Scharpf, F. W. (2006). The joint-decision trap revisited. *Journal of Common Market Studies, 44*(4), 845–864.

Spicer, Z. (2016). *The boundary bargain: Growth, development, and the future of city-county separation*. McGill-Queen's University Press.

Taylor, Z. (2019a). Pathways to legitimacy. *Planning Theory, 18*(2), 214–236. https://doi.org/10.1177/1473095218806929

Taylor, Z. (2019b). *Shaping the metropolis: Institutions and urbanization in the United States and Canada*. McGill-Queen's University Press.

Taylor Z. (2020). Theme and variations: Metropolitan governance in Canada. *IMFG Papers on Municipal Finance and Governance*.

Taylor, Z. (2022). Regionalism from above: Intergovernmental relations in Canadian metropolitan governance. *Commonwealth Journal of Local Governance, 26*, 139–159. https://doi.org/10.5130/cjlg.vi26.8141

Taylor, Z., Chapple, K., Elliott, M., Smith, A., & Eidelman, G. (2023). *Strong(er) mayors in Ontario—What difference will they make?* Institute on Municipal Finance and Governance, University of Toronto. https://hdl.handle.net/1807/127410

Taylor Z., & Dobson, A. (2019). Power and purpose: Canadian municipal law in transition. *IMFG Papers on Municipal Finance and Governance*.

Trounstine, J., & Valdini, M. E. (2008). The context matters: The effects of single-member versus at-large districts on city council diversity. *American Journal of Political Science, 52*(3), 554–569. https://doi.org/10.1111/j.1540-5907.2008.00329.x

Open Access This chapter is licensed under the terms of the Creative Commons Attribution 4.0 International License (http://creativecommons.org/licenses/by/4.0/), which permits use, sharing, adaptation, distribution and reproduction in any medium or format, as long as you give appropriate credit to the original author(s) and the source, provide a link to the Creative Commons license and indicate if changes were made.

The images or other third party material in this chapter are included in the chapter's Creative Commons license, unless indicated otherwise in a credit line to the material. If material is not included in the chapter's Creative Commons license and your intended use is not permitted by statutory regulation or exceeds the permitted use, you will need to obtain permission directly from the copyright holder.

Chapter 3
Decentralization Within Urban Areas in India: A Study of Delhi Metropolitan Governance

Asha Sarangi and Lipika Ravichandran

Abstract The re-amalgamation of the Municipal Corporation of Delhi (MCD) in 2022 has opened the debate on municipal governance regarding decentralisation, federalism, and participative democracy. Delhi is distinct from the rest of urban India as it is the seat of the central government, which plays a significant role in managing the city's affairs. Thus, three levels of government participate in Delhi's governance: the central government, the government of the National Capital Territory of Delhi (NCTD) or Delhi government and the MCD. Delhi's municipal body is subject to the decisions of the central government. The unification and trifurcation process of Delhi municipal body(ies) is made by an act of Parliament, unlike other metropolitan cities in India. Further, the geographical jurisdiction of the Delhi government and the MCD is largely coterminous, so their civic services overlap. As the functioning is coterminous, there exists a lot of conflict in budgetary allocation, and the performance of MCD is strained. In contrast, the New Delhi Municipal Corporation (NDMC), with its high budgetary allocation from the central government, topped the municipal civic service delivery in India.

Keywords Decentralisation · Unification · Municipal Corporation of Delhi · Delhi Government

A. Sarangi (✉)
Centre for Political Studies, Jawaharlal Nehru University, New Delhi, India

L. Ravichandran
Chennai, India

© The Author(s) 2026

K. Kössler, E. M. Belser (eds.), *Local Government Structure and Intergovernmental Relations*, Local and Urban Governance,
https://doi.org/10.1007/978-3-031-99820-1_3

3.1 Introduction

In 2022, Delhi's three urban local bodies (ULBs) were re-amalgamated into a single entity of the erstwhile Municipal Corporation of Delhi (MCD). In 2012, the MCD had been trifurcated into North Delhi Municipal Corporation (North DMC), East Delhi Municipal Corporation (EDMC) and South Delhi Municipal Corporation (SDMC). The trifurcation was justified by better administrative efficiency, with each smaller local body managing the heterogeneous distribution of the population (Shukla, 2016). Financial constraints were cited a decade later as the rationale behind the re-amalgamation. To elaborate further, the South Delhi Municipal Corporation (SDMC) has greater revenue-generating potential than the other two municipal bodies due to its demographics and the nature of business activities. Due to the increased revenue, SDMC had big budgetary spending and efficient civic service deliveries. However, this is not the case with the other two municipal bodies of Delhi. It is argued that after the unification, SDMC's surplus revenue can be shared with the other two and, in turn, facilitate a holistic development of the city. With a population of over 21.88 million people, the re-amalgamated MCD has become the second largest municipal body in the world, next to Tokyo. The MCD's re-amalgamation has opened the debate on municipal governance regarding decentralization, functionalities, and finances. With the constant influx, municipal governance in the city-state of Delhi has become a case for classic representation of decentralization, federalism, and participative democracy.

3.2 Delhi's Governance: A Complex Labyrinth

Delhi, with its distinct identities as a state, a city, and the nation's capital, faces a range of unique challenges and contradictions. Having served as the capital of multiple empires in medieval and modern India, the city's rich history is reflected in its urban landscape and the iconic architectural design of its monuments and famous structures. Old Delhi, located in the northern part of the city, was established by the Mughal Emperor Shah Jahan in 1649 and remains a bustling trade hub today. Positioned between Old Delhi and South Delhi, British India designed New Delhi as a garden city when the capital was moved from Calcutta to Delhi in 1911 (Jain, 2016, p. 651–672). Currently, the area serves as a high-security zone housing the central government's seat of power, numerous offices, political party headquarters, high-level establishments, and diplomatic enclaves. South and West Delhi experienced significant development after India gained independence in 1947, with the partition profoundly impacting the city's social and economic fabric. A large influx of people migrated from Western Punjab in Pakistan and surrounding regions, shaping these areas into middle-class residential and commercial hubs. In contrast, the Trans-Yamuna region, located east of the city, began development in the 1990s, initially as a relocation site for evicted slum residents and later as a residential area for migrants from other Indian states. This rich history has significantly influenced Delhi's governance structure.

Following India's independence in 1947, Delhi was administered as a Chief Commissioner's province. With the adoption of the Constitution in 1950, Delhi was designated as a Part C State, a category encompassing the former Chief Commissioner's provinces and certain princely states (Austin, 1966, p. 243–244). The Government of Part C States Act of 1951 established a legislative assembly for Delhi, granting it the authority to legislate on matters listed in the State List and Concurrent List, with certain exceptions. These excluded areas were (1) public order, (2) police, (3) the structure and powers of municipal corporations and other local bodies managing water supply, drainage, electricity, transport, and other public utilities in Delhi or New Delhi, and (4) lands and buildings owned or controlled by the Union government within Delhi or New Delhi (Goyel & Sharma, 2014, p. 29).

In 1956, the State Reorganisation Act led to the dissolution of Delhi's legislature, transitioning it into a Union Territory under the direct administration of the central government. The Delhi Municipal Corporation Act, passed by the Indian Parliament in 1957, established an urban local body for the city. As a result, Delhi's first municipal government was elected in 1958. However, the democratic process faced frequent disruptions due to the central government's repeated supersession of the municipal administration. (Goyel & Sharma, 2014, p. 39). To elaborate further, the central government has the dominant role in Delhi's municipal governance. Delhi's municipal body is subject to the decisions of the central government. The unification and trifurcation process of Delhi municipal body(ies) is made by an act of Parliament, unlike in other metropolitan cities in India. The following facts substantiate the argument. The friction between the central government and the Delhi government has explicitly increased after implementing the Delhi Municipal Corporation (Amendment) Act 2022, which gave the central government a direct role in administering the Municipal Corporation of Delhi (MCD). This amendment replaced the word "government" with "central government" (Ministry of Law and Justice, 2022, p. 2). Before the amendment act, the three municipal corporations were overseen by the Director (Local Bodies) of the Urban Development Department of the Delhi government. After the unification, the central government's Department of Home Affairs took the administrative role.

The constitutional amendments of the 1990s significantly restructured Delhi's governance framework. The 69th Constitutional Amendment Act established the National Capital Territory of Delhi (NCTD), granting it a unique status with limited features of a full-fledged state. It provided for a legislative assembly with members directly elected by the people and an executive branch headed by a chief minister, supported by a council of ministers. However, key domains such as land governance, police, and law and order remained under the central government's control (Goyel & Sharma, 2014, p. 42).[1] Complementing this, the 74th Constitutional

[1] The land governance is under the Delhi Development Authority which reports to the Central Ministry of Urban Development and the law and order in Delhi falls under the Central Ministry of Home Affairs.

Amendment Act delineated the powers and functions of urban local bodies across India, leading to the empowerment of the Municipal Corporation of Delhi (MCD), which held its first general elections on 24th February 1997, marking a milestone in local self-governance in the capital.

3.3 Decentralized Metropolitan Governance in Delhi

Along with the MCD, the urban local governance of the city-state of Delhi is managed by other urban local bodies, namely the New Delhi Municipal Council (NDMC) and Delhi Cantonment Board (DCB) in charge of small territories and specific constituencies. The former is responsible for the municipal administration of New Delhi, and the latter is for army personnel. MCD comprises approximately 92% of the area of NCTD, which is 1400 km^2. NDMC and DCB separately administer around 4% of the area of NCTD, which is about 45 km^2 each (NDMC, 2023a, 2023b). The scope of discussion in this chapter is restricted to the MCD and NDMC.

3.3.1 Municipal Corporation of Delhi (MCD)

Municipal corporations are established to manage large cities like Delhi, Mumbai, Chennai, Kolkata, Hyderabad, and Bangalore. In states, they are formed through acts passed by state legislatures, while in union territories, they are created by acts of the Indian Parliament. Typically, a municipal corporation in India has three main authorities: the council, led by a mayor; standing committees; and the commissioner, who oversees the executive functions of the corporation. Delhi is unique among Indian cities in terms of governance because it hosts the central government, significantly influencing its administration. Governance in Delhi involves three levels: the central government, the Government of the National Capital Territory of Delhi (NCTD), and the Municipal Corporation of Delhi (MCD) (Goyel & Sharma, 2014, p. 59–60). The jurisdiction of the Delhi government and the MCD largely overlaps, and this relationship is explored further in the chapter. According to the population census of 2011, the NCTD spans an area of 1483 km^2, consisting of 369.35 km^2 of rural and 1113.65 km^2 of urban areas (Development Department, Government of Delhi, 2023).[2]

[2]According to the official Indian census, a rural area is classified as an area with a population of less than 5000, a Density of population less than 400 per sq. km and more than 25% of the male working population is engaged in agricultural pursuits. For example, the number of rural villages has reduced in Delhi from 300 in 1961 to 165 in 2001 and 112 in 2011.

The MCD operates under the "commissioner system,"[3] in which the municipal commissioner plays a significant role. The municipal corporation's role and functions are divided between the executive headed by the municipal commissioner and the deliberative wing, headed by the mayor and the standing committee (Goyel & Sharma, 2014, p. 63). The standing committee approves the budgetary decisions while the commissioner makes the policy and the contract allocation. The mayor's role is ceremonial; they are elected for a 1-year term among the councillors.[4]

To discuss this in detail, MCD comprises a deliberative and executive wing. The deliberative wing consists of directly elected councillors and a few persons nominated by the lieutenant governor with knowledge or experience in municipal administration. The nominated members are eminent personalities in fields like science, public affairs, etc. A mayor heads the council and is assisted by deputy mayors. The mayor in the Municipal Corporation is usually chosen through indirect election by the councillors from among themselves for a term of 1 year, which is renewable. The mayor generally lacks executive authority (Delhi Councillors Hand Book, 2017, p. 32).

The executive wing implements the policies. The central government appoints the administrative/executive head (municipal commissioner) and senior officials. As the executive head, the municipal commissioner is responsible for implementing the decisions made by the council and its standing committees. Thus, he/she is the chief executive authority of the corporation appointed by the central government. (Goyel & Sharma, 2014, p. 63) The commissioner's powers are those provided by the Statute and those delegated by the corporation or the standing committee.

The MCD's highest decision-making executive body is the standing committee. This was created to facilitate the council's work, and it had 18 members. Out of these, the house directly elects six members, and the ward chooses the remaining committee (Delhi Councillors Hand Book, 2017, p. 33). The standing committee is headed by a chairperson and a deputy chairperson, elected from among the members. The standing committee carries out the financial functioning of approving and implementing projects for the city with the assistance of the steering committee. The standing committee also appoints sub-committees if and when needed to look into environmental matters, education, etc. The political party with the majority in the standing committee has control over the policy and financial decisions of the MCD house, which is the large chamber that accommodates all the 250 municipal councillors (Kumar, 2024).

The 74th Constitutional Amendment Act (CAA) provides a pan-India common framework for decentralized local government. State governments were required to modify their municipal legislation to ensure conformity with the 74th CAA. The latter was expected to change how locally-elected representatives participate in

[3] Also known as the "Bombay system." This model is established under the Bombay Municipal Corporation Act of 1888.

[4] According to the Delhi Municipal Corporation Act (1957), the MCD should hold elections every 5 years and elect a mayor when they members meet for the first time at the start of each financial year.

local governance in at least four ways: (1) by instituting mandatory elections; (2) by extending the mandate of municipal councils, notably through the addition of new functions[5] and more systematic access to funds[6]; (3) by modifying the demographic makeup of the councils through reservations[7]; and (4) by decentralizing local government deliberative processes through the creation of ward committees (WC) at the sub-municipal level (Ministry of Housing and Urban Affairs, 1993).

The creation of ward committees at the sub-city level is a key aspect of the 74th Constitutional Amendment Act (CAA). Significant changes were introduced to the Delhi Municipal Corporation Act in 1993, altering its structure, functions, governance, and administration. The amendments mandated the establishment of Ward Committees (WCs) at the zonal level and enhanced their financial authority. These changes also required administrative support for the WCs to facilitate decentralised urban governance in Delhi (Bhattacharya, 2022). To implement these reforms, the Municipal Corporation of Delhi (MCD) bolstered its zonal administration, which became effective on January 1, 1997, following the first elections conducted after the 1993 amendments. Article 243S of the Indian Constitution further mandated the formation of WCs, each encompassing one or more wards within a municipal, territorial area with a population of at least 300,000 (Parth & Makarand, 2006).

To decentralize administration and settle the day-to-day complaints of citizens, the area falling under the jurisdiction of MCD has been divided into 12 zones. Each zone consists of several wards. At present, there are a total of 250 wards. Each Zone has a ward committee, which consists of all the councillors elected from that ward. These ward committees are structures meant to decentralize administrative powers and provide local solutions for local problems. A total of 12 WCs have been constituted by the MCD, i.e., one for each zone. The 12 ward committees are: (1) City ward committee, (2) Rural Narela ward committee, (3) Karol Bagh ward committee, (4) Rohini ward committee, (5) Sadar Paharganj ward committee, (6) Civil Lines ward committee (7) Central ward committee (8) Westward committee (9) Southward committee (10) Najafgarh ward committee (11) Shahdara North ward committee (12) Shahdara South ward committee (Urban Governance Report Mumbai and Delhi, 2017, p. 11).

Each zone is led by a deputy commissioner, who holds all the delegated powers of the commissioner and has the authority to make key decisions at the zonal level. The deputy commissioner is supported by an assistant commissioner, a superintending engineer, a deputy health officer, a joint assessor and collector, a deputy

[5] The 74th CAA added the 12th schedule to the Constitution which contains a list of functions to be performed by the ULBs.

[6] The 74th CAA prescribes every state government to constitute a state finance commission to assess the financial resources of the state as well as rural and urban local bodies and make recommendations for devolution of funds from the former to the latter.

[7] The 74th CAA mandates a minimum of one-third of seats and offices of chairpersons in panchayats (local governments in rural areas) and municipalities be reserved for women. It also mandated reservation for Scheduled Castes and Schedules Tribes based on their percentage of the population and enabled states to reserve seats for Backward Classes.

education officer, and a deputy chief accountant (Parth & Makarand, 2006, p. 22). Ward Committees (WCs) have been operational in Delhi since 1997, with a tenure of 5 years. Each WC oversees several wards, typically ranging from 4 to 16, and consists of two wings: a deliberative or political wing and an executive wing. The deliberative wing is chaired by a chairman, assisted by a deputy chairman, and includes elected ward councillors as members. The executive wing, led by a deputy commissioner with delegated powers of the commissioner, is responsible for significant ward-level decision-making (Jha, 1988, p. 45). The WCs are composed solely of ward councillors, while MCD executive officers collaborate with councillors in the committees to facilitate policy implementation. Weekly WC meetings serve as a critical platform for discussing ward-specific issues, making decisions, and passing resolutions to implement those decisions (Parth & Makarand, 2006, p. 31). Municipal officials have observed that strengthening WCs in Delhi has positively impacted the quality of life for residents. Powers and Functions of the wards committee are as given in the 15th Schedule of the Delhi Municipal Corporation Act (1957), on behalf of a corporation in relation to that Zone [Section 52 (1)].

The 15th Schedule outlines the powers and functions of the Wards Committees as follows:

> Approve estimates and plans for municipal works within the Zone costing up to Rs. one crore, excluding works that apply to Delhi as a whole or span multiple Zones, provided that specific provisions exist in the corporation-approved budget.
>
> Request reports, returns, plans, estimates, statements, accounts, or statistics from the Commissioner concerning municipal administration matters within the Zone.
>
> Review monthly statements of receipts, expenditures, and progress reports on revenue collection in the Zone.
>
> Examine and provide recommendations on proposals related to revenue and expenditure estimates for the Zone under various budget headings before submitting them to the Commissioner.
>
> Advise or report on any matters referred to the Wards Committee by the corporation under the Act.
>
> Handle other matters delegated to the Wards Committee by the corporation.

Generally, exercise all municipal powers and functions of the corporation specific to the Zone, excluding matters pertaining to Delhi as a whole or involving multiple Zones.[8]

The WCs have the potential to enhance the effectiveness of elected councillors by facilitating interaction with different branches of the administration through regular meetings and to favour greater participation of citizens and neighbourhood groups. The members of the ward committees have periodic interaction with the municipal executive officers who implement the policies. The MCD has several important executive departments, such as Community Services, Environmental Management, Education, Finance, and Hospital Administration. However, guidelines were not provided regarding the size, membership, and specific functions to be included in ward committees. As a result, each state government has crafted its own

[8] Schedule 15 Sect. 52 (1) Delhi Municipal Corporation Act (1957).

rules. One of the most common differences is the demographic size of ward committees (Kennedy, 2012, p. 61).

The zones formulate mid-level planning between the MCD and the wards. Their function and role are mainly limited to the geographical area of the zone.

As discussed above, the implementation of the 74th CAA has been very limited in Delhi as it has no Metropolitan Planning Committee (MPCs),[9] and the municipal functions are devolved to the Delhi government and numerous parastatal bodies (Bakore, 2006, p. 13–14). Delhi's WCs do not respect the spirit of the 74th CAA. The powers and functions of municipal councillors in Delhi are greatly undermined. The same is reflected in the functioning of the WCs. The executive departments of the MCD do not consult with the WC of a zone in policy implementation due to the undermined role of municipal councillors (Ahmad et al., 2013, p. 645).

What is referred to as "ward committees" in Delhi are considered zonal committees, which are part of the administrative division in the rest of India. In other metropolitan municipal corporations, there are no ward committees. Instead, the executive wing of the municipal corporation is divided into multiple zones for administrative efficiency (Map 3.1; Table 3.1).

Unlike the other states in India, from the above discussion, it is evident that Delhi's state government doesn't directly control municipal governance (MCD). The central government makes decisions about the establishment of the municipal corporation, the division of Delhi into zones, and the delimitation of wards. Moreover, decentralization in Delhi suffers from a democratic deficit since elected councillors are limited in their action by the institutional set-up and are not close to their constituents. The scope and the functions of the municipal councillors are very limited as many of the functions are devolved to the Delhi government. In Delhi, out of 18 functions to be devolved to cities under the 74th CAA, only four are under the Municipal Corporation of Delhi (MCD), while the remaining 11 functions are under multiple agencies, and three are with the state government.[10] Consequently, MCD's scope of action is more limited than most municipal bodies. Moreover, as Tawa Lama-Rewal points out, fierce competition exists between the various types of 'local' representatives in delivering public services (Lama-Rewal, 2007, p. 23–24).

To elaborate in detail, due to the small geographical spread of an MLA's constituency in Delhi, much of their civic service delivery overlaps with the MCs. The

[9] MPCs were to be constituted in every metropolitan area. The purpose was to accord constitutional recognition to metro-regional planning with a view to augmenting investment in economic activities and infrastructure. MPCs would be responsible for functions such as the preparation of draft development plans for the metropolitan areas, spatial coordination of plans prepared by the municipalities and panchayats in the metro area and recommending modifications in the local area plan. The MPCs would also advise local bodies in the preparation of development plans and, thereafter, monitor effective implementation of an approved development plan of the region.

[10] For instance, drinking water and drainage, slum improvement and urban poverty reduction, functions usually devolved to municipalities, are the responsibility of the Delhi government. Praja Foundation (2020). Status of governance and service delivery in Delhi. https://praja.org/praja_docs/praja_downloads/Report%20on%20Status%20of%20Governance%20 and%20Service%20Delivery%20in%20Delhi.pdf

Map 3.1 The 12 zones/ward committees (WC) of MCD. (Source: MCD official website)

Table 3.1 Ward Committees of MCD. Source: MCD official website

Municipal corporation	No. of elected councilors	No. of WCs	No. of electoral wards in each WC	Population of each WC (approx.)	Membership, in addition to municipal officers
Delhi	250	12	~20	1,700,000	MCs

Members of Legislative Assembly Local Area Development (MLA-LAD) Scheme can explain the service delivery overlap. This scheme aims to establish local need-based infrastructure to create public utility assets. Under the MLA-LAD scheme, each MLA in Delhi can recommend works for up to Rs. 100 million yearly to the district administration that implements the work. During the monsoon season, an

MLA in Delhi recommends fogging and mosquito eradication to gain popular support, as Dengue fever will be the most pertinent civic issue. However, sanitation and vector-borne disease control/eradication are the primary functions of MCD. The overlap might sometimes lead to conflict and negligence of civic service delivery. Further, their functions overlap with the MLA, as mentioned with respect to the MLA-LAD scheme. Due to the small geographical spread of the constituency, the scope of delivery of civic functions is limited. There are only three MCs for one MLA in Delhi, as opposed to six or eight in other megacities of India.[11]

Further, to elaborate on the argument, the Delhi government's and MCD's territoriality is coterminous, so their civic services mostly overlap. There is an overlap in some duties between the MCD and the Delhi government. For example, both are involved in the education sector. The MCD is entrusted with the responsibility of supporting the primary schools, while the Delhi government has to take care of the higher and secondary schools and colleges. However, the Delhi government also runs primary schools. Regarding healthcare service delivery, the MCD is responsible for running dispensaries and hospitals catering to primary healthcare, while the Delhi government is entrusted with taking care of bigger and more specialized hospitals. However, MCD runs hospitals which cater to tertiary healthcare. As the functioning is coterminous, there exists a lot of conflict in budgetary allocation and regarding the outcome of the civic service delivery, which is discussed below.

The National Achievement Survey Report 2021 surveyed 3.4 million students in grades 3, 5, 8, and 10 to evaluate children's progress and learning competence. Under the survey, the students in grade 3 assessed in language, mathematics, and environmental studies showed an average performance of 48.7% in Delhi, against the national average of 59%. In addition, grade 8 students who were assessed in language, mathematics, science and social science received an average grade of 43.6% in Delhi, against the national average of 41.9%. Similarly, the national average for grade 10 students was 37.8%, while Delhi's average was 45.4%. The poor performance of Delhi's grade 3 students is mainly attributed to the MCD, as it controls more primary education schools. MCD schools' performance has been ranked amongst the bottom five in India. The National Commission for the Protection of Child Rights (NCPCR) said that MCD is responsible for imparting primary education. Therefore, the MCD is somewhat accountable for the dismal performance of grade 3 students.

The poor performance of MCD schools is directly related to the poor budgetary allocation, which has resulted in poor infrastructure and teacher allocation. The MCD, in its total budget outlay of approximately Rs. 16 billion for the financial year 2023–2024, has allocated around 17% for the educational sector. In contrast, the NCTD government has an educational sector allocation of 22% for the same period in its total budget outlay of nearly Rs. 79 billion (Department of Planning, 2023) (Chart 3.1).

[11] For instance, Mehrauli, a neighborhood in South Delhi, has one MLA constituency and three MC wards. Following the new delimitation of wards undertaken for the 2023 municipal elections, there are presently 250 municipal wards in Delhi.

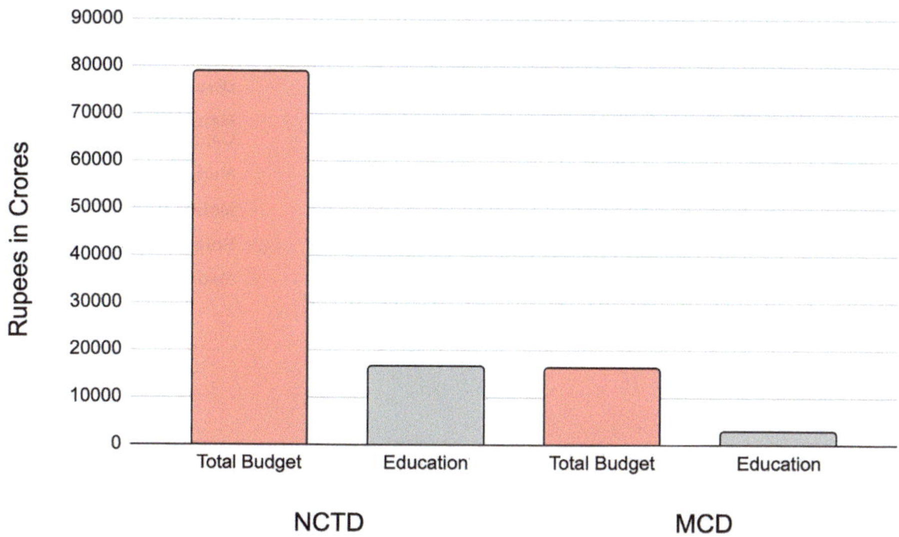

Chart 3.1 Educational spending by NCTD government and MCD

The less educational spending by MCD has severely affected the school infrastructure and poor pupil-teacher ratio (PTR). Out of 1707 MCD-run schools, 753 (almost 44%) were found to be non-compliant with the RTE-mandated PTR.[12] On the contrary, 2% (21 out of 1068) of NCTD government-run schools have a low PTR (Department of School Education and Literacy, 2020). High budgetary allocation has led to better infrastructural facilities, teacher appointment, and training, resulting in better learning outcomes in NCTD government-run schools. In 2022, 384 Delhi Government School students qualified for JEE Mains[13] and 485 students qualified for NEET.[14] A survey in 2015 and 2021 reported that the NCTD-run schools have witnessed high enrolment compared to MCD-run schools. During the same period, MCD has shut down 102 schools.

The public health responsibilities in Delhi lie with the MCD and Delhi state. MCD and the Delhi government provide municipal health through two branches of medical and public health services. The medical service branch constitutes maternal and child health (MCH) services, including contraception, antenatal care, delivery, postnatal care, and immunization. The public health branch focuses on preventing

[12] The Right of Children to Free and Compulsory Education (RTE) Act of 2009 describes the Pupil Teacher Ratio (PTR) for both primary and upper primary schools. At primary level the PTR should be 30:1 and at the upper primary level it should be 35:1.

[13] It is an Indian standardized computer-based test for admission to various technical undergraduate programs in engineering, architecture, and planning programs in premier technical institutes across India.

[14] The National Eligibility cum Entrance Test (NEET) is an all-India pre-medical entrance test for students who wish to pursue undergraduate medical (MBBS) and dental (BDS) courses in government and private institutions in India.

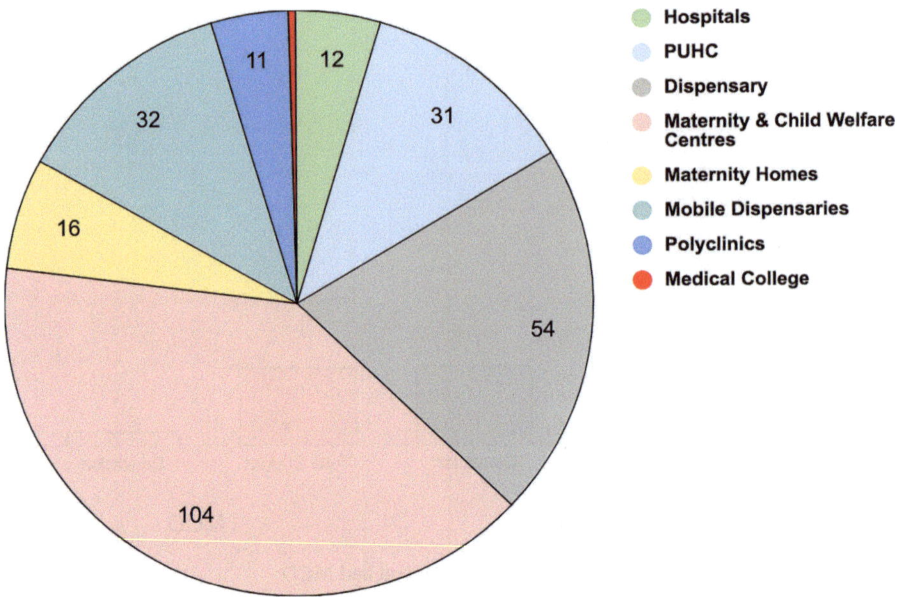

Chart 3.2 Medical institutions under MCD

communicable diseases, mosquito breeding, personal/domestic hygiene, and environmental sanitation.

There is no clear distinction between MCD and the Delhi government in terms of providing public health services. MCD manages around 280 health institutions, which include one medical college, 12 hospitals, 54 dispensaries and other ancillary health institutions described in the chart.[15] The Delhi government manages a similar number of health institutions, around 277, which include 30 hospitals and 247 ancillary health institutions (Chart 3.2).[16]

Though both levels of government manage a similar number of health institutions to provide similar healthcare services to the same population, the disparity in budgetary spending between the two is enormous. The Delhi government's health budget outlay for the period 2023–2024 is almost six times more than that of MCD health spending (Development Department, Government of Delhi, 2023) (Chart 3.3).

The poor health spending by MCD is reflected in its dire infrastructure and shortage of healthcare professionals. Though the MCD and Delhi government have an equal number of medical institutions with better budgetary spending, the bed capacity of Delhi government medical institutions is four times higher than that of the MCD. Further, MCD dispensaries and hospitals had a 21% shortage of medical staff

[15] Data retrieved from the official website of MCD. https://mcdonline.nic.in/portal/downloadFile/zone_wise_list_of_all_health_institutions_220908100116916.pdf

[16] Data retrieved from the official website of the Government of NCT Delhi https://health.delhi.gov.in/health/delhi-govt-hospital

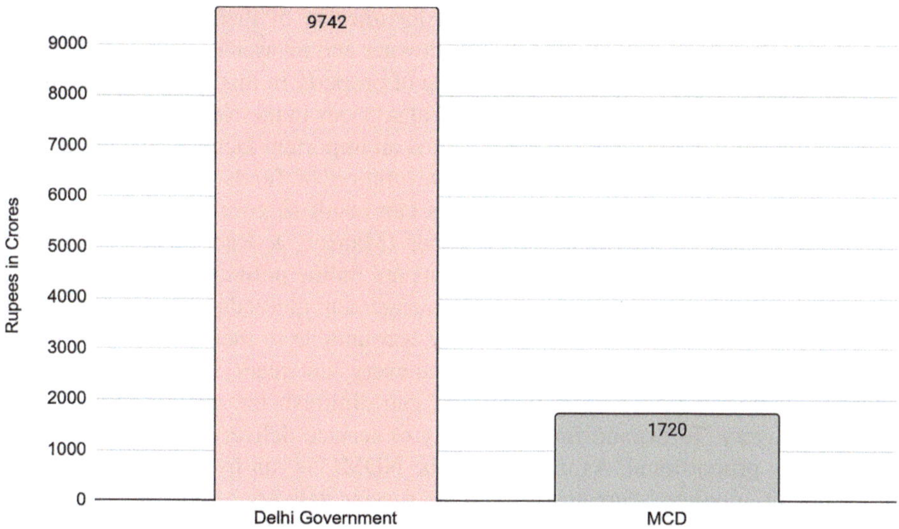

Chart 3.3 Health Expenditure of Delhi Government and MCD in the Budget 2023–2024

and a 50% shortage of para-medical staff as of 2018 (Report on the state of health in Delhi, 2019, p. 26).

To conclude, Delhi's municipal and state governments seem more fragile than those of other Indian states. At the municipal level, needs more human and material necessary to fulfil its mandate. At the state level, any conflict between the Delhi government and the central government can result in a near-complete paralysis of the former. Therefore, urban governance in Delhi is characterized by a multiplicity of institutional actors, overlap of services and a general lack of coordination.

3.3.2 New Delhi Municipal Council (NDMC)

The NDMC area comprises the territory that has been described as Lutyens's Delhi or New Delhi. It comprises important buildings like the Rashtrapati Bhawan (President's Estate), Parliament House, Supreme Court, North and South Blocks[17] and buildings abutting Central Vista,[18] and all the diplomatic missions that function

[17] North and South Blocks contain offices of important central government Ministries of Home Affairs, Defense, Finance and External Affairs.

[18] Central Vista is a 3 km long path, officially named Kartavya Path, which connects Rashtrapati Bhawan with the India Gate (a war memorial monument). Office buildings of various central government ministries occupy both sides of the Kartavya Path.

as territorial entities under the sovereign jurisdiction of their Flag States.[19] The Government of India is nearly the sole landowner and owns about 80% of the properties in the NDMC area. Private ownership of property in this area is marginal.[20]

The efficient functioning of the municipal services in the New Delhi area is crucial for the internal image of the country. It is an important factor which has a bearing on the functioning of the NDMC. Devolution of funds and responsibilities without strong accountability mechanisms can result in poor service quality and reduce the focus on providing public goods (Mansuri & Rao, 2012, p. 177). As Besley and Ghatak point out, "[b]ureaucrats are unlike politicians in that they can be held to formal contracts and standard management methods" (Besley & Ghatak, 2007, p. 136). Politicians are only directly accountable to their constituents at the time of the next election, which takes place every few years. Under these circumstances, democratic devolution to NDMC can diminish the quality of municipal service delivery. To expand further, quality of service delivery and accountability are directly proportional. As mentioned, the NDMC is run by non-elected central government-appointed bureaucrats, and the service delivery of NDMC is high due to the highly accountable nature of bureaucrats. In India, bureaucrats' accountability is achieved through the Annual Performance Appraisal Report (APAR), which monitors their performance annually. On the contrary, an elected representative is made accountable only once in 5 years, as elections are held every 5 years for many elected posts in India.

The council is the deliberative and legislative wing of the corporation. It consists of the councillors, directly elected by the people, and a few nominated persons with knowledge or experience in municipal administration.

Thus, NDMC comes directly under the center. No elections are held to this council, and the center nominates its members in consultation with the state government. However, to give it a more representative character, some sitting MLAs of the Delhi government have also been nominated to the council.

According to Chapter 2 of NDMC act 1994, "the council shall consist of the following members: (a) A Chairperson, from amongst the officers, of the central government, of or above the rank of Joint Secretary to the Government of India to be appointed by the central government in consultation with the Chief Minister of NCTD government, (b) Two MLAs of the Delhi Legislative Assembly representing constituencies, which comprise wholly or partly the New Delhi area, (c) Five members from amongst the officers of the central government or the government of their undertakings, to be nominated by the central government, and (d) Four members to

[19] Chanakyapuri is a neighborhood and diplomatic enclave established in the 1950s in New Delhi. It hosts the majority of foreign embassies in New Delhi. Chanakyapuri, meaning "city of Chanakya", is named after Chanakya, an ancient Indian philosopher, politician and military strategist.

[20] Data retrieved form the official website of NDMC: www.ndmc.gov.in

be nominated by the central government in consultation with the Chief Minister of NCTD government to represent from amongst lawyers, doctors, chartered accountants, engineers, business and financial consultants, intellectuals, traders, laborers, social workers including social-scientists, artists, media persons, sports persons and any other class of persons as may be specified by the central government in this behalf" (NDMC, 2023a, 2023b).

The 2011 amendment to the NDMC Act states that the sitting member of parliament (MP) of the New Delhi Constituency is a member of the council. Furthermore, two members must belong to the Scheduled Castes, of which one member shall be from the members nominated under clause (d). In consultation with the Chief Minister of Delhi, the central government shall nominate a vice-chairperson from amongst the members specified in clauses (b) and (d). In other words, following the NDMC Act of 1994, a 13-member council headed by a chairperson governs the NDMC. Out of 13 members, two members of Delhi's legislative assembly and five from amongst the officers of the central government, or the government of their undertakings, are to be nominated by the central government. In addition, four members are to be nominated by the central government in consultation with the Chief Minister of Delhi. Finally, the council shall continue to function for 5 years from the appointment date.

The NDMC achieved good outcomes due to better fiscal grants from the central government and a better management structure. NDMC ranks very high in the periodic urban sanitation surveys, while the MCD that serves 96% of Delhi's population languishes far behind.[21] NDMC also receives grants from the Smart City Mission,[22] which has extensive funds explaining the high-quality housing and urban infrastructure compared to MCD. Further, with the surplus funds, the NDMC has taken several IT-based initiatives through technology intervention for strengthening of e-Governance and m-Governance to improve efficiency and effectiveness in providing civic services to citizens in an equitable, non-discretionary and transparent manner.[23]

---

[21] NDMC was adjudged the 'cleanest small city' in the Swachh Survekshan 2022 Ranking. The Ministry of Urban Development, Government of India, and the Central Pollution Control Board (CPCB) of India annually publish National City Rating under the Swachh Bharat Abhiyan scheme. Swachh Bharat Abhiyan, or Clean India Mission, is a country-wide campaign initiated by the Government of India to eliminate open defecation and improve solid waste management.

[22] Smart Cities Mission (SCMs) is an urban renewal and retrofitting program by the Government of India with the mission to develop smart cities across the country, making them citizen-friendly and sustainable. Urban local bodies play a vital role in SCMs.

[23] For example, the NDMC-311 app serves multifaceted civic services like payment of bills and taxes, disaster helpline, women and children helpline and complaint registration. As of Januaty 2011, the 98% of grievances registered in the app has been resolved.

3.3.3 Decentralization Through Associations of Civil Society

The participation of civil society in managing urban affairs can further accelerate the democratization process. In Delhi, municipal governance is essentially politically driven. That is to say that the recipients of urban civic services are seen as vote banks. Against this backdrop, a ward of the municipal councillor belonging to the ruling party of the MCD receives better civic services than a ward belonging to an opposition party.

The concept of "good governance," introduced and popularized by the World Bank, extends beyond the mere provision of civic amenities. It embodies a quasi-moral framework that emphasizes key political values such as participation, transparency, accountability, and collaboration between the public and private sectors. These principles became the foundation for several initiatives the Delhi government undertook during the 1990s.

In 2003, the NCTD government introduced the Bhagidari scheme to encourage widespread civic engagement in local governance. The initiative aimed to enhance "transparency and accountability in administration" while improving "the quality, efficiency, and delivery of public services." As the cornerstone of Delhi's "good governance" policy, the Bhagidari scheme significantly promoted public participation beyond just voting, enabling citizens to take an active role in managing civic matters. The program also facilitated the establishment of Resident Welfare Associations (RWAs) and Market Traders Associations (MTAs).

Resident Welfare Associations (RWAs), primarily active in middle-class neighborhoods, are typically formed through self-selection and co-optation. Despite this, they have gained recognition as significant players in urban governance over the past decade. The growing legitimacy can be attributed to several factors: (1) the emphasis on participation as a core principle of good governance, (2) backing from local and state authorities, and (3) the sociopolitical standing of their active members, which provides them with resources to effectively engage with the media and judiciary (Mooij & Lama-Rewal, 2012, p. 93). RWAs operate within the boundaries of their respective neighborhoods. While their primary role is to ensure the area's security, they also take on additional responsibilities, such as managing street lighting, maintaining parks, and promoting the community's overall welfare.

For the past few years, Delhi has witnessed heightened air pollution during winter months. The ambient air quality is severely deteriorated due to the lingering toxic haze. The Delhi government and MCD, with their resources and expertise, were capable of dealing with the air pollution crisis, and the RWAs were doing their bit to combat the pollution. Most RWAs have taken proactive steps to assist residents in housing societies and apartment buildings. They issued advisories with guidelines on what to do and what to avoid and have enforced a ban on thrash burning. They have also discouraged residents from using firecrackers during Diwali celebrations.

3.4 Conclusions

The re-amalgamation of the Municipal Corporation of Delhi (MCD) in 2022 has ignited renewed discussions about the intricacies of municipal governance and decentralization, particularly within a city that serves as the seat of the central government. This unique governance environment means that Delhi's administrative framework involves a complex interplay between the central government, the National Capital Territory of Delhi (NCTD), and the MCD, leading to overlapping jurisdictions that often result in conflicts regarding service delivery. Significant challenges remain despite the establishment of the MCD and its Ward Committees (WCs) to enhance local governance. These include limited budgetary allocations, which hinder effective service provision, and administrative inefficiencies that reduce the responsiveness of local government to the needs of residents. In contrast, the New Delhi Municipal Council (NDMC) has demonstrated notably effective governance, benefiting from substantial central funding and a management structure that relies on appointed bureaucrats who are accountable to the central government.

Additionally, civil society plays a crucial role in the urban governance landscape through Resident Welfare Associations (RWAs). These organizations are intended to give a voice to citizens and facilitate community engagement in governance; however, their influence is often constrained by bureaucratic barriers and a lack of institutional recognition. The chapter underscores the pressing need for improved coordination and accountability mechanisms within Delhi's urban governance framework. Key areas of focus include examining the relevance of local government size and its impact on citizen engagement, understanding the origins of urban subdivisions—whether based on historical amalgamations or modern administrative planning and clarifying the legal status of these subdivisions. Furthermore, insights into decision-making structures, inter-agency coordination mechanisms, and methods for assessing the legitimacy and efficiency of local governance are paramount, fostering a more participatory governance model that aligns governmental actions with the needs and expectations of the diverse population.

References

Books and Journals

Ahmad, S., Balaban, O., Christopher, N. H. D., & Dreyfus, M. (2013). Delhi revisited. *Cities, 31*, 641–653.

Austin, G. (1966). *The Indian Constitution: Cornerstone of nation*. Oxford India Paperbacks.

Bakore, M. (2006). *74th Constitutional Amendment and its implementation in Delhi—A comparison*. Centre for Civil Society.

Besley, T., & Ghatak, M. (2007). Reforming public service delivery. *Journal of African Economies, 16*, 127–156.

Bhattacharya, R. (2022). *Ward committees as "invited space": Is it successful? A literature review of urban India*. Institute for Social and Economic Change.
Goyel, P., & Sharma, S. K. (2014). *Polity and governance of Delhi*. National Book Trust.
Jain, A. K. (2016). The significance of Shahjahanabad and Lutyens' Delhi. *International Journal of Environmental Studies, 73*(4), 651–672.
Jha, G. (1988). *Local finance in metropolitan cities: A study of Delhi*. Mittal Publications.
Kennedy, L. (2012). New patterns of participation shaping urban governance. In J. Ruet & S. T. Lama-Rewal (Eds.), *Governing India's metropolises* (pp. 55–80). Routledge India.
Lama-Rewal, S. T. (2007). Urban governance through the prism of primary level health services provision: A study of Delhi. In *Seminar on urban actors, policies and governance in four Indian metropolitan cities* (pp. 23–24). Center de Sciences Humaines de New Delhi (CSH) and the India International Center.
Mansuri, G., & Rao, V. (2012). *Localizing development: Does participation work?* Policy Research Report: 177. World Bank.
Mooij, J., & Lama-Rewal, S. T. (2012). Class in metropolitan India: The rise of the middle classes. In J. Ruet & S. T. Lama-Rewal (Eds.), *Governing India's metropolises* (pp. 81–104). Routledge India.
Parth, S., & Makarand, B. (2006). *Ward power: Reforms in urban governance*. Centre for Civil Society.
Shukla, S. (2016). Trifurcated MCD: Challenge to survive politico-economic crisis. *The Discussant, 4*, 34–38.

Newspaper and Documents

Delhi Councillors Hand Book. (2017). Praja.
Delhi Municipal Corporation Act. (1957). https://www.mha.gov.in/sites/default/files/DMC-Act-1957_0.pdf
Department of School Education and Literacy. (2020). *Unified District Information System for Education (UDISE) plus 2019–20 report*. Government of Delhi.
Development Department, Government of Delhi. (2023). Retrieved November, 2023, from https://development.delhi.gov.in/development/introduction
Kumar, K. (2024, September 4). What makes Standing Committee of Delhi civic body more powerful than mayor? *India Today*.
Ministry of Housing and Urban Affairs. (1993). *The Constitution (74th Amendment) Act, 1992*.
Ministry of Law and Justice. (2022). *The Delhi Municipal Corporation Amendment Act 2022*. The Gazette of India.
NDMC. (2023a). https://www.ndmc.gov.in/ndmc/NDMCAct/NDMC%20ACT%201944%201.1.pdf
NDMC. (2023b). Retrieved November, 2023, from https://www.ndmc.gov.in/ndmc/introduction.aspx
Report on the State of health in Delhi. (2019). Praja.
Urban Governance Report Mumbai & Delhi. (2017). Praja.

Open Access This chapter is licensed under the terms of the Creative Commons Attribution 4.0 International License (http://creativecommons.org/licenses/by/4.0/), which permits use, sharing, adaptation, distribution and reproduction in any medium or format, as long as you give appropriate credit to the original author(s) and the source, provide a link to the Creative Commons license and indicate if changes were made.

The images or other third party material in this chapter are included in the chapter's Creative Commons license, unless indicated otherwise in a credit line to the material. If material is not included in the chapter's Creative Commons license and your intended use is not permitted by statutory regulation or exceeds the permitted use, you will need to obtain permission directly from the copyright holder.

Chapter 4
Local Government and Its Urban Subdivisions in Mexico: The Case of Mexico City

José María Serna de la Garza

Abstract The purpose of this chapter is to explain the evolution and current institutional and normative design of the local government structure and intergovernmental relations of Mexico City and of the Valley of Mexico. Accordingly, I will examine the origins and the rationales of Mexico City's urban subdivisions, as well as their legal status, institutions, structures, and competences. Moreover, in this chapter I discuss the rules concerning the subdivision and amalgamation of local government units in Mexico City and the institutions and forums that guarantee coordination across the subdivisions. Furthermore, I analyze the relationship between civil society and institutional reform of Mexico City's governmental structures. Finally, a reflection is developed on the legitimacy and efficiency of Mexico City's urban subdivisions and on possible future developments.

Keywords Local government · Mexico City · Urban subdivisions · Intergovernmental relations · Metropolitan zone

4.1 Introduction

Mexico City, which is Mexico's capital, is located in the center of the country, in an area of 1495 km^2 where, according to the 2020 census, 9.2 million people live as permanent residents.[1] The population density in this area amounts to 6163 inhabitants per km^2 (in contrast with 64 in the country as a whole) (INEGI, 2021, p. 1–2). To deal with size, Mexico City is divided into 16 territorial units which, since the

[1] Mexico City's "floating population" is of around 1.5 million people who travel daily to work or study in the city, coming from neighboring states.

J. M. S. de la Garza (✉)
Institute of Legal Research, National Autonomous University of Mexico (UNAM), Mexico City, Mexico
e-mail: josemar@unam.mx

© The Author(s) 2026

K. Kössler, E. M. Belser (eds.), *Local Government Structure and Intergovernmental Relations*, Local and Urban Governance,
https://doi.org/10.1007/978-3-031-99820-1_4

constitutional reform of 2016, are called *alcaldías*. Until 2016, the official denomination of Mexico's capital was "Federal District", but the constitutional reform of that year changed the official denomination to "Mexico City". Furthermore, Mexico City is at the center of a large metropolitan zone located in the Valley of Mexico which, in addition to the 16 *alcaldías* already mentioned, is formed with 59 municipalities of the State of Mexico and one of the State of Hidalgo. According to the 2020 census, 22 million people live in this zone of 7954 km^2.

As I will explain in this chapter, the legal status and internal organization of Mexico City has changed over the years. Today, Article 122 of the Constitution defines it as a "federated entity with autonomy in everything concerning its internal government and its political and administrative organization". The purpose of this chapter is to explain the evolution and current institutional and normative design of the local government structure and intergovernmental relations of Mexico City and of the Valley of Mexico. Accordingly, Sect. 4.2 of this chapter examines the origins and explains the rationales of Mexico City's urban subdivisions. Section 4.3 analyses the legal status, institutions, structures, and competences of Mexico City's urban subdivisions. Section 4.4 discusses the rules concerning the subdivision and amalgamation of local government units in Mexico City. Section 4.5 examines the institutions and forums that guarantee coordination across the subdivisions. Section 4.6 discusses the relationship between civil society and institutional reform of Mexico City's governmental structures. Finally, Sect. 4.7 develops a reflection on the legitimacy and efficiency of Mexico City's urban subdivisions and on possible future developments.

4.2 Origins and Rationales of Mexico City's Urban Subdivisions

The 16 urban subdivisions of Mexico City are called territorial demarcations and have their origin in the colonial municipal government structure, which has remained even after independence. The first Mexican Constitution, approved in 1824, created a federal system in Mexico and empowered the Congress of the Union to establish the seat of the federal powers wherever it deemed convenient, as well as to exercise in that area the powers of the local legislative branch. In 1824, the federal Congress established that the central part of Mexico City would be a Federal District and that this district would be administered by a governor appointed by the President of the Republic. In addition, the federal Congress determined in the same year that the rest of Mexico City's territory would be governed by municipal town councils elected according to the norms of the 1812 Spanish Constitution of Cadiz.

Throughout the nineteenth century and the beginning of the twentieth century, there were several reform proposals to the 1824 Constitution. These reform proposals stemmed from the population growth and territorial extension of the city, as well as the need to better organize public services (such as transportation and public lighting), and the need for drainage (Mexico City is located on what used to be a large lake and the area experiences frequent flooding as a result. In 1901, President Porfirio Díaz successfully promoted a constitutional reform that abolished the popular election of the Federal District's municipal presidents. The latter were substituted by prefects who were freely appointed and removed by the President of the Republic through the Minister of the Interior and subordinate to the governor of the Federal District. Moreover, in 1903, the Law of Political and Municipal Organization of the Federal District was enacted by the federal Congress, which determined that the Government of Mexico City would depend on the President of the Republic through the federal Ministry of the Interior and three officials who depended on that Ministry: the Governor of the Federal District; the President of the Superior Health Council and the Director of Public Works. These three officials, freely appointed and removed by the President of the Republic, made up the Superior Council of Government which was in charge of the administration of the Federal District. Finally, according to this law, all legislative power concerning the Federal District and its (then) 13 municipalities[2] was vested in the Congress of the Union (Article 18).

After the 1910 Mexican Revolution a new national Constitution was approved in 1917. This constitution established at the normative level the so-called "free municipality", and the regime of popularly elected municipal government was re-established in the Federal District. However, the constitution also stipulated that a governor, freely appointed and removed by the President of the Republic, would govern the Federal District. It was also expected that the governor would have to report to the President of the Republic. In the same year, the Law of Organization of the Federal District and Territories was issued, establishing in its Article 7(2) that the Governor of Mexico City (and not the municipal presidents) would have the supreme command of the city's police force. Notably, Article 49(2) of said statute, established that the Government of the Federal District had the power to annex a municipality to another, provided that it could not finance its expenses with its own resources. This article also established that this determination could not be carried into effect if the council of the municipality concerned was not in agreement with it.

In 1928, a new constitutional reform promoted by presidential candidate Alvaro Obregón decreed the suppression of municipal governments in Mexico City. As explained in my previous work (Serna, 2013, p. 155–156), in 1928, General Obregón sponsored a reform to the legal regime of the Federal District, whose main point was the elimination of the municipal form of organization. The reasons given by Obregón in his proposal were that municipalities had never really worked in the city. On the contrary, the president of the Republic through the governor, provided most public services and functions, and the federal Congress was the main provider of rules and statutes for the Federal District. For Obregón, this was a logical course of action because of the need to have unified and homogenous public services and

[2] In 1903 there were 13 (and not 16) subdivisions in the Federal District, and they were called "municipalities". In 1928 these "municipalities" were transformed into "delegations". In 1970 new subdivisions ("delegations") were created to reach the number of 16. The constitutional reform of 2016 substituted the term "delegations" for "*alcaldías*".

functions in Mexico City. Under those conditions—according to the proposal—municipal power had no reason to exist.

The reform proposal was approved and published in August 1928. The 13 municipalities that existed at that moment disappeared, and instead, 13 new territorial demarcations called "delegations" were created. The heads of these "delegations" would be appointed by the Chief of the Federal District Department with the approval of the president of the Republic. In turn, the Chief of the Federal District Department would be appointed by the president of the Republic. Notably, there were two main effects of this reform: the tightening of the president's political control on a nerve-centre such as Mexico City; and the significant reduction of political rights for the citizens of the Federal District who, under the new rules, would not be able to elect their local authorities (Serna, 2013, p. 155–156).

Between 1987 and 1996, a series of constitutional reforms led to the progressive democratization of the Federal District's government structure. By 1996, the Chief of Government of the Federal District and the heads of the delegations were directly elected by the citizens of the Federal District. Moreover, the legislative power was vested in a Legislative Assembly of the Federal District, which included the power to pass legislation on matters that were expressly indicated in Article 122 of the national Constitution. However, the Congress of the Union still retained the power to legislate on matters relating to the Federal District not mentioned in this provision.

This regime, which existed until 2016, created an ambiguous legal framework that (as some scholars noticed) was the product of intense tension between two camps. On one side you had those advocating for greater control and centralization (given that Mexico City is the seat of federal institutions). On the other side there were those advocating for greater decentralization, given the growth in population density and the increase in social demands from more local instances (Botero & Carvajal, 2011, p. 8). The result was ambiguity with parallel powers of the federal Congress and of the Legislative Assembly of the Federal District.

In 2016, a reform to the national Constitution modified the regime described above (Olvera Acevedo, 2019). As a consequence of this reform: (1) a constituent assembly was called to discuss and approve the Constitution of Mexico City (CMC) of 2017 which established a broad bill of rights and regulated the government structures of Mexico City, among them the *alcaldías* (boroughs)[3]; (2) instead of "Federal District" the official name of this entity became "Mexico City"; (3) Mexico City entered into the logic of the residual clause found in Article 124 of the national Constitution. According to this clause, what is not expressly made federal by the national Constitution is reserved to the states or to Mexico City. Thus, in contrast to the preceding regime, residual competence would now lie with Mexico City and no longer with the national government; and (4) the 16 delegations were transformed

[3] The CMC was drafted by a Constituent Assembly formed with 100 members. 60 of them were democratically elected by Mexico City's citizens; but 40 of its members were appointed in the following way: 6 by the president of the Republic; 6 by Mexico City's chief of government; 14 by the federal Chamber of Deputies; and 14 by the Senate.

into *alcaldías*, which have a regime different from that of municipalities which exist in the rest of the country.

It should be noted that with this reform, it was not considered appropriate to return to the regime of the municipality in Mexico City, because, as some scholars noticed, this would have implied an excess of regulations and authorities in a reduced territory with a demographic continuity and with an integrated scheme for the provision of public services to serve the 16 territorial demarcations of the city (Pérez López, 2013, p. 768 and 784). In this regard, it is important to mention that until 1928 the subdivisions of Mexico City were organized under the regime of municipalities. In 1928 the municipalities of Mexico City disappeared and were transformed into "delegations". In 2016 there was a debate on whether Mexico City subdivisions should return to the regime of "municipalities" (that existed before the reform of 1928), or if "delegations" should be transformed into some other kind of entity. The result of this debate was the transformation of "delegations" into "alcaldías" (and not a return to the regime of "municipalities").

4.3 The Legal Status, Institutions, Structures, and Competences of Mexico City's Urban Subdivisions

Article 122(6)(a) of the national Constitution establishes that the *alcaldías* (boroughs) are political-administrative bodies made up of a mayor and a council both? elected by universal, free, secret and direct vote for a 3-year term.

For its part, Article 52 of the CMC states that the territorial demarcations are the basis of the territorial division and the political and administrative organization of Mexico City and that they shall be autonomous in their internal government (which will be in charge of the *alcaldías*). This article also states that these territorial demarcations are made up of their inhabitants, their territory, and their democratically elected political authorities. Finally, the article also makes it clear that the *alcaldías* are the order of government that is closest to the population of the city and that their institutions are based on a democratic, representative and citizen participation regime, as well as on the precepts of good government.

Furthermore, Article 122(6)(a) of the national Constitution establishes that the government of the *alcaldías* is formed by a mayor and a council, who will be elected by free and secret vote of citizens. This article also provides that the members of the *alcaldía* will be elected by lists of between seven and ten candidates, as the case may be, in progressive order, beginning with the candidate for mayor and then the councilpersons, in the number determined by the CMC for each territorial demarcation. This article also states that in no case may the number of councilpersons be less than ten or more than 15 which shows that the right of the *alcaldías* to organize themselves is subject to certain constitutional limits.

In Mexico City, all *alcaldías* have the same constitutional and legal status. This is also the case of Mexican municipalities: they all have the same constitutional and legal status. In other words, there is no asymmetry among them.

For its part, Article 21 of the CMC determines that the public administration of the *alcaldías* corresponds to the mayor (*alcaldesa* or *alcalde*), and that in each *alcaldía* there shall be a council, which is the elected collegiate body in each territorial demarcation. The functions of the council are: (1) to supervise and evaluate governmental actions by the mayor; (2) to approve the draft budget of the *alcaldía*; and (3) to control the exercise of the *alcaldía*'s public expenditure (Article 81 of the Organic Law of *Alcaldías* of Mexico City). Likewise, Article 83 of this same statute establishes that the councils shall in no case exercise government and public administration functions. This means that councils have no decision-making power to adopt laws or regulations of any kind.

Decisions in the *alcaldías* are implemented by the mayor, who is assisted by different administrative units. The mayor determines and establishes the number, structure, integration, and organization of these administrative units, according to the characteristics and needs of the corresponding territorial demarcation (Article 71 of the Organic Law of *Alcaldías* of Mexico City).[4]

According to Article 53(a)(12) of the CMC, the *alcaldes* have competence, within their respective jurisdictions, in the following matters:

1. Government and internal regime;
2. Public works and urban development;
3. Public services;
4. Mobility;
5. Public roads;
6. Public space;
7. Public safety;
8. Economic and social development;
9. Education, culture and sports;
10. Environmental protection;
11. Legal affairs;
12. Accountability and social participation;
13. Regulations, circulars and administrative provisions of general observance;
14. Digital City Hall; and
15. Other competences as defined by laws.

However, in connection with each of the subject-matters mentioned above, the *alcaldes* of the 16 territorial demarcations of Mexico City exercise one of three

[4]Article 71 of the Organic Law of *Alcaldías* of Mexico City establishes that the functions and powers of each administrative unit shall be set forth in the Organizational Manual to be drafted by the *alcalde*, in accordance with the provisions of this law. Likewise, such Manual shall have the purpose of establishing the powers and functions of the administrative units of the *alcalde*'s office. Finally, this article states that the Manual shall be submitted by the *alcalde* to the Chief of Government of Mexico City for its publication in the Official Gazette of Mexico City.

types of competences. Some of them are exclusive of the *alcaldes*; others are exercised in coordination with the Chief of Government of Mexico City; and others are exercised subordinated to the Chief of Government of Mexico City.

As argued by some analysts, a shared and coordinated power structure emerged, which reflects a relationship of "institutional subordination" and a consequent "institutional ambiguity", particularly within the *alcaldías* that make up Mexico City, which is far from having the same autonomy as any Mexican municipality, something that is valid currently just as valid as it was before 2016 (Botero & Carvajal, 2011, p. 33).

Regarding fiscal resources of the *alcaldías*, Article 21(d) of the CMC states that they are composed of: (1) participations, contributions and other federal revenues, in accordance with the laws of the matter[5]; (2) resources that they generate for the provision of certain services and red tape[6]; (3) allocations raised by Mexico City's Government and determined for the budgets of the *alcaldías*, as approved by the Congress of Mexico City money; and (4) revenues coming from the fund established in Article 55 of the CMC (which is oriented to the construction of infrastructure to be used in projects that benefit the sectors of the population that are in a situation of vulnerability, with the objective of gradually reducing the inequality gap).

Unlike the municipalities, the *alcaldías* do not have the power to collect property tax. They depend to a great extent on the budget approved by the Mexico City Congress, which, in order to determine the amounts that correspond to each *alcaldía*, must take into account criteria such as: the resident and floating population; the population living in poverty; the levels of marginalization and social backwardness; the territorial extension, green areas and conservation land; investment in infrastructure, public services and urban equipment, as well as their maintenance. In addition, this budget may not be less in percentage terms than what it represented in the immediately preceding fiscal year with respect to the total budget of Mexico City, except in exceptional cases determined by law (Article 21(d)(2) of the CMC).

Comparing municipalities with the *alcaldías*, Méndez and Salguero conclude that they still lack a number of requisites to be a true local government with full political, fiscal, and administrative powers (Méndez Bahena & Salguero, 2019, p. 57). Or, as stated in a comparative study between municipalities and *alcaldías*, the latter are under the tutelage of the central government of Mexico City and therefore do not enjoy the same autonomy as municipalities (Guzmán Correa, 2018, p. 4).

---

[5] The federal Law of Fiscal Coordination establishes different kinds of federal transfers to the States, to Mexico City, to municipalities and to *alcaldías*. Summarizing, the most important federal transfers are the "participations" (non-targeted, that is, these resources can be used freely by states, municipalities and *alcaldías*); and "contributions" (in Spanish *aportaciones*, which are targeted, that is, they have to be spent on the items indicated by the Federal Budget approved by the Chamber of Deputies each fiscal year).

[6] For example, fees charged for issuing a permit to engage in commerce on public spaces; or fees for the registration of a construction permit to build, expand, repair or modify a construction site or facility for non-housing or mixed use.

The spending forecasts in the Mexico City Budget for the year 2021 give us an idea of the predominance of Mexico City's central government in the exercise of the available fiscal resources: 72.5% corresponded to Mexico City's central government. In contrast, the spending forecast for the *alcaldías* was equivalent to 18.3% and that of the so-called Autonomous Governmental Bodies[7] (Mexico's regulatory agencies) was 9.3% (Congreso de la Ciudad de México, 2020, p. 9).

Concerning staff remunerations by *alcaldía*, the data in the following table shows that, on average, they spent 46% of their total fiscal resources on that item (Table 4.1).

Table 4.1 Gross expenditures of Mexico City's *Alcaldías* (fiscal year 2018)

	Total fiscal resources (in billions of Mexican pesos)	Staff remunerations (as a percentage of total fiscal resources)
Álvaro Obregón	2.6	44
Azcapotzalco	1.8	53
Benito Juárez	2.5	44
Coyoacán	3.0	42
Cuajimalpa	1.9	44
Cuauhtémoc	3.4	58
Gustavo A. Madero	4.3	48
Iztacalco	2.2	45
Iztapalapa	5.6	36
Magdalena Contreras	1.7	40
Miguel Hidalgo	2.3	40
Milpa Alta	1.4	48
Tláhuac	1.9	51
Tlalpan	2.3	41
Venustiano Carranza	3.0	52
Xochimilco	2.0	51
	Total: 41.9	**Average: 46**

Source: INEGI (taken from *El Economista*, 15 July 2019)

[7] In Mexico, Autonomous Governmental Bodies or Autonomous Constitutional Agencies are government bodies created through a reform or addition to the national or subnational constitutional text, with a sphere of powers and competences defined directly by the corresponding Constitution and with an important degree of financial autonomy in the management of their budget. These agencies, which can be compared to other countries' independent regulatory agencies, perform relevant functions of the State. Specifically, it is understood that they have been created to perform technical functions which should be maintained far from political party politics. They exist both at the national and at the subnational level. In Mexico City, examples of this type of agencies are the Human Rights Commission and the Institute of Transparency and Access to Public Information.

4.4 Subdivision and Amalgamation of Local Government Units in Mexico City

4.4.1 Subdivision

In the case of Mexico City, the law allows for subdivision of the existing *alcaldías*. However, several analysts have stated that if such a subdivision were ever decided, there would be great resistance on the part of the existing territorial units. Discussing this matter when "delegations" still existed, Marván Laborde stated that: "It is foreseeable that since there are already elected heads of delegations there will be greater resistance to modify the political division of the city, given that, although there would be a distribution of responsibilities with a greater probability of efficiency, this would also mean a reduction in budget, human and material resources for the larger delegations" (Marván Laborde, 2001, p. 66). As we will see below, this is exactly what has happened.

In fact, Article 52(4) of the CMC establishes that the territorial demarcations may be modified in the terms established in said constitution, "without being able to be less in quantity than the established at the time of its entry into force". In other words, the number and territorial limits of the 16 territorial demarcations of Mexico City may be modified by dividing them (thus creating more demarcations), but they cannot be amalgamated. The rationale behind this rule results from the fact that the existing territorial demarcations are already very big. Amalgamation would create even bigger ones, and this could create greater difficulties in governing them.

Before the constitutional reform of 2016, some scholars identified a series of questions that had to be answered in case a decision was taken to divide one or several of the 16 units (delegations) that composed the Federal District. For example, Marván Laborde stated that some of these questions were: what is the ideal number of inhabitants per delegation so that they can be represented and properly cared for at this level of government?; what is the adequate maximum and minimum number of inhabitants per delegation that can be proposed for the delegations of the Federal District?; which of the current delegations should be divided, and, if so, how would the eventual territorial division be carried out?; what would be the budgetary cost of establishing each new delegation? (Marván Laborde, 2001, p. 65–66).

During the reform process that led to the approval of the CMC, there was a debate about the possibility of dividing the delegations (*alcaldías* since the reform of 2016), to the point that Transitory Article 22 of said constitution established that: "Once the electoral process corresponding to 2018 is concluded, the Congress of Mexico City must initiate the process of reviewing the configuration for the territorial division of the demarcations that make up Mexico City, in accordance with the criteria of balancing the population sizes among the *alcaldías* and those set forth in Article 52(3) of this constitution. This process must be concluded no later than December 2019." However, this process did not take place because of vested interests that favored the maintenance of the status quo.

4.4.2 Amalgamation

In contrast with the rules applicable to Mexico City and its *alcaldías*, amalgamations are possible in the states. In fact, most subnational constitutions provide for this possibility. For example, Article 5 of the Constitution of Veracruz provides that the State Congress may create, suppress, or merge municipalities, as well as modify their extension, by a vote of two thirds of its members, having previously heard the opinion of the State Governor and the City Council or City Councils of the municipalities concerned.

In spite of this possibility, amalgamations of municipalities do not usually occur. On the contrary, the creation of new municipalities is more frequent. For example, between 2011 and 2021, 17 new municipalities were created in Mexico (Galicia, 2021).

4.5 Institutions and Forums Guarantee Coordination Across the Subdivisions

Metropolitan governance in Mexico City is organized through: (1) the city council (*cabildo*); (2) Metropolitan commissions created through agreements; and (3) the Law on Metropolitan Coordination, which seeks to organize the governance of the entire metropolitan area whose center is Mexico City (with its 16 territorial demarcations), but also includes two other states (the State of Mexico and the State of Hidalgo), and 60 municipalities that form part of the latter.[8]

*4.5.1 City Council (*Cabildo*)*

It is stated in Article 54 of the CMC that a City council will be formed by the mayors of the 16 *alcaldías* and the Chief of Government of Mexico City. The City council functions as a planning, coordination, consultation, and decision-making body. Its decisions are made by consensus and its main function is to establish general agreements on matters of the public administration of the City and of the territorial demarcations.

In practice, the *cabildo* has had great difficulties functioning due to the enormous political polarization between the political forces occupying government positions in Mexico City. Currently, Mexico City's Chief of Government belongs to the MORENA party, as do 7 *alcaldías*; but 9 *alcaldías* are governed by other political parties, and the relationship between these two blocks tends to be one of confrontation rather than coordination. Certainly, the consensus rule adds to the stalemate and

[8] The total population living in this area is equivalent to about 22 million people.

polarization mentioned above. However, there have not been any debates to change this rule.

4.5.2 Metropolitan Commissions

In 2008, the legislature of the then Federal District passed the Act on Metropolitan Coordination, which empowers the Chief of Government of the city (though the Secretary of Government), to enter into agreements with the national government, the governments of the *alcaldías*, and the governments of the states and municipalities, in order to create metropolitan commissions in charge of coordinating planning and actions for the provision of different kinds of public services.

However, even though the Act on Metropolitan Coordination empowers the Chief of Government of Mexico to enter into agreements to form metropolitan commissions, the Chief is not the only one that can initiate agreements. Ultimately, according to Article 53(a)(2)(20) of the CMC, the *alcaldías* can "establish mechanisms of local collaboration with other *alcaldías* and municipalities of the federal entities". For its part, Article 64 of the Organic Law on the *Alcaldías* of Mexico City establishes that the *alcaldías*, "with the agreement of their Council, may associate with each other and with neighboring municipalities of other federative entities for the coordination in the provision of public services of regional and metropolitan impact, in matters of human settlements, environmental human settlements, environmental management, mobility, transportation, water, sanitation, waste management, public safety and other concurrent matters, through the subscription of the corresponding coordination agreement, in full compliance with the applicable legislation." However, in practice the *alcaldías* do not frequently make use of these rights.

Prior to the Act on Metropolitan Coordination mentioned above, metropolitan commissions were created in the 1990s so that the governments of Mexico City and the State of Mexico could address in a coordinated manner issues related to water and drainage, transport and transit, public security, human settlements, environment and civil protection (Serna, 2009, p. 163–172).

A current example of this type of coordination mechanism is the so-called Megalopolis Environmental Commission, which is in charge of planning and implementing actions related to environmental protection, preservation and the restoration of the ecological balance in the region that extends to the 16 territorial demarcations of Mexico City and to other 224 municipalities that exist within the States of Mexico, Hidalgo, Morelos, Puebla and Tlaxcala.

4.5.3 *Federal Law on Metropolitan Coordination for the Megalopolis Formed by Mexico City and Neighboring States and Municipalities*

It is worth mentioning that since the 2016 reform, Article 122(c) of the national Constitution provides that the Federation, Mexico City, as well as its territorial demarcations, and the States and Municipalities bordering the Metropolitan Zone, shall establish administrative coordination mechanisms in matters related to planning and the implementation of regional actions for the provision of public services, in terms of the law issued by the Congress of the Union. The reform also asserts that to achieve this coordination, the law shall establish the bases for the organization and operation of the Metropolitan Development Council, which will be responsible for agreeing on actions in the areas of human settlements; mobility and road safety; environmental protection; preservation and restoration of the ecological balance; transportation; transit; potable water and drainage; collection, treatment and disposal of solid waste; and public safety. However, to date, this federal statute has yet to be enacted by the Mexican Congress. Regardless of the fact that said Metropolitan Development Council still has not been created, the way in which the existing metropolitan coordination mechanisms are designed and function in Mexico has been criticized by some scholars (Iracheta Cenecorta, 2009, p. 85–86).

In relation to the metropolitan zones existing in Mexico, we must distinguish between those that include municipalities or *alcaldías* of two or more federated entities (interstate metropolitan zones); and those that include municipalities or *alcaldías* of only one federated entity (intrastate metropolitan zones).

The metropolitan zone encompassing Mexico City is located in an interstate metropolitan zone which, like all of this kind, is regulated by the General Law of Human Settlements, Territorial Planning and Urban Development, approved by the Congress of the Union. Chapter Six of this general law establishes several rules related to metropolitan governance. For example, Article 36 asserts that, in order to achieve effective metropolitan governance, mechanisms and instruments of a mandatory nature shall be established, to ensure the coordinated institutional action of the three levels of government and the participation of society. Likewise, it is established that the management of the metropolitan zones will be carried out through the following instances, such as a metropolitan planning commission; an advisory council for metropolitan development; bodies with technical expertise that may be required; agencies that allow the provision of common public services; and mechanisms and resources to finance metropolitan actions.

The above means that metropolitan areas that include municipalities or *alcaldías* of two or more states must follow a metropolitan governance scheme defined by a federal statute. However, there are not many such metropolitan areas in Mexico. The three that exist today are located in the Valley of Mexico (it includes *alcaldías* and municipalities of Mexico City, the State of Mexico and the State of Hidalgo), in the States of Puebla and Tlaxcala, and in the region known as La Laguna (which includes three municipalities of the State of Coahuila and two of the State of Durango).

4.6 Civil Society and Institutional Reform of Mexico City's Governmental Structures

The topic I would like to discuss in this section is the relationship between local civil society and the institutional and normative evolution of Mexico City's governmental structures. In my view, the examination of this topic can be divided into two major issues. One has to do with the democratization of the government bodies of Mexico City. The other is related to the specific organization and structure of these bodies, and the relationship between them.

Regarding the democratization of Mexico City's governmental bodies, it can be said that there was intense citizen pressure to modify a scheme that prevented citizens of Mexico City from electing their local governors. As explained above, between 1928 and 1996, the person who governed the then Federal District was an official appointed and freely removed by the President of the Republic. During this period, there was no local government elected by the inhabitants of the Federal District. However, a series of social mobilizations beginning in the 1980s (Loaeza, 1995, p. 148–149) led to the progressive democratization of the Federal District's Government.

As for the second issue, referring to the organization and structure of the Federal District's government bodies and the relations between them, I would argue that specialists and various politicians are more concerned about this issue than the general public. In addition, as argued by Marván, the motivation for the reforms initiated by the Federal Distrct to the regulartory scheme was not theoretical questions of federalism. Instead, it was the need to solve specific political, financial, administrative, and urban problems which arose from debates on: "the territorial extension of Mexico City, the political rights of its inhabitants, the definition of the relations between the governing bodies of Mexico City and those of the Federation, particularly with the Congress and the Executive, and finally the representative character and degree of autonomy, both of the Federal District's government and that of its territorial units" (Marván Laborde, 2001, p. 52).

4.7 Conclusions: A Final Reflection on the Legitimacy and Efficiency Mexico City's Urban subdivisions and on Possible Future Developments

Overall, I believe that the delegations, known today as *alcaldías*, have gained democratic legitimacy because, since he constitutional reform of 1996, their authorities have been elected by universal and direct suffrage. Moreover, in theory, the councils were created in the *alcaldías* to give participation to citizens in the government, as well as to open spaces for the representation of neighbors and avoid unilateral decisions of the mayor and serve as a counterweight. In practice, however, this has not worked. The list system by which they are elected makes them subordinate to the mayor. In my view, the democratic weight of the council could be strengthened by substituting the list system with a system in which councilpersons are elected in electoral districts within the corresponding *alcaldía*. In this way, each of them would have a direct electoral connection with a specific constituency to whom they are accountable.

In addition, the councils lack normative power, as they have no authority to draft any kind of rules or regulations (Santiago, 2021). They only have oversight and budgetary powers. Moreover, in many cases they do not comply with basic rules for their proper functioning, such as the duty to meet at least once a month (Cosme, 2023).

Likewise, according to some observers, the Organic Law of *Alcaldías* of Mexico City, approved by the Legislative Assembly in 2018, did not carefully outline the essential details needed for councilpersons to carry out their functions, such as timely access to all information regarding the exercise of public spending, the fulfillment of the actions and goals of the government program, and the administrative acts and resolutions on which the councils have supervisory powers. Additionally, councilors lack the material conditions (e.g. budget and infrastructure) to carry out their work effectively and with autonomy from the mayor (Muñiz Toledo, 2018).

An important aspect to point out is that in the public administration of the *alcaldías* there is no real career civil service, which affects the efficiency of the administration. Ultimately, every time there is a new mayor, a large part of the first and second level administrative personnel is removed from office. This prevents the formation of a professional, technical, and specialized local public administration.

An issue that can be explored for the future that will improve the efficacy of local government both in Mexico City and in the municipalities has to do with the creation of a true civil service career. In fact, such a service needs to be created at the federal and state levels as well. Currently, the alternative to professionalize local public administration in some municipalities or *alcaldías* has been the creation of the so-called "city manager". However, when tried, it has not yielded the expected results, as explained by Chávez and Villasana, who have examined the experiences with the city manager role in four municipalities[9] and one delegation of the then Federal District.[10] Moreover, after making an analysis of the debates on the city manager that have taken place in multiple states and municipalities, these authors reach the basic conclusion that this institutional option has not managed to expand its presence or to establish itself permanently where it has been tried. This is due to various factors, such as: political-partisan polarization, resistance of mayors to giving up spaces of power to the benefit of the city manager, weak social demand of in-depth local government reforms, and the lack of consensus of academics, specialists and those interested in modernizing local government (Chávez Alzaga & Villasana Dávila, 2019, p. 276–298).

[9] In Tijuana, Baja California (2001–2004); in Texcoco, State of Mexico (2006–2012); in Navolato, Sinaloa (2014–2016), and in Ciudad Juárez, Chihuahua (2016–2017).

[10] Miguel Hidalgo delegation of the then Federal District (2000–2006).

Another attempted route to professionalize local public administration has involved establishing minimum requirements that must be met by persons holding certain public positions within the local government. For example, by amendment of 18 October 2018 to the Organic Law of the *Alcaldías* of Mexico City, it was established that the head of the unit of Administration of the *alcaldías* of Mexico City, must "(a) Hold a degree or have the respective professional license for the practice of the profession in the areas of Accounting, Public Administration, Business Administration, Finance, Economics, Law, Actuary, Engineering or sciences in areas related to administration; or (b) Have a minimum experience of 2 years in the exercise of a position within the Federal, State, City or Municipal Public Administration, related to the branches of budget, administration, auditing or similar; or 2 years in the exercise of the profession as an administrator, accountant, comptroller or auditor in the private sector".

In the same way, special requirements were established to be head of the administrative units of Legal Affairs, Public Works and Urban Development, Government and Urban Services of the *alcaldías* of Mexico City. It is important to mention that these requirements have been implemented, with no observable or mesurable result.

Finally, I would like to say that there has been a discussion in Latin American academic circles that propose the introduction of a series of "democratic innovations" in public decision-making processes in order to reinvigorate the legitimacy and efficacy of representative democracies (Selee & Peruzzotti, 2009; Cameron & Sharpe, 2012; Serna, 2024). This implies the creation of "entry points" of civil society actors into legislative, administrative, and judicial processes (Fishkin, 2013). It would be worth exploring whether mechanisms of this sort could be created in the governmental structures and processes of Mexico City and its *alcaldías*. In my view, there is no potential clash between citizen involvement and coordination. Moreover, participatory democracy should (and could) mostly be strengthened on the level of the territorial demarcations.

References

Botero, M. H., & Carvajal, D. (2011). *El proceso de descentralización intraterritorial en el Distrito Federal mexicano: La ambigüedad generada por la tensión entre descentralización y centralización en la gestión de los territorios*. Centro de Estudios Políticos e Internacionales de la Universidad del Rosario.

Cameron, M. A., & Sharpe, K. E. (2012). La voz institucionalizada en las democracias de América Latina. In M. A. Cameron, E. Hershberg, & K. E. Sharpe (Eds.), *Nuevas Instituciones de democracia participativa en América Latina: La voz y sus consecuencias*. FLACSO.

Chávez Alzaga, O., & Villasana Dávila, J. (2019). Crónica del administrador municipal y del City Manager en México a 2018. In T. R. Huerta (Ed.), *500 años del municipio en México. Perspectivas multidisciplinarias* (pp. 276–298). Universidad de Guanajuato.

Congreso de la Ciudad de México. (2020). *Análisis Comparativo del Gasto del Gobierno de la Ciudad de México: 2020 vs 2021*. Reporte de Trabajo, Unidad de Estudios de Finanzas Públicas del Congreso de la Ciudad de México.

Cosme, M. (2023, July 10). Councils of 10 Alcaldías do not meet their monthly work. *El Sol de México*.

Serna de la Garza, J. M. (2009). Mechanisms of cooperation in Mexico's federal system. In B. de Villiers (Ed.) *Crossing the line: Dealing with cross-border communities*. Konrad Adenauer Occasional Papers (pp. 163–172).

Serna de la Garza, J. M. (2013). *The Constitution of Mexico: A contextual analysis*. Hart Publishing.

Serna de la Garza, J. M. (2024). *Acceso a la Ciudadanía. Estudio sobre diversos mecanismos de participación de la sociedad civil en los procesos decisionales del Estado*. UNAM.

Fishkin, J. (2013). Deliberation by the people themselves: Entry points for the public voice. *Election Law Journal, 12*(4), 490–507.

Galicia, D. (2021). En 10 años, 17 nuevos municipios. *Alcaldes de México* 133. https://www.alcaldesdemexico.com/revista/sin-categoria/en-10-anos-17-nuevos-municipios/

Guzmán Correa, P. R. (2018). *Alcaldías y Municipios, un análisis comparativo*. Instituto de Investigaciones Parlamentarias, Asamblea Legislativa del Distrito Federal, VII Legislatura.

INEGI. (2021). *Comunicado de Prensa Núm. 98/2021*.

Iracheta Cenecorta, A. (2009). *Políticas públicas para gobernar las metropolis mexicanas*. Miguel Angel Porrúa.

Loaeza, S. (1995). Perspectivas para una historia política del Distrito Federal en el siglo XX. *Historia Mexicana, El Colegio de México, XLV*(1)

Marván Laborde, I. (2001). La cuestión del gobierno representativo en el Distrito Federal mexicano. *Cuestiones Constitucionales, 4*, 49–83.

Méndez Bahena, B., & Salguero, A. L. (2019). Mexico City's boroughs: Not yet local governments. *Revista de Direito da Cidade, 11*(4), 57–83.

Muñiz Toledo, R. (2018, October 20). Para qué sirven los Concejos de las Alcaldías. *Aristegui Noticias*. https://aristeguinoticias.com/2010/opinion/para-que-sirven-los-concejos-de-las-alcaldias/

Olvera Acevedo, A. (2019). *Ciudad de México. La Reforma Jurídico-Política en el Distrito Federal*. Tirant lo Blanch.

Pérez López, M. (2013). Hacia la Constitución Política de la Ciudad de México, Antecedentes, fundamentos y propuestas. *Alegatos, 85*, 761–788.

Santiago, D. (2021). Councils of Mexico City: Invisible players in the electoral process of 2021. *Expansión Política*. https://politica.expansion.mx/cdmx/2021/03/23/voces-concejales-de-la-cdmx-un-jugador-invisible-en-el-proceso-electoral-2021

Selee, A., & Peruzzotti, E. (2009). *Participatory innovation and representative democracy in Latin America*. Johns Hopkins University Press.

Open Access This chapter is licensed under the terms of the Creative Commons Attribution 4.0 International License (http://creativecommons.org/licenses/by/4.0/), which permits use, sharing, adaptation, distribution and reproduction in any medium or format, as long as you give appropriate credit to the original author(s) and the source, provide a link to the Creative Commons license and indicate if changes were made.

The images or other third party material in this chapter are included in the chapter's Creative Commons license, unless indicated otherwise in a credit line to the material. If material is not included in the chapter's Creative Commons license and your intended use is not permitted by statutory regulation or exceeds the permitted use, you will need to obtain permission directly from the copyright holder.

Chapter 5
Governing Large Urban Areas in Spain: Multiple Scales, Models and Challenges

Esther Pano and Carmen Navarro

Abstract Managing large urban areas poses two main institutional challenges: decentralizing city governance to sub-municipal units such as districts to better respond to local needs and coordinating government action in fragmented metropolitan spaces. Spain faces these challenges in local governance without being able to solve either of them effectively. Within cities, the implementation of decentralized districts does not seem to have developed the potential for which they were intended. In metropolitan terms, the model provided by the national framework legislation has hardly been developed, and instead each metropolitan region has followed a different institutional arrangement with different degrees of legitimacy. As an example, while Barcelona displays a strong inter-municipal component and bases legitimacy on a multilevel and coordination logic, Madrid has chosen to steer the management of metropolitan affairs towards the regional level of government that enjoys more effectiveness than municipal inclusion.

Keywords Local government · Cities · Decentralization · Districts · Metropolitan areas

5.1 Introduction

As populations tend to concentrate in cities, managing large urban areas becomes increasingly complex. Just in institutional terms, two key challenges emerge. Firstly, to bring local action closer to citizens and to the specificities of the territory within large cities by decentralization to sub-municipal units such as districts. Secondly, to

E. Pano (✉)
Fundació Carles Pi i Sunyer and Universitat de Barcelona, Barcelona, Spain
e-mail: epano@ub.edu

C. Navarro
Institute of Local Government Law, Autonomous University of Madrid, Madrid, Spain
e-mail: c.navarro@uam.es

© The Author(s) 2026

K. Kössler, E. M. Belser (eds.), *Local Government Structure and Intergovernmental Relations*, Local and Urban Governance,
https://doi.org/10.1007/978-3-031-99820-1_5

coordinate governmental action in metropolitan spaces when the boundaries don't align with government jurisdictions but are a patchwork of authorities. Spain faces both challenges in its local governance.

Confronted with the first challenge, the decentralization within large cities has extended to most urban territories in Spain. This was facilitated by the establishment of districts. Districts, which had already been in existence during the pre-democratic era only in the most populates cities in the country, began to gain momentum in the 1980s with the democratization of local governments. The pace of districts implementation accelerated two decades ago, catalyzed by a reform of the Local Government Act adopted in 2003. This reform mandated the compulsory establishment of districts in large municipalities.

In this new legislation, districts were envisaged as instruments of administrative decentralization aimed at enhancing participation in local governance and improving service delivery processes. The reform also established that the regulation of these entities falls within the responsibility of each individual city council which determines the key aspects of its management including territorial delineation, political structure and election methods, as well as functions and internal organization. This has led to considerable variation between municipalities in the allocation of tasks, funding and human resources in districts, ranging from negligible differences to significant impacts on local organizational structures. Years after its implementation, studies on the actual functioning of districts report that cities have not made widespread use of the potential for decentralization this opportunity offers (Galindo Caldés, 2014) and assess them as a "tool with high potential but weakly explored by municipal governments" (Navarro & Pano, 2018, p. 242).

As for the second challenge, the difficulty in articulating an institutional and juridical framework for the metropolitan reality has been extensively explored and analyzed (Tomàs, 2023; Hildenbrand, 2017). Hildenbrand (2017) identifies a wide range of contributions from different disciplines (from legal studies to urban planning, architecture, geography, and economy) that observe the failure of an effective metropolitan institutionalisation. This lack of a clear metropolitan institutional framework leaves municipalities as the main actors in the governance of large urban spaces. The relevance of municipal governments in metropolitan governance is the result of two factors: the impossibility of amalgamations in the Spanish context as a way to address metropolitan challenges and the difficulty of creating new metropolitan entities that may hinder the well-established principle of municipal autonomy.

Indeed, the Spanish legal framework provides for the possibility of giving an institutionalized status to large urban conglomerations. It does so through the possibility to create so-called "metropolitan areas" which have to be created and regulated by the autonomous communities (the regional level of government). However, the regions have hardly made use of the possibilities offered by the law and only two (Catalonia and Valencia) have set up metropolitan formal entities. Generally, they have been reluctant to create metropolitan legal entities that could rival them for power. Instead, the metropolitan reality in Spain is channelled through other mechanisms that meet functional needs rather than the existence of formal institutions (e.g. inter-municipal cooperation agreements, public enterprises, consortia, etc.).

Even in Barcelona, the case of the highest level of institutionalization, the Metropolitan Area of Barcelona is a second-level entity without any mechanism of direct election or legitimation by the citizens. Therefore, the concept of internal decentralization of metropolitan areas may not precisely fit the specific Spanish reality. Nevertheless, concerns about distance and scale are common, as are the challenges in coordinating interests, regardless of the legal formula used.

In this context of diversity in how the Spanish political system deals with urban areas and the lack of real metropolitan institutions, the local government structures of Madrid and Barcelona constitute two contrasting scenarios. This chapter systematically explores the principal features of both realities—decentralization within cities and metropolitan institutional arrangements—and the diverse mechanisms employed for integrating territorial preferences into the decision-making process. The following section puts this reality into context by presenting the characteristics of the Spanish municipal map. This is followed in subsequent sections by systematic analysis of the way in which both districts and metropolitan spaces have been institutionally addressed in the Spanish system. In the final section, the chapter examines the metropolitan arrangements of Madrid and Barcelona, presenting and analyzing the two contrasting models with particular attention to legitimacy.

5.2 The Spanish Municipal Map

Looking at the constellation of Spanish municipalities for the first time does not leave one indifferent. The high number of units, the predominance of small municipalities, and the concentration of the population in a small number of big cities define the Spanish map. 50% of the 8131 existing municipalities have less than 500 inhabitants, and 1360 have less than 100 inhabitants. However, big cities like Madrid (3.2 million inhabitants), Barcelona (1.6), Seville (0.8), ten other cities with more than 300,000 and an additional 50 cities with more than 100,000 inhabitants are also part of this diverse landscape. This implies that the 60 largest municipalities account for 40% of the population. The Spanish pattern of big and small units is more extreme than in other southern European countries like Italy and France, which also have a large number of small municipalities but where the disproportion in population distribution is not so acute.

This fragmented map does not result from a specific design or a global territorial reform. On the contrary, the Spanish municipal map is a historical product with medieval roots (Magre Ferran et al., 2019) and a strong historical inertia that has marked the (non)evolution of the local map. The current number of municipalities and their territorial boundaries are very similar to what we could find a century ago. In 1813, there were about 12,000 villages, while the census of 1900 gave a figure of 9214 (Calonge Velázquez, 2015). Today, the number of municipalities (1831) is lower, but it does not represent a substantial change in the local map. The historical determinants are so present that there is still a clear north-south divide that differentiates the country: in the south, larger municipalities predominate, and in the north, small ones. This difference is due to the different phases of the *reconquista* between the eighth and the sixteenth centuries (Ribero & Lladós 2014).

The wave of territorial consolidation reforms that began in the Scandinavian countries in the 1950s and continues to this day has never affected Spain. Swianiewicz and colleagues report that, in the twenty-first century alone, 21 European countries have implemented amalgamation reforms (Swianiewicz et al., 2022), all intending to create economies of scale and give municipalities more policy scope. In contrast to this trend, Spain has not only been spared this wave of reform, but the number of municipalities has actually slightly increased over the last decades (from 8022 in 1980 to 8131 in 2020).

The only substantial amalgamations conducted in the country date back to the mid-twentieth century, when two types of consolidation processes were implemented during Franco's authoritarian rule. The first occurred in the 1940s and affected Madrid and other big cities. Surrounding towns and villages were amalgamated into the big cities to create large metropolitan urban settings. The second took place in the 1960s and concerned small municipalities in inner rural Spain and followed the intense process of migration from these areas to the emerging industrial poles. The legislation adopted in 1966 allowed for the merging of municipalities in order to make the resulting entity politically and administratively viable in areas where depopulation had been more intense. Other than these reforms made more than half a century ago, the system has not responded to recent changes in the territorial distribution of the population.

The non-evolution of the Spanish local map has resulted in a combination of very large, large, medium, small, and very small municipalities. In terms of democratic legitimacy, this feature does not pose major problems Indeed, local democracy is experienced differently in small municipalities compared to large ones, as shown, for example, by the fact that electoral participation in local elections is higher in small municipalities, even higher than in general elections (Magre Ferran & Delgado Sotillos, 2019), indicating a greater appreciation of local institutions by residents of villages and small towns. However, municipalities are highly accepted by the population as they are. They have been, at the beginning of the democratic transition in the 1970s, the spaces where citizens learned to socialize in a new culture of freedom, competitive elections, and participation in public affairs, and they played a decisive role in laying the foundations—in terms of services and infrastructure—for economic activity (Magre Ferran et al., 2019). In addition, surveys show that Spaniards tend to value local governments more than the regional level of government.

5.3 Decentralization in Large Cities

Against this background, large cities are a challenge for the realization of local democracy. The much-praised value of closeness and participation that local government embodies suffers when talking about political communities with millions of inhabitants. Political systems cannot decide on the size of urban spaces. It is rather a structural trend in our societies that citizens tend to move more and more to urban areas and mega-cities have become a fact. These spaces are internally diverse, and political institutions must provide effective institutions that are responsive and accountable to their diverse constituencies. This is usually achieved through the political or administrative decentralization in districts or neighbourhoods.

Decentralizing the different parts that make up the municipal territory (i.e. districts or neighborhoods) is the strategy more commonly used in large municipalities to overcome the lack of proximity between the municipal government and citizens. It is argued that doing so improves the efficiency and effectiveness of local action by taking administration closer to citizens and promoting citizens' participation (Lowndes & Sullivan, 2008).

Districts have been part of the larger cities' functioning for already more than four decades of our recent democratic history (e.g. Madrid, Barcelona, Bilbao, Valencia). However, the practice of decentralizing districts has become even more popular because of the 2003 Reform of the Local Government Act. Already before this reform, all cities *could* establish districts in their organizational structure. But the so-called Measures of the Modernization of Local Government made, in addition, the establishment of these structures *mandatory* for what the law defined as "large cities".[1] The specific purpose of that was to encourage citizen participation. The adopted legislation gives local authorities considerable autonomy in the organization of their territorially decentralized bodies. They can choose from a wide range of options: individual or collective bodies, with advisory, management, control, or sanctioning functions, funded with more or less human and financial resources, etc.

The lack of an official register for districts combined with the autonomy of cities to organize districts means that the assessment of its implementation has to be done surveying municipality by municipality or relying on specific academic studies. Galindo Caldés (2014) has counted a total of 85 municipalities where the establishment of districts has been implemented. Despite only accounting for 1% of the country's local governments, this strategy encompasses nearly half of the Spanish population. The adoption of districts correlates directly with municipality size; all municipalities with populations exceeding half a million inhabitants have implemented them, whereas only about one-third of cities with populations ranging between 50,000 and 100,000 have done so, and a minority of smaller towns have followed suit.

For instance, in the two most populous cities in the country, the figures are relatively comparable. Madrid, with a population of 3.2 million inhabitants, has 21 districts, while Barcelona has 10 districts with half the population of Madrid. This results in an average district size of approximately 150,000 inhabitants in these

[1] According to Section 138 of the Local Government Act (Law 8/1985), the status of large cities (*ciudades de gran población*) is granted to (a) municipalities with more than 250,000 inhabitants, (b) capital cities of provinces and regions and (c) municipalities with populations above 75,000 inhabitants with special economic, social, historical and cultural circumstances when this status is approved by the regional parliament. There are currently 65 large cities in Spain.

cities, although some territories boast around 250,000 inhabitants, while others have fewer than 100,000. Notably, figures are significantly lower in other Spanish cities.

National legislation provides general guidelines that municipalities must adhere to when establishing districts. These guidelines are outlined in the Local Government Act and in the Royal Decree 2568/1986. However, the national legal framework remains quite broad and does not delve into specifics. It simply authorizes municipalities to establish territorial bodies for deconcentrated management to facilitate citizen participation in local affairs, allowing each municipality to determine the organization, tasks, and functions of such bodies (Section 24(1) of the Local Government Act). It further stipulates that the members, organization, and territorial boundaries of districts shall be determined by the municipal council. Additional regulations can be found in the laws of autonomous communities. However, similar to national legislation, regional parliaments have rarely developed detailed regulations on districts. Only half of them have provided their own guidelines for municipalities, which again are broad and general, granting local governments autonomy in determining the specifics of district organization.

Despite their general and broad principles, what is clear from the national and regional regulations is that among the various forms of decentralization/deconcentration described by Kuhlmann and Wayenberg (2016), the transfer of tasks to districts is an example of vertical deconcentration of functions. This is because government functions are delegated to territorially operating field offices within districts, which remain part of the organisational structure of local governments.

Given the substantial autonomy granted to municipalities, it would be necessary to refer to each municipality's legal framework set in the Municipal Organic Regulation to understand the characteristics of the functioning of its districts. These specific legal instruments encompass instructions on organization, tasks, financing, and coordination mechanisms with central city government departments. But although district organization is autonomously decided by each municipality, common patterns exist (Galindo Caldés, 2014). In political terms, districts are typically structured around three key actors: the president, district councilor, and district council.

The *district president* holds representative functions and limited executive authority. S/he may be appointed by the mayor, elected by district councilors, or chosen based on local election results. Often, a councilor from the municipal council serves as president. The *district councilor* serves as the executive head within the district, often holding multiple mandates and being a member of the local council appointed by the mayor. The district councilor oversees executive, managerial functions, and citizen participation within the district. Many cities consolidate the roles of district councilor and president into a single office: the District Councilor-President, combining mayoral delegation, executive duties, and presidency responsibilities.

The *district council* is the collective assembly within the district, chaired by the district president and composed of district councilors (*vocales vecinos)*. Their election is based on an indirect election or appointment, and cities have varied systems to choose their members. Among district council members we find city councillors themselves as well as members appointed by the political groups, by city associations, or by ordinary citizens (Galindo Caldés, 2014). If the model is that district councillors are elected by the political groups represented in the city council, the district council majority can mirror either the city's electoral results in municipal elections, as in the case of Madrid, or the district's electoral results, as in the case of Barcelona.

Besides these primary actors and institutions, certain municipalities have incorporated specific additional frameworks to facilitate citizen engagement in the decision-making processes of districts. While some models involve territorial citizen participation directly through district councils themselves (Rodríguez Herrero & Ajangiz, 2007), others set up specific collective bodies with diverse compositions including association representatives, city councilors and/or citizens. Examples of these new bodies include neighborhood assemblies, territorial councils and participatory councils, among others.

Regarding their administrative structures, districts are supported by public administration structures overseen by the district councilor or, in some cases, by CEOs known as district managers or directors. Tasks and responsibilities decentralized to districts are determined by each municipality's internal organization rules, with no national or regional requirements. The challenge is to bring administration closer to citizens while preventing fragmentation and inequality in service provision among city residents in similar circumstances. The practical landscape offers a wide range of situations, from municipalities in which only the area of citizen participation has been decentralized to districts, to cities—especially the largest ones—where these sub-municipal units develop a wider range of tasks, including decentralized municipal decision-making processes (reports, proposals, budgeting), management (permits, contracts, subsidies, sanctions), provision of services (cultural, sports, education), and support to associations (Navarro & Pano, 2018).

Funding allocation to districts varies widely, with municipalities deciding the share of financial resources. City government must declare the amount allocated to districts in their internal regulations, whether as a percentage of the total budget or a fixed amount. Funding levels fluctuate based on the range of functions transferred, with some cities allocating approximately 15% of total revenues to district administration, while others allocate less than 1% (Galindo Caldés, 2014).

5.4 Managing Metropolitan Areas

When socio-economic and mobility dynamics in urban areas go beyond municipal boundaries, their challenges must be addressed with a metropolitan view. A single municipal government is unable to meet the governance challenges derived from the daily mobility of residents, and new forms of governance are needed.

Over decades, countries have adopted different approaches to this problem. The approaches span a spectrum. One alternative is the consolidation of municipalities within the metropolitan agglomeration. This is in accordance with the reformist perspective, which contends that reducing institutional fragmentation enhances efficiency, democratic quality, and social equity. Another approach involves maintaining a passive stance and depending on the capacity of municipalities in the metropolitan area to coordinate their actions. This echoes the public choice school of the 1970s, which advocates for minimal governmental intervention. Alternatively, intermediary strategies involve establishing metropolitan structures as an additional tier of government with authority limited to metropolitan policy domains, such as transport, planning, waste management, and water provision (Kübler & Heinelt, 2004).

Spain has opted for the latter model, which gives regional governments the flexibility to decide whether to establish metropolitan institutions, but it has not been widely implemented. The Local Government Law stipulates that the regional governments, i.e. the Autonomous Communities, are responsible for the creation, modification and suppression of metropolitan political structures. However, the Autonomous Communities have been extremely reluctant to create formal metropolitan structures in accordance with these provisions. So much so that, although the Institute of Statistics recognizes, based on the Eurostat methodology, 73 functional urban areas (which can be regarded as metropolitan areas), only in Barcelona do we see a metropolitan government following the stipulation of the Local Government Act. In the remaining areas, different models of metropolitan governance coexist. Studies on this topic identify up to a dozen different hard and soft institutional settings: sectoral metropolitan agencies, inter-municipal cooperation agreements, consortia, public and mixed enterprises, territorial plans, sectoral plans (mobility, waste management, water), counties, associations of municipalities, strategic plans, European projects and working groups (Sevillano et al., 2023, p. 56). Each of these implies a different way of dealing with the metropolitan phenomenon.

5.5 Madrid: A Case of a Metropolitan Region

Madrid is the country's largest and most populated urban area, with over six million inhabitants. Its development as a metropolitan area started in the 1940s under the authoritarian rule of General Franco following a strategy of territorial consolidation of annexation of municipalities to the City of Madrid. In the late 1940s and early 1950s, the central government annexed 13 surrounding municipalities to the central city. This meant that the urban area to be governed by a single local authority increased from 68 to 607 km^2, and the local administrations of the annexed municipalities were abolished. Today, those merged territories make up the districts where the City of Madrid decentralizes part of its action. In the 1960s, a special metropolitan body (Metropolitan Planning and Coordination Commission—COPLACO) was set up to coordinate urban planning in the area, covering 23 municipalities, including the City of Madrid.

These reforms prioritised effective urban planning as one of their objectives. Both were top-down reforms carried out during the authoritarian period. At the time, municipalities did not provide many services or policies themselves. Urban planning was one of the few tasks they did perform. Other potential public issues for a metropolitan agenda (transport and infrastructure, economic development, etc.) corresponded to services provided by the central government in a highly centralized system.

Soon after the adoption of the 1978 Constitution—based on the principle of territorial autonomy—a quasi-federal state emerged, in which political power and public action were highly decentralised to governments in the regions, the so-called Autonomous Communities. In this context, the coordination of the Madrid metropolitan area underwent a significant change. The metropolitan mechanism of COPLACO was abolished, and no other similar mechanism of metropolitan governance emerged. Instead, the newly created government—the Government of the Autonomous Community of Madrid—has since acted as the only de facto metropolitan arrangement mechanism.

The creation of the Madrid regional government prevented the emergence of another type of metropolitan governance mechanism. This is because of the responsibility it entails and the territory it covers. Since (1) the boundaries of the government's jurisdiction practically coincide with the boundaries of the metropolitan area, and (2) it has powers typically associated with metropolitan issues (urban and physical planning, housing, environmental issues, mobility), we could say that a consolidated metropolitan government emerged by accident in this large urban area. The fact that regional governments in Spain are extremely strong and reluctant to devolve power to municipalities has hindered the possibility of creating the legal structure of a "metropolitan area" based on cooperation between municipalities. Due to the characteristics of the model, Madrid's arrangement wins in terms of efficiency of decision-making processes but loses in terms of local autonomy and the possibility of municipalities coordinating their action in fields they are responsible for.

Indeed, the resulting model applied in Madrid has produced positive effects in terms of identifying clear responsibilities and the existence of a structure of public administration to implement adopted policies. While some authors see problems of legitimacy and citizen acceptance in other metropolitan governments set up with top-down strategies (Lefèvre, 1998), Madrid avoids this problem. The Autonomous Community of Madrid is one of the 17 regional governments created under the new democratic regime, and there is considerable popular acceptance and support for this decentralised form of government. It also enjoys legitimacy in the output dimension, as the political-administrative structures are powerful and autonomous, with the financial means to effectively develop metropolitan policies.

Madrid would stand out as a case of metropolitan governance carried out in two stages. First, through a consolidation reform in the 1940s accomplished by annexing the surrounding municipalities to the City of Madrid. Second, through the creation of a new governmental layer in the early 1980s—the regional government—as a result of the decentralization system designed in the new democratic Constitution of 1978. This regional government de facto exercises power in key metropolitan fields (e.g. mobility and spatial planning). This arrangement does not make use of the legal possibility of to establish a formal "metropolitan area". But, in fact, the regional government is heavily involved in metropolitan policies, as well as in many other areas of responsibility (health, education, etc.), as defined by the Spanish system of decentralisation. In this regional government we find clear powers, representative institutions, public employees in charge of many metropolitan policies' implementation, and adequate budgets—all of which result in significant governing capacity. However, these indicators of metropolitan legitimacy and performance would mainly emphasise the input and output aspects of the system.

When assessing the throughput legitimacy of the model though (the way decision-making processes are constructed, emphasising the need for transparent, inclusive and participatory methods), we begin to see weaknesses. In the Madrid model, we see the regional authority as the only institution in place and a very limited presence of municipalities and private actors (groups, civil society associations or NGOs) in formal metropolitan decision-making processes (Navarro & Tomas, 2007). Municipalities have legal responsibilities for urban planning, mobility, waste treatment and water supply, and this model hampers their ability to take coordinated action. It is only in the field of public transport that we find a typical metropolitan governance mechanism involving municipalities in coordination with the regional government. The Regional Consortium for Public Transport (CRTM) stands out for its approach of vertical (regional and municipal levels of government) and horizontal (municipalities) cooperation in the field of metropolitan mobility. Consortia are public law entities with legal personality, set up by several public authorities and sometimes with the participation of private entities for the development of activities of common interest to all of them. But even in this mechanism, the presence of the regional government and the City of Madrid marks the governmental arrangement at the expense of the representation of other municipalities. Its executive board is presided over by the regional minister of transportation, the vice president is a member of the municipal council of the City of Madrid and only three members in a board of 20 members represent other municipalities.[2]

The mechanisms for horizontal coordination between municipalities provided for in the Local Government Act could have been implemented in Madrid for certain policy areas. However, the strength and power of the regional government has prevented the emergence of other, more inclusive forms of metropolitan governance. The throughput legitimacy of the model suffers from this lack of inclusiveness of municipalities in decision making processes. However, despite its weaknesses, there does not seem to be an alternative for it in the near future. Nobody, whether political parties, citizens or their associations, is calling for new ways of managing the metropolitan phenomenon (González Medina & de Gregorio Hurtado, 2023).

[2] See https://transparencia.crtm.es/informacion-institucional/?lang=.

5.6 Barcelona a Case of Municipal Coordination

The creation of the Metropolitan Area of Barcelona has been marked by the political challenges of each moment and context. It is worth noting that the current municipal term of Barcelona is the result of a process of division and annexation of neighbouring localities, taking place between the mid-nineteenth century and the early-twentieth century, that ended in the first decades of the twentieth century with the aggregation of partial zones or areas (Busquets, 2004).

In 1974, still during the Franco regime, the Metropolitan Corporation of Barcelona was established, serving as an initial precursor to the current institution. This entity was dissolved by the Territorial Planning Law in 1987, and its services were transferred to the Generalitat of Catalonia, which then created the Metropolitan Entity of Transport, the Metropolitan Entity of Hydraulic Services and Waste Treatment, and the Association of Municipalities of the Metropolitan Area of Barcelona. All of these were cooperative entities dedicated to service provision and planning. However, these mechanisms did not fully meet the territorial needs and demands.

Thus, in 2010, after a period that was not without difficulties, Law 31/2010 of the Parliament of Catalonia was approved, which created or reinstated, depending on the perspective, the Metropolitan Area of Barcelona. The Metropolitan Area of Barcelona is a local administration created by Law 31/2010 of the Parliament of Catalonia, which establishes its competences, financing, and political structure. Its main functions include a wide range of tasks such as urban planning, transportation, environment, economic development, and social cohesion. The functions are mostly concurrent between the metropolitan area and the municipalities, and, among them, service provision related to public transportation and environmental activities are the most visible and recognizable for the citizens. The fiscal system of the Metropolitan Area of Barcelona is essentially based on transfers, notably those from participating municipalities. Regarding the mode of election, it is entirely indirect, with mayors and municipal councils being the main actors in the process.

The political structure comprises four essential mechanisms: the President, the Metropolitan Council, the Governing Board, and the Council of Mayors. The Metropolitan Council serves as the main deliberative body and functions as a plenary. The process for electing its members is intricate and stems from the outcomes of municipal elections. A certain number of metropolitan councillors are assigned to each municipality. Barcelona has a fixed number of councillors while the rest of the municipalities have a different number depending on population. At present, the Metropolitan Council comprises 90 councillors. The election of councillors occurs during local council plenaries, guided by two criteria: all mayors are *ex officio* members, and the remaining councillors are elected based on the results obtained by political parties in the municipal elections. The election period aligns with the municipal mandate, and the loss of the mayor or councillor status also results in the loss of the councillor status. The system ensures Barcelona's prominence and generates an essentially supra-municipal model based on the composition of municipal councils.

The plenary of the Metropolitan Council is organized into groups that follow the party logic of political forces. Thus, the council operates under a dual logic: through their election, councillors are tied to their municipality of origin, and by their position on the council, they are grouped based on party criteria. It is important to note that the political composition of the metropolitan council does not reflect the results obtained by political parties across the entire territory of the metropolitan area. Instead, it is based on the aggregation of results in terms of the composition of each municipal council with some adjustments. Thus, the political distribution among forces on the council does not reflect the overall preferences of the metropolitan population but rather those of the municipal councils.

On the other hand, the Metropolitan Area of Barcelona also has a Council of Mayors. The Council of Mayors, composed of the mayors of the municipalities in the Metropolitan Area, can submit to the Metropolitan Council proposals for actions of interest to the Metropolitan Area. It must provide a preliminary report on the approval of the action program and the matters determined by the internal regulations. One of the most formally relevant functions of the Council of Mayors is to formulate the proposal for a candidate for the president of the Metropolitan Area. Specifically, the law states that it is necessary for the presidential candidacy to have the support of the Council of Mayors, with the favourable vote of mayors from municipalities representing two-thirds of the population of the Metropolitan Area. This fact implies that, in practice, the mayor of the City of Barcelona would have the ability to wield veto power. However, this has never been an effective problem since its reinstatement by the law of 2010, and although the law neither establishes nor requires it, the mayor of Barcelona has always been appointed president of the Metropolitan Area of Barcelona.

Thus, the process of electing the president commences with a proposal from the Council of Mayors and requires the support of the Metropolitan Council. The legislation outlines precise procedures in the event that no candidate garners the requisite backing from the Council of Mayors. The president possesses the authority to designate vice-presidents and members of the governing board who provide assistance in the execution of their duties. Historically, metropolitan governments have often forged coalitions of political forces, a practice persisting even when not essential to ensure the election or operation. Upon examination of this reality in conversations with mayors and other political figures engaged in metropolitan affairs, their position is grounded in the defence of municipal interests and the pursuit of extensive territorial consensus, prioritizing it over partisan preferences. This phenomenon encapsulates the dual dimension discerned in the organizational framework: the foundational aspect of the election process at the municipal level and subsequent alignment contingent on party dynamics. As a conceivable dysfunctional consequence of this dynamic, it is pertinent to note the challenge in of formulating effective control by the opposition.

The political structure and the election process already highlight the supra-municipal nature of the institution. Likewise, the competences and functions also have a strong concurrent component and very often require prior agreement for their proper development. This fact, which can be considered one of the strengths of the model as it guarantees municipal autonomy and the precedence of local interests, also represents one of the major challenges for metropolitan institutions. The model hinders the establishment of priorities and strategic visions that do not have the support of municipalities. In turn, continuous coordination and effort in the process of consensus-building are essential to develop the institution's functions.

The financing of the metropolitan area underscores the necessity for municipal support. The majority of metropolitan revenues stem from transfers from member municipalities. In essence, municipalities fund a substantial portion of the entity's activities. In this context, it is evident that municipalities, seldom endowed with abundant resources, consistently evaluate the benefits derived from the metropolitan area's activities. An inevitable analysis based on the comparison between contributions and receipts exists, consequently fostering certain expectations regarding the services and activities provided by the metropolitan area. This aspect is particularly pronounced in the case of one of the few revenues directly received by the entity from citizens—the so-called metropolitan tax—eliciting a specific reaction among the populations of certain localities.

In terms of legitimacy, the distinction between input, throughput, and output legitimacy (Scharpf, 1999; Mosley & Wong, 2021) can be useful for analysing the specific nature of the institutional arrangement in the Barcelona metropolitan area. The Barcelona model exhibits a dual political nature: it functions as a territorial institution, but its internal bodies, election processes, and decision-making procedures closely resemble those of an inter-municipal governance tool. Such entities may encounter legitimacy issues (Swianiewicz, 2010), especially concerning their connection with citizens and accountability.

The Metropolitan Area of Barcelona lacks any decision-making mechanism that involves citizens of the municipalities and lacks a consultation or participatory system. The election process is strictly indirect. In fact, the political composition of the Metropolitan Council does not reflect the aggregated results of municipal elections in the area but rather the distribution in the plenaries of local councils. However, in terms of intergovernmental arrangements, mayors may have a voice in the two deliberative bodies, and policies must be designed to include the preferences of municipalities. Considering the nature of the functions and funding system, it is improbable that the metropolitan entity operates without alignment with municipal views. The question of the election process and the adoption of a direct system has arisen in public debate (Tomàs, 2018), but there has never been a strong citizen demand for such changes.

In summary, the Metropolitan Area of Barcelona represents the most institutionalized model of metropolitan governance in Spain. It is noteworthy that over time, it has encountered various political challenges and crisis contexts, and in most instances, it can be argued that the municipalities themselves have supported and propelled its development. This municipalist foundation endures both in its formal structure and its internal practices and dynamics. The challenges confronting the institution are primarily associated with overcoming this framework. On the one hand, there is a clear challenge in formulating a shared narrative that articulates a unified strategic vision. On the other hand, beyond the strictly institutional sphere, the entity lacks mechanisms for direct engagement with citizens that are not mediated by municipal governments.

5.7 Conclusions

This chapter has shown how the Spanish system has faced the governance challenges of articulating institutional models for large urban areas. The development of proximity mechanisms within cities and the legitimation of decisions in metropolitan spaces have followed highly diverse trajectories which depend on the particular model adopted. Spain has faced both challenges without having been able to solve either of them effectively.

For decentralization within cities, each council was granted the authority to determine key aspects of management, including territorial delineation, political structure, election methods, functions, and internal organization. Consequently, there exists significant variation among municipalities regarding the allocation of tasks, funding, and human resources in districts. This ranges from minor discrepancies to substantial impacts on local organizational frameworks. Studies assessing the actual functioning of districts indicate that cities have not fully capitalized on the decentralization potential that this opportunity presents (Galindo Caldés, 2014). The districts are often regarded as a "tool with high potential but underutilized by municipal governments" (Navarro & Pano, 2018, p. 242).

In metropolitan terms, the Spanish political system has not been able to provide a coherent answer to how to organize metropolitan areas and design and implement policies. The lack of a national model has resulted in each metropolitan governance arrangement developing in its own way, without following common patterns or guidelines (Navarro, 2012). Some authors have referred to this situation as "metropolitan misgovernment" (*desgobierno metropolitano*) (Tomàs, 2023).

The analysis has shown that Madrid is a case of a non-decision on metropolitan governance. The territorial peculiarities of Madrid have probably led to this result. In a small metropolitan territory where the boundaries almost coincide with the reach of the regional government, any additional layer of metropolitan government would have been difficult to implement. The outcome is clear. Efficiency stands out as the model's main advantage, at the expense of inclusiveness of municipalities and local autonomy. The case of Barcelona highlights the relevance of municipalities in metropolitan coordination. This circumstance, which can be seen as a strength, also constitutes one of the potential weaknesses. The political vicissitudes of the metropolitan entities in Barcelona underscore some of the debates surrounding this type of local entity. The design and functioning of the metropolitan area ensure that the interests and preferences of the municipalities are clearly represented. Simultaneously, building a shared discourse and narrative, as well as expanding functions and competencies beyond territorial consensus are still pending challenges. Seeking avenues for direct engagement with the public is also a goal yet to be achieved.

References

Busquets, J. (2004). *Barcelona: La construcción urbanística de una ciudad compacta*. Ediciones del Serbal.

Calonge Velázquez, A. (2015). La fusión de municipios, único instrumento de la Ley 27/2013, de 27 de diciembre, de racionalización y sostenibilidad de la Administración Local para la modificación de la planta municipal: una oportunidad perdida. *Revista de Estudios de la Administración Local y Autonómica*, Extra, 47–58.

Galindo Caldés, R. (2014). *La organización territorial en los municipios: Los distritos*. CEMCI.

González Medina, M., & de Gregorio Hurtado, S. (2023). El Área Metropolitana de Madrid: Un caso singular de (des)institucionalización. In M. Tomàs (Ed.), *Metropolis sin gobierno. La anomalía española* (pp. 157–191). Tirant lo Blanch.

Hildenbrand, A. (2017). *Gobernanza y planificación territorial en las áreas metropolitanas. Análisis comparado de las experiencias recientes en Alemania y de su interés para la práctica en España*. Publicacions de la Universitat de València.

Kuhlmann, S., & Wayenberg, E. (2016). Institutional impact assessment in multi-level systems: Conceptualizing decentralization effects from a comparative perspective. *International Review of Administrative Sciences, 82*(2), 233–254.

Kübler, D., & Heinelt, H. (2004). Metropolitan governance, democracy and the dynamics of place. In *Metropolitan governance in the 21st century: Capacity, democracy and the dynamics of place* (pp. 8–28). Routledge.

Lefèvre, C. (1998). Gouvernements métropolitains et gouvernance dans les pays occidentaux. *Politiques et management public, 16*(1), 35–59.

Lowndes, V., & Sullivan, H. (2008). How low can you go? Rationales and challenges for neighbourhood governance. *Public Administration, 86*(1), 53–74.

Magre Ferran, J., & Delgado Sotillos, I. (2019). Las elecciones municipales de 2019 en España. *Anuario del Gobierno Local, 1*, 93–122.

Magre Ferran, J., Gómez, C. N., & Riascos, M. Z. (2019). El gobierno local en España. In *Gobierno y política en España* (pp. 679–704). Tirant lo Blanch.

Mosley, J. E., & Wong, J. (2021). Decision-making in collaborative governance networks: Pathways to input and throughput legitimacy. *Journal of Public Administration Research and Theory, 31*(2), 328–345.

Navarro, C. (2012). Metropolitanization of Spanish urban areas: Trends, challenges and the special case of Madrid. *European Political Science, 11*(3), 420–429.

Navarro, C., & Pano, E. (2018). Rural and urban sub-municipal governance in Spain: The contrasting worlds of Lilliput and Brobdingnag. In *Sub-municipal governance in Europe: Decentralization beyond the municipal tier* (pp. 227–246). Palgrave.

Navarro, C., & Tomàs, M. (2007). Madrid et Barcelone conceptions alternatives de la gouvernance métropolitaine. In J. P. Collin, & M. Robertson (Eds.), *Le gouvernement des métropoles: Enjeux et portraits des expériences sur quatre continents*. Presses de lUniversité Laval.

Ribero, J. B., & Lladós, M. G. (2014). El mapa municipal de España. *Una caracterización geográfica*. Boletín de la Asociación de Geógrafos Españoles.

Rodríguez Herrero, G., & Ajangiz, R. (2007). Descentralización municipal y participación ciudadana: Evaluación de una experiencia consolidada. *Revista Española de Ciencia Política, 17*, 181–197.

Scharpf, F. W. (1999). *Governing in Europe: Effective and democratic?* Oxford University Press.

Sevillano, A., Tomàs, M., Capéans, J., & Roselló, M. (2023). La complicada definición del hecho metropolitano en España. In M. Tomàs (Ed.), *Metropolis sin gobierno. La anomalía Española* (pp. 43–61). Tirant lo Blanch.

Swianiewicz, P. (2010). If territorial fragmentation is a problem, is amalgamation a solution? An East European perspective. *Local Government Studies, 36*(2), 183–203.

Swianiewicz, P., Gendźwiłł, A., Houlberg, K., & Klausen, J. E. (2022). *Municipal territorial reforms of the 21st century in Europe*. Routledge.

Tomàs, M. (2018). Els governs metropolitans d'elecció directa. Reflexions per a l'Àrea Metropolitana de Barcelona. *Revista Papers, 61*, 52–59.

Tomàs, M. (2023). *Metropolis sin gobierno. La anomalía española.* Tirant lo Blanch.

Open Access This chapter is licensed under the terms of the Creative Commons Attribution 4.0 International License (http://creativecommons.org/licenses/by/4.0/), which permits use, sharing, adaptation, distribution and reproduction in any medium or format, as long as you give appropriate credit to the original author(s) and the source, provide a link to the Creative Commons license and indicate if changes were made.

The images or other third party material in this chapter are included in the chapter's Creative Commons license, unless indicated otherwise in a credit line to the material. If material is not included in the chapter's Creative Commons license and your intended use is not permitted by statutory regulation or exceeds the permitted use, you will need to obtain permission directly from the copyright holder.

Part II
Mergers and Inter-municipal Cooperation in Rural Areas

Chapter 6
Tackling Structural Challenges in Rural Areas: Mergers, Inter-Municipal Cooperation, and Innovation in Australasia

Andy Asquith, Carol Mills, and D'Arcy Blaxell

Abstract This chapter discusses system and structural innovations in rural local government within Australia and New Zealand, focusing on capability building, amalgamations (mergers) and collaboration (inter-municipal cooperation). It identifies the primary themes driving reform, such as shifts in community expectations, challenging financial positions, the need for local governments to provide 'local voice, local choice', difficulties in delivering key services, and challenges in attracting and retaining talented staff and councilors. Many rural councils in both countries are attempting to deliver more comprehensive services while simultaneously experiencing funding shortfalls and operating without an overarching policy framework to guide them. Rounds of amalgamations have often failed to have the desired efficiency effect and councils are increasingly turning to voluntary systems of cooperation, including through the formation of joint organizations, to create economies of scale and drive improvements in capacity and capability. Such voluntary cooperation has proven successful in certain areas, such as waste management and the provision of library services. However, it remains to be seen how and whether the trend of increasing cooperation can offset deep-seated structural challenges and meet ever-evolving community expectations of local government.

Keywords Rural governance · Local government · Local council · Amalgamation · Inter-municipal cooperation · Council merger

A. Asquith · C. Mills (✉) · D. Blaxell
Institute for Public Policy and Governance, University of Technology Sydney, Sydney, Australia
e-mail: andy.asquith@uts.edu.au; Carol.Mills@uts.edu.au; DArcy.Blaxell@uts.edu.au

© The Author(s) 2026

K. Kössler, E. M. Belser (eds.), *Local Government Structure and Intergovernmental Relations*, Local and Urban Governance,
https://doi.org/10.1007/978-3-031-99820-1_6

6.1 Introduction

In this chapter we explore directions in system and structural innovation in rural local government in Australia and New Zealand, with a particular focus on capability building, amalgamations (mergers), and collaboration (inter-municipal cooperation). In doing so, we identify the dominant themes driving reform and explore how these have been dealt with to date. What is clear is that there have been long-term, underlying challenges for the local government sector in attempting to grapple with shifts in community expectations, challenging financial positions, capability demands, and the concept that local governments (referred to as councils) should provide "local voice, local choice".

Within both Australia and New Zealand, this has meant that the respective local government systems, structures, and institutions are faced with a dilemma. Generally, citizens are demanding a wider, more complex, and more comprehensive mix of services from all tiers of government, including local councils (Chou et al., 2023). At the same time, and in the absence of an overarching policy framework, these councils continue to be impacted by a legacy of multiple government decisions that have impacted their role and funding.

In the absence of guiding policy directions, the emphasis has been on improving efficiency and effectiveness through mechanisms such as mergers, cooperation, and shared services. Given their size, structures, and financial foundations, these aims have proven challenging for many councils in Australia and New Zealand, particularly those in rural areas.

6.2 Local Government in Australia and New Zealand

To understand the significance of these trends, it is useful to first establish the position of the local government systems within both countries.

6.2.1 Australia

Australia is a federation which contains three distinct tiers of government. The national or federal level is known as the Commonwealth. Beneath the Commonwealth are six states (New South Wales, Queensland, South Australia, Tasmania, Victoria, and Western Australia) and two territories (Australian Capital Territory and Northern Territory). Below that sits local government.

Across all jurisdictions, there are a total of 537 local government entities—a number reduced from a peak of over 1000 in 1900 through the ongoing process of efficiency and effectiveness-seeking amalgamations (Mills, 2021). Despite these changes, there remains an immense disparity in the sizes of local councils in

Australia. Brisbane City Council in Queensland, for example, serves a population in excess of one million, covers an area of 1318 km^2 (Asquith, 2022) and has an operating budget of over AU$3 billion. At the other end of the scale, in Western Australia, the Shire of Sandstone covers nearly 33,000 km^2—around the size of Belgium—providing services for its 81 residents with an annual budget in 2020 of just AU$5.6 million (Shire of Sandstone, 2023).

Although Australia is a highly urbanized country, it contains a large number of rural councils which make up a high proportion of overall council numbers. In New South Wales, for example, there are 34 metropolitan, 37 regional, and 57 rural councils.

Each state and territory has its own distinct system of local government which is specified in their respective constitutions. As a result, different arrangements are in place within each jurisdiction, although the fundamentals remain quite consistent.

Councils in Australia primarily depend on a mix of rates (property tax) and, to a lesser extent, service user charges, fines, and business activities for their earned income. Ratings methods vary somewhat between state and territory governments but are essentially based on unimproved land value. This means that both the value and number of ratable properties within a locality combine to generate what is, in principle, intended to be a council's core income. For a growing proportion of councils, especially in rural areas, however, this model is no longer working. While the national average of total council revenue from rates is just under 40%, the figure rises to around 80% for larger, well populated councils. Other councils, particularly those covering large, sparsely populated rural areas, may not be generating enough even to support their base, statutory services. Numerous rural councils, for instance, have a population density of under two persons per km^2 and for Winton Shire, in remote Central Western Queensland, income from rates makes up just 11% of its revenue (LGPA, 2021).

Long-term challenges from the rates system have been exacerbated in the last decade by the imposition in several jurisdictions of multi-year caps on rate rises that are not linked to running costs or inflation rates. For example, the Victorian "Fair Go Rates System", in place since 2016, capped rate increases for the 2022/23 financial year at 1.75% (DJPR, 2022) while inflation was running at over 6%.

The dominance of rates revenue in part derives from the fact that, in contrast to its role internationally, local government in Australia was historically associated with a narrow focus on property and limited service provision revolving around the collection of rates, the building and maintenance of roads, and the collection and disposal of rubbish (Dollery et al., 2006). This model has, however, evolved considerably recent in decades in response to ever increasing citizen expectations for public service provision (Busbridge et al., 2024) and as responsibilities for services have been increasingly transferred from the higher tiers of state and federal government. These have included fire services, health and welfare, libraries, and local airports.

The combination of these systemic factors—limited rates growth, increases in community expectation, unplanned increases in the range of council responsibilities, plus the impact of ageing assets and practical limits to service charges—has meant that many councils are increasingly financially stressed. As a result, a growing number of councils across Australia, especially in rural and remote areas, are reliant on federal and state grant funding to provide even their statutory services (Rural Councils Victoria, 2022).

Rural councils in particular are heavily reliant on Commonwealth government grants. There are two principal types of grants—untied and tied. The former are known as Financial Assistance Grants (FAGs) which, for constitutional reasons, are distributed to the State and Territories who then allocate to local councils. These grants were established to promote financial equalization between councils and as a result over two thirds are allocated to non-metropolitan areas. When the current iteration of the FAGs model was introduced in 1996 it equated to 1% of annual commonwealth tax revenue. Limits to its growth have meant it is currently just half of that level.

While the value of FAGs has diminished in real terms, other grants are often short-term, for capital purposes, and do not include recurrent support for operating costs, repair or renewal. Commonwealth grants tend to be tied to specific activities like infrastructure development and road building. Grants for the latter, for example, equated to AU$7.3 billion nationally between 2000 and 2019 (Mills, 2021). This is also the case for State and Territory Governments grants, which are commonly ring-fenced for programs such as community facility upgrades.

In addition to being short-term, these tied grants—unless specifically bid for by a council—can also be said to reduce a council's capacity for local decision-making and expenditure prioritization. This, it can be argued, equates to central administration replacing local democracy for some or, in many cases in rural areas, the majority of a council's activities.

This pressure on the grants system has led to local councils and their peak body, the Australian Local Government Association (ALGA), lobbying for an overhaul of arrangements. In 2019, ALGA argued that the value of FAGs amounted to only 7% of total local government revenue around Australia, despite councils delivering a large number of services and programs delegated from the Commonwealth government (ALGA, 2019).

While reform of the current grants model remains a core policy objective of ALGA, as of mid-2024, there has been little progress and most policy levers have focused on increasing efficiency through means such as amalgamation.

6.2.2 New Zealand

New Zealand is a unitary state with an unwritten constitution. Local government operates within the boundaries of structures and activities set out in national legislation. In practice, this has meant that the scope and scale of local government actions can differ considerably, depending on the political flavor of a national government (Asquith, 2016; Molineaux & Asquith, 2022).

As in Australia, the size of councils in New Zealand varies significantly. By far the largest is Auckland. Created in 2010 through the amalgamation of seven territorial authorities and one regional council, Auckland Council provides services to 1.7 million people—one-third of the country's total population—and covers 4941 km^2. In contrast, the Chatham Islands Council has a population of around 600. Geographically, Southland District is the largest council, covering 29,552 km^2, and with a population of 33,000. At the other end of the scale, Kawerau District covers just 24 km^2, and has 7000 residents.

Over the last two decades there have been several attempts by national governments to affect the role of local government. Left-leaning governments have tended to champion the idea of the "general power of competence", while conservative governments have conceived of local government in a more minimalist form, seeking to restrict areas where councils can act. This contrast can be seen in the passage of legislation between 2002 and 2019. In 2002, the Labour Government's Local Government Act empowered local government to act to enhance the social, economic, cultural, and environmental wellbeing of its citizens (Asquith, 2012). In 2012, a National Party-led Government amended the legislation and replaced "wellbeing" with "interest", only for the sixth Labour-led Government to reinstate the "wellbeing" concept in 2019. Molineaux and Asquith (2022) described this as "local government political ping pong".

Despite this degree of uncertainty, local governments in New Zealand have a much higher level of financial autonomy than their Australian and many international counterparts (Asquith, 2012, 2023). In general, approximately 80% of local government revenue is raised locally, typically from rates (property tax) or service user charges. However, as in Australia, councils are facing increasing demands from residents and also managing additional costs associated with devolved responsibilities. These pressures have been exacerbated by a history of chronic underinvestment in infrastructure—notably the provision of water services.

There have been several attempts by government to strategically examine these issues. In 2006, the Labour Government commissioned a report on local government finance (Asquith, 2007, Shand Report 2007). The Shand Report contained 96 recommendations, however, the election of a conservative National Government in 2008 meant that they were not progressed. In 2019, a Productivity Commission review of Local Government Funding found that existing arrangements met the needs of most local council activities, but that some councils, especially in rural areas serving low-income communities, were under significant funding pressure and that targeted strategies were needed (New Zealand Productivity Commission, 2019).

The Productivity Commission's findings in part reflected the impact of earlier reforms. In 1989, a program of local government amalgamations was imposed nationally, reducing council numbers from 227 to 86 and introducing a two-tier system of 11 regional councils and 66 territorial authorities.

Regional councils are empowered with planning, transport, environmental protection, biosecurity and civil defense functions, while city and district councils are focused on community wellbeing, building control, culture, and infrastructure—especially roads and water. Territorial authorities are empowered to create community boards, of which there are currently 110, to ensure the representation of specific communities (Molineaux & Asquith, 2022). Members are remunerated and have decision-making powers on matters categorized as "local", as well as agreeing local annual budgets with the governing body and agreeing and overseeing annual work programs. For example, the board of the rural area of Hastings in the North Island can make representations to council on spending on roads, recycling, and disaster recovery and resilience (HDC, 2025). The effectiveness of the boards model has not been evaluated, but in 2024 a review commenced to examine issues such as the "optimal number" and the "range and scope" of their responsibilities.

The most recent wide-ranging review of local government in New Zealand was commissioned by the then Labour Government in early 2021 and reported in mid-2023. Its broad aim was to identify "how [the] system of local democracy and governance needs to evolve over the next 30 years" (Te Tari Taiwhenua Department of Internal Affairs, 2021). This included examining "what local does, how it does it, and how it pays for it" (Te Tari Taiwhenua Department of Internal Affairs, 2021). The review concluded that: "The current local government system is not set up for future success. Decisions by successive governments have marginalised local government and left it in a precarious position in terms of focus, resourcing, and viability" (Te Tari Taiwhenua Department of Internal Affairs, 2023, p. 2). October 2023 saw a change of government in New Zealand and as a result it is unclear how the report will be taken forward.

6.3 Issues Impacting Rural Councils

Having provided a contextual background to the local government systems in Australia and New Zealand, we now turn our attention to considering examples of key issues impacting contemporary directions for rural councils in both countries.

6.3.1 Capacity and Capability Challenges

At a local level, the financial and performance pressures on rural local governments in Australasia are most readily seen through their impact on levels of service delivery—an issue directly affecting and visible to residents and businesses. This relates to the *capacity* of councils to deliver services. There are also direct and indirect impacts on the *capability* of a council. For example, its ability to attract and retain high caliber staff with the requisite skills and competencies is a significant issue.

From a staffing perspective, small and geographically isolated rural councils have long faced ongoing challenges in offering career paths and attracting experienced senior personnel from other locations (Cameron et al., 2023). There is evidence in Australia that the lack of financial resources is exacerbating this situation and directly impacting the ability of individual councils to attract and retain employees with the requisite expertise (Rainey et al., 2021). ALGA estimates that the national staff turnover rate for local government is about 15%, rising to 20% in rural areas, that 90% of local governments are facing skills shortages (ALGA, 2022b), and that two thirds have unmet training needs (ALGA, 2022a).

In locations such as New South Wales, where chief executives are employed under contracts with "no cause no notice" clauses that can be triggered by a majority of councillors, it can be especially hard to entice experienced managers to relocate to a rural area.

Capability gaps in New Zealand regional and rural councils have also been identified by researchers including Asquith (2023) and in the *Review into the Future for Local Government* (Te Tari Taiwhenua Department of Internal Affairs, 2023) report.

These gaps have also been seen to extend to elected representatives in many locations. This tends to be spotlighted whenever a State or Territory Minister uses their legislative power to intervene in a council over performance or corruption issues. A recent case that highlights the significance of the issue is that of the Central Coast Council, just north of Sydney. The council was created as part of a series of statewide amalgamations in New South Wales in 2016 and covers a population of 350,000 spread over 1681 km^2. In 2020 it was placed into administration by the state government following a 50% blowout in the council's deficit over a 7-month period (Persson, 2020). The administrator found "catastrophic budget mismanagement" at many levels (Central Coast Council, 2020) and, following further reviews, all councillors were dismissed and elections postponed. As a result of the findings, it was recommended that all local councillors undertake mandatory financial and company director level management training.

This call for professional training mirrored earlier recommendations from the New South Wales Independent Local Government Review Panel (2013) and the Western Australian Local Government Review Panel (2020), which both argued for the ongoing education of councillors.

In some jurisdictions, there are now compulsory pre-election training requirements for aspirant councillors, but these are generally short, online modules that cover only basic accountabilities. More robust courses, such as an Executive Certificate for Elected Representatives in New South Wales, are voluntary, and only a small proportion of councillors attend. These courses are delivered by the UTS Centre for Local Government and run on demand. Approximately 50 councillors a year enroll.

In summary, as Australasian councils have taken on additional functions and been expected to perform more efficiently and effectively, there has been increased interest in improving the capability of council staff and elected officials. Implementation is, however, still very much a work in progress and is proving to be particularly challenging for rural councils with limited resources.

6.3.2 Amalgamations as a Tool for Structural Change

Given the capability, financial, and related challenges facing local governments in Australasia, it is not difficult to see why amalgamations emerged as a preferred strategy within the higher levels of government. Numerous reports, including in New South Wales (2014), Western Australia (2020) and Tasmania (2023), have advocated for council amalgamations as a means of creating local councils of sufficient size to create economies of scale and to attract and retain appropriately qualified leaders.

In most instances, the amalgamation process has been top-down, with either the Australian state or territory, or the New Zealand central government mandating a reduction in the number of local government areas. In many cases, ambitious savings estimates have been promoted as the primary benefit. For example, as part of its rationale for the round of mergers in New South Wales in 2016, the state government cited savings of AU$20 million over 20 years based on a report commissioned from KPMG which it refused to publicly release (Bajkowski, 2017).

The top-down approach of imposed mergers has often met with robust local council and resident opposition, with concerns expressed about a lack of influence in the new entities and a loss of local representation, identity, and engagement (Uddin, 2018). In rural areas, where councils tend to be major employers, there has also been concern about the "well-known snowballing effect of the loss of jobs and services on fragile rural economies" (LGNSW, 2015, p. 25).

Whilst such opposition saw limited success in preventing amalgamations through the 1990s and early 2000s, there have been notable recent examples where, such has been the outcry from residents and councils, that mergers have not proceeded. While action tended to focus on individual proposed mergers, the quantum of opposition also resulted in some governments committing to no further compulsory amalgamations in their jurisdiction. Examples include the cessation of reforms in Western Australia in 2015 (Jones, 2016) and those proposed in New Zealand by the then Local Government Minister Paula Bennett in 2015 (Bennett, 2015).

While much of the opposition was based on concerns about loss of local identity and autonomy, the financial experience of amalgamated rural councils has also been an issue. Even after merging, many rural councils remain small and have been unable to reap the envisaged economic benefits of scale. In many cases, individual property rates have actually risen, leading to disaffection among residents.

As a result, some councils have formally sought to demerger (Dollery & Drew, 2023). For example, in October 2023 the Minister for Local Government in New South Wales announced that he would support the break-up of Cootamundra-Gundagai Regional Council if it could be shown that a demerger would "enhance local democracy" and that the two new councils would be "sustainable and able to continue to deliver services and infrastructure to their community' (Hoenig, 2023, p. 2).

The Cootamundra-Gundagai experience provided the impetus for the recently elected (March 2023) New South Wales Labour Government to introduce a bill allowing forcibly amalgamated councils to de-amalgamate, provided that they can present a compelling business case to do so, have the support of the electorate, and are approved by the Minister for Local Government. This was recently tested by the Inner West Council in Sydney, which had been created by the merger of three councils in 2016. The independent NSW Boundaries Commission, recommended in early 2024 that the Council's application for a demerger should not proceed on the basis that the "financial disadvantage associated with a de-amalgamation significantly outweigh[s] any potential financial benefits" (LGBC, 2024, p. 37) and the Minister concurred.

Interestingly, as New South Wales was retreating from amalgamations in 2023, the Tasmanian Future of Local Government Review recommended significant structural reforms for local governments in the state, including amalgamations to reduce the total number of councils from 29 to 15 (Tasmanian Government Department of Premier and Cabinet, 2023). However, the review noted the prospect of significant opposition from local governments and the reticence of the state government to mandate unpopular changes, and so advocated for changes to begin with the voluntary amalgamation of willing councils.

In New Zealand, as in Australia, attempts to amalgamate local councils have become a political minefield. The recent Review into the Future for Local Government report (Te Tari Taiwhenua Department of Internal Affairs, 2023) stopped short of calling for forced amalgamations but did suggest a substantial restructuring of local government. The report offers scope for councils to reorganize according to their needs and those of their constituents. Councils can choose to either move towards a new unitary model, taking on some of the responsibilities of current regional councils, or to work with neighboring councils to form "combined councils". These combined councils would not replace existing local councils, and so should not be considered amalgamations. Instead, they would take on regional responsibilities like environmental management and regulation and allow for the creation of economies of scope and scale when required, leaving local councils to deal with place-shaping, wellbeing, and local issues and services. However, community reaction to the new arrangements is still clouded by concerns about forced amalgamations. For example, the mayor of tiny Kawerau council responded to the report by saying that the "community is not in favour of amalgamation around anything", and instead suggested increasing the councils' boundaries to safeguard its viability (Milne, 2023).

6.3.3 Inter-Governmental Cooperation as an Alternative to Amalgamation

As the focus has moved from "top down" amalgamations as a key strategy to enhance local councils' viability in Australasia, the concepts of inter-council cooperation and formal collaboration have become more prominent. For local governments, arrangements for voluntary cooperation, systemic resource sharing and special project collaboration are being increasingly recognized as alternative means of gaining many of the purported benefits of amalgamation—including the creation of economies of scope and scale and enhanced capabilities—without sacrificing local representation and council autonomy.

Regional cooperation, in various forms, has a long history in Australia. For example, Regional Organisations of Councils (ROCs) have existed in New South Wales since the 1980s. These are voluntary structures, usually formed by neighboring councils. They may operate as incorporated associations, companies, or without a formal structure. ROCs can undertake a range of activities on behalf of their member councils including advocacy, strategic planning, service delivery, and shared services.

In 2018, these were supplemented by a more structured arrangement in New South Wales known as Joint Organisations (JOs). While membership remains voluntary, the JOs are underpinned by legislation and receive some support funds from state government. Interestingly, the Greater Sydney area was deliberately excluded from the model, which is very much focused on engendering collaboration between rural and regional councils with a view to enhancing their efficiency.

Although the practice of inter-council cooperation can be fraught with difficulties, ranging from overcoming parochialism to having a sufficiently detailed understanding of existing costs of services to be confident that efficiencies are being achieved, a growing number of rural and regional councils are joining JO type arrangements or establishing purpose-specific partnerships. A survey of New South Wales Councils by the state's Auditor-General in 2018 found that 84% of responding councils were involved in shared services and only 6% reported that they had not had any involvement in shared services (NSW Auditor-General's Report to Parliament 2018). That survey also found that the most common arrangements covered waste and recycling, road maintenance, environmental services, procurement, asset management and human resources.

One area in which significant intermunicipal cooperation exists—and which has shown considerable success—is in the shared provision of library services. In the state of Victoria, for example, five local governments—four rural councils plus the major regional center of the City of Geelong—joined together to establish the Geelong Regional Library Corporation (Geelong Regional Libraries, 2023). The smallest member council, the Borough of Queenscliff, has a population of only 3000, while Geelong has 270,000 residents. This network offers the structure and scope to provide rural constituents with library services that were otherwise impractical or uneconomical for its smaller members. The Geelong Regional Library Corporation is itself part of the peak body Public Libraries Victoria, which represents libraries across the 79 Victorian local governments and uses its size, reach, and bargaining power to advocate on their behalf and provide shared services in marketing, IT, and training (Public Libraries Victoria, 2023). With 80% of Public Libraries Victoria's funding provided by Victorian local governments, and most of the balance coming from the state government, Libraries Victoria offers a powerful example of the potential of local government cooperation.

Waste management is another area of established inter-council cooperation in Australia (Dollery et al., 2016). A 2022 review identified 49 intermunicipal cooperation arrangements for waste management, including a large number operating in rural environments across the country (Tobin & Zaman, 2022). The majority of waste management partnerships are built on a foundation of equality, with member councils having equal voting and decision-making powers, although a small number of partnerships are run by entities such as steering committees whose membership may extend beyond the council members. These arrangements are based on horizontal connection and collaboration towards a common goal.

The Covid-19 pandemic provided excellent examples of how local councils can take the lead in intra-organizational and cross-sector cooperation to benefit their communities. McNeill and Asquith (2022) and Stoney et al. (2023) outline how local councils, working in partnership with state governments, other councils, non-government organizations, and local businesses put protocols in place within each locality in an attempt to minimize the disruption caused by the Covid-19 pandemic. To a certain extent, within an international context, local councils across Australia were well prepared to deal with the challenges provided by the pandemic, given the considerable experience many rural councils have in dealing with the natural disasters that affect Australia. An example is Carayannopoulos's (2018) discussion of the 2011 Queensland floods. In addition, the very nature of the Covid-19 pandemic in effect compelled all local councils in Australia to collaborate to mitigate the more extreme impacts on their local communities. In many ways, the challenge is to learn how to sustain and normalize such productive levels of cross-sectoral engagement.

Future inter-council cooperation is likely to include a wider range of partners and partnership forms. Given the trend towards the general power of competence in local government, the ideas advocated by Stewart and Clarke (1987) have merit. They advocate for the coming together of government, business, and the non-profit sector to combine expertise, resources and, importantly, democratic legitimacy to fulfil community expectations. Irrespective of the motivations for inter-council cooperation, the success or failure of such measures rests upon factors such as the personalities and motivations of individuals involved, the strength of governance, business acumen and the presence of shared objectives. Further work in each of these areas is essential if councils are to successfully pursue sustained rather than crisis-driven arrangements.

6.4 Conclusions: The Future of the Structural Challenges in Rural Areas

With a high proportion of rural councils under financial stress and with service and staffing levels and quality highly variable, the future of rural and regional local government relies on change. Given the scope, scale, and remoteness of Australia and New Zealand, and the sheer vastness of some of their local councils, it is difficult to generalize what any "best fit" might be. Experience has shown that the "traditional" route favored by policymakers in the higher tiers of government—amalgamation—offers potential only if it has clearly defined objectives, quantitatively and qualitatively measurable (and measured) results, and actively engaged communities. Inter-municipal cooperation, on the other hand, offers the opportunity for councils to build economies of scope and scale on their own terms, but still tends to be ad hoc, small scale, and occasionally beset by issues of competitiveness and competing priorities.

With current political headwinds and public opinion against mandated amalgamations, advocates of such mergers must find a way to demonstrate—and communicate—their benefits beyond often unrealized economic dividends. Irrespective of that direction, inter-council cooperation is increasingly important, particularly in rural areas where infrastructure and service demands outstrip individual capacity and capability.

In this context, the specifics of which council structures and governance models are selected are perhaps less important than having a clarity of objectives and a strong commitment to the viability of local government at all levels of government. In both Australia and New Zealand, change needs to encompass national funding arrangements to enhance certainty and autonomy; increases in council capabilities, whether achieved internally, through co-operation, or by contracting; enhanced engagement with citizens to ensure the right services are being delivered to the right people; improved long-term planning and budget management; and improved role clarity between the levels of government, especially regarding responsibilities for service delivery and asset maintenance. Many rural councils are well advanced on pursuing parts of this agenda, but others are still at the beginning, and no council can achieve these aims in isolation from their peers or the other levels of government.

References

ALGA (Australian Local Government Association). (2019). *Stronger safer together: 2020–21 pre-budget submission*. Australian Government Treasury. Retrieved April 22, 2024, from https://treasury.gov.au/sites/default/files/2020-09/115786_australian_local_government_association.pdf

ALGA (Australian Local Government Association). (2022a). *2022 local government workforce skills and capability survey*. ALGA. Retrieved April 23, 2024, from https://alga.com.au/app/uploads/LG-Workforce-Skills-and-Capability-Survey-National-Report.pdf

ALGA (Australian Local Government Association). (2022b). *Final submission to the 5-year productivity inquiry interim report*. ALGA. Retrieved April 22, 2024, from https://alga.com.au/app/uploads/ALGA-Sub-to-Productivity-Commission-Oct-2022.pdf

Asquith, A. (2007). The Shand report: The view of an interested observer. *Public Sector, 30*(3), 23–24.

Asquith, A. (2012). The role, scope and scale of local government in New Zealand: Its prospective future. *Australian Journal of Public Administration, 71*(1), 76–84. https://doi.org/10.1111/j.1467-8500.2012.00751.x

Asquith, A. (2016). Public sector management in New Zealand's local government. In J. Drage & C. Cheyne (Eds.), *Local government in New Zealand: Challenges and choices* (pp. 205–217). Dunmore Publishing.

Asquith, A. (2022). *Governance that goes bump in the night: The mysterious case of local government*. Governance Directions. Retrieved April 12, 2024, from https://www.governanceinstitute.com.au/news_media/governance-that-goes-bump-in-the-night-the-mysterious-case-of-local-government/

Asquith, A. (2023). False dawn or false hope? An assessment of the 2022 local elections. In J. McNeill & C. Cheyne (Eds.), *Candidates, voters and voting in New Zealand's 2022 local government elections* (pp. 9–15). Titipounamu Press.

Bajkowski, J. (2017, March 28). Secret KPMG report brings NSW council mergers unstuck. *The Mandarin*.

Bennett, P. (2015). *Speech to LGNZ annual conference*. Scoop NZ. Retrieved April 22, 2024, from https://www.scoop.co.nz/stories/PA1507/S00320/hon-paula-bennett-speech-to-lgnz-annual-conference.htm

Busbridge, R., Chou, M., & Rutledge-Prior, S. (2024). The three Rs and beyond: Public perceptions on the role of Australian local government today. *Urban Policy and Research, 42*(2), 204–216. https://doi.org/10.1080/08111146.2024.2320637

Cameron, R., Burgess, J., Archer, B., Millcock, S., & Graves, P. (2023). *Research report: Local government career pathways and workforce toolkit for Regional SA*. Northern & Yorke Local Government Association. Retrieved April 17, 2024, from https://nylga.sa.gov.au/wp-content/uploads/2023/12/Local-Government-Career-Pathways-Report.pdf

Carayannopoulos, G. (2018). *Disaster management in Australia: Government coordination in a time of crisis*. Routledge.

Central Coast Council. (2020, December 2). *Office of the Administrator media release – Administrator delivers damning report of Council's financial mismanagement*. Central Coast Council. Retrieved April 22, 2024, from https://www.centralcoast.nsw.gov.au/council/media-release/office-administrator-media-release-administrator-delivers-damning-report

Chou, M., Busbridge, R., & Rutledge-Prior, S. (2023). *The changing role of local government in Australia: National survey findings*. Analysis & Policy Observatory. Retrieved August 28, 2024, from https://apo.org.au/sites/default/files/resource-files/2023-02/apo-nid321483.pdf

Department of Premier and Cabinet. (2023). *The future of local government review: Final report*. Tasmanian Government. Retrieved August 29, 2024, from https://www.futurelocal.tas.gov.au/wp-content/uploads/2023/11/The-Future-of-Local-Government-Review-Final-Report.pdf

DJPR (Department of Jobs, Precincts and Regions). (2022). *Analysis of the 2022–2023 adopted budgets of Victorian councils*. Local Government Victoria. Retrieved April 23, 2024, from https://www.localgovernment.vic.gov.au/__data/assets/pdf_file/0033/189816/Report-on-adopted-budgets-2022-23.pdf

Dollery, B., & Drew, J. (2023). New South Wales State Government failure? An empirical analysis of the Cootamundra Gundagai Regional Council forced merger. *Public Administration Quarterly, 47*(2), 200–222. https://doi.org/10.37808/paq.47.2.6

Dollery, B., Wallace, J., & Allan, P. (2006). *Perspectives on the changing role of Australian local government: Working paper series in economics no. 2006-3*. University of New England. Retrieved August 28, 2024, from https://www.une.edu.au/__data/assets/pdf_file/0005/67982/econ-2006-3.pdf

Dollery, B., Kortt, M., & Drew, J. (2016). Fostering shared services in local government: A common service model. *Australasian Journal of Regional Studies, 22*(2), 225–242.

Geelong Regional Libraries. (2023). *Annual report 2022/2023*. Geelong Regional Libraries. Retrieved August 28, 2024, from https://www.grlc.vic.gov.au/sites/default/files/GRLC%20Annual%20Report%202022-23.pdf

HDC (Heretaunga Hastings District Council). (2025). *Rural Community Board: Te Poari Hapori Tuawhenua*. HDC. Retrieved August 21, 2025, from https://www.hastingsdc.govt.nz/our-council/rural-community-board/

Hoenig, R. (2023). *Media release: New pathway to guide Cootamundra-Gundagai Regional Council de-amalgamation*. Office of Local Government. Retrieved April 17, 2024, from https://www.olg.nsw.gov.au/wp-content/uploads/2023/10/MMR-03102023.pdf

Independent Local Government Review Panel. (2013). *Revitalising local government: Final report of the NSW Independent Local Government Review Panel*. Narrabri Local Council. Retrieved August 29, 2024, from https://www.narrabri.nsw.gov.au/files/assets/public/v/1/1.-your-council/strategic-and-corporate-plans/fit-for-the-future/other-files/revitalising-local-government-ilgrp-final-report-october-2013-rs.pdf

Jones, R. (2016). Local government amalgamation and the lack of a metropolitan government: A political geography. In S. Biermann, D. Olaru, & V. Paül (Eds.), *Planning boomtown and beyond* (pp. 103–128). UWA Publishing.

LGBC (Local Government Boundaries Commission). (2024). *Examination of a proposal to de-amalgamate Inner West Local Government Area*. Office of Local Government. Retrieved May 09, 2024, from https://www.olg.nsw.gov.au/wp-content/uploads/2024/03/Final-Report-by-the-Local-Government-Boundaries-Commission-to-the-Minister-for-Local-Government.pdf

LGNSW (Local Government New South Wales). (2015). *Submission to general purpose standing committee no 6 – Inquiry into local government in NSW*. NSW Parliament. Retrieved May 09, 2024, from https://www.parliament.nsw.gov.au/lcdocs/submissions/37185/0142%20Local%20Government%20New%20South%20Wales.pdf

LGPA (Local Government Professionals Australia). (2021). *Local government professionals 2020–21 pre-budget submission*. Australian Government Treasury. Retrieved April 23, 2024, from https://treasury.gov.au/sites/default/files/2020-09/115786_local_government_professionals_australia.pdf

Local Government Review Panel. (2020). *Final report recommendations for a new Local Government Act for Western Australia*. Department of Local Government, Sport and Cultural Industries. Retrieved August 29, 2024, from https://www.dlgsc.wa.gov.au/docs/default-source/local-government/local-government-review-panel-final-report.pdf?sfvrsn=acefce14_1

McNeill, J., & Asquith, A. (2022). End of the world: New Zealand's local government and Covid-19. In C. N. Silva (Ed.), *Local government and the Covid-19 pandemic: A global perspective* (pp. 757–781). Springer.

Mills, C. (2021). The structure of local government in Australia. In E. M. Belser, K. Kössler, & T. Morandell (Eds.), *Structure of local government* (pp. 244–251). Zenodo. https://doi.org/10.5281/zenodo.10105799

Milne, J. (2023, June 20). *NZ's tiniest council shows attack is the best defence against amalgamation*. Newsroom.

Molineaux, J., & Asquith, A. (2022). Local government and governance in Aotearoa New Zealand. In C. Copus, R. Kerley, & A. Jones (Eds.), *Modern guide to local and regional politics* (pp. 315–334). Edward Elgar.

New Zealand Productivity Commission. (2019). *Local government funding and financing: Final report*. New Zealand Treasury. Retrieved August 29, 2024, from https://www.treasury.govt.nz/sites/default/files/2024-05/pc-inq-lgff-final-report-local-government-funding-and-financing.pdf

Persson, D. (2020). *Administrator's 30 day interim report*. Central Coast Council. Retrieved August 28, 2024, from https://cdn.centralcoast.nsw.gov.au/sites/default/files/Administrator/Administrators_30_Day_Interim_Report_-_2_December_2020.pdf

Public Libraries Victoria. (2023). *Annual report 2022/23*. Public Libraries Victoria. Retrieved August 27, 2024, from https://www.plv.org.au/wp-content/uploads/2023/10/PLV-Annual-Report-2022-23_FINAL_web-3.pdf

Rainey, H., Fernandez, S., & Malatesta, D. (2021). *Understanding and managing public organizations*. Jossey Bass.

Rural Councils Victoria. (2022). *Alternative sources of income for local government*. Rural Councils Victoria. Retrieved August 28, 2024, from https://media.ruralcouncilsvictoria.org.au/

wp-content/uploads/2022/12/13085030/20220153-RCV-own-source-income-Updated-Final-report-221212.pdf

Shire of Sandstone. (2023). *Annual report 2022/2023*. Shire of Sandstone. Retrieved August 29, 2024, from https://sandstone.wa.gov.au/documents/21859/annual-report-20222023

Stewart, J., & Clarke, M. (1987). The public service orientation: Issues and dilemmas. *Public Administration, 65*(2), 161–177. https://doi.org/10.1111/j.1467-9299.1987.tb00654.x

Stoney, C., Asquith, A., Kipper, K., McNeill, J., Martin, J., & Spano, A. (2023). Policy-making, policy-taking and policy-shaping: Local government responses to the Covid-19 pandemic. *Australian Journal of Public Administration, 82*(4), 440–461. https://doi.org/10.1111/1467-8500.12585

Te Tari Taiwhenua Department of Internal Affairs. (2021). *Future for local government review*. Te Tari Taiwhenua Department of Internal Affairs. Retrieved August 21, 2025, from https://www.dia.govt.nz/Future-for-Local-Government-Review

Te Tari Taiwhenua Department of Internal Affairs. (2023). *Review into the future for local government: He piki tūranga, he piki kōtuku*. Retrieved August 21, 2025, from https://www.dia.govt.nz/diawebsite.nsf/Files/Future-for-Local-Government/$file/Te-Arotake_Final-report.pdf

Tobin, S., & Zaman, A. (2022). Regional cooperation in waste management: Examining Australia's experience with inter-municipal cooperative partnerships. *Sustainability, 14*(3), 1578. https://doi.org/10.3390/su14031578

Uddin, K. (2018). NSW local government reform: Council amalgamation, antagonism, and resistance. *Journal of Public Affairs, 18*(4), 1–8. https://doi.org/10.1002/pa.1725

Open Access This chapter is licensed under the terms of the Creative Commons Attribution 4.0 International License (http://creativecommons.org/licenses/by/4.0/), which permits use, sharing, adaptation, distribution and reproduction in any medium or format, as long as you give appropriate credit to the original author(s) and the source, provide a link to the Creative Commons license and indicate if changes were made.

The images or other third party material in this chapter are included in the chapter's Creative Commons license, unless indicated otherwise in a credit line to the material. If material is not included in the chapter's Creative Commons license and your intended use is not permitted by statutory regulation or exceeds the permitted use, you will need to obtain permission directly from the copyright holder.

Chapter 7
Local Government in Ethiopia: Territorial Reforms and Horizontal Intergovernmental Cooperation

Zemelak Ayitenew Ayele

Abstract Ethiopia has been implementing a local-level decentralization program beginning from the early 2000s with an eye to mainly empowering rural local government so that it can be efficient in terms of delivering basic services. While it has significantly contributed to enhancing basic service provisions, the decentralized system was constrained, among others, by two major challenges. The first was the arbitrary and often politically motivated splitting of *woredas* (the most important rural local government units in Ethiopia which are the equivalent of districts or municipalities in other systems). While it was necessary to create smaller and more efficient *woredas*, considering the territorial size of the country, the splitting of *woredas* was however introduced in a context where there was no legal framework for it. The second challenge was the absence of forums for *woreda-to-woreda* cooperation within a state and across a state boundary. This was despite the fact that the efficient provision of certain services, such as primary healthcare, education, and the like, required such cooperation.

Keywords Ethiopia · *Woredas* · Ethnicity · Local government · Cooperation · Decentralization

7.1 Introduction

Once an extremely centralized unitary state, Ethiopia has undergone a decentralization process, which was implemented in two phases. The first phase began in May 1991, after the military regime of the Derg was overthrown, and culminated when the country became a federal state with the adoption of the 1995 Constitution (Ayele, 2014; Gebre-Egziabher & Berhanu, 2007). The 1995 Constitution

Z. A. Ayele (✉)
Centre for Federalism and Governance Studies, Addis Ababa University, Addis Ababa, Ethiopia
e-mail: zemelak.ayitenew@aau.edu.et

© The Author(s) 2026

K. Kössler, E. M. Belser (eds.), *Local Government Structure and Intergovernmental Relations*, Local and Urban Governance,
https://doi.org/10.1007/978-3-031-99820-1_7

established a federal system with two levels of government. Originally, the Constitution established nine states, which were demarcated along lines, and a federal capital at the subnational level.[1] With the dissolution of one of the nine constituent units, the Southern Nations Nationalities and Peoples State (SNNP), the number of states has risen to 13.[2]

The second phase of the decentralization program was launched in the early 2000s (Ayele, 2014; Gebre-Egziabher & Berhanu, 2007). This phase was meant, at least officially, to empower local government so that the latter could be democratic, well-resourced, and efficient in providing basic services to citizens. This stage of the decentralization process included adjusting local government boundaries by dividing or merging existing local units. Dividing local units continued for several years after the second phase of decentralization was implemented. This begs the question, how the decision to alter local government boundaries has been passed and implemented? What is the constitutional and legal basis for doing so? How does the alteration of local boundaries impact local government autonomy? What institutional mechanism exist for the local government units to cooperate with each other? The chapter attempts to answer these and related questions.

The chapter begins with an introduction to the local government system of Ethiopia. It then assesses whether local government, rural local government in particular, delivers on its mandates. It then discusses the legal framework for merging or splitting local government units and issues of how the splits and amalgamation of local governments have impacted the capacity of local government to deliver on its mandate. This is followed by a discussion on whether and how local government units cooperate with each other.

7.2 Local Government Structure in Ethiopia

The federal constitution allows the states to regulate all matters relating to local government. Practice shows that the states have established two types of local government: ethnic and regular local government (Ayele & Fessha, 2012). Ethnic local government is a sub-state extension of the federal structure and is meant to provide territorial autonomy to intra-state ethnic minorities at the sub-state level (Ayele & Fessha, 2012; Van der Beken, 2016). In this category are ethnic zones and ethnic (*liyu*) *woredas*. The ethnic zone is larger both in population and territorial terms than the ethnic *woreda* and is made up of several *woredas* (districts) and towns/cities. An ethnic or special *woreda* is a single *woreda* (district) whose boundaries are demarcated along ethnic lines. These are found in Amhara, Gambella, Benishangul-Gumuz, Afar, and the states that emerged following the dissolution of the former

[1] The original members of the federation were Tigray, Amhara, Afar, Oromia, Somali, Hareri, Benishangul-Gumuz, Gambella, Southern Nations, Nationalities and Peoples (SNNP).

[2] The four new states are Sidama, South-West, South-Ethiopia, and Central Ethiopia.

SNNPR (South-West, Central Ethiopia, and South Ethiopia). There are about 25 nationality zones and ethnic *woredas* in Ethiopia. Functional competencies of ethnic zones are restricted to regulating cultural matters, such as selecting the working language and language of instruction and (for ethnic zones) coordinating the works of the *woredas* and cities within them. Having barely any internal source of revenue, they are almost entirely dependent on state fiscal transfers. (Ayele, 2014). Ethnic *woredas*, in addition to dealing with cultural matters, like any *woreda*, are responsible for providing basic services (Fig. 7.1).

Regular local government is made up of cities and rural *woredas*. There is an administrative zone in some states which comprises several *woredas*. However, it is not a local government with devolved power but a sub-state structure with deconcentrated power run by state appointees. Thus, *woredas* (including ethnic *woredas*) and cities form the main tiers of local government. As a rule, a *woreda* is supposed established in a territorial area with a population of about 100,000 people—a rule that is seldom practiced. Practice shows that *woredas* have, on average, a population of 76,000. However, in sparsely populated states, such as Somali, Benishangul-Gumuz, and Afar states, the average *woreda* population is much less than the national average. For instance, Benishangul Gumuz state has an estimated population one million and 77% the population lives in rural areas. This means the 21 *woredas* of this state have on average about 36,000 population which is much less than the population requirement set in the policies on decentralization and the national average of woreda population. *Woredas* in the densely populated states of the highland areas—Amhara, Tigray, Oromia—tend to be, relatively small in territorial size as compared to those in sparsely populated low land states, such as, Afar and Somali states. For instance, the average size of a *woreda* in Somali and Afar

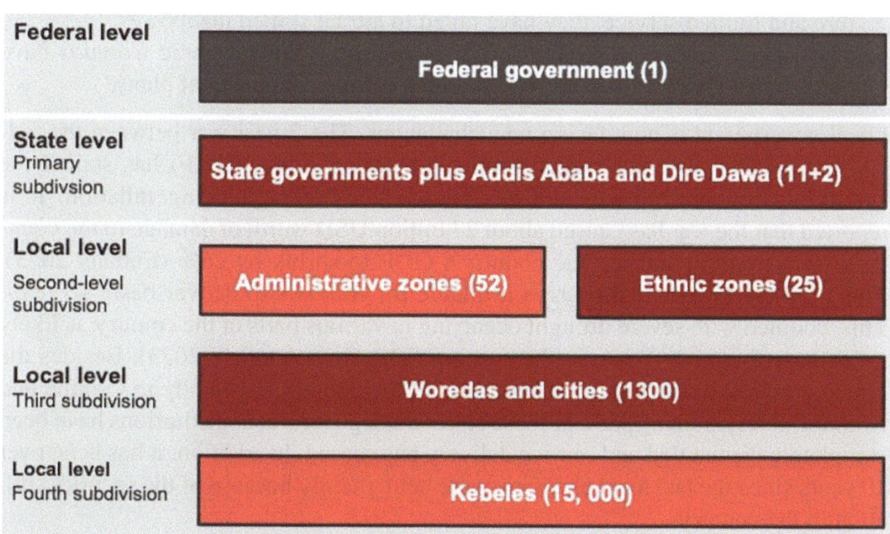

Fig. 7.1 Structure of local government in Ethiopia. Source: Local Public Sector Alliance (2023)

states are 3280 and 2183 km^2, respectively. The average size of a *woredas* in Amhara and Oromia states on the other hand are 840 and 1022 km^2, respectively.

Functions within the competencies of *woredas* and cities include primary education, primary health care, rural roads, water, and the like (Ayele, 2014). Ethnic *woredas*, which are simply *woredas* except that they are established primarily based on ethnic criteria (with an eye to allow intra-state ethnic minority communities to enjoy a degree of autonomy) have the same functions as regular *woreda* as far as the delivery of basic services is concerned. Cities have additional urban-specific functions, such as garbage collection, streetlights, abattoirs, etc. *Woredas* and cities are allowed to collect revenue in the form of service charges and taxes. However, *woredas,* including ethnic *woredas,* are dependent on state financial transfers, which cover over 70% of their annual budget (Ayele, 2014).

Woredas (including ethnic *woredas*) and cities play critical role in terms of basic service provision. Yet several challenges limit their effectiveness in this respect:

1. Local government does not enjoy constitutional protection, and its very existence is at the mercy of the states.
2. The second decentralization program was conceived and designed at the federal level. This left the states with little room to design their local government system or consider their own contexts, which rendered the decentralization program a one-size-fits-all project (Nigussie, 2006).
3. *Woredas* functional competencies are not clearly defined in state constitutions, which opened room for mandate confusion and occasional recentralization of certain functions (Ayele, 2014).
4. Local government, rural *woredas*, in particular, lacked an internal source of revenue and depended for over 70% of their expenditure.
5. *Woredas* lacked human capacity since, being rural where there is poor infrastructure and limited service, they have failed to attract skilled manpower.
6. The endless territorial structuring of *woredas,* including ethnic *woredas* have made it difficult for *woredas* to make long-term developmental plans.

Local government is now facing new challenges. The 2-year war between the federal government and the Tigray People Liberation Front (TPLF) has stalled the country's economic growth and has been a cause for galloping inflation. It is reported that the war has caused about 27 billion USD worth of damage to the country's infrastructure and led the country's GDP to shrink by 26% (Endale, 2023). This is likely to reduce resources available for *woredas* to deliver basic services. This, coupled with severe drought occurring in various parts of the country, is likely to increase the poverty rate in the country (The Humanitarian, 2023). Besides the armed conflicts occurring in various parts of the country, especially in Oromia and Amhara states, in many parts of these states local government institutions have been completely dismantled and service delivery has ceased. In addition, it has been over 10 years since the last local elections were held, mainly because of the security situation in the country.

7.3 Revising Local Boundaries

As mentioned, the endless revisions of the boundaries is one of the biggest challenges that *woredas*, which have a double function (a cultural and the basic service delivery function), are facing. This is because the revisions are impacting their ability to deliver services. This begs the question about the constitutional and legal framework for restructuring the boundaries of *woredas* and cities. The federal constitution authorizes the states to determine the number of tiers and units of local government that they may want to establish. It provides neither substantive criteria nor procedure requirements for the territorial structuring of *woredas*. The states are at liberty to determine whether and how to create new *woredas* and divide and amalgamate the existing ones. This raises the question, what criteria do states use for demarcating the boundaries of nationality zones, special *woredas*, *woredas*, and city boundaries? Who has the authority to decide on local government boundaries? What is the procedure that must be followed to create local governments, whether regular or ethnic? How do local communities participate in the process of local government boundary demarcation?

7.3.1 Ethnic Local Government

As mentioned, ethnic local governments are meant to give effect to the right to self-determination of sub-state ethnic minorities. The principle that underpins its establishment is stipulated under Article 39 of the 1995 Constitution, which allows each ethnic community to form self-government in the territory it inhabits. Having the status of an ethnic community is the only criterion that a community must meet to qualify for its own ethnic zone or ethnic *woreda*. The House of Federation, the second chamber of the federal parliament, has the final say on whether a community is a distinct ethnic community (Constitution 1995, Art 62(3)). The settlement pattern of the relevant ethnic community is thus the only consideration that has to be taken into account for demarcating the boundaries of ethnic local government. There are no other criteria that must be taken into account such as population size and economic context (Van der Beken, 2015; Ayele & Fessha, 2012). Currently, there are 76 recognized ethnic communities in the country, with populations ranging from 40 million (Oromo) to a few thousand.[3] In principle, each of these ethnic communities is entitled to a state or, at least, a local government of its own.

State constitutions detail whether and how ethnic local government would be established. The Afar, Amhara, and Gambella State Constitutions create ethnic local

[3] It should be noted that in 1992 when Ethiopia began the journey towards the ethnic federal system, there were 63 recognized ethnic communities. The increase in number means 13 communities have received recognition as distinct ethnic communities that fulfill the criteria defined under Article 39(5) of the Constitution.

government for specific ethnic communities (Van der Beken, 2015; Fiseha, 2017). In the Afar, the Argoba, a sub-state minority in the Afar State, has its own special *woreda*. In the Amhara State, the Wag-Himra, Awi, and Oromo zones are established for the three sub-state minority communities. The Anywaa Nuer and Mejenger communities have ethnic zones. The former SNNP, which was home to over 50 ethnic communities, has been divided into four smaller ethnic-based states: the Sidama, South West, South Ethiopia, and South-Central states. Before its dismemberment into four states, the NNP had 14 ethnic zones and four *ethnic woredas. Almost all the ethnic zones of the SNNP have retained their status in the newly established states. The exception is the Sidama, which has become a state in its own right.*

As implied in the federal constitution, every ethnic community is entitled to its own state, ethnic zone or ethnic *woreda*. However, petitions for ethnic zones and *woredas* seldom found positive responses from the states and the federal government. The states (politicians hailing from the dominant ethnic communities in each state) are not interested in establishing autonomous ethnic zones and ethnic *woredas* since doing so would reduce their power to control those areas and the resources in them. In fact, they often deny claims of distinct identity by minority communities the establishment of which is the basis for demanding territorial autonomy at any local level. Besides, establishing ethnic zone and ethnic *woredas* is often seen as a first step towards internal secession through the establishment of a state (Ayele et al., 2023; Ayele & Fessha, 2022). The states are thus relucent to grant petitions by sub-state ethnic minority communities for own ethnic zones and ethnic woredas.

The Ethiopian Peoples' Revolutionary Democratic Front (EPRDF) was, as a rule, against establishing ethnic local government units since it deemed that they would undermine its developmental agenda (Vaughan, 2006; Aalen, 2008). It often violently suppressed demands for ethnic zones and *woredas*, and, as was the case with ethnic *woredas* of the former SNNP which merged into the Segen zone, it even abolished some of the existing ones (Dejen, 2010). It allowed the creation of ethnic zones only when it found it necessary to deal with inter-ethnic conflicts. Following the rise to power of Abiy Ahmed in 2018, the demand for ethnic local government intensified. Communities having their own ethnic zones demanded their own states, and several new ethnic zones and *liyu* woredas were established. The federal government, partly overwhelmed by the inter-ethnic conflict, agreed to the creation of several ethnic zones, and even reluctantly agreed to the formation of four new states out of the former SNNP (Ayele et al., 2023).

7.3.2 Regular Local Government

When the 1995 Constitution was adopted, the old *woreda* boundaries were generally kept intact. There were approximately 600 *woredas when the second phase of decentralization was launched in the early 2000s.* No major local boundary re-demarcation took place as part of the implementation of the second phase of the decentralization program. Yet, in the past two decades, the number of *woredas* has increased even though the exact number of *woredas* is not known. Data obtained from the National Electoral Board of Ethiopia (NEBE) shows that there are today over 1200 rural *woredas*. The number of *woredas* has doubled in the past two decades, which implies that there has been a territorial restructuring of *woredas*. The restructuring was more towards dividing existing *woredas* than amalgamating them. This is partly because of the country's massive territorial size and growing population which require rationalizing the sizes of *woredas* so that they can be efficient in terms of service provision. The other, perhaps the main, reason for the increase in the number of *woredas* is political. A promise of *woredas* is often used to secure political support from rural communities for the ruling party (Berhanu, 2017).

It is however unclear on what constitutional or legal basis the changes of the boundaries of *woredas* were introduced. Most states have not adopted laws clearly regulating the creation of new *woredas,* as well as the splits and/or amalgamation of existing ones. Indeed, some states, such as the Tigray and Benishangul-Gumuz states, have enacted proclamations that, among other things, deal with *woreda* boundaries. The two proclamations formally recognize the existing *woredas* and authorize the respective state councils to create new *woredas*, and/or to divide, amalgamate, or eliminate any existing *woreda* within the states. Article 6(1) of Proclamation 99/2006 of the Tigray State authorizes the state executive council to define, through executive regulation, the criteria for creating a new *woreda*. Article 6(3) of the Proclamation also provides that the criteria, to be defined by the executive council, should include the capacity to deliver services, administrative convenience, and the communities' culture and preferences. The criteria for dividing or merging *woredas* in Amhara State is defined in a regulation issued by the executive council (Workneh, 2021). It should be noted that executive regulation is a legal instrument that the executive council can easily adopt and revise thereby making changing *woreda* boundaries easily achievable. This means *woredas* are exposed to the risk of arbitrary division or amalgamation. Article 11(1) of Proclamation 86/2010 of Benishangul-Gumuz provides certain criteria for creating a new *woreda*. These are population size, capacity to cover 25% of own expenses from own resources, population settlement structure, and the history, culture, and interest of the community. When deciding to create a new *woreda,* or to divide or amalgamate an existing one, the Benishangul-Gumuz State Council must consider studies and proposals of the state bureaus of finance and administrative and security affairs.

Clearly not every state has adopted a legal farmwork for splitting or merging *woredas*. The existing ones are, as is the case in the Amhara state, executive regulation that the executive branch of a state government can change at whim (Workneh, 2021). In any case it is unclear to what extent the state follow in practice the procedures for splitting *woredas* that are laid down in their laws. There are indeed instances where states have established *woredas* in response to petitions lodged by local communities. However, a study by Ayenew Berhanu shows that in most cases states would create new *woredas* or amalgamate existing ones based on political considerations: as a reward for votes received or punishment for votes denied in elections (Berhanu, 2017). Besides, the decision to alter *woreda* boundaries is seldom based on genuine public participation. About the creation of new *woredas*, Workneh (2021) writes: "Observation of regional government finds that there are limitations in public participation in regard to claims for new local governments. This is also evident in discontentment among the people and in the inefficiency of institutions after splits have occurred. The local elites, including public servants, merchants, and government officials, are crucial in initiating, framing, and facilitating requests for new local government status. They call for public participation with some predetermined outcome, basically the inevitability of splits. Public gatherings are neither inclusive nor genuine."

7.4 Inter-Municipal Cooperation

Little attention was given to inter-municipal cooperation in the constitutional architecture of the Ethiopian federal system, even though co-operation among local government units is indeed critical. For example, in several cases, schools and clinics are situated in one *woreda* but serve residents of other *woredas* (Negussie, 2006). Financing and administering these facilities require cooperation between or among *woredas*. Moreover, cities and municipalities serve as political seats and economic and political centers of several *woredas*. This also requires institutionalised city-*woreda* cooperation.

In some states, such as Oromia, Amhara, and the like, *woredas* are found within one of the administrative zones. An administrative zone, which encompasses several *woredas, is a* "deconcentrated arm" of the state government, not an autonomous sub-state government. In states, such as Gambella, in some parts of Amhara, and the states that seceded from the SNNP other than the Sidama state, *woredas* are found within ethnic zones. The administrative and ethnic zones often play the role of coordinating the works of *woredas* within them (Ayele, 2014). However, the role that administrative and ethnic zones play in terms of coordinating the works of *woredas* cannot be strictly considered facilitating 'cooperation' among *woredas* since they serve as an apparatus of supervision by the state governments. The zones thus use hierarchical top-down approach to coordinate the activities of *woredas* within them (Ayele, 2014). Some states have enacted proclamations that provide for the establishment of associations of *woredas* within their respective jurisdiction. These would then act to represent local governments collectively, express their views on matters of common interest [and] lobby [the regional] government for revision of laws. State laws also provide that an association of cities can be established within the respective states and that these associations can represent cities collectively and express their views on matters of common interest to state governments (Article 60 of Proclamation 195 (2015) of the Oromia State; Proclamation 103 (2006) of the SNNPR). There is no report indicating that such an association exists in any of the states.

Some state laws provide for cooperation among *woredas* and the cities within the states. A case in point is Proclamation 86 (2010) of Benishangul-Gumuz, which provides that *woreda*-to-*woreda* and *woreda*-to-city cooperation within the state may be conducted through joint committees that these local government units can establish to deal with common issues. As mentioned, it is unclear though if such a committee exists in practice. Cooperation between local government units of two or more states is left unregulated even though there are common issues that are likely to require such cooperation, particularly when *woredas* of different states share borders. Service delivery, boundary disputes, inter-communal conflicts (especially regarding the pastoralist communities who move across state boundaries) require cooperation between *woredas* of two or more states if they are to be successfully resolved. However, no federal law regulates interactions between local government units of two or more states. Cities use what is called Cities' Day, Cities' Forum and Mayors' Forum Fana Broadcasting Corporate, 2021) to come together once a year. These are special events that take place in a host city and last for several days, with more than a hundred cities taking part and each being represented by their mayor and officials. While this is not an ideal occasion for policy discussions, the forum has been used for experience sharing. On the other hand, *woredas* do not have such forums to meet and discuss common issues.

7.5 Conclusions

Ethiopia has implemented a two-phased decentralization program, including measures that sought to empower especially rural local government. The decentralization program was implemented in a top-down manner. The policy of restructuring local government and decentralizing power to *woredas* was initiated by the federal government despite the federal system that makes local government an exclusive state matter. In any case *woredas* had also served as fora of electoral participation even though local elections, as all elections in the country, are far from free and fair.

The decentralization program has contributed to a significant poverty reduction and enhanced social service provision which the country achieved in the past three decades. A World Bank Report (2015) shows that in the early late 1990s, just before the decentralization program was launched, about 44% of the population lived under below the national poverty line. Less than 30% and 17% of the population had access to education and clean water, respectively. Life expectancy was just above 50, and close to 60% of children had stunted growth due to malnutrition. The rate of poverty was reduced to 30% in 2011 and 19% in 2022 (World Bank, 2015; Policy Study Institute, 2023). The poverty reduction is often attributed to the sustained economic growth that the country achieved between 2005 and 2015.

However, the works of *woredas* were constrained by various challenges. *Woredas* in Ethiopia have operated in a context where their very existence was not constitutionally guaranteed, their mandates not clearly demarcated, and they suffered from acute financial constraints. The political context in which a single political party controls every level of government also allowed little autonomy to *woredas*. Their amalgamation has not been a major challenge in Ethiopia but arbitrary splitting of woredas by states had undermined the autonomy of woredas and their works in the areas of service delivery. There were about 600 large *woredas* when Ethiopia began implementing the decentralization program. Given the territorial size of the country, the 600 *woredas* were too large and, therefore, too far from the people. It was thus necessary that boundaries were re-demarcated to create smaller *woredas* which were more manageable and closer to the people. Almost every state introduced reforms that led to the splitting of the *woredas*. Now there are about 1200 *woredas* in Ethiopia. Thus, the splitting of the *woredas* was not a problem in itself. The problem was rather that this process was often top-down and arbitrary since several states did not have a clear legislative framework for dividing and amalgamating the *woredas*. The states did not have clear substantive criteria and strict procedures to be followed in deciding splits and amalgamations of *woredas*. Besides the splitting of woredas were not implemented as a well-thought-out policy response to the challenges that *woredas* faced. They were rather politically motivated and often implemented on a top-down basis. Such arbitrary splits render long-term development planning at the *woreda* level difficult. In addition, intergovernmental cooperation among political institutions of *woredas* was virtually non-existent despite the many factors that necessitated such cooperation. *Woredas* and cities, inter-*woreda* cooperation across state boundaries was unknown, while cities of different states interact at least once a year in the form of Cities' Day. While this is not an ideal occasion for policy discussions, the forum has been used for experience sharing. The constitutional recognition of local government as a democratically constituted level of government could provide a degree of protection and prevent the arbitrary splitting and amalgamation of *woredas* and cities. While every aspect of *woreda*-state and inter-*woreda* cooperation cannot be, and need not be, regulated, a legal framework at the state level could provide a structure to such interactions.

Ethiopia implemented limited political and institutional reforms since the rise to power of Abiy Ahmed in 2018. However, the reforms were superficial which did not meet demands of the different political actors. Besides the reforms are restricted at the federal level and local government was not on the agenda. Now in the name of bringing about a lasting political settlement in the country, the federal government has initiated a process of "national dialogue". A National Dialogue Commission (NDC) is legislatively established which is responsible for facilitating the dialogue. The plan is that the national dialogue would result in constitutional reform or amendment. It is expected that local government would be on the agenda in this national dialogue. Some political parties have proposed local government reforms as part of the agenda of the national dialogue. Assuming that this initiative, which is fraught with numerous challenges, goes ahead as planned, any reform in relation to local government, territorial or institutional, is likely to be the outcome of the process of the nationaldialogue.

Acknowledgement This research was financially supported by the UK Research and Innovation (UKRI, GCRF) Award reference number ES/T014946/1 under the project title Partnership Programme for Capacity Building Centre of Excellence in Good Governance (CoE in Good Governance), Addis Ababa University.

References

Aalen, L. (2008). *Institutionalizing the politics of ethnicity: Actors, power and mobilization in Southern Ethiopia under ethnic federalism.* Dissertation submitted for the degree of PhD in political science University Oslo.

Ayele, Z. (2014). *Local government in Ethiopia: Advancing development and accommodating ethnic minorities*. Nomos.

Ayele, Z., & Fessha, Y. (2012). The place and status of local government in federal states: The case of Ethiopia. *African Today, 58*, 89–109.

Ayele, Z., & Fessha, Y. (2022). Internal secession: The Ethiopian experience in comparative perspective. In M. Belov (Ed.), *Territorial politics: Constitutional and international law perspective* (pp. 265–287). Palgrave Macmillan.

Ayele, Z., Fuller, B., & Raleigh, C. (2023). Ethno-federalism and subnational conflicts in Ethiopia. *Civil Wars*. https://doi.org/10.1080/13698249.2023.2214500

Berhanu, A. (2017). *The politics of local government creation and boundary demarcation within Ethiopian Federation: Challenges and implications*. Unpublished PhD thesis, Addis Ababa University.

Dejen, M. (2010). Amalgamating five special local governments into a single administrative zone vs self-government rights of ethnic groups in SNNPRS. In Z. Ayele (Ed.), *Local government in Ethiopia: Responses to urban-rural challenges* (pp. 65–70). Zenodo. https://doi.org/10.5281/zenodo.5718741

Endale A. (2023, May 20). Conflict pushes 3m deeper into poverty. *The Reporter*. https://www.thereporterethiopia.com/34088/

Fana Broadcasting Corporate. (2021). የከንቲባዎች ፎረም በአዲስ አበባ ከተማ የሚገኙ ፕሮጀክቶችን ጎበኙ (‘*[Participants of] Mayors’ forum visited different projects of Addis Ababa*’). Retrieved June 11, 2021, from https://bit.ly/3vph2MX

Fiseha, A. (2017). Intra-unit minorities in the context of Ethno-National Federation in Ethiopia. *Utrecht Law Review, 13*, 171–189.

Gebre-Egziabher, T., & Berhanu, K. (2007). A literature review of decentralization in Ethiopia. In T. Assefa & T. Gebre-Egziabher (Eds.), *Decentralization in Ethiopia* (pp. 9–18). Forum Social Studies.

Nigussie, S. (2006). *Fiscal federalism in the Ethiopian ethnic based federal system*. Wolf Legal Publisher.

Policy Study Institute. (2023). *PSI researchers released preliminary findings on dynamics of multi-dimensional poverty in Ethiopia*. https://psi.org.et/index.php/blog/161-psi-researchers-released-preliminary-findings-on-dynamics-of-multidimensional-poverty-in-ethiopia#:~:text=In%20Ethiopia%2C%2068.7%25%20of%20the,risk%20of%20becoming%20multidimensionally%20poor

The Humanitarian. (2023, August). *Boom to bust: Fallout of war and drought leaves Ethiopians mired in poverty*. https://www.thenewhumanitarian.org/news-feature/2023/08/01/boom-bust-fallout-war-and-drought-leaves-ethiopians-mired-poverty

Van der Beken, C. (2015). Federalism, local government and minority protection in Ethiopia: Opportunities and challenges. *Journal of African Law, 59*, 150–177.

Van der Beken, C. (2016). Subnational constitutional autonomy and the accommodation of diversity in Ethiopia. *Rutgers University Law Review, 68*, 1535–1571.

Vaughan, S. (2006). Responses for ethnic federalism in Ethiopia’s southern region. In D. Turton (Ed.), *Ethnic federalism: The Ethiopian experience in comparative perspective* (pp. 181–207). Addis Ababa University Press.

Workneh, Y. (2021). Splitting local government and its (un)expected outcomes: The case of Amhara National Regional State. In Z. Ayele (Ed.), *Local government in Ethiopia: Responses to urban-rural challenges* (pp. 71–75). Zenodo. https://doi.org/10.5281/zenodo.5718743

World Bank. (2015). *Ethiopia poverty assessment.* https://www.worldbank.org/en/topic/poverty/publication/ethiopia-poverty-assessment

Yonatan, F., & Ayele, Z. (2022). Inter-governmental relations and ethnic federalism in Ethiopia. In Y. Fessha, K. Kössler, & F. Palermo (Eds.), *Inter-governmental relations in divided societies* (pp. 113–132). Palgrave Macmillan.

Open Access This chapter is licensed under the terms of the Creative Commons Attribution 4.0 International License (http://creativecommons.org/licenses/by/4.0/), which permits use, sharing, adaptation, distribution and reproduction in any medium or format, as long as you give appropriate credit to the original author(s) and the source, provide a link to the Creative Commons license and indicate if changes were made.

The images or other third party material in this chapter are included in the chapter's Creative Commons license, unless indicated otherwise in a credit line to the material. If material is not included in the chapter's Creative Commons license and your intended use is not permitted by statutory regulation or exceeds the permitted use, you will need to obtain permission directly from the copyright holder.

Chapter 8
Rural Areas and Institutional Sustainability: Assessing the Nexus Between Population Decline and Rescaling of Municipal Government in Italy

Elisabeth Alber

Abstract This chapter explores the critical nexus between population decline and the rescaling of local government in Italy, with a focus on small rural municipalities. Through a detailed assessment of demographic data, municipal traditions, constitutional guarantees, and policy interventions, the chapter highlights the importance of including the populations affected in rescaling reforms. It argues that successful strategies require a balance between top-down and bottom-up approaches, coordination between the national and regional legislatures, and collaborative governance between the public sector and civil society. The chapter examines the current state of municipal government, and the theory and practice of municipal mergers and inter-municipal cooperation as potential solutions to enhance the administrative capacity and service delivery in small municipalities, showcasing and explaining the significant variations between Italian regions. It concludes that Italy's fragmented territorial governance suffers from unfinished reforms and centralized policies that negatively impact the effectiveness of both rescaling reforms and policy interventions that aim at enhancing the institutional sustainability of rural local government.

Keywords Local government · Mergers · Inter-municipal cooperation · Institutional sustainability · Depopulation

---

E. Alber (✉)
Institute for Comparative Federalism, Eurac Research, Bolzano/Bozen, Italy
e-mail: elisabeth.alber@eurac.edu

© The Author(s) 2026

K. Kössler, E. M. Belser (eds.), *Local Government Structure and Intergovernmental Relations*, Local and Urban Governance,
https://doi.org/10.1007/978-3-031-99820-1_8

8.1 Introduction

The most recent studies of the European Commission's Joint Research Centre (JRC) show that 75% of the world population currently live in urban areas (European Commission, Joint Research Centre, 2016). JRC projections to 2030 also show that most European regions hosting major cities are expected to experience urban population growth and that this increase is significantly at the expense of the surrounding smaller cities and towns, and rural areas. Although not a linear process (Doignon et al., 2016), population decline is thus one of the biggest challenges rural areas face (Raugze et al., 2017). Its effects are visible not only in demographic terms (rural-urban migration as well as net population change due to changing age structures) but also in the lack of service provision and loss of social cohesion (quality of life), and the economic viability of rural areas (GDP, investment in research and development, employment, and innovation).

Italy is no exception to this trend. The exodus of the population from rural areas to urban centers first intensified after World War II. Back then, Italy moved from a moderate to a strong regional divergence, with the North, unlike the South, profiting from modernization efforts put forward by local entrepreneurs that managed to innovate in the period during World War I and II. Hence, in the early 1950s, southern regions had fallen behind the northern regions in economic-industrial terms (Felice, 2017). The consolidation of northern urban poles was matched by a massive depopulation of rural areas, and South to North migration (Bonifazi & Heins, 2000), with significant consequences in terms of land abandonment, land maintenance, agricultural and pastoral practices (De Rubertis, 2019). The resident population in municipalities with fewer than 10,000 inhabitants decreased dramatically, from 45% in 1951 to 35% in 1971. Similar trends were recorded between the 1970s and 1990s, when, despite losing intensity, population decline in rural areas continued.

It was young people in particular who migrated, which is why migration in Italy and elsewhere led to a concentration of elderly people in rural areas that impacts municipal governance in three ways (OECD, 2009, pp. 50–61). First, the large concentration of elderly people in rural areas poses challenges regarding labor productivity and the amount of utilized agricultural areas. Second, it undermines the sustainability of education services. Third, it impacts the delivery of health care services, as the need for such services is increasing. Although foreign workers may counteract ageing and population decline, rural municipal government does not necessarily have the capacity to sustain adequate integration and repopulation policies, financially and in terms of personnel. Thus, replacement migration—the idea implying that international migration might be a tool to offset population ageing and its negative effects—is no optimal solution to face depopulation (Saczuk, 2013). On the contrary, mergers of local governments and inter-municipal cooperation as well as place-based policies involving autochthonous population in collaborative governance between the public sector and civil society may decelerate population decline and increase the sustainability of municipal government in rural areas.

Institutions are considered sustainable when they aptly contemplate, balance, and support the concerns and interests of their peoples and territories; when their functioning is grounded in a clear institutional vision that considers how formal and informal actors from various levels of government shape and affect behavior and expectations, so that their capacity to perform their functions lasts over the long term (Pfahl, 2005; Fedeli, 2017). However, a clear institutional vision is absent in Italy's territorial governance. Regions, provinces, metropolitan cities, municipalities, and associative forms thereof are the plaything of centralized, short-sighted policies, and they are incapable of renewing themselves because of parochialism (Alber et al., 2024). In other words, despite some attempts to institutionally innovate, conformism prevails (Palermo, 2009).

This chapter addresses the institutional dimension of municipal government in Italy. It focuses on small municipalities with less than 5000 inhabitants and on mergers and inter-municipal cooperation (IMC) as instruments to rescale municipalities, a need that has been part of the academic debate and political agendas for many years (Bolgherini et al., 2018; De Donno & Tubertini, 2020). The choice of this focus has three main motivations. The first motivation relates to the fact that mergers and IMC are among the most relevant manifestations in municipal government (Teles, 2016; Hulst & van Montfort, 2007). The purpose of mergers and IMC is to address the mismatch between existing structures and underlying realities, that is to bridge the gap between (administrative) capacity and (service delivery) expectations (Nørgaard, 1996). The second motivation refers to the scarce attention that research has given to the systemic (empirical) analysis of the topics of mergers and IMC, and (comparative) evaluation studies thereof, despite being a widespread institutional phenomenon in European domestic contexts (Teles & Swianievicz, 2018). The third motivation relates to the notion of institutional sustainability and, more precisely, to the part of the notion that points to the need to properly include affected populations in any rescaling reform. In the end, rescaling reforms reformulate the relationships between a municipality seen as the main provider of services and the citizen as the user of these services.

Within the framework of this introduction, this chapter demonstrates that Italy is amid unfinished reforms regarding the optimal dimension for the exercise of municipal powers, in general and in relation to combating population decline in rural areas. The chapter is structured as follows. Section 8.2 presents data on demography, municipalities, and rural regeneration programs. Section 8.3 explains the tradition and evolution of municipal government, while Sect. 8.4 outlines how municipal government is constitutionally recognized and guaranteed, and which functions it has. Understanding the role of municipal government as a pawn of multiple interests is crucial for the discussion of the theory and practice of top-down and bottom-up rescaling measures in Sects. 8.5 (mergers) and 8.6 (IMC). The chapter ends with Sect. 8.7, which offers concluding remarks and suggests future directions for research.

8.2 Population Decline and Strategies of Rural Regeneration

Italy is one of the 48 European countries where population decline is underway (UN, 2019). It is also among the countries where the share of the population aged 65 years and over constantly grows (Statista—Italy, 2024). The country's population density is very uneven. The largest number of people live in the northern region of Lombardy (about one–sixth of the entire population). Lazio, in the center, and Campania, in the south, are the second and third most populous regions. The largest cities are in each of these three regions: Milan, Rome, and Naples. The Basilicata plateaus, the Alps and Apennines highlands, and the island of Sardinia have very sparse populations. Geographically, the plains comprise about one-fifth of the country and are confined to the northern triangle of the Po Valley; the rest of the territory is divided almost evenly between hilly and mountainous land.

The heterogeneity of the Italian territory, the unequal population density, and the effects of population decline due to the "desertification" of services in small municipalities (Cipolloni, 2021, p. 53) have led to a progressive fragility of the territory and its social system (Benassi et al., 2022). Although not a linear process (Rizzo, 2016), depopulation in small (rural) municipalities has been ongoing for some years. Indeed, more than 40% of Italy's population now live in urban areas. Out of 7899 Italian municipalities, 5525 are small (with less than 5000 inhabitants), and account for just over ten million residents (Tuttitalia.it, 2024). Most small municipalities have populations between 1001 and 3000 inhabitants, while 2014 municipalities have a population under 1000. In many regions, more than 70% of the land area falls under the control of small municipalities; and small municipalities in all regions continue to lose inhabitants. According to the National Association of Italian Municipalities (*Associazione Nazionale Comuni Italiani*—ANCI), small municipalities lost 3% of their inhabitants from 2012 to 2017 (Falconio, 2018). On top of this, growth and decline contrasts continue to be evident between northern and southern Italy (Reynaud et al., 2020), with estimates for urban population growth of over 35% in the northern Italian regions (European Commission, Joint Research Centre, 2016, pp. 27–28).

It is important to note that the number of municipalities varies greatly from one region to another (Alber & Valdesalici, 2023, pp. 262–263). So does the number of small municipalities. Piedmont (25,386 km^2) is the region that has the greatest number of small municipalities: 1045; Lombardy region (23,863 km^2) follows with 1034, while Emilia-Romagna (22,444 km^2) has only 135. Lombardy is the region with the greatest share of inhabitants living in small municipalities: two million of its ten million inhabitants reside in small municipalities (Tuttitalia.it, 2024).

Regarding mountain municipalities (about ten million inhabitants), the National Union of Municipalities, Communities and Mountain Entities (*Unione Nazionale Comuni Comunità Enti Montani*—UNCEM) further distinguishes between those municipalities that are "totally" mountainous (3524) and those defined "partially" mountainous (652), for an overall total of 4176 municipalities (Senato della Repubblica, 2022). In terms of territorial extension, out of a total of 302,073 km^2, which define the Italian territory, 147,517 km^2 are occupied by mountain municipalities, representing 49% of the national territory. UNCEM highlights the constant population decline, particularly notable in recent years, and its constant ageing: from 2011 to 2019 in "totally" mountainous municipalities the population loss totaled 149,371 units and the average population density settled at 61 inhabitants/km^2 compared to a national average of 197 inhabitants/km^2. Population decline is especially visible in remote areas characterized by considerable masses of land with altitudes of no less than 600 m in northern Italy and 700 m in southern and island Italy.

Recent central programs counteracting population decline include the 2022 National Plan for the Redevelopment of Small Municipalities (*Piano nazionale per la riqualificazione dei piccoli comuni*). In 2023, a call for proposals invited municipalities with a population of up to 5000 inhabitants to submit applications for projects. Among the aims of the call, the safeguarding and urban redevelopment of historical centers, the securing of road infrastructures and educational institutions, and the promotion of economic and social development are mentioned. The maximum amount of funding for each project is EUR 700,000 if submitted by the municipality individually and EUR 700,000 multiplied by the number of municipalities that are part of IMC forms, such as a convention or a union of municipalities.[1] 67.3% of municipalities applied as single municipalities, the rest by means of IMC, for a total of 2638 submitted projects that involve 3359 municipalities (Presidency of the Council of Ministers Casa Italia Department, 2023).

Another program, the National Strategy for Inner Areas (*Strategia Nazionale Aree Interne*—SNAI), initially promoted in 2013 by the then newly formed Agency for Territorial Cohesion, promotes social cohesion objectives to decelerate and reverse Inner Areas' depopulation. Inner Areas are defined as fragile territories, far away from centers of supply of essential services with a travel distance of 45–75 min (peripheral area) and over 75 min (ultraperipheral area). Thus, spatial inequality is the parameter in selecting Inner Areas, although the dichotomy rural-urban is overly simplified. Inner Areas stretch over 60% of the national surface, and host 53% of Italian municipalities and 23% of Italy's population. Resources available for the SNAI amount to more than EUR 591 million, in addition to the allocations from programs financed by the European Structural and Investment Funds and other public/private programs. The SNAI funds individual projects according to a three-step method. First, municipalities are selected through a public investigation procedure by the inter-ministerial Inner Areas Technical Committee (*Comitato Tecnico Aree Interne*—CTAI), in cooperation with the concerned regions or autonomous province. Second, projects are funded after approval of the Area Strategy by the Department for Cohesion Policies of the Presidency of the Council of Ministers. Third, details are defined in the Framework Program Agreement for implementing the Inner Area Strategy through the commitment of all concerned administrations. The National Strategy currently addresses 72 Inner Areas, including 1077

[1] See Sect. 8.6.

municipalities with about 2.1 million inhabitants. Observed with interest by many European countries, the SNAI undoubtedly constitutes a paradigmatic case of public policies benefiting the most marginal territories by, among others, aiming at the creation of a permanent system of IMC (Falcone, 2020). According to the latest data (CIPESS, 2020), almost all Inner Areas have set up (or are well-advanced in setting up) processes of IMC. The regions with the greatest number of Inner Areas constituting IMC are Emilia-Romagna, Lombardy and Sicily, followed by Veneto, Umbria and Marche.

Of course, support programs originating from the regional level of government can also make a difference in decelerating population decline (Cipolloni, 2021, pp. 64–70). But such programs differ in their frequency and scope. They depend on the effective scope of autonomy, the political-administrative culture, and the fiscal capacity of each region; these differ from one region to another, and, in most cases, they are driven by the national government because of Italy's centralized political system that approaches (fiscal) federal reforms halfhearted and assigns local governments the role of bystanders (Alber & Valdesalici, 2023; Valdesalici & Trettel, 2023).

8.3 Municipal Government as the Pawn of Multiple Interests

Italy's municipal tradition extends back to the late Middle Ages and relates to the setting of parish communities. As other Southern European models (Kuhlmann & Bouckaert, 2016), it is rooted in the ideas of the 1798 French Revolution (Scarciglia, 2021). After the collapse of Napoleon's rule over Italy in 1814, the nation-state was declared in 1861 after more than 40 years of civic conflict. Administrative unification was a priority of the Kingdom of Italy, and laws were enacted to establish decentralized ministerial bodies that could exert control over powerful currents of local identity in the presence of, back then, 7720 municipalities. However, the highly centralized structure of government proved unable to standardize local realities; territorial inequalities grew even stronger after unification.

With the adoption of the Constitution of 1948, the promotion of local autonomies and administrative decentralization became a basic principle (Article 5 of the Italian Constitution). Most importantly, Articles 117 and 118 grant legislative and administrative powers to ordinary regions. Accordingly, the 15 ordinary regions co-determine the scope of municipal government. However, they were only created in 1970, and in most cases the broad margin of legislative autonomy has remained on paper. Thus, regional legislation on municipal government mainly replicates the measures adopted at the central level of government; and the system of municipal government is overall uniform. The situation is different for the five special regions. They were created in 1948, or shortly after, and they have the upper hand over municipal government. However, there are profound differences between the municipal government in one special region and another (Valdesalici & Trettel, 2023, pp. 268–269). The respective system is laid forth in an autonomy statute and implemented with by-laws of quasi-constitutional rank that are adopted by bilateral commissions between the national government and the special regions (Palermo & Valdesalici, 2019). One of the special regions—Trentino-Alto Adige/Südtirol—has a further characteristic. This northernmost constituent unit of Italy is composed of two autonomous provinces: the Autonomous Province of Trentino, and the Autonomous Province of Bolzano/Bozen (Alto Adige/Südtirol, or South Tyrol). In terms of powers, these two provinces are comparable to a region, and they both have their very own system of municipal government.

In 1990, central legislation significantly addressed local government with the first general law on local government (Law 142/1990). Throughout the 1990s, further reforms enabled municipal governments to become more active and autonomous. These reforms included an increase in financial autonomy, the reduction of the preventive control over the legitimacy of administrative acts, and the introduction of the direct election of mayors and presidents of provinces (a district type local authority of a larger geographical scope between the region and municipalities). In addition, several changes to the regime of administrative functions were pivotal in empowering local governments, with the most important being Law 59/1997 that, along with its implementing legislation, introduced the principle of subsidiarity. This principle was constitutionalized with the 2001 constitutional reform that turned the distribution of legislative powers upside-down: the exclusive legislative powers of the central level of government as well as subject-matters that relate to concurrent legislation are now specifically listed in the Italian Constitution, with regions retaining residual powers.

Most importantly, Italian constitutional law makes a distinction between vertical and horizontal subsidiarity. Vertical subsidiarity pertains to the allocation of powers across different levels of government, ensuring that administrative functions are carried out by the institutions closest to the citizens, unless those functions are already attributed to the provinces, metropolitan cities, and regions, or to the national government. Horizontal subsidiarity refers to collaborative governance between the public sector and civil society, forming the basis of Italy's model of "shared administration" that enables municipalities to enter collaboration pacts with citizens for managing public goods (Salati, 2023).

The constitutional reform, however, has led to numerous interpretative challenges due to the lack of interim rules. Regional governments have frequently appealed to the Italian Constitutional Court to set aside central measures that infringe on regional powers, prompting the Constitutional Court to take on a quasi-political role in implementing the reform. In its judgment 303/2003, the Constitutional Court invoked the subsidiarity principle "as a Trojan horse to reshape the distribution of competences" (Martinico, 2021, p. 195). The central question of the judgment was whether it is legitimate for the national government to retain administrative functions over matters for which it does not have exclusive legislative power. The Constitutional Court concluded that a strict, principled allocation of powers is ineffective, and that, under certain conditions, administrative functions can be retained, and thus affect the powers the regions have. The Constitutional Court, however, emphasized the relevance of the principle of loyal cooperation. It must also be stressed that, regarding the constitutional autonomy of municipalities, constitutional case-law upheld the principle of subsidiarity as classically applied. Indeed, it is used as a safeguard against regional laws (judgment 179/2019).

At last, to fully understand local governance, the 2014 national government reform must be kept in mind. Law 56/2014 called for a significant reorganization of the sub-regional scale of government. It mandated the transformation of provinces (not the autonomous provinces) into non-elected bodies and redefined their functions. It finally also established the tier of the metropolitan cities, replacing the provinces in 14 major cities. However, the limit of the Law 56/2014 is that, despite the new responsibilities for strategic planning, metropolitan cities are considered successors of the previous provinces rather than new institutions. As a result, they inherit the same challenges—critical budgetary conditions and a fragile political role—that were already present in the provinces.

8.4 Constitutional Recognition and Guarantees of Municipalities

Municipalities are put on an equal footing together with all other constituent units of the Italian Republic, with their own statutes, powers, and functions (Article 114(1) of the Constitution). However, equality is not meant in absolute and substantial terms. The different types of constituent units have different powers, and they weigh differently in the practice of territorial governance, also impacting the unfolding of mergers and IMC. Municipalities have no legislative powers and their power to adopt their own statute is constrained by the exclusive power of the national government to determine the electoral system and the governing bodies thereof (Article 117(2)(p) of the Constitution). Municipalities regulate their organization, and the functions attributed to them (Article 117(6) of the Constitution). Fundamental functions of municipalities include: general organization of administration, financial and accounting management and control; organization of public services of general interest, including municipal public transport services; land registry, with some exceptions; urban and building planning as well as participation in territorial planning at supra-municipal level; activities of civil protection planning and coordination of first aid; organization and management of municipal waste collection, disposal and recovery services and collection of related taxes; school building for the part not assigned to the provinces, organization and management of school services; municipal police; maintenance of civil status and population registers; tasks relating to registry services and electoral service; planning and management of the local social services system. In accordance with the principles of subsidiarity, differentiation, and proportionality (Article 118 of the Constitution), municipalities take precedence in the allocation of administrative powers to local autonomies; and they are liable for all of them, if and to the extent that a certain function shall not be assigned to the higher level of government.

Absent original powers of taxation, municipalities may set and regulate taxes only when the national or regional legislatures provide for this, which is rare. Municipal finance is thus based on devolved taxes (Valdesalici & Trettel, 2023, p. 275) and, in ordinary regions, mainly driven by the national government. However, because of the requirement of balanced budgets, regions have leverage on the spending autonomy of municipalities. As budgets must only be balanced on a regional scale, a municipality may borrow financial room to the detriment of others by the practice of intra-regional agreements, though only for investment spending (Valdesalici & Trettel, 2023, p. 276). In special regions, municipal finance differs as some have a great scope of financial autonomy; in practice, however, only the northern special regions run municipal finance, whereas the island special regions (Sicily and Sardinia) do not (Valdesalici & Trettel, 2023, p. 276–277). In general, the financial autonomy of regions and local autonomies (Article 119 of the Constitution) is greatly limited by the actions the national government undertakes, particularly regarding the coordination of public finance, which is a concurrent power (the national government is responsible for the principles and the regions for the details; Article 117(3) of the Constitution).

Regarding intergovernmental relations, the Italian Constitution is silent as to how municipalities represent their interests vis-à-vis the national government. An advisory Conference System is in place, born out of political practice in the 1980s and regulated only in 1997. This system has gradually established itself as the expression of the principle of loyal cooperation (Woelk, 2021). It consists of three bodies of which two foresee the participation of municipalities: the State-Cities-Local Autonomies Conference and the Unified Conference, that is the body in which the State-Cities-Local Autonomies Conference meets with the State-Regions Conference. Within the regions, a regionally regulated Council of Local Autonomies (CAL) is the consultative body for the coordination of the relations between the regions and the municipalities. Ordinary regions must provide for a CAL (Article 123 of the Constitution). Special regions are exempt from this legal requirement, but they all have set up a CAL. The functions and composition of CALs vary from one region to another, and they overall have a limited impact (Di Carpegna Brivio, 2018). Most importantly, a CAL delivers compulsory advice in several matters such as the amendment to the region's statute, the procedure for approving the budget and the legislative process for delegating regional functions to municipalities; the CAL also expresses its opinion on mergers of municipalities and it may also be entitled to propose them.

In short, constitutional guarantees regarding the autonomy of municipalities are weak. Provisions are not self-executing; and both the national government and the regions affect the concrete scope and structural dimension of municipalities. This is the reason why the system of municipal government (in ordinary regions) is considered one of the most emblematic elements that distinguishes Italy's highly decentralized model from traditional federations (Valdesalici & Trettel, 2023), and why practices of mergers and IMC vary from one region to another.

8.5 Mergers of Municipalities

Mergers aim to reduce the number of units of municipalities by creating new entities. Although with little success, they have been encouraged by the national government starting from Law 142/1990 (Vandelli, 2017). Their main objective is to achieve efficiency gains by the reorganization of municipalities that are considered too small to perform effectively. Among mergers, incorporation is also considered, which is the process in which the larger municipality incorporates the smaller one/s (Article 130 of Law 56/2014).

The establishment of the new municipality is a matter of regional power (Article 133 of the Constitution) (Filippini & Maglieri, 2015). So are procedures for the obligatory consultation of the concerned populations, and the interpretation of its results. As a rule, the merger is approved by the regional legislature if the consultation is positive. However, differences exist. Regions may apply a "dirigiste" role and not entirely respect the result of the consultation or be the mere executor of the popular will (Alber, 2021a). A few examples clarify the different approaches.

Emilia-Romagna (Regional Law 24/1996) adopts for an open-ended rather than a "dirigiste" approach. Indeed, the regional legislature, in 2018, committed itself to halt any merger process if just one municipality votes against it. Interestingly, the successful merger of Valsamoggia in 2013–2014, which involved five municipalities and a total of 30,000 inhabitants, would have never been approved following this approach.

Lombardy, in contrast, showcases a mixed approach. On the one hand, it provides limited incentives for municipalities created from mergers. On the other hand, it introduces a simplified procedure that gives municipal councils the authority to take the final decision on mergers. Specifically, Regional Law 29/2006 allows for a consultative referendum prior to the initiation of a regional draft law for mergers by incorporation. Hence, local administrators can effectively manage the consultation process and carefully assess the results.

Tuscany has been experimenting with mergers for many years, though often without success. The reason for this is following: several attempts were too ambitious and aimed at merging too many municipalities (for example, 'del Casentino' with 13 municipalities). Regional Law 62/2007 does not specify clear parameters on how to interpret the results of the consultation. However, in 2016, the regional legislature introduced a new approach by approving mergers if the majority of votes in each municipality supported it or if the overall yes votes equal two-thirds of the valid casted votes, provided that no concerned municipality had more than a quarter of its votes opposing the merger ("anti-merger clause").

The Veneto model, established by Regional Law 25/1992, introduces a time constraint for merger proposals. If a merger proposal is rejected, it cannot be resubmitted for 3 years. Regarding the interpretation of the popular vote, both the overall votes cast as well as the votes in each involved municipality are considered. Notably, the legislature decided to approve mergers involving four or more municipalities if only one municipality rejects the proposal, in which case the regional council can exclude the municipality from the merger process.

Research shows that the (administrative) capacity of the municipality resulting from the merger depends on its formation process (Mussari & Ruggiero, 2017). Most importantly, for mergers to be successful, the involvement of the populations cannot be limited to the period of the strictly merger-related consultation but must be started well in advance and continue afterwards to ensure the municipality's institutional sustainability and strengthen it from an identity viewpoint (Fissi & Scalone, 2020). The concerned populations must be enabled to contribute to the construction of the new self that will characterize the governance of the municipality born through a merger process.

The initiation of a merger is up to the municipalities who are also responsible for approving a by-law that regulates the new municipality. Differences exist between one region and another (Alber, 2021a). The by-law of the new municipality may be approved as a provisional one by all municipal councils that initiated the merger before the new municipality is established. In addition, it is foreseen that the new municipality's by-law lays down appropriate detailed measures that ensure the participation of all former independent municipalities, and the effectiveness of decentralized service provision throughout the new municipal territory. Both the national government and the region can provide financial incentives. The national government, for example, currently foresees extraordinary revenues for the following 10 years. To this end, each year, the Minister of the Interior, after hearing the Conference of the State, Cities and Local Autonomies, defines the modalities of allocation of the contributions.

The highest number of mergers was recorded in 2018 (Fondazione Think Tank Nord Est, 2023): 30 consultations yielded a positive outcome in that year, compared to 27 in 2015 and 26 in 2013. Undoubtedly, the introduction and then the strengthening of financial incentives stimulated the amalgamations. However, interest in mergers has waned in recent years: in fact, only five have been created from 2019 onwards. From an analysis of the consultation processes, out of 268 merger referendums that were held, 54.5% were approved, for a total of 146 mergers (Fondazione Think Tank Nord Est, 2023). The highest number of consultations is in Lombardy with 61 and a success rate of 54.1%; 48 referendums, approved in 60.4% of cases, were held in the Autonomous Province of Trentino. No mergers were carried out in South Tyrol that, together with Trentino, forms one out of five special regions. However, a recent analysis shows that the municipal structure of the Autonomous Province of Bolzano/Bozen (South Tyrol) is institutionally sustainable (i.e. it performs well), even though selective improvements in the form of a few mergers could be envisaged to increase local resilience capacity, particularly in remote areas (Penn, 2021). In the ordinary regions of Tuscany, Veneto, and Emilia Romagna (with 33, 31 and 27 consultations respectively) the success rate is less than 50%. In Piedmont, the region with the largest number of small municipalities, the result was excellent: 27 referendums with an approval percentage of 85.2%, with regional authorities actively promoting mergers. The functions and the weight of the CAL in relations between regional and local autonomies also impact the practice and success of mergers.

The analysis of the territorial distribution of mergers confirms the following trend. Mergers are especially present where the region has been exercising an active role; or where the region has allocated significant resources, both financial and technical, to support merger processes, in a context already strongly inclined to IMC (as in Emilia-Romagna, Tuscany and Marche); or where—in particular in Lombardy, Piedmont, and Veneto—a large number of small municipalities has forced the most fragile communities to seek definitive solutions to emerge from the global financial crisis of 2007–2008 and the subsequent austerity measures imposed by national legislation that not only affected financial intergovernmental relations at the expense of subnational entities, but also structural aspects in municipal government (Alber, 2021b).

Data on the size of merged municipalities confirm that in a limited number of cases, mergers resulted in municipalities with a population of more than 10,000 inhabitants; and in a fair number of municipalities with a size close to or slightly above the critical threshold of 5000 inhabitants. Thus, the choice of national and regional legislatures to not set a minimum size for the establishment or the incentivization of merged municipalities should be reassessed in systemic and place-based political discourses.

Whether mergers, a phenomenon mainly related to the North and Center of the country, can achieve gains is yet understudied. A recent study analyzed 135 municipalities born from mergers in the period between January 1995 and March 2019 (Fissi & Scalone, 2020). The research focused on budgetary performance, the possible recognition of national and/or regional funding related to mergers, the degree of perceived satisfaction of the population and the ways in which it was measured, the degree of qualitative-quantitative improvement of local public services, and the process of personnel reorganization carried out in the new municipality. Municipalities were categorized into six population classes belonging to four geographical areas: Northeast (Trentino-Alto Adige/Südtirol, Veneto, Friuli Venezia Giulia, Emilia-Romagna); Northwest (Piedmont, Aosta Valley, Liguria, Lombardy); Center: (Tuscany, Umbria, Marche, Lazio); South (Abruzzo, Molise, Campania, Puglia, Basilicata, Calabria, Sicily, Sardinia). More than half of the mayors of the municipalities involved filled out the questionnaire (68 out of 134, corresponding to 50.75%). In general, they showed satisfaction with the improvement of public services obtained through the merger. However, a large part of the population affected by the mergers were not given surveys to express their un/satisfaction with administrators. Mayors also stressed the complexity of reorganizing personnel and the long period of time required for the conclusion of a merger (from 6 months to more than 2 years in relation to the municipalities subject to the study).

8.6 Inter-municipal cooperation (IMC)

The 2015 edition of the Italian Atlas of Small Municipalities, edited by ANCI and the Institute for Local Finance and Economy (*Istituto per la Finanza e l'Economia Locale*—IFEL), interprets IMC as a growingly relevant issue that may improve the quality of local services and enhance institutional sustainability and social cohesion. IMC comes in different forms, initially regulated by the national Law 142/1990: the conventions (Article 30), the consortia (Article 31) and the unions of municipalities (Article 32).

The conventions are agreements between two or more municipalities for the delivery of a service or the fulfillment of a task. As a rule, they represent a flexible, adaptable tool. They can be of "closed" type (with a fixed and predetermined number of members) or of "open" type (with the possibility for others to join at a later stage, prior to the consent of all municipalities that cooperate in the convention). Conventions do not foresee the establishment of further bodies; one municipality is normally identified as the coordinator of all parties. For the exercise of fundamental functions in the form of a convention, Law 56/2014 establishes a minimum demographic limit of 10,000 inhabitants or 3000 inhabitants in case of municipalities belonging to mountain communities (and if the regional legislature that holds exclusive powers on IMC does not foresee any exceptions to these parameters due to territorial conditions). Conventions are widely used, sometimes also straddling two regions, and the services mostly managed through this form of IMC are municipal secretariat, municipal police, school services, social services, and technical services.

Unlike the conventions, consortia are fully recognized as local entities with an assembly that is composed of the representatives of the associated bodies in the person of the mayor, the president or their delegate, and a management board. Municipalities form a consortium if they intend to manage one or more public services together. In practice, the use of consortia is very limited; and they are in the process of being surpassed (Carloni & Cortese, 2020, p. 154).

The union of municipalities (UoM) is an instrument—mandatory and voluntary—to jointly exercise an array of functions. Two or more municipalities may create a UoM with their own by-law and organs. UoMs are the most common and long-lasting form of IMC (Piazza, 2017). One of the success factors of a UoM is its flexibility and adaptability to large-scale collaboration and to the enhancement of the institutional sustainability of small municipalities. It is not by chance that UoMs came to be the solution suggested by the national government for small municipalities when the economic crisis imposed and made it necessary to collaborate in order to cope with the contraction of resources, from 2009–2010 onwards (De Donno & Tubertini, 2020, p. 305–310). Municipalities with up to 5000 inhabitants (3000 if part of a mountain community) must exercise basic functions in a joint manner, by a convention or by a UoM, in a gradual manner, initially by jointly exercising three functions (single-municipal islands and the enclave municipality of Campione d'Italia are exempt from this rule). Defaulting municipalities are given a peremptory deadline within which to act; and in case of inactivity, sanctions incur, and an external commissioner can take over. For the first time ever, the national legislature set a minimum size threshold for the newly established UoM (10,000 inhabitants), which can be waived by the region. The national government also accompanied the mandatory provision of the joint exercise of fundamental functions by small municipalities with incentives that consider the number and importance of the associated functions. Fundamental functions are grouped into the following six areas: general administration and management; early childhood education and care as well as schooling and schools; local mobility, transport, and roads; land management and environmental development; and social services.[2]

Regarding personnel, resources invested in the UoM shall not exceed the sum of staff costs previously incurred by each municipality now part of the UoM; and once fully operational, progressive savings must be the aim. Because of this, UoMs have been viewed—or have so been interpreted by the national government—as a precursor of amalgamations (Bolgherini et al., 2018). When national Law 265/1999 made clear that UoMs are an acceptable instrument, UoMs have been more frequently established. However, the distribution of UoMs throughout the country is not homogeneous. Regions differently incentivize IMC. There are regions that strongly encourage UoMs, while others promote UoMs and conventions indifferently. For ordinary regions, it must be reiterated that their legislative scope in the field of UoMs has been reduced. In fact, the national government has been granted by the Constitutional Court the power to establish the object, conditions, limits, and thresholds of the joint exercise of functions (judgments 22/2014, 44/2014 and 33/2019), and to legislate on the organizational model of UoMs (judgment 50/2015). UoMs do not constitute an additional, diverse constituent entity; and thus, according to Article 117(2)(p) of the Constitution, and following the Italian Constitutional Court, the national government has exclusive power to legislate on the organizational model of UoMs. In addition, the Court legitimized the national government's interference by interpreting mandatory IMC as a tool that is instrumental to the rationalization of public finance. In other words, by extensively interpreting the concurrent national-region power "coordination of public finance", the Constitutional Court almost nullified the regional space in IMC (among others, see judgments 237/2009; 68/2011; 108/2011; 182/2011; 151/2012; 77/2013; 120/2013; 22/2014; 44/2014). However, the Court (judgment 33/2019) also stressed that small municipalities shall have the possibility to demonstrate that the joint management is not economically favorable or that it does not ameliorate the delivery of public services. In the end, there might be circumstances in which IMC does not achieve cost savings and service delivery benefits. Special regions, instead, have their own IMC models (D'Orlando & Grisostolo, 2018).

Studies on the efficiency gains of IMC are complex. Research tends to focus on a few regions, rather than on common trends on a national basis and comparative evaluation studies. In relation to IMC in Emilia-Romagna, results show that the participation of a municipality in a UoM reduces the total current per-capita

[2] See Sect. 8.4.

expenditure by around 5%, compared to municipalities not in a UoM. The effect is persistent and increases up to 6 years from entering a UoM. In addition, the quality of local public services remains high (Ferraresi et al., 2018). Another study, on the evaluation of the responses of Emilia-Romagna's UoMs in case of natural disasters, confirms the relevance of UoMs for coordination purposes and as strong interlocutor in vertical inter-institutional relations (Pattaro & Ranuzzini, 2017). Back in 2013, a study explored whether IMC has any impact on the efficiency of small municipalities by focusing on municipalities in the 15 ordinary regions (Luca & Modrego, 2021). Its results did not find any statistically significant effect of IMC on local efficiency across 12 key policy areas; this is because IMC, in absence of a clear institutional vision of sustainable policymaking, suffers from implementation failures. Although formal and informal actors from the same and other levels of government co-shape IMC, there is a lack of political culture to implement them. Similarly, the analysis of data from 280 small municipalities on the effects of IMC confirms that in more than two-thirds of the municipalities participating in IMC there were benefits in terms of cost reduction and better public services, whereas greater institutional legitimacy was detected only in about half of the cases (Giacomini et al., 2018). This additionally demonstrates that the success of IMC and any rescaling processes depend on a clear political will and vision of all actors involved, including the populations concerned.

8.7 Conclusions

In Europe, the first continent where population decline is set to overtake population growth by 2025 (UN, 2019), rural areas face depopulation in favor of urban and intermediate areas, with small- and medium-sized municipalities in rural areas typically oriented towards the acceleration of population decline in comparison with larger rural areas. This results from a study on the trajectories of depopulation in a total of 696 subnational areas across 33 countries over the period from 2000 to 2018 (Newsham & Rowe, 2022). However, population decline does not occur uniformly across the continent; and it is not pre-destined. How rural areas evolve depends on the capacity of the respective municipality; on how municipal government adjusts its functions and structures to external changes; and on how institutions manage to become sustainable.

Indeed, research shows that future approaches for regional development must go beyond strategies for targeting economic growth (Dax & Fischer, 2018) and address in-between (Cattivelli, 2021) and rural areas from the viewpoint of institutional sustainability (Cipolloni, 2021; De Donno & Tubertini, 2020). Issues of local participation, social innovation, and transparency are key for strengthening the relationship between institutions and governance, to combat depopulation and counteract its effects in rural areas, and to face urban-rural flows and peri-urban areas that combine urban and rural features beyond the respective administrative boundaries and thus demand innovation from the region as the lawmaker in territorial planning.

Although crucial, a discussion on how municipal government can be rescaled by considering the concept of institutional sustainability surely is no easy endeavor. First, the concept of institutional sustainability is polysemous. Second, municipal government is characterized by significant differences. In Italy, these include the urban/rural and the North/South divide, but also the differing number, characteristics and definitions of rural areas and small municipalities from one region to another. Third, the different regions—relevant actors in co-determining municipal government—do not necessarily adopt a systemic approach in dealing with the rescaling of municipal government.

The findings of this chapter show that mergers and IMC, though to a different extent from one region to another, remain of particular interest to all regions. Two are the reasons. First, the region (in theory) plays a fundamental role in merger processes and IMC. Second, mergers and IMC are part of long overdue national programs of territorial reorganization of rural areas and small municipalities. Although the SNAI is still in its infancy and is experiencing delays in implementation, the following merit must be acknowledged. The objectives of the territorial reorganization of small municipalities are, for the first time, combined with planning and incentive strategies aiming at sustainable local development. The hope is that the creation of permanent IMC systems can truly augment the (administrative) capacity of small municipalities and improve service delivery in view of decelerating and reversing population decline in rural areas. The SNAI, however, should not remain isolated but rather have continuity with the principles of inter-institutional collaboration and administrative coordination pursued by Law 56/2014; it needs to be part of a broader discussion on how to reassess the role of all levels of government in territorial governance. Because place-based policies aiming at combating depopulation, to be successful and thus institutionally sustainable, must necessarily be grounded in loyal cooperation between the different levels of government; and loyal cooperation, from the viewpoint of tackling structural challenges of municipal government, means to adopt a sustainable perspective that succeeds in combining the interdependent needs of the local dimension within the regional and the national spheres.

Future directions in research should thus focus on more extensive and comprehensive studies of the institutional account of mergers and IMC, and on (comparative) evaluation studies. Studies of this kind would surely serve inter-regional learning and policy coordination and contribute to a better conceptualization of institutional sustainability in municipal government and rural-urban relations.

References

Alber, E. (2021a). Mergers of municipalities—A comparison of procedures and their implications. In K. Kössler & T. Morandell (Eds.), *Local government in Italy: Responses to urban-rural challenges* (pp. 54–58). Zenodo. https://doi.org/10.5281/zenodo.5254948

Alber, E. (2021b). The structure of local government in Italy: An introduction. In K. Kössler & T. Morandell (Eds.), *Local government in Italy: Responses to urban-rural challenges* (pp. 42–49). Zenodo. https://doi.org/10.5281/zenodo.5254844

Alber, E., & Valdesalici, A. (2023). Italy. In J.-F. Tremblay (Ed.), *The Forum of Federations handbook of fiscal federalism* (pp. 257–296). Palgrave Macmillan. https://doi.org/10.1007/978-3-030-97258-5_7

Alber, E., Valdesalici, A., & Klotz, G. (2024). Italy. In N. Steytler (Ed.), *The Forum of Federations' handbook on local government in federal systems* (pp. 281–311). Palgrave Macmillan.

Benassi, F., Busetta, A., Gallo, G., & Stranges, M. (2022). Local heterogeneities in population growth and decline. A spatial analysis of Italian municipalities. In N. Salvati, C. Perna, S. Marchetti, & R. Chambers (Eds.), *Studies in theoretical and applied statistics* (pp. 297–314). Springer. https://doi.org/10.1007/978-3-031-16609-9_19

Bolgherini, S., Casula, M., & Marotta, M. (2018). Pursuing defragmentation at the municipal level: Signs of a changing pattern? *Modern Italy, 23*(1), 85–102. https://doi.org/10.1017/mit.2017.44

Bonifazi, C., & Heins, F. (2000). Long-term trends of internal migration in Italy. *International Journal of Population Geography, 6*(2), 111–131. https://doi.org/10.1002/(SICI)1099-1220(200003/04)6:2<111::AID-IJPG172>3.0.CO;2-L

Carloni, E., & Cortese, F. (2020). *Diritto delle autonomie territoriali*. Wolters Kluwer.

Cattivelli, V. (2021). Planning peri-urban areas at regional level: The experience of Lombardy and Emilia-Romagna (Italy). *Land Use Policy, 103*(C). https://doi.org/10.1016/j.landusepol.2021.105282

CIPESS—Dipartimento Politiche di Coesione. (2020). *Relazione annuale sulla Strategia Nazionale per le aree interne*. Retrieved January 5, 2024, from https://temi.camera.it/leg18/post/la-strategia-nazionale-per-le-aree-interne.html

Cipolloni, C. (2021). Le politiche di contrasto al fenomeno dello spopolamento nelle Aree interne. *Italian Papers on Federalism 3*. https://www.ipof.it/le-politiche-di-contrasto-al-fenomeno-dello-spopolamento-nelle-aree-interne/

D'Orlando, E., & Grisostolo, E. F. (2018). La disciplina degli enti locali tra uniformità e differenziazione. In F. Palermo & S. Parolari (Eds.), *Le variabili della specialità: Evidenze e riscontri tra soluzioni istituzionali e politiche settoriali* (pp. 99–160). Edizioni Scientifiche Italiane.

Dax, T., & Fischer, M. (2018). An alternative policy approach to rural development in regions facing population decline. *European Planning Studies, 26*(2), 297–315. https://doi.org/10.1080/09654313.2017.1361596

De Donno, M., & Tubertini, C. (2020). Frammentazione comunale e contrasto allo spopolamento: La prospettiva italiana. *Istituzioni del Federalismo, 2*(2020), 297–321. https://www.regione.emilia-romagna.it/affari_ist/rivista_2_2020/Indice.html

De Rubertis, S. (2019). Dinamiche insediative in Italia: Spopolamento dei comuni rurali. *Perspectives on Rural Development, 3*, 71–96.

Di Carpegna Brivio, E. (2018). Il CAL tra sogno e realtà. Problemi attuali delle istituzioni di raccordo nel sistema regionale delle fonti. *Federalismi.it 2018*(5). https://www.federalismi.it/nv14/articolo-documento.cfm?artid=35863

Doignon, Y., Oliveau, S., & Blöss-Widmer, I. (2016). L'Europe méridionale depuis 20 ans: Dépeuplement, dépopulation et renouveau démographique. *Espace populations sociétés* 2015/3–2016/1. https://journals.openedition.org/eps/6171

European Commission, Joint Research Centre. (2016). *Atlas of the human planet 2016—Mapping human presence on Earth with the global human settlement layer*. Publications Office. Retrieved January 5, 2024, from https://data.europa.eu/doi/10.2788/889483

Falcone, M. (2020). Le politiche europee per le città: Agenda urbana e "aree interne". In E. Carloni & F. Cortese (Eds.), *Diritto delle autonomie territoriali* (pp. 239–263). Wolters Kluwer.

Falconio, E. (2018). *Ricerca Anci: L'esodo svuota i piccoli borghi italiani, in sei anni sono spariti 75 mila abitanti*. Retrieved January 5, 2024, from https://www.anci.it/ricerca-anci-lesodo-svuota-i-borghi-italiani-in-sei-anni-spariti-75-mila-abitanti/

Fedeli, V. (2017). Institutions matter: Governance and citizenship in a post-metropolitan perspective. In A. Balducci, V. Fedeli, & F. Curci (Eds.), *Post-metropolitan territories. Looking for a new urbanity* (pp. 266–273). Routledge.

Felice, E. (2017). *The roots of a dual equilibrium: GDP, productivity and structural change in the Italian regions in the long-run (1871–2011)*. Banca d'Italia.

Ferraresi, M., Migali, G., & Rizzo, L. (2018). Does inter-municipal cooperation promote efficiency gains? Evidence from Italian municipal unions. *Journal of Regional Science, 58*(5). https://doi.org/10.1111/jors.12388

Filippini, R., & Maglieri, A. (2015). Il procedimento legislativo di fusione di Comuni nelle leggi regionali. *Istituzioni del Federalismo, 2*(2015), 313–329. https://www.regione.emilia-romagna.it/affari_ist/Rivista_2_2015/indice2.html

Fissi, S., & Scalone, G. (2020). Il fenomeno della fusione di comuni in Italia: Profili evolutivi ed evidenze empiriche. *Economia Aziendale Online, 11*(3), 285–305.

Fondazione Think Tank Nord Est. (2023). *"Resistono" i campanili in Italia meno di 150 le fusioni tra comuni realizzate*. Retrieved January 5, 2024, from https://www.fondazionethinktank.it/ricerche/resistono-i-campanili-in-italia-meno-di-150-le-fusioni-tra-comuni-realizzate/

Giacomini, D., Sancino, A., & Simonetto, A. (2018). The introduction of mandatory inter-municipal cooperation in small municipalities: Preliminary lessons from Italy. *International Journal of Public Sector Management, 31*(3), 331–346. https://doi.org/10.1108/IJPSM-03-2017-0071

Hulst, R., & van Montfort, A. (2007). *Inter-municipal cooperation in Europe*. Springer.

Kuhlmann, S., & Bouckaert, G. (2016). *Local public sector reforms in times of crisis: National Trajectories and international comparisons*. Palgrave.

Luca, D., & Modrego, F. (2021). Stronger together? Assessing the causal effect of inter-municipal cooperation on the efficiency of small Italian municipalities. *Journal of Regional Science, 61*(1), 261–293. https://doi.org/10.1111/jors.12509

Martinico, G. (2021). Federalism, regionalism, and the principle of subsidiarity. In A. Erika, G. Martinico, & F. Palermo (Eds.), *Federalism and constitutional law: The Italian contribution to comparative regionalism* (pp. 189–205). Routledge.

Mussari, R., & Ruggiero, P. (2017). Merging for capacity and a capacity for merging: Politicians, citizens, and discourses in public administrations. *Financial Accountability and Management, 33*(1), 27–47. https://doi.org/10.1111/faam.12102

Newsham, N., & Rowe, F. (2022). Understanding the trajectories of population decline across rural and urban Europe: A sequence analysis. *Population, Space and Place, 29*(3), 1–16. https://doi.org/10.1002/psp.2630

Nørgaard, A. S. (1996). Rediscovering reasonable rationality in institutional analysis. *European Journal of Political Research, 29*(19), 31–57. https://doi.org/10.1111/j.1475-6765.1996.tb00640.x

OECD—Organization for Economic Co-operation and Development. (2009). *Rural policy reviews: Italy*. Retrieved January 5, 2024, from https://www.oecd-ilibrary.org/urban-rural-and-regional-development/oecd-rural-policy-reviews-italy-2009_9789264056237-en

Palermo, P. C. (2009). *I limiti del possibile. Governo del territorio e qualità dello sviluppo*. Donzelli.

Palermo, F., & Valdesalici, A. (2019). Irreversibly different: A country study of constitutional asymmetry in Italy. In P. Popelier & M. Sahadžić (Eds.), *Constitutional asymmetry in multinational federalism: Managing multinationalism in multi-tiered systems*. Palgrave Macmillan. https://doi.org/10.1007/978-3-030-11701-6_11

Pattaro, A. F., & Ranuzzini, M. (2017). Il ruolo delle Unioni di comuni in situazioni di emergenza naturale: Considerazioni da un caso di studio. *Agriregionieuropa 51*. https://agriregionieuropa.univpm.it/it/content/article/31/51/il-ruolo-delle-unioni-di-comuni-situazioni-di-emergenza-naturale.
Penn, A. (2021). *Potentialanalyse für Gemeindefusionen in der Autonomen Provinz Bozen*. Universität Innsbruck.
Pfahl, S. (2005). Institutional sustainability. *International Journal of Sustainable Development, 8*(1/2), 80–96. https://doi.org/10.1504/IJSD.2005.007376
Piazza, I. (2017). Le Unioni di comuni e i processi di riforma del governo locale nell'ordinamento italiano. In W. Gasparri (Ed.), *L'associazionismo municipale. Esperienze nazionali e europee a confronto* (pp. 23–57). Giappichelli.
Presidency of the Council of Ministers Casa Italia Department. (2023). *Bando piccoli Comuni. Conclusa la Fase 2 per la presentazione delle domande 17 novembre 2023*. Retrieved January 5, 2024, from https://www.casaitalia.governo.it/generali/notizie/bando-piccoli-comuni-conclusa-la-fase-2-per-la-presentazione-delle-domande/
Raugze, I., Daly, G., & van Herwijnen, M. (2017). *Shrinking rural regions in Europe. Towards smart and innovative approaches to regional development challenges in depopulating rural regions*. https://www.espon.eu/rural-shrinking
Reynaud, C., Miccoli, S., Benassi, F., Naccarato, A., & Salvati, L. (2020). Unravelling a demographic 'mosaic': Spatial patterns and contextual factors of depopulation in Italian municipalities, 1981–2011. *Ecological Indicators, 115*(12), 106356.
Rizzo, A. (2016). Declining, transition and slow rural territories in southern Italy characterizing the intra-rural divides. *European Planning Studies, 24*(2), 231–253. https://doi.org/10.1080/09654313.2015.1079588
Saczuk, K. (2013). Development and critique of the concept of replacement migration. In M. Kupiszewski (Ed.), *International migration and the future of populations and labor in Europe* (Vol. 32). Springer. https://doi.org/10.1007/978-90-481-8948-9_13
Salati, C. (2023). The forgotten meaning of the EU principle of subsidiarity—Horizontal subsidiarity in Italian local governments. *EURAC Research*. https://doi.org/10.57749/HCDQ-2P97
Scarciglia, R. (2021). Local self government in Italy. In B. Brezovnik, I. Hoffman, & J. Kostrubiec (Eds.), *Local self-government in Europe* (pp. 246–275). Institute for Local Self-Government.
Senato della Repubblica. (2022). *Dossier: Disposizioni per lo sviluppo e la valorizzazione delle zone montane, 15 luglio 2020*.
Statista—Italy. (2024). Retrieved January 5, 2024, from https://www.statista.com/topics/5925/demographics-in-italy/#topicOverview
Teles, F. (2016). *Local governance and inter-municipal cooperation*. Palgrave Pivot.
Teles, F., & Swianievicz, P. (2018). *Inter-municipal cooperation in Europe. Institutions and governance*. Palgrave Macmillan.
Tuttitalia.it. (2024). *Comune per fasce demografiche*. Retrieved January 5, 2024, from https://www.tuttitalia.it/comuni-per-fasce-demografiche/
UN. (2019). *World population prospects 2019 I: Comprehensive tables* (ST/ESA/SER.A/426). United Nations, Department of Economic and Social Affairs, Population Division.
Valdesalici, A., & Trettel, M. (2023). The system of local government in Italy: A stress-test to traditional paradigms? In M. Nicolini & A. Valdesalici (Eds.), *Local governance in multi-layered systems*. Springer. https://doi.org/10.1007/978-3-031-41792-4_12
Vandelli, L. (2017). La difficile recherche de l'optimum dimensionnel des communes italiennes: Entre fusions et coopérations. *Revue Française D'administration Publique, 162*, 327–338. https://doi.org/10.3917/rfap.162.0327
Woelk, J. (2021). Loyal cooperation: Systemic principle of Italy's regionalism? In E. Arban, G. Martinico, & F. Palermo (Eds.), *Federalism and constitutional law—The Italian contribution to comparative regionalism* (pp. 170–188). Routledge.

Open Access This chapter is licensed under the terms of the Creative Commons Attribution 4.0 International License (http://creativecommons.org/licenses/by/4.0/), which permits use, sharing, adaptation, distribution and reproduction in any medium or format, as long as you give appropriate credit to the original author(s) and the source, provide a link to the Creative Commons license and indicate if changes were made.

The images or other third party material in this chapter are included in the chapter's Creative Commons license, unless indicated otherwise in a credit line to the material. If material is not included in the chapter's Creative Commons license and your intended use is not permitted by statutory regulation or exceeds the permitted use, you will need to obtain permission directly from the copyright holder.

Chapter 9
Responding to Structural Challenges in Rural Areas: Mergers and Inter-municipal Cooperation in Poland

Andżelika Mirska

Abstract The deteriorating demographic situation of many rural local governments means that they are faced with the challenge of how to carry out their own tasks and provide basic public services while revenues are declining and their ability to finance their development is increasingly limited. This chapter mainly addresses the question of how governments (both at central and subnational level) are responding to the growing crisis. In order to examine the possible strategies for dealing with this problem on the example of Poland, it is first necessary to take a nuanced look at the term "rural municipality", as the economic health of rural municipalities depends largely on their geographical location. Depopulation is a problem primarily for those rural municipalities which are located on the periphery of large cities or important transport routes. This chapter contains a diagnosis of the condition of Polish local government in rural areas, presents an analysis of the problems it currently faces and outlines the possible strategies for responding to this crisis, along with an assessment of the importance of each of these strategies. It differentiates between top-down and bottom-up processes. Among these, the processes of voluntary cooperation between local governments, which is stimulated by a system of financial incentives from the central government and the European Union, are becoming increasingly important.

Keywords Local government · Rural area · Rural municipality · Poland · Inter-municipal cooperation · Voluntary cooperation · Depopulation

A. Mirska (✉)
Faculty of Political Sciences and International Studies, University of Warsaw, Warsaw, Poland
e-mail: amirska@uw.edu.pl

© The Author(s) 2026

K. Kössler, E. M. Belser (eds.), *Local Government Structure and Intergovernmental Relations*, Local and Urban Governance,
https://doi.org/10.1007/978-3-031-99820-1_9

9.1 Introduction

In Poland, rural areas are designated following the basic territorial division of the country using the identifiers of the National Official Register of the Territorial Division of the Country (Statistics Poland, 2022c). Rural areas are those which remain outside the administrative borders of cities; they consist of rural municipalities and rural parts of urban-rural municipalities. A city (town)[1] is defined in Polish law as "a settlement having mostly concentrated housing and non-agricultural functions, possessing the status of a city under provisions of distinct laws" (Act of 2003). Granting a rural commune (or a locality within a rural commune) the status of a city is carried out in a way that considers the social and technical infrastructure as well as the urban layout and the type of construction (Act of 1990). The decision in this respect shall be by the Council of Ministers assessing whether the above requirements are complied with.

Research covering the period 1980–2015 shows that the main factors contributing to granting the status of a city include:

1. historical background i.e. having had urban status in the past (82.3% of localities);
2. demographic potential of the locality (84.1% of new cities had over 2000 inhabitants at the time they were granted city status);
3. aspirations to obtain the city status. According to local communities, the city status is a sign of prestige and greater opportunities to obtain financial resources for local development (Szmytke, 2015, p. 303; Wytrążek, 2020, p. 155).

However, in every instance, the decision to change the status of a commune from a rural commune to an urban commune is up to the Polish government. The smallest urban commune (Krynica Morska) has 1390 inhabitants and the smallest town located within an urban-rural commune is inhabited by only 336 people (Opatowiec).

The municipalities are the first level of the basic territorial division in Poland, the counties are the second one, while voivodeships form the third level. This territorial structure was introduced by an ordinary law and has been in force since 1999. There is a local government at each level of the basic territorial division in Poland: municipal self-government (*samorząd gminny*), county self-government (*samorząd powiatowy*) and voivodeship self-government (*samorząd województwa*). It should be noted that Poland has adopted a symmetrical approach to the legal status of local governments. This means that the legal status of all municipalities is the same, regardless of their category or size and socio-economic importance. However, larger municipalities, especially the 66 cities with county rights, most with a population of over 100,000 inhabitants, clearly have greater political, economic, and demographic potential (Mirska, 2021b).

As of January 1, 2024, Poland has 16 voivodeships, 314 counties, 66 cities with county rights and 2477 municipalities. Rural communes dominate among them,

[1] In Polish there is no distinction between the concepts of "city" and "town". There is only one word, i.e. *miasto*, which means both town and city.

numbering 1464 at present. 302 cities, or urban municipalities, have been designated, 66 of which have the status of a city with county rights. There are also 711 municipalities in Poland which have both an urban centre and rural areas within their administrative boundaries, i.e. urban-rural communes. Comparing the average size of municipalities in European countries, we can say that Polish communes are medium-sized units with an average population of around 15,000.

Rural areas, that is, those comprising rural communes as well as rural areas within urban-rural communes, cover a total of 92.5% of Poland's territory (Statistics Poland, 2023a). However, rural areas vary enormously in terms of their demographic, economic, and social potential (Statistics Poland, 2022b).

As far as population potential is concerned, municipalities with up to 5000 inhabitants account for 37.8% of all rural and urban-rural communes. One in four municipalities have a population of 5000–6000, and one in five 7000–10,000. In turn, the share of the most populous communes, i.e. those with more than 10,000 people, is 18.4%. It is worth noting that compared to 2010, there has been an increase in the number of the least and most densely populated communes, while the number of communes with a population of between 5000 and 10,000 people has decreased (Statistics Poland, 2022a).

Since 2000, the number of rural inhabitants has been growing slightly yet steadily. This phenomenon is mainly due to the fact that the population has been moving from urban areas to rural areas, most often to rural communes concentrated around large cities. Thus, the number of city inhabitants has been decreasing and their share in the total population has dropped to 60%, down from almost 62% in 1990–2000 (Statistics Poland, 2023b).

However, it should be noted that inhabitants are particularly attracted to the areas where the largest growing multifunctional urban agglomerations are located. Thus, the process of de-urbanization is deepening, which should be associated mainly with the so–called "urban sprawl" and suburbanization—rural areas which surround urban areas become de facto urbanized areas while still remaining rural areas in the administrative sense (Statistics Poland, 2023b).

However, it should be emphasized that the most important general feature of Poland's current demographic situation is the actual decrease in its population, which has continued since 2012. The aging process of Poland's population has also been accelerating. Forecasts indicate that Poland's population will decrease by 6.8 million people by 2060 relative to 2022 (Statistics Poland, 2022a).

Regarding the economic and social situation, the authors of a report on the state of rural areas in Poland point to the growing polarization of socio-economic development in rural areas (Stanny et al., 2023). Ongoing processes are leading to excessive disparities in the quality of life between inhabitants of zones around large urban centres and peripheral areas located at the borders of administrative regions. The latter are marked by a high outflow of inhabitants, mainly young people, which results in negative natural growth and changes in the social structure. Emigration from the countryside generally results from a lack of jobs, which stems from the inadequate development of the non-agricultural sector in rural areas. Local politicians hold a similar view. For example, the mayor of an urban-rural commune with

18,000 inhabitants, emphasized that there is a clear correlation between the geographical location of a municipality and its resources and development opportunities (Mirska, 2023). On the nationwide scale, the main factors differentiating rural communes are their location relative to the influence of metropolises/large cities and transport routes. There are also large regional differences. “Peripheral municipalities” (or “marginalized municipalities”, as they are called by the National Strategy of Regional Development 2030[2] and voivodeship development strategies[3]) exist in every region. If one looks at rural areas, there are also large disparities among communes with rural status. The above-mentioned mayor referred to the research conducted by the Institute of Rural Development and Agriculture of the Polish Academy of Sciences, which categorized seven types of communes in rural areas: from traditionally agricultural to highly urbanized. For this reason, the division into the city and the countryside is slowly becoming meaningful only in statistical terms (Mirska, 2023).

The Ministry of Digitalization and Administration report entitled “Assessment of the Situation of Local Governments” found that many municipal self-governments are small and financially weak. In the long term, they may be unable to cope with the more difficult and expensive public tasks for an aging population. The report further stated that demographic processes will increasingly undermine the financial foundations of the smallest local government communities, increase the burden on the state budget from financial transfers to local governments and weaken their ability to provide public services (Ministry of Administration and Digitization, Assessment of the Situation of Local Governments in Poland, 2013).

Therefore, the central government is aware of the potential structural problems that local governments will face. These problems have also been recognized by local politicians and felt by the inhabitants of rural areas. Thus, there is no doubt that in the face of such dynamic demographic changes, it is necessary to ask about the legal possibilities and feasible strategies for dealing with these structural problems, especially in the areas most affected by these changes. The following strategies of action are possible:

1. radical top-down territorial reform to consolidate local government units;
2. partial changes in the territorial structure of the state;
3. creating incentives for voluntary mergers of territorial units;
4. enabling and creating additional incentives for cooperation between local government units in carrying out public tasks;

[2] Resolution No. 102 of the Council of Ministers of September 17, 2019 on the adoption of the National Strategy for Regional Development 2030.

[3] The voivodeship development strategy is the basic and most important document of the voivodeship government, defining the areas, goals and directions of the development policy conducted on a regional scale in Poland. Their legal basis is the Act of June 5, 1998 on Voivodeship Self-Government.

5. strengthening the potential of peripheral rural centres through additional financial transfers and investments, especially with the support from the European Union.

9.2 Top-Down Reforms

The number of local government units in Poland has remained relatively stable over time with 2383 when local government was restored in 1990 and 2477 in 2024 (an increase by 3.9%). In 1990, commune self-government was restored without any interference in the territorial structure of the state. The second stage of state decentralization took place in 1999 with a reform that included two elements. First, counties were established as an additional level of local government with their own county self-government. Secondly, the third level of territorial division was consolidated with the creation of 16 large territorial units to replace 49 voivodeships in order to allow them to act as regions in the European Union and perform the tasks of a regional government. In contrast to the introduction of these new entities at the county and voivodeship levels, no comprehensive top-down changes have been made to Poland's territorial structure at the municipal level. Thus, territorial units in Poland have not been consolidated, which goes against the dominant trend that has been seen in the last few decades in several European countries, including Germany, Sweden, Switzerland, Denmark, and the Netherlands (Swianiewicz et al., 2017).

Although the scientific literature frequently discusses the idea of consolidating territorial units as one of the strategies for managing the state's territorial development, there have been no concrete recommendations for political decisions (Babczuk & Kachniarz, 2016). In turn, political discussions and programs have diagnosed the problem of the inefficiency of small communes (under 5000 inhabitants) and examined solutions to the unavoidable demographic processes that will exacerbate the inequalities between rural peripheral areas and the rest of the country. However, there have been no clear political signals that a top-down territorial reform is planned for the near future (Ministry of Administration and Digitization, Assessment of the Situation of Local Governments in Poland, 2013); on the contrary, the Polish government has explicitly denied that it intends to introduce top-down changes to the territorial division that would merge small communes.[4] Moreover, the Polish government stated that it would not implement mergers due to the lack of such will and initiative from the municipalities. According to the government, municipalities

[4] A reply by the undersecretary of state at the Ministry of Administration and Digitization to parliamentary interpellation no. 17492 on the reform of local government in Poland, May 31, 2013. The parliamentary interpellation asked whether the government planned to merge small communes. https://www.sejm.gov.pl/sejm7.nsf/interpelacja.xsp?typ=INT&nr=17492. Accessed 26 October 2023.

do not want to merge with other municipalities into larger territorial units and the legal procedure for merging municipalities is not complicated.[5]

This is certainly due to the fact that politicians are too afraid of the political costs of such a reform. Poland is deeply attached to its "small homelands" and the values of local democracy. This certainly stems from the fairly recent experience of a centralized state. As one observer points out, this attachment to tradition and the desire for independence are still the reason for the reluctance to change the borders of communes (Kaczmarek, 2016). Instead, political declarations and government programs tend to focus on financial support for small rural communes, such as assistance with infrastructure projects, or the creation of financial incentives for voluntary cooperation.

9.3 Partial Changes to the Territorial Structure

Pursuant to the Act of March 8, 1990, on commune self-government, the Council of Ministers is authorized to make ongoing adjustments to the territorial structure of municipalities. Such an adjustment may involve: the establishment of a new commune, a merger of communes, a division of a commune, or the liquidation of a commune. Additionally, the Council of Ministers has a special authorization to adjust the borders of communes. These changes may be initiated by the Council of Ministers itself, the municipal council(s) concerned, or the inhabitants of the commune(s). Importantly, the issuance of a regulation on the adjustment of the structure of municipalities requires the consultation of the commune councils concerned, and prior to that, these councils should hold consultations with the inhabitants. However, these opinions are not binding on the Council of Ministers.

As far as the number of communes is concerned, there were 2383 units when local government was restored in 1990 (Statistics Poland, 1992). Currently, there are 2477 units. This represents a 3.9% increase in the number of municipalities (Mirska, 2021). The numerous causes for the fragmentation of the commune structure in Poland, include the following:

1. the establishment of new communes was a manifestation of grassroots social movements in the process of democratization and restoration of local government after 1990. Local government was often seen as an important value in localities; and
2. the lack of statutory provisions on the criteria for the establishment of new communes resulted in spontaneous and uncontrolled splits of local governments.

[5]A reply by the undersecretary of state at the Ministry of Interior and Administration to parliamentary interpellation no. 26935 on simplifying procedures for merging municipalities, October 6, 2021. https://www.sejm.gov.pl/Sejm9.nsf/InterpelacjaTresc.xsp?key=C7JHJ5. Accessed 26 October 2023.

It was only in 2015 that a legal provision was introduced to counter the fragmentation of the territorial structure in Poland. It adopted the alternative criteria of commune revenue and population size. This provision prohibits the establishment of municipalities in which:

1. the revenue would be lower than the lowest tax revenues per capita provided for individual communes in the Act of November 13, 2003, on Revenue of Local Government Units, or
2. the population of the newly established commune would be lower than that of the least populous commune in Poland (Mirska, 2021).

9.4 The Problem of Territorial Expansion of Cities at the Expense of Rural Municipalities

In the context of the Council of Ministers' power to make ongoing changes to the territorial structure of communes, issues concerning the interests of rural communes located around cities are particularly controversial (Mirska, 2021). For a long time, we have seen large cities increasingly adopt the strategy of expanding their territories at the expense of adjacent rural municipalities. In each case, the central government decides on the adjustment of the borders between the territorial units by considering the requests of the cities to take over a part of the area, i.e. the "urbanised" area, of the neighbouring rural commune. Although the procedure includes the obligation that the rural municipal council must give its opinion on such a change and that the inhabitants must be consulted, territorial changes, which are disadvantageous for the rural commune and its inhabitants, often go ahead despite clear opposition. This leads to a significant reduction in the potential of the rural commune as it loses some of its territory, and some of its taxpaying inhabitants and may face difficulties in maintaining its capacity to perform public tasks (Mirska, 2021a).

Rural local governments refer to the principle of the communes' identity and territorial stability. The Association of Rural Communes,[6] a national organization that represents the interests of rural communes, has repeatedly expressed its disapproval of, and urgent objection to, the expansion of urban communes at the expense of rural areas.[7] The Association of Rural Communes has highlighted the issue of spatial urban sprawl that causes cities to strive to incorporate territories surrounded by communes, which is supposed to be a panacea for the problems of urban

[6] The Association of Rural Communes of the Republic of Poland is the largest local government organization, currently comprising 664 municipalities, including 576 rural municipalities and 88 urban-rural communes. This means that 38.5% of rural communes and 13% of urban-rural communes in Poland are members of this organization.

[7] Position of the XVII Congress of Polish Rural Communes of October 20, 2017, on changes to the law regarding the division of communes and changes to their borders, https://www.zgwrp.pl/attachments/article/1227/ws.%20ochrony%20granic%20gmin.pdf. Accessed 15 March 2021.

depopulation. Rural local governments reject such moves to deprive them of a part of their territory for economic reasons in order to increase the area and wealth of urban areas.[8]

In another statement, the Association of Rural Communes has called on the Polish Parliament to change the procedures for making territorial changes at the expense of rural municipalities.[9] Rural communes have highlighted the problem that the current law does not regulate the frequency of border changes, creating a sense of instability and uncertainty that hinders municipal planning and development. There are many examples of cities planning for territorial expansion and submitting requests each year to the Council of Ministers to incorporate more areas from adjacent communes. It also happens that after receiving a refusal from the Council of Ministers, the following year they resubmit a request to incorporate the same territory. In addition, rural communes have been demanding the introduction of a judicial review of the Council of Ministers' decisions on border adjustments (Mirska, 2021a). Interestingly, an association of municipalities called "Defending the Borders of Rural Communes" operated between 2009 and 2022 with the primary aim of working to change the legislation on establishing municipal borders. The association included municipalities scattered throughout Poland such as Ełk, Szczecinek, Łomża, Będzino, Białe Błota, Sicienko, Tyczyn i Wiżajny.

The problem was also discussed in a Polish parliamentary committee, which considered a proposal put forward by the Association of Rural Communes to amend the legislation on changes to administrative borders. Representatives of rural municipalities pointed out that the current regulations cause rural communes to live in constant uncertainty over the possible absorption by a neighbouring city. They also mentioned the need to regulate financial settlements between local governments whose borders undergo changes: "We need to think about how to approach this so that units which lose territory can function and adapt their budgets to the new realities."[10] The discussion on this topic is still present, but without any effect of changing the applicable law.

[8] Position of the XXXII General Assembly of the Association of Rural Communes of the Polish Republic of June 19, 2018 on changes to the law regarding the division of communes and changes to their borders, http://www.zgwrp.pl/attachments/article/1354/XXXIIZO_stanowisko_granice.pdf. Accessed 15 October 2023.

[9] Position of the XXXVII General Assembly of the Association of Rural Communes of the Polish Republic of May 15, 2023 on speeding up legislative work on the act on local government in the context of changes to the administrative borders of local governments; https://www.zgwrp.pl/wp-content/uploads/2023/05/37ZO_15.05.2023_stanowisko-ws-granic.pdf. Accessed 15 October 2023.

[10] Transcript of the meeting of the Sejm's standing subcommittee on the system of local government of April 12, 2023. Subject of the meeting: Assessment of the functioning of the legislation on the establishment and amendment of municipal borders. https://www.sejm.gov.pl/sejm9.nsf/biuletyn.xsp?skrnr=STR04S-5. Accessed 26 October 2023.

9.5 Incentives for Voluntary Mergers

To encourage the voluntary merger of communes or counties, a range of incentives has been provided. One type of incentive is financial bonuses, which have been stipulated in Polish law since 2003. The "reward" for local governments that voluntarily merge is subsidies from the Polish state budget. These subsidies are to be paid over a period of 5 years in amounts specified in the Act of November 13, 2003, on the revenues of local government units.

Despite this, Polish communes have shown little interest in this proposal.[11]To further encourage mergers, the financial bonus was increased, but this still failed to produce significant results in terms of voluntary mergers. So far, there has only been one voluntary merger of communes in Poland: two territorial units were consolidated: (1) Zielona Góra, a city with county rights, and (2) the rural commune of the same name which surrounded the city.

The initiative for the merger was proposed by the city of Zielona Góra. The city authorities were highly engaged in promoting and encouraging residents of both the city and the rural commune to support the idea. On the other hand, the local government authorities of the rural commune were rather opposed to the plan and did not endorse the merger.

To measure the opinion of the residents of the rural commune, a consultative referendum was held. With a turnout of 55.18%, 53.45% of the residents voted in favour of merging the two communes. Taking this into account, the Council of Ministers, which in Poland has the authority to decide on territorial unit mergers, announced the decision to establish the new urban commune of Zielona Góra. The area of this commune now covers 275.36 km^2, making it the sixth-largest city in Poland in terms of territorial area. Its population stands at 139,000 residents, ranking it 24th in the country.

The significance of voluntary commune mergers as a way of addressing structural challenges in Poland is rather minimal. Even financial bonuses fail to persuade communes to adopt this solution. Yet, it could be a method for fostering the development of less-developed rural areas. As demonstrated by the merger of Zielona Góra, the extra financial bonus from the state budget was allocated to investments in the area of the annexed rural commune. This was one of the promises made by the mayor of Zielona Góra to encourage the residents of the rural commune to support the idea of merging the two communes into one city.

As studies on the opinions of former rural commune residents have shown, the expected investments in infrastructure played a key role in their support for the merger (Dubicki & Kułyk, 2018).

[11]The Ministry of Administration and Digitisation's response to parliamentary question no. 24063 on the consequences of administrative reform, February 26, 2014. http://www.sejm.gov.pl/sejm7.nsf/InterpelacjaTresc.xsp?key=0F92DD9D. Accessed 30 September 2023.

9.6 Additional Incentives for Cooperation Between Local Government Units in Carrying Out Public Tasks

Inter-municipal cooperation is seen as another way to solve problems related to territorial fragmentation. Based on the assumption that the main problem of fragmented territorial structures is the difficulty in providing certain public services to residents, it has been suggested that the development of inter-municipal cooperation could become a viable alternative to the consolidation of small municipalities (Herzog, 2010).

Some studies on territorial organization, in particular those inspired by public choice theory, have pointed out that the issue of economies of scale ceases to be a problem for small municipalities if they can join forces with adjacent municipalities on key tasks and thus manage to increase their capacity to perform public tasks and also reduce the unit costs of these services (Swianiewicz, 2014).

One of the principles of the political system in Poland is the liberty of free collaboration between local government units. Chapter VII of the Constitution of the Republic of Poland and the several laws indicate that cooperation may be undertaken differently. Three forms of joint activities are of fundamental importance in Polish law. Namely, local government units may create municipal *unions*, then enter into *agreements* between local government units, or establish local government *associations*.

The legal form of a municipal union means the establishment of a new legal entity. The actors that create a municipal union are local government units. The goal is to transfer specific local government task(s) to be performed by the municipal union. Therefore, this task(s) is no longer performed by these local government units. The resolution on the founding of the union is adopted by the representative bodies of the interested local government units. The joint obligation of local governments is to adopt a statute regulating the tasks, organizational structure and method of operation of the established union. In terms of the organizational structure, each municipal union is managed by two bodies: the union assembly (the decision-making and control body) and the executive board. The union's assembly includes mayors from all municipalities or counties that formed the union. The management board is appointed and dismissed by the assembly from among its members. If the union's statute so provides, it is permissible to elect management board members from outside the members of the union's assembly in a number not exceeding 1/3 of the union's management board All municipal unions established in Poland must be entered into the state register for transparency purposes. The central authority that maintains the register is the Minister of Interior and Administration.

The legal form of an agreement between local government units does not entail the establishment of a new legal entity. It is a type of agreement under which one local government unit transfers tasks to another unit for execution. This requires the transfer of financial resources for the execution of this task. The third legal form of cooperation between local government units does not concern the performance of public tasks in the strict sense. The purpose of associations is to represent and support the interests of local government. An association may be established by at least three local government units, has a separate legal personality and its own statute and operates through its bodies.

Since the restoration of democratic local government in Poland in 1990, it has been possible for municipalities to establish unions, agreements, and associations with one another and thus engage in inter-municipal cooperation. Moreover, counties have been able to cooperate with one another in these three legal forms.

From the perspective of performing public tasks, unions play a leading role. In this way, administrative boundaries are crossed and certain tasks are carried out over larger territorial areas than individual local government units. Initially, this method of task execution was only possible through horizontal cooperation, meaning between communes or between counties. In 2016, a significant change was introduced in Poland, namely, the horizontal perspective was expanded to include a vertical perspective of cooperation. Since that year, Polish law has allowed the formation of unions between communes and counties. Polish local governments eagerly use this form, for example, to provide integrated local transport services in areas covering both counties and communes. (Mirska, 2021c).

It is quite difficult to assess whether communes cooperate willingly with each other. On the one hand, it can be said that, for example, unions of communes are a very popular form of performing local government tasks. Currently, there are 323 of them registered in Poland and they include between 2 to 49 communes.[12]

The range of tasks they perform is very broad. These include spatial planning environmental protection, economy, waterworks and water supply, sewerage, urban wastewater treatment, and many others. However, many of these unions are registered but are not operating as they fail to meet their budgetary reporting obligations (Bober et al., 2013). The report of the Chambers of Audit for 2022 regarding state control of the finances of local government units and their unions indicates that the financial statements were submitted by 168 communal unions.

Commune-county unions are also important for performing tasks in rural areas. 62 such unions were established in 2016–2023. Their tasks mainly involve the organization of local public transport. Recently, unions have also been formed to create joint tourist products, to build a brand promoting the region, and to implement projects related to the development of tourist infrastructure, and environmental protection.

The assessment of the need and real prospects for cooperation seems to vary between different types of municipalities. The mayor of a medium-sized urban-rural commune with 25,000 inhabitants assessed that "looking at the neighboring rural communes, I can agree with the opinion that small rural communes do not have a rationale for existence. They do not provide their inhabitants with all services, for example in the field of culture. Inhabitants of the neighbouring rural communes take advantage of the cultural and sports offer which our city provides to its residents.

[12] A list of inter-municipal unions can be found on the website of the Ministry of the Interior and Administration. https://www.gov.pl/web/mswia/zarejestruj-zmien-statut-lub-wyrejestruj-zwiazek-miedzygminny-zwiazek-powiatow-zwiazek-powiatowo-gminny. Accessed 30 September 2023.

Rural communes do not have any housing resources for their inhabitants. Furthermore, cooperation between local government units is very difficult. There is more competition and lack of interest in implementing common public services. For example, our city has a modern water supply and sewage system which could be used by the neighbouring rural communes, but they lack interest in using it. I also do not think that voluntary mergers of small, rural communes will be feasible in the near future" (Mirska, 2022).

In contrast, the mayor of a rural commune with a population of 8000 said that, in his opinion, "one of the methods of strengthening the position of smaller local government units (rural, urban-rural) is cooperation." Pointing to the example of his municipality, the mayor stated that he did not see competition between communes. On the contrary, communes are integrating, and creating new structures (unions and associations) to become stronger and pursue their common interests more effectively while also being able to compete with large cities in the region. Thus, they demonstrate the need to create programs to ensure financial support for such cooperation, not only for individual communes. The mayor mentioned the several examples of various legal forms of cooperation in which his commune has been successfully involved such as associations focused on wastewater management, tourism infrastructure and military infrastructure, as well as a foundation, able to also apply for EU funds not intended for local governments, that is concentrated on tourism:

1. the Mazury Inter-Communal Waste Management Association—12 local government units have built their own waste collection system (the lowest prices for waste collection in the Warmińsko-Mazurskie voivodeship), a local waste segregation system and have been preparing to launch their own incineration plant;
2. the Association "Great Masurian Lakes"—17 local government units have associated and built infrastructure around Lake Śniardwy after receiving EU financing;
3. the Foundation "Great Masurian Lakes"—consists of 24 members and has the legal form of a foundation, which allows it to apply for EU funds that are not intended for local governments;
4. an association of local governments where NATO training grounds and military units are located—a nationwide union established in response to the problem of infrastructure degradation (mainly roads) by the military. The associated municipalities have effectively pursued their interests and received additional funds from the government to reconstruct infrastructure (Mirska, 2023).

This statement highlights two issues. Firstly, communes can undertake joint activities not only in the form of unions, agreements, and associations but also as foundations. In addition, communes can cooperate under private law by establishing commercial companies. This is possible under the Act on Municipal Management of 1996. Secondly, it is clear that external funding, primarily from the European Union, is a great motivator for communes to enter into institutionalized cooperation.

Poland's membership in the European Union is undoubtedly one of the key factors that stimulate the development of cooperation processes at the local level in

Poland. The existence of areas which generate social and economic problems translates into intra-regional differentiation, which contradicts the European Union's fundamental principle of cohesion. The 2007 Lisbon Treaty introduced the aspect of *territorial* cohesion into the EU's cohesion policy, making it as important as achieving social and economic cohesion. The main assumption of the new way of implementing the cohesion policy in the context of territorial development is to consider the individual features of the territories that receive financial support, while moving away from viewing these territories through the prism of administrative borders.

The European Union's launch of a new financial instrument called Integrated Territorial Investments (ITIs) was quite important from the point of view of promoting and supporting cooperation between communes in Poland. According to Article 7(1) and 7(2) of the EU Regulation 1303/2013, the European Regional Development Fund supports sustainable urban development through strategies that set out integrated actions to tackle the economic, environmental, climate, demographic and social challenges faced by urban areas, taking into account the need to promote links between urban and rural areas. Thus, the European Commission's main goal is to increase the involvement of cities in the implementation of its cohesion policy, but rural self-governments have also become participants in these activities. The European Commission has obliged all member states in the Multiannual Financial Framework (MFF) of 2014–2020 to allocate a minimum of 5% of the funds from the European Regional Development Fund (ERDF) to the implementation of this instrument. The provisions in the EU regulations for 2021–2027 imply that a minimum of 8% of ERDF funds should be allocated to the implementation of territorial investments.

In Poland, ITIs are implemented in the functional areas of the largest cities (these are voivodeship capitals) and in smaller regional and sub-regional cities with areas that are functionally linked to them. The designation of ITIs for voivodeship cities has been obligatory and taken place in accordance with the guidelines of the Ministry of Infrastructure and Development. In contrast, the designation of ITIs areas for regional/sub-regional cities have depended on the decisions of voivodeship self-governments within which these cities are located.

24 areas for the implementation of ITIs have been designated in Poland, including seven functional areas of regional/sub-regional cities. One of the necessary elements for the creation of an ITI area is the establishment of an institutionalized form of partnership, i.e. the establishment of an "ITI Union" or "ITI Partnership" by local government units and the development of a joint, coordinated strategy for territorial development and subsequent implementation of joint projects.

Thus, Integrated Territorial Investments are implemented not only in cities but also in communes around these cities. The condition is the existence of strong socio-economic links between the neighboring communes and the urban core. This means that both urban and rural communes can be beneficiaries of ITIs.

ITI areas vary greatly in size: this depends on the degree of development of functional links between the city and the adjacent municipalities. The number of municipalities that make up ITIs areas ranges from 5 to 81.

For example, the ITI area for Warsaw includes the territory of the capital city of Warsaw as well as 14 urban, 12 urban-rural and 13 rural municipalities. The aim is to implement projects that are important for the entire functional area. The projects concern both the problems of rural areas (e.g. educational programs for rural schools in the municipality to provide equal educational opportunities for children) and metropolitan areas (the provision of childcare facilities for children in nurseries in one of Warsaw's districts with the highest birth rate). There are also projects implemented jointly by several communes, such as the construction of bicycle paths connecting six communes, as well as projects with an impact on all local governments, for example, in the field of e-services. One example is the project entitled "Construction and implementation of an integrated support system for care services in the Warsaw Functional Area (E-Care)" (Mirska, 2021d).

In the opinion of Katarzyna Kuć-Czajkowska, the cooperation of local government units within ITIs varies greatly, from conciliatory cooperation of local governments in the implementation of joint projects to very bad practices and the lack of harmonious cooperation based on partnership. Cooperation within ITIs is most effective in those areas where local governments have already cooperated. The expert points out that the success factors promoting cooperation between local governments include effective leadership, i.e. the determination of local authorities to build cooperative relations and mutual trust. Among the problems, the expert points to the subjective feeling of representatives of small local self-governments (rural communes) that they are less significant partners: communes believe that the central city is somehow privileged by its very position and that they should compete with it. In addition, there is a lack of trust between partners, a lack of human resources for the substantive preparation of cooperation and a belief that there are no clear results from the implementation of joint projects. However, Katarzyna Kuć-Czajkowska notes that while conducting empirical research (2018) with all local governments that were implementing ITIs, nearly 95% of respondents stated that such cooperation was needed. When asked if cooperation would continue even if there was no financial support from the European Union programme, 52% of the respondents said yes. 38% stated that cooperation would continue, provided EU funds are available (Mirska, 2023a).

Polish law also provides for legal instruments to encourage local governments to cooperate. A new and very important instrument is the supra-local development strategy introduced with an Act of 2020.[13] Communes that are adjacent to each other and functionally linked may develop such a document as their joint development strategy. The supra-local development strategy serves primarily to coordinate activities and cooperation at the commune level, but counties can also participate. The supra-local development strategy, in a way, complements the ITIs strategy and encourages cooperation between all local government units, regardless of whether they are located in functional areas of large cities or outside them.

---

[13] The supra-local development strategy was introduced by the Act of July 15, 2020, amending the Act on the principles of development policy.

The supra-local development strategy is an integrated document, which combines social and economic perspectives. In addition, compulsory elements of the strategy include the development of a model of the functional and spatial structure and recommendations for spatial policy. This comprehensive document is intended to ensure spatial coordination of planned activities in line with the principles of sustainable development and spatial planning The supra-local development strategy is a universal instrument and can be used by all communes, regardless of their demographic potential and location. A financial incentive for municipalities to jointly develop supra-local development strategies was included in the document that defines European Union funding for programs in Poland, i.e. the Partnership Agreement for the Implementation of the Cohesion Policy 2021–2027. Namely, communes with a supra-local strategy can hope for additional EU funds under the fifth European Union policy objective called "Europe closer to citizens" (Partnership Agreement 2022). For many local politicians, working on a supra-local strategy, based on common problems, development factors, opportunities and risks, will be one of their first experiences of cooperation with other local governments, which until now have been seen as rivals in the competition for residents, tax revenues, and EU funds. Additionally, although 521 communes, including 272 rural and 124 urban-rural communes, participated in Integrated Territorial Investments in 2014–2020, accounting for more than 20% of all communes in Poland, many local politicians still feel that they are accountable only for investments made within their own commune and cannot accept solutions that are located in a neighboring commune even if they are beneficial from the perspective of the development of their own commune and its residents (Cieślińska, 2021).

9.7 Conclusions

The deteriorating demographic situation of Polish local governments, particularly in peripheral rural areas, means that they are facing the challenge of how to perform their own tasks and provide basic services in the event that public expenditure rises while revenues fall. Due to reluctance of small local governments to be merged, it is unlikely that any amalgamations will take place in the near future. Even the introduction of financial incentives has proved insufficient to convince local government units.

Therefore, it appears that the only possible strategy at present is to consistently encourage local governments to cooperate in various areas. Such cooperation may involve above all public transport, environmental protection, water and sewage management, and education.

Certainly, instruments such as ITIs and supra-local planning will gradually contribute to a change in the mentality of local politicians and foster a culture of cooperation, as ITIs are partly mandatory, and collaboration is incentivized through financial means. The fact that the EU maintains ITIs in the next MFF 2021–2027 will probably have a positive impact on local government cooperation in Poland.

The Polish central government itself also supports this direction of development: in 2026, legal provisions will come into force under which a commune that has devised a supra-local development strategy with other communes will be able to opt out of adopting a separate development strategy for itself.

Due to the lack of real plans to implement reforms involving the creation of larger territorial units, Poland is an example of a country that tries to encourage local government units to cooperate through a system of financial incentives and legal regulations. Poland has had no top-down territorial reforms aimed at merging small communes. Such changes in the structure of municipalities should not be expected soon, as this is not a topic which is present on the political agenda of the central government.

References

Babczuk, A., & Kachniarz, M. (2016). Czy konsolidowanie małych jednostek samorządu terytorialnego w Polsce jest uzasadnione?/Are justified the consolidation of small local government units in Poland? *Studia KPZK, 167*.

Bober, J., Hausner, J., Izebski, H., Lachiewicz, W., Mazur, S., Nelicki, A., Nowotarski, B., Puzyna, W., Surówka, K., Zachariasz, I., & Zawicki, M. (2013). *Narastające dysfunkcje, zasadnicze dylematy, konieczne działania: Raport o stanie samorządności terytorialnej w Polsce/growing dysfunctions, fundamental dilemmas, necessary actions: Report on the state of local self-government in Poland*. Uniwersytet Ekonomiczny w Krakowie.

Cieślińska, J. (2021). *Strategia rozwoju ponadlokalnego to katalizator współpracy samorządów, opinia/The supra-local development strategy is a catalyst for cooperation between local governments, opinion*. Retrieved October 26, 2023, from https://www.prawo.pl/samorzad/strategia-rozwoju-ponadlokalnego-ma-sluzyc-wspolpracy-z-innymi,506955.html

Dubicki, P., & Kułyk, P. (2018). Proces integracji miasta z gminą wiejską. Przykład Zielonej Góry/The process of urban-rural integration. Using the example of Zielona Góra. *Studia Miejskie, 32*, 113–124. https://doi.org/10.25167/sm2018.032.08

Herzog, R. (2010). Inter-municipal cooperation: A viable alternative to territorial amalgamation? In P. Swianiewicz (Ed.), *Territorial consolidation reforms in Europe* (pp. 285–308). Open Society Institute.

Kaczmarek, T. (2016). Gminny podział administracyjny w świetle 25 lat funkcjonowania samorządu terytorialnego w Polsce. *Przegląd Politologiczny, 1*, 63–80. https://doi.org/10.14746/pp.2016.21.1.5

Ministry of Administration and Digitization, Assessment of the Situation of Local Governments in Poland. (2013). Retrieved October 1, 2023, from http://eregion.wzp.pl/sites/default/files/ocena-sytuacji-samorzadow-lokalnych.pdf

Mirska, A. (2021). The structure of local government in Poland: An introduction. In A. Mirska (Ed.), *Local government in Poland: Responses to urban-rural challenges* (pp. 56–61). Zenodo. https://doi.org/10.5281/zenodo.5556083

Mirska, A. (2021a). Decisions on expanding the city territory at the expanse of the rural area. Consultations with residents or a local referendum? In A. Mirska (Ed.), *Local government in Poland: Responses to urban-rural challenges* (pp. 106–114). Zenodo. https://doi.org/10.5281/zenodo.5556138

Mirska, A. (2021b). The system of local government in Poland. In A. Mirska (Ed.), *Local government in Poland: Responses to urban-rural challenges* (pp. 3–10). Zenodo. https://doi.org/10.5281/zenodo.5556031

Mirska, A. (2021c). County-commune unions as a new form of intergovernmental relations in Poland. The Beskidian County and Commune Union. In A. Mirska (Ed.), *Local government in Poland: Responses to urban-rural challenges* (pp. 88–100). Zenodo. https://doi.org/10.5281/zenodo.5556120

Mirska, A. (2021d). Integrated Territorial Investment (ITI). In A. Mirska (Ed.), *Local government in Poland: Responses to urban-rural challenges* (pp. 46–49). Zenodo. https://doi.org/10.5281/zenodo.5556074

Mirska, A. (2022). *LoGov Poland Interview Report n°2 [Data set]*. Zenodo. https://doi.org/10.5281/zenodo.6498109

Mirska, A. (2023). *LoGov Poland Workshop Report n°1 [Data set]*. Zenodo. https://doi.org/10.5281/zenodo.10075817

Mirska, A. (2023a). *LoGov Poland Workshop Report n°2 [Data set]*. Zenodo. https://doi.org/10.5281/zenodo.10198393

Partnership Agreement for the Implementation of the Cohesion Policy 2021–2027 in Poland. (2022). Retrieved October 10, 2023, from https://www.funduszeeuropejskie.gov.pl/media/109763/Umowa_Partnerstwa_na_lata_2021_2027.pdf

Stanny, M., Rosner, A., & Komorowski, L. (2023). *Monitoring rozwoju obszarów wiejskich. Etap IV. Dekada przemian społeczno-gospodarczych*. Fundacja Europejski Fundusz Rozwoju Wsi Polskiej Instytut Rozwoju Wsi i Rolnictwa PAN. Warszawa. Retrieved October 26, 2023, from https://www.irwirpan.waw.pl/dir_upload/site/files/badania/MROW_IV.pdf

Statistics Poland. (1992). *Small Statistical Yearbook 1991*. Retrieved October 26, 2023, from https://statlibr.stat.gov.pl/exlibris/aleph/a22_1/apache_media/941J6LGBUXMDVRBKGGP4X3BM4NRNGH.pdf

Statistics Poland. (2022a). *Demographic situation in Poland up to 2021*. Retrieved October 26, 2023, from https://stat.gov.pl/obszary-tematyczne/ludnosc/ludnosc/sytuacja-demograficzna-polski-do-roku-2021,40,2.html

Statistics Poland. (2022b). *Rural areas in Poland in 2020*. Warsaw. Retrieved October 26, 2023, from https://stat.gov.pl/files/gfx/portalinformacyjny/pl/defaultaktualnosci/5507/2/5/1/obszary_wiejskie_w_polsce_w_2020_r_pl.pdf

Statistics Poland. (2022c). *Types of municipalities and urban and rural areas*. Retrieved October 26, 2023, from https://stat.gov.pl/en/regional-statistics/classification-of-territorial-units/administrative-division-of-poland/

Statistics Poland. (2023a). *Area and population in the territorial prole in 2023*. Warsaw. Retrieved October 26, 2023, from https://stat.gov.pl/obszary-tematyczne/ludnosc/ludnosc/powierzchnia-i-ludnosc-w-przekroju-terytorialnym-w-2023-roku,7,20.html

Statistics Poland. (2023b). *Demographic situation in Poland up to 2022*. Warsaw. Retrieved October 26, 2023, from https://stat.gov.pl/obszary-tematyczne/ludnosc/ludnosc/sytuacja-demograficzna-polski-do-roku-2022,40,3.html

Swianiewicz, P. (2014). *Ocena podziału terytorialnego państwa z uwzględnieniem efektywności funkcjonowania urzędów organów jednostek samorządu terytorialnego—Wnioski i rekomendacje*. Raport przygotowany na zlecenie Ministerstwa Administracji i Cyfryzacji/Assessment of the territorial division of Poland in the perspective of the effectiveness of the functioning of offices of local government units—Conclusions and recommendations. Report prepared on behalf of the Ministry of Administration and Digitization, Warsaw

Swianiewicz, P., Gendźwiłł, A., & Zardi, A. (2017). *Territorial reforms in Europe: Does size matter?*. Centre of Expertise for Local Government Reform, Council of Europe. Retrieved October 1, 2023, from https://rm.coe.int/territorial-reforms-in-europe-does-size-matter-territorial-amalgamatio/168076cf16

Szmytke, R. (2015). Miasta zdegradowane w Polsce jako potencjalne nowe miasta/Degraded towns in Poland as potentially new towns. In K. Robert & D. Mirek (Eds.), *Miasta zdegradowane i restytuowane w Polsce. Geneza, rozwój, problemy/degraded and restituted towns in Poland: Origins, development, problem*. University of Gothenburg.

Wytrążek, W. (2020). Administracyjnoprawny charakter nadania statusu miasta na wniosek gminy. *Roczniki Nauk Prawnych, XXX*(2). https://doi.org/10.18290/rnp20302-10

Open Access This chapter is licensed under the terms of the Creative Commons Attribution 4.0 International License (http://creativecommons.org/licenses/by/4.0/), which permits use, sharing, adaptation, distribution and reproduction in any medium or format, as long as you give appropriate credit to the original author(s) and the source, provide a link to the Creative Commons license and indicate if changes were made.

The images or other third party material in this chapter are included in the chapter's Creative Commons license, unless indicated otherwise in a credit line to the material. If material is not included in the chapter's Creative Commons license and your intended use is not permitted by statutory regulation or exceeds the permitted use, you will need to obtain permission directly from the copyright holder.

Part III
The Role of Local Authorities in Intergovernmental Conferences

Chapter 10
The Role of Italian Local Authorities in Conferences with Other Government Levels

Greta Klotz and Sara Parolari

Abstract This chapter focuses on the intergovernmental relations between local authorities, Regions and the State in Italy. It provides an overview of intergovernmental relations involving local authorities and assess their impact on national and regional policy-making. The chapter describes Italy's local governance system and discusses the importance of collaboration mechanisms between local authorities and higher levels of government, highlighting the lack of parliamentary representation for municipalities and formal forms of collaboration with the municipalities at national and regional level. The chapter shows that there have been no significant legal changes in formal relations at the national level in recent years. However, local actors' political influence has grown in practice, even if it is fragile due to its dependence on leaders' abilities and terms.

Keywords Intergovernmental relations · Italy · Conference system · State-regions · State-local authorities · Regions-local authorities

10.1 Introduction: The Political-Territorial Architecture of Italy

Italy is known as an asymmetrical regional state (Palermo, 2021) or a quasi-federal state (Lippi, 2011). According to Article 114(1) of the Constitution, municipalities, provinces, metropolitan cities, regions and the state make up the republic. All these territorial entities are defined as "autonomous bodies with their own statutes,

This chapter is the product of a joint effort. However, Greta Klotz wrote the Sects. 10.1 and 10.4, while Sara Parolari authored the Sects. 10.2 and 10.3. Section 10.5 has been co-authored.

G. Klotz (✉) · S. Parolari
Institute for Comparative Federalism, Eurac Research, Bolzano/Bozen, Italy
e-mail: greta.klotz@eurac.edu; sara.parolari@eurac.edu

© The Author(s) 2026

K. Kössler, E. M. Belser (eds.), *Local Government Structure and Intergovernmental Relations*, Local and Urban Governance,
https://doi.org/10.1007/978-3-031-99820-1_10

powers and functions in accordance with the principles laid down in the Constitution" (Article 114(2)).

In the Italian regional system 15 out of 20 regions are ordinary, while five are special due to historical or political reasons, one of which (the Trentino-Alto Adige/Südtirol region) comprises the autonomous provinces of Trento and Bolzano/Bozen. Both provinces are comparable to a Region in terms of powers and competences (Article 116(2) of the Constitution). Each special region has a different system of powers due to bilateral negotiations with the state (central government), which is guaranteed by a basic law with the rank of a national constitutional law. A central distinguishing feature between ordinary and special regions is also their system of local authorities (Klotz, 2024). Unlike the other regions, the five special regions can regulate the system of their municipalities with an own regional law. The municipalities within the ordinary regions, by contrast, are subject to the exclusive legislative power of the state with regard to their electoral legislation, government bodies and basic tasks (Article 117(2) of the Constitution). However, as the regions are responsible for all areas that are not expressly reserved to state legislation (Article 118(4)), the division of powers regarding local authorities between the national and subnational level is closely interwoven (Bin & Falcon, 2012, p. 250; Villamena, 2013, p. 195).

Other than the regions, the territorial entities are 83 provinces, 14 metropolitan cities and 7896 municipalities. All of them have no legislative powers. According to the Constitution (Article 117(6) of the Constitution), they have the power to issue regulations governing the organization and performance of the tasks assigned to them. Moreover, they have financial autonomy and their own sources of revenue (Article 119). Administrative powers are in principle granted to the municipalities, unless they have been transferred to other levels of government for reasons of unity (Article 118(1)). Municipalities form the lowest level of government and administrative unit. Like the provinces and metropolitan cities, they have statutory autonomy, but they also have directly elected bodies (mayors and councils) and their own tasks. As a special type of a municipality, Italy also knows associative forms: Law 267/2000 provides for certain "communities" (*comunità*) and "associations" (*forme associative*). The former include the so-called mountain communities (Article 27). This is an association of municipalities (*unione di comuni*) that can be established between individual mountain municipalities to jointly carry out functions. It is therefore partly a form of local cooperation, but also an intermediary institution between the provincial and municipal level of government (Bolgherini, 2015, p. 60). In addition to these mountain communities, there are island communities (*comunità isolane o di arcipelago*, Article 29).

Overall, local autonomy in Italy has developed slowly but gradually (Villamena, 2013), and its actual capacity remains limited. The system of local entities in Italy can be defined as hybrid (Valdesalici & Trettel, 2023) especially due to the allocation of powers between the national and subnational level and the local finance regulations. Additionally, municipalities in regions with ordinary statutes have been repeatedly subject to national or regional reforms (Alber et al., 2024).

In the context of slow but increasing local autonomy in the last decades, it is worth looking at the collaboration mechanisms of local authorities with other levels of government. Possibilities for local governments to influence the decision-making of higher levels of government can tell us a lot about the legal and political role which they fulfill. As Ladner rightly underlines (Ladner et al., 2019, p. 194), available instruments show if they serve as a compensation or confirmation of limited functions of local institutions. In the case of Italy where no parliamentary representation of municipalities exists the extent of intergovernmental relations is crucial. The objective of this chapter is therefore to provide an overview of intergovernmental relations involving local authorities and to assess the impact of the local level on national and regional policy-making.

10.2 Instruments of Intergovernmental Relations Involving the Local Level

The institutions that connect regions, local autonomies and the center in Italy are manifold and tend to reflect the asymmetrical nature of the Italian regional design. As in most countries that have decentralized progressively, the second chamber of parliament performs no role in terms of linking the regions with the center, despite a generic reference to this effect in the text of the Constitution (Palermo & Kössler, 2017, p. 177). The chamber is equally not a vehicle for representing local governments. Consequently, intergovernmental relations have mainly been developed through cooperation among the executives of the various government levels rather than by means of the legislature.

Originally developed as informal channels of cooperation in the 1980s, and subsequently regulated by national legislation (ministerial decrees in 1996, reformed by Legislative Decree 281/1997), a complex system of conferences dominated by the executives has gradually been established as an expression of the constitutional principle of loyal cooperation (Bifulco, 2006; Del Prete, 2020). This is an unwritten principle, which has been developed and shaped by the Constitutional Court,[1] demands coordination and cooperation among the various levels of government as a guarantee for subnational autonomy. It influences all provisions and procedures for regulating intergovernmental relations, ranging from mutual information duties to the realization of unanimously agreed action (Woelk, 2021). Loyal cooperation is particularly relevant for the system of conferences.

This system is made up of three bodies, namely the State-Regions Conference, the State-Cities and Local Autonomies Conference and the Unified Conference, which is the union of the first two and addresses matters and tasks of common interest for all three levels of government. This means that local governments are

[1] See the Judgments 64/1987, 341/1996 and 242/1997.

involved in two of these conferences, namely the State-Cities and Local Autonomies Conference and the Unified Conference.

As for its composition, the State-Cities and Local Autonomies Conference is a collective body chaired either by the Prime Minister or, if this task is delegated (and this frequently occurs), by the Minister of Home Affairs or the Minister of Regional Affairs.

Members of the conference are the ministers of economy and finance, of economic development, of infrastructures, transport and health, the President of the National Association of Municipalities (*Associazione Nazionale dei Comuni Italiani*—ANCI), the President of the Union of the Italian Provinces (*Unione Province d'Italia*—UPI) and the President of the National Union of Mountain Towns and Municipalities (Unione Nazionale Comuni, Comunità e Enti Montani—UNCEM), six presidents of provinces appointed by the UPI and 14 mayors appointed by ANCI. Through the stipulation that five of the 14 mayors appointed by ANCI must represent major Italian cities,[2] special attention is given to urban areas.

The State-Cities and Local Autonomies Conference holds meetings (not open to the public) at least every 3 months (mandatory meetings), and in any case in which the Prime Minister sees the need for convening it or the president of ANCI, UPI or UNCEM ask for it (non-mandatory meetings). However, in the latter case the power to convene the conference still rests with the Prime Minister (Bifulco, 2006, p. 256). As to functions, the primary purpose of the State-City-Local Autonomies Conference is to coordinate relations between the State and local entities and to guarantee local autonomies a way to directly interact with the national government. This includes advisory and information activities, discussions on issues that may affect functions of provinces, municipalities, and metropolitan areas, as well as financial and budgetary policies or national legislative initiatives.

The Unified Conference brings the previous conference and the State-Regions Conference[3] together. It is convened by the Prime Minister and is chaired either by the Prime Minister or, by delegation, by the Minister of Regional Affairs or by the Minister of Home Affairs. Its standing members are the same as for the two mentioned conferences. Other members of the central government and representatives from central government and local administrations or public bodies may also be invited to take part in the conference sessions.

As regards its functions, the Unified Conference promotes and signs intergovernmental agreements and memoranda of understandings, expresses opinions, designates representatives in relation to matters and tasks of common interest to the

[2] According to Law 267/2000, this refers to Torino, Milano, Venezia, Genova, Bologna, Firenze, Bari and Napoli. But Roma can be added as well.

[3] This conference is a collective body headed and convened either by the President of the Council of Ministers (the Prime Minister) or by the Minister of Regional Affairs by delegation or another minister by special appointment of the Prime Minister. The standing members are the presidents of the 20 regions and of the two autonomous provinces, while the responsible ministers are invited to participate in the conference sessions, depending on the matters in the agenda. The same applies to the representatives of state administrations and public agencies.

regions, provinces, municipalities and mountain communities. The Unified Conference is competent in all cases in which regions, provinces, municipalities and mountain communities or the State-Region Conference and the State-City and Local autonomies have to express themselves on the same subject. It delivers advice, which is mandatory (but not binding) whenever draft laws affect regional or local affairs (according to Legislative Decree 281/1997), and appoints representatives from the regions, provinces, municipalities and mountain communities to several bodies dealing with matters and tasks of common interest.

While the conference system represents national-local intergovernmental relations, the main instrument for the interaction between local-subnational actors was provided with the constitutional reform of 2001. This reform amended Article 123 of the Constitution by foreseeing that the regional statutes, at least those of ordinary regions, must provide for a specific body aimed at representing the interests of the local entities at the regional level, i.e. the Council of Local Authorities (*Consiglio delle Autonomie Locali*—CAL). It has to be considered that many administrative functions fall under the responsibility of the local level in accordance with the principle of subsidiarity stated in Article 118 of the Constitution. Consequently, there is an increasingly need to create an institutional setting that gives to municipalities the possibility of expressing their views whenever a regional legislation impacts on local affairs. After some delay, most of the Regions established CALs (see section below). According to the Constitutional Court's Judgment 370/2006, special regions are not obliged to establish such councils, given their exclusive legislative competence over the organization and the functioning of local authorities. In practice, however, all of the special regions (and the two autonomous provinces of Trento and Bolzano) set up such CALs, thus aligning their intergovernmental institutional structure to that of the ordinary regions.

Each regional Statute regulates this organ differently. The CALs are composed of all local authorities (sometimes representatives of local executives, sometimes of local councils, sometimes of both) plus, in some regions, other organizations, such as Chambers of Commerce.

As to functions, CALs have no decision-making power, but they are expected to issue mandatory opinions on certain matters, including amendments to the regional statutes and approval of budgets and financial laws (Carloni & Cortese, 2020, p. 123). Regarding the possibilities for local entities to defend their autonomous status and interact with the national institutions, it is also interesting to consider that—despite the constitutional recognition of local entities—no legal provision grants them instruments to directly access the Constitutional Court in order to ensure that their prerogatives are respected. This impediment has led to a search for ways of safeguarding municipal autonomy. The Constitutional Court identified a solution in its Judgment 196/2004, stating that Article 123(4) of the Constitution has configured the Council of Local Authorities as a necessary organ of the region and that Article 32(2) of Law 87/1953 (as replaced by Article 9(2) of Law 131/2003) has attributed precisely to this organ the power to propose to the regional parliament to promote judgments of constitutional legitimacy directly against the laws of the state (Valdesalici & Trettel, 2023).

10.3 The Role of Intergovernmental Institutions in the Decision-Making Process at National and Subnational Level

As many legal scholars pointed out, it is evident that—as composite legal orders evolve—any significant government activity requests the combined and coordinated effort of both the central government and territorial autonomies (Carrozza, 1989). It is therefore clear that arranging for the devolution of competences merely in view of a constitutional catalogue of functions cannot adequately ensure the recognition of distinct areas of expertise (Ceccherini, 2009). This is true also when considering the Italian system.

At a first stage, the leading interpretation of Title V Part II of the Constitution concerning the relations between the central government and regional/local authorities were shaped by a dualist theory, based on a rigid system of strictly separated spheres of competences (Woelk, 2021). Later on, thanks to a constitutional reform of 2001, the direction of regionalist development has been inverted: the jurisprudence of the Constitutional Court, the legislation regarding relations between the central government and the regions, as well as the legal doctrine on the topic, all contributed to the definition of a new model of national-subnational relations, founded on the principle of collaboration (the so-called "cooperative regionalism") (Ceccherini, 2009). Cooperative regionalism was favored by the concurrent introduction by the Constitutional Court of the principle of loyal collaboration, as a fundamental principle to be taken into account when relations between the different levels of government are at stake. The court's Judgments 64/1997 and 242/1997 are cases in point (Bilancia, 2001).

As regards the local level, the issue of loyal collaboration has been mainly approached through the triadic conferences system described above where political representatives of local authorities meet regularly with members of the national government, and in some cases, also regional governments.

However, although the liaison function and advisory role of the two conferences where local authorities are represented are of paramount importance to the political process, it can be observed that the mechanism is not well-functioning, and it is difficult to determine in general the real impact of the system on policymaking. Discussions are often limited to technical issues that have been already decided at other levels of government, and its decisions are non-binding but merely advisory (Carpani, 2009). Nonetheless, this conference system has allowed for strong but informal relations to develop between individual members, although there are considerable differences in the nature of these relations, depending mostly on the expertise and the effective leadership of the local politicians involved (Bolgherini et al., 2018).

Moreover, the two conferences where local authorities are represented are often criticized for their alleged democratic deficit. This is because the local representatives are appointed by ANCI and UPI, which are private law associations. It is therefore a "trade union-type" representation of interests rather than of territories. This is because in the case of ANCI, its appointees, who must be mayors, act in the conference as representatives of the "category" of entities being part of the association and not—more directly—as representatives of the people that elected them. It is quite odd for democratically elected representatives of territorial communities and "union" representatives of category interests to be in the same assembly: whether they are mayors or province presidents, thus holding elected office, has no relevance since they sit in the conference not as delegates democratically elected by their community, but as representatives of the category of entities that appointed them (Bin & Ruggiu, 2006).

This issue is particularly relevant when considering the Unified Conference where, on the contrary, each region has one member representing the respective territory. In this regard, some commentators suggest that, instead of ANCI, it should be up to CALs to appoint the local members representing their territory. On the one hand, it would facilitate the linkage between regional and local representatives of each regional area by adopting a single common position, on the other hand, it would strengthen an institution—the CAL—which so far have played only a marginal role (Bin & Ruggiu, 2006).

In the end, even if the 2001 constitutional reform brought about several remarkable changes, especially with regard to the duties and functions of the regions, it did not carry out a systematic review of the instruments to promote greater collaboration between the different institutional levels that constitute the Italian Republic (Rolla, 2003). These instruments—the conference system as well as the CALs—need some sort of revision to ensure, on the one hand, the effective representation of the interests of local authorities and, on the other hand, the concrete possibility for them to influence regional and national policies.

10.4 The Impact of Local Authorities in Decision Making from an Empirical Perspective

Apart from the mere existence of intergovernmental structures such as the abovementioned conferences, it is significant how the institutions function in practice and what position the municipalities have within them.

As emphasized, the most important "speaker" of Italian municipalities at national level is ANCI. First, it is besides the UPI the only association which elects its representatives to sit within the State-City-Local Autonomies Conference. Secondly, the ANCI members of the intergovernmental conference are also members of the national assembly and the steering committee of the association itself so that a continuous liaison between the two institutions is guaranteed.

As to the frequency of the conference activity, Table 10.1 gives an overview about the number of meetings in the last 10 years as well as on the number of topics on the agenda in the specific years and, finally, how many of these topics were requested by the two local government associations ANCI and/or UPI.

Table 10.1 ANCI/UPI and the State-City-Local Autonomies Conference meetings

Year	Number of meetings	Number of topics on order of business (opinions, agreements…)	Request by ANCI or UPI	Percentage of ANCI/UPI requests
2023	17	61	9	14.7%
2022	17	72	5	6.9%
2021	14	68	4	5.8%
2020	14	66	2	3%
2019	12	44	11	25%
2018	14	58	18	31%
2017	18	73	13	17.8%
2016	19	77	31	40.2%
2015	16	75	17	22.6%
2014	10	61	15	24.5%

Source: Own elaboration based on official data at: www.conferenzastatocitta.it, access date: 26 March 2024, annual reports 2013–2023

The data show that the two local authorities' organizations have been more active in the years 2014–2019 than over the last several years. However, regarding the overall frequency of meetings, a steady increase in the activities of the State-City-Local Autonomies Conference between 2014 and 2017 can be confirmed. It then became less meetings in the years 2018–2021 and again more in 2022 and 2023. However, as the data show, more meetings do not always result in more agenda items and more decisions. Furthermore, the instable political landscape and short-term governments in Italy must be taken into consideration when looking at such kind of summaries. For example, between April and June 2018, there was a period of slowdown in the conference's activities due to the formation of the government following the national elections held on March 2018. The same must be taken into consideration for other years, as Italy also voted in February 2021 and September 2022.

If we look at the topics which are on the agenda of the intergovernmental organ, the topics for common discussion are mostly shaped by national actors, that is, the national government and single ministries. In 2023, the topics discussed at the conference meetings affected more than ten different ministries. Often a single issue concerns more than one ministry (Conferenza Stato-cittá ed autonomie locali, 2024a, 2024b). Most of the points for discussion concerned the Ministry of Interior and the one of Economics and Finance (see Table 10.2).

To evaluate the role of local authorities in national decision-making it is useful to take a look also at the kind of topics which were discussed in the State-Cities-Local Authorities Conference over the last 10 years. The matters mostly touch on economic-financial challenges affecting municipalities, provinces and metropolitan cities. Based on the activity reports produced by the official offices, most of the measures concern the organization and operation of local governments. These measures can be on financial policies, the organization or even human resources of local entities. Following the classification by the reports based on the criterion of the main subject, it can be summarized that almost all topics examined in the last

Table 10.2 Arguments affecting national ministries in the State-City-Local Autonomies Conference

Type of Ministry	Number of arguments affecting national ministries
Interior	35
Economics and Finance	36
Education	6
Family, birth and equal opportunities	6
Europan affairs	5
Public administration	5
Technical innovation	4
Prime Minister's Office	4
Disability	3
Infrastructures	2
Regional affairs and autonomies	1

Source: Own elaboration based on official data at: www.conferenzastatocitta.it, access date: 26 March 2024, annual reports 2013–2023

10 years with regard to the organization of local government fall within financial and budgetary policies (Conferenza Stato-cittá ed autonomie locali, 2024b). Conversely, also the topics which ANCI and UPI brought on the agenda mostly concern financial issues. They speak about deferrals, observations or clarifications linked to financial statements or other financial regulations. Only one out of nine issues requested in 2023 by ANCI/UPI concerned a practical challenge and this was the regulation of waste separation in public schools. Apart from economic-financial issues, topics also concern practical issues. In 2022, these have been, among others, the mitigation of the social and economic consequences of the Covid-19 emergency and the increase in energy costs (Conferenza Stato-cittá ed autonomie locali, 2023). In 2023, among others, the simplification of relations between the public administration, citizens, and businesses through interconnected platforms was discussed. In this year, the conference also dealt with measures aiming to strengthen social services, including nursery schools or summer camps for children. The conference also discussed measures for investments for urban regeneration in favor of municipalities with a population of <15,000 or interventions in favor of small municipalities (Conferenza Stato-cittá ed autonomie locali, 2024a).

As mentioned above, there are different types of decisions through which the State-Cities-Local Authorities Conference operates: opinions (*pareri*), agreements (*intese*), accords (*accordi*), designations (*designazioni*) and deliberations (*delibere*). Despite this diversity of acts, only two of them play a major role, i.e. the opinions and agreements. In fact, in the last 10 years most of the decisions of the conference were opinions. This is true for all years except of 2021 and 2022 when most points resulted in agreements. In 2023, out of 61 questions on the agenda meetings, 26 were opinions and 18 agreements which corresponds to a percentage of 72%. The instrument of the opinion is, however, politically less impactful than the agreement. Indeed, for the adoption of an opinion the majority of the members of the conference is sufficient, and this type of decision does not bind the national government to comply with its content. By contrast, an agreement needs a unanimous decision by the members of the conference and is binding. Opinions can therefore be classified as a form of weak cooperation whereas agreements are one of strong cooperation (Bolgherini et al., 2018).

In contrast to the different types of influence of local authorities within the conference, they have at the regional level a purely advisory role in the legislative process of the single Italian regions. As stated, the ordinary regions have the obligation to establish an advisory body to include the municipalities in the regional decision-making process (Article 123 of the Constitution). It is important to underline that the institution is implemented very differently throughout the country. As mentioned before, regions had to introduce a Council of Local Authorities (CALs) in their respective statute to ensure a formal consultation mechanism between the subnational and the local level. As foreseen by constitutional law, all CALs are regulated in the statutes of the respective ordinary regions. The exceptions are the five special regions which regulate the intergovernmental institution in an ordinary law at provincial/regional level. The special Region of Aosta Valley was the first and is an innovative pioneer, having introduced an institution to encourage the participation of local authorities in regional policy already back in 1998. On the other hand, there is the special Region of Sicily which has to date no functional CAL—much to the chagrin of the regional ANCI and the Sicilian Association of Local Government Administrators. Since 2018, it only has a draft law to establish a so-called "regional council of local autonomies". Albeit Sicily has at least another institution of cooperation, the so called a "Conference Region-Local Autonomies" since 2002 which was established by decree of the President of the Region as a means of liaison between the Region and local government executives. Members are representatives of the regional government as well as of local authorities. The remaining special regions and the autonomous provinces of Trento and Bolzano/Bozen have established the institutions between 2005 and 2010. Looking at the situation in the ordinary regions, the implementation of the CALs leads to the assumption that not much importance is given to intergovernmental cooperation with the municipalities by the regional level. The fact that some regions have not yet introduced the CAL or that it is not active at all tells a lot about the (limited) weight the local authorities enjoy. Though all ordinary Regions introduced the institution in their statute, it took several years for the adaption of the respective regional laws (see Table 10.3; Zuddas, 2005; Di Carpegna Brivio, 2018). The first two Regions following the national regulation were Piedmont and Apulia which introduced the institutions already in 2006. We do not count the Region of Toscana which established a representative organ for local authorities, similar to the Aosta Valley, already years before and therefore without top-down initiative by the state. In contrast to these trailblazers, there are

Table 10.3 The CALs and other institutions of liaison in the Italian regions and autonomous provinces

Region or Autonomous Province	Year of foundation (regional law)	Operational	Number of members	Number of meetings in 2023 or 2022
Abruzzo	2007	Yes	20	2023: 1
Basilicata	2021	No	24	–
Calabria	2016	Yes	32	2023: 1
Campania	2011	No	40	–
Emilia Romagna	2009, 2012	Yes	36	2023: 13
Friuli Venezia Giulia	2006	Yes	22	2023: 16
Lazio	2007	Yes	40	2023: 1
Liguria	2011	Yes	30	2023: 9
Lombardia	2009	Yes	45	No data
Marche	2007	Yes	30	No data
Molise	1999 (not a CAL but a Conference of local autonomies)	No	–	–
Piemonte	2006	Yes	29	2023: 18
Puglia	2006	No	57	–
Sardegna	2005	Yes	32	No data
Sicilia	2002 (not a CAL but a Standing Conference Region-Local Autonomies); CAL: draft law only	No	–	–
Toscana	2000	Yes	50	2023: 12
Aut. Prov. Trento	2010	Yes	31	2023: 31
Aut. Prov. Bolzano/Bozen	2010	Yes	17	2023: 35
Umbria	2008	Yes	41	2023: 12
Val d'Aosta	1998 (not a CAL but a permanent Council of local entities); 2017	Yes	83	2022: 16
Veneto	2017	Yes	24	2023: 20

Source: Own elaboration based on official websites of the regional CALs

also regions which still do not have a functioning CAL. For instance, Basilicata adopted the respective regional law only in 2021.

Regarding their composition and tasks, the CALs are heterogenous. As Table 10.3 shows, the regional CALs has between 17 (Autonomous Province of Bolzano) and 83 members (Autonomous Region of Aosta Valley). The high number of members in the Aosta Valley CAL is due to the fact that each mayor of the 74 municipalities is granted representation. In most regions the majority of the members are representatives of the local executives, e.g. mayors or presidents of the provinces. The mayors are mostly members by law (e.g. the mayor of a certain capital city), while other mayors are elected, either only by a mayors' assembly or an election which also includes local councilors. The latter obviously means stronger participation and more democracy. In some regions attention is also given to the inclusion of local councilors in the CALs and therefore integrating more political plurality in the advisory organs. As an example, the Region of Liguria includes several presidents of the local councils and the Region of Apulia (even if the CAL is not active) would foresee a number of members who are elected by the local councilors with lists at provincial level. The Autonomous Province of Trento even includes the president of the provincial association of municipalities. Also the composition of other CALs indicates a central role at regional level for the associations representing local entities, especially the ANCI. In many CALs the representatives of the regional ANCI, UPI or other organizations (UNCEM, ANPCI) are members. Representatives of the regional ANCI can be direct members of the CAL (e.g. Lombardy) or have at least the right to participate in its meetings (e.g. Abruzzo). This shows the importance of networking and the strong connection between the local authorities and their regional representative institutions. An even closer connection can be observed in the Autonomous Province of Bolzano where the member of the provincial CAL, the so-called "Council of Municipalities", are exactly the same persons as in the council of the provincial association representing the municipalities. The regional ANCI in Liguria also has a pivotal role in collaborating with the CAL. It is determined by regional law that it supports the CAL with an operational structure.

The regions also attach importance to a balance between the various interests of municipalities within the Council of Local Autonomies. In many CALs (e.g. Lazio, Umbria) the representation of both larger municipalities and smaller municipalities is guaranteed, as a certain number of elected mayors has to come from municipalities within a specific range of population (the thresholds vary). In many cases, the larger municipalities correspond to the capital cities of the provinces whose mayors are usually compulsory members (e.g. Marche). In other CALs the mayor of the capital city of the region has also an automatic membership (e.g. the Mayor of Milan or Venice in the CALs of Lombardy and Veneto, respectively). In addition to the different types of municipalities according to population, some CALs also take the geographical position of the municipalities into consideration. In the CALs of Abruzzo and Calabria the members consist, on the one hand, of the presidents of the provinces and the mayors of the capital cities of the provinces and, on the other hand, also of members elected by all mayors of the non-capital municipalities. Some CALs (e.g. Lazio) even include representatives of the mountain communities, thereby guaranteeing also these small local authorities a voice.

As to the tasks, empirical research confirms that the CALs have several functions which are very similar throughout Italy. They are organs of representation, consultation and coordination. In this sense, the CALs have advisory functions for the regional parliament and government as well as proposing, monitoring and informative ones. The concrete activities include not only compulsory statements on regional draft laws or acts concerning the functioning, tasks or interests of local authorities but can also concern legislative initiatives or the possibility to make proposals to the regional government or parliament. In most regions, the CALs have the mandatory task to express itself on regional laws or modifications of the statute which concern local authorities or the allocation of competences between regions and municipalities. However, these opinions are of advisory nature. Many CALs are also requested to make a statement on the regional financial planning document. Some have additional functions: For example, in Liguria and Marche they have a legislative initiative. In Calabria, Lazio or Veneto, the institution may be called upon to make agreements with local entities on relevant issues related to local autonomy. Others (e.g. Abruzzo) can nominate experts for different regional institutions. Some CALs (e.g. Veneto, Emilia Romagna and Sardegna) also have the possibility of a joint meeting with the regional parliament.

A last issue concerns the political autonomy of the CALs. The case of the Region of Abruzzo shows that at the meetings also members of the regional government have the right to participate. This can guarantee, on the one hand, a close collaboration between local entities and the regional governments and can provide a direct channel of communication for the local authorities. On the other hand, one could argue that municipalities are thus "under control" and maybe influenced by the regional executives.

Lastly, the CALs also vary in their yearly activity and as a consequence in their political weight within a certain region. The research shows that some institutions are very active and meet more than once a month (e.g. Friuli Venezia Giulia with 16 meetings or the Autonomous Province of Bolzano/Bozen with 35 meetings in 2023). Others seem to play only a limited role within the decision-making process as they meet less or have at least none or very rare information on their websites. This shows a weak organizational structure and also less political relevance. The fact that for many of the CALs no data is available regarding their activity in the last 2 years (2022–2023) can be seen as an indicator for limited activity or at least low transparency. Given the number of meetings which goes from 1 to 31 it can be concluded that there exists a huge heterogeneity. Also previous research confirmed that the CALs, so far, have played a rather marginal role in decision-making, at least in the Regions with ordinary statute (Di Carpegna Brivio, 2018). However, interestingly, the CALs of some regions (Lazio, Marche, Sardegna, Toscana, Umbria) established in 2012 a Permanent Coordination Body in order to promote inter-regional collaboration between the institutions, as well as to exchange experiences and best practices.

10.5 Conclusions

The main conclusions that we reached on the topic of intergovernmental relations involving local authorities in Italy can be summarized in three points.

First, the chapter demonstrates that the involvement of local authorities in the decision-making process in Italy is formally acknowledged through mechanisms such as the conference system and CALs, which, however, are not stipulated in the constitution. CALs are at least mentioned in the regional statutes. The rationale behind the establishment of the conferences as well as CALs is very important, as their aim is to reinforce the position of local authorities in intergovernmental relations, giving the latter an official voice regarding policies that concern them (but not only). These institutions provide therefore important platforms for the representation of the local actors in the territorial system and guarantee them visibility and possibilities to voice their opinions. But they also offer formal options of exchange and collaboration with other levels of government (Alber et al., 2024). Thus, they strengthened the position of the local level of government.

Nonetheless, the actual impact of the conferences and CALs on the national and regional policy making is questionable, as their role typically involves non-binding recommendations and is therefore limited to advisory function. In spite of their potentially crucial role granted by law, the conferences are in fact criticized as being limited to discussing relatively minor technical issues instead of big policy issues and as being imbalanced in terms of power. This is underlined by the fact that the Prime Minister (or the delegated minister) chairs both conferences and sets the agenda. Furthermore, the opinions of the conferences are not binding, with the consequence that they are frequently ignored by the national government. Only agreements have to be unanimous and therefore create obligations for the government. Only they play a more direct role in shaping the substance of legislative acts, making any departure from an agreed-upon normative act legally problematic. But, compared to opinions, they are less frequently used. Arguably even more problematic is the fact that there is no mechanism for verifying compliance with what was agreed upon. In fact, as some scholars have pointed out, it was only the Covid-19 pandemic which eventually seems to have prompted the national government to take the conference system more seriously (Bolgherini & Lippi, 2022). Even if the formal integration of local entities into the legislative process contributes to the strengthening of local autonomy (D'Orlando & Grisostolo, 2018, p. 152), it clearly emerges in our chapter that the value local authorities could add to the decision making in Italy is not fully realized.

As regards the CALs, they are often inactive or barely operational even if the formal basis exists to guarantee the local authorities a specific role in regional decision-making. There are even two regions which did not introduce the institution formally. The additional value of the CALs does not only lie in the inclusion of local governments in regional policy-making but also in bringing together political representatives from heterogenous territories with specific challenges within the same region (urban/rural dichotomy, size, economic strength). The fact that many CALs, over 20 years after their formal introduction, do not operate shows that not all regions value the potential local authorities can add to make decision-making more inclusive and therefore in the long term sustainable. On the other hand, there are some regions which have a very active CAL elaborating many positions and statements.

As a second point the chapter underlines the central position of politicians in developing and shaping the relations between the state, regions and municipalities. There are two dimensions of political access and representation of local interests in Italy, i.e. through the formal channels such as the conference system and CALs and through (party-)political informal channels. This is particularly true for mayors of major Italian cities who became increasingly visible in the public arena over the last years, influencing the political agenda at national level and ending the career as mayor in favor of a run in national elections. The important role of mayors is also seen within intergovernmental relation mechanisms, as they have an almost purely executive representation. This is especially the case for the conferences (mayors), whereas in the CALs representatives from the local councils are sometimes involved besides the mayors and other representatives. However, it seems that the capacity of a territory to effectively influence intergovernmental relations heavily relies on political leadership and capacity.

Thirdly, our chapter shows that urban areas are disproportionately represented in intergovernmental bodies, despite the fact that 70% of municipalities have fewer than 5000 inhabitants (Klotz, 2024). This imbalance is shown due to the significant roles that mayors of major cities hold in the conference system, as well as within most of the CALs (even if some CALs also reserve seats for mayors of small and/or rural municipalities). In addition, a challenge for local authorities in general remains to speak with one voice vis-à-vis the regional or national level of governance. The broad spectrum of different views on specific policies by local governments from urban and rural territories might be not visible. As a result, they focus on political contacts with other government levels through ANCI or outside of it.

To conclude, there has not been for many years at the national level a legal change or development in formal intergovernmental relations which is true for the conferences and the CALs. However, the political influence by local actors increased in practice (Bolgherini et al., 2018). This reliance on leadership can make intergovernmental relations quite fragile, as they depend on leaders' ability and the duration of their term in office. While waiting for a comprehensive reform to take place that gives voice to all types of local authorities in a uniform way and take the opinions of local authorities more seriously into account, a better dialogue, coordination and cooperation between government levels could be reached by increasing the use of the agreements within the conference system and by implementing well-functioning CALs in all regions.

References

Alber, E., Valdesalici, A., & Klotz, G. (2024). Italy. In N. Steytler (Ed.), *The Forum of Federations' handbook on local government in federal systems* (pp. 281–312). Palgrave Macmillan.

Bifulco, R. (2006). Il modello italiano delle conferenze Stato-autonomie territoriali (anche) alla luce delle esperienze federali. *Le Regioni*, 2–3, 233–268.

Bilancia, P. (2001). Verso un federalismo cooperativo? In G. Marchetti et al. (Eds.), *Problemi del federalismo* (pp. 67–85). Giuffré.

Bin, R., & Falcon, G. (2012). *Diritto regionale*. il Mulino.

Bin, R., & Ruggiu, I. (2006). La rappresentanza territoriale in Italia. Una proposta di riforma del sistema delle conferenze, passando per il definitivo abbandono del modello Camera delle Regioni. *Le Istituzioni del Federalismo, 6*, 903–954.

Bolgherini, S. (2015). *Navigando a vista. Governi locali in Europa tra crisi e riforme*. Il Mulino.

Bolgherini, S., Di Giulio, M., & Lippi, A. (2018). From the change of the pattern to the change in the pattern: The trilateral game in the Italian intergovernmental relations. *European Policy Analysis, 4*(1), 48–71.
Bolgherini, S., & Lippi, A. (2022). Dal Giano bifronte al baricentro statale. Le relazioni intergovernative tra Stato e Regioni in Italia nel primo biennio della pandemia. In F. Palermo & S. Parolari (Eds.), *Le tendenze del decentramento* (pp. 269–293). ESI.
Carloni, E., & Cortese, F. (2020). *Diritto delle autonomie territoriali.* Wolters Kluwer.
Carpani, G. (2009). La collaborazione strutturata tra Regioni e tra queste e lo Stato: Nuovi equilibri e linee evolutive dei raccordi "verticali" ed "orizzontali". *federalismi.it, 20.* Retrieved April 20, 2024, from https://www.federalismi.it/nv14/articolo-documento.cfm?Artid=14154&content=&content_author=
Carrozza, P. (1989). Principio di collaborazione e sistema delle garanzie procedurali (la via italiana al regionalismo cooperativo). *Le Regioni, 2*, 473–509.
Ceccherini, E. (2009). Intergovernmental relations in Italy: The permanent state-regions-autonomous provinces conferences. *Revista de la Facultad de Ciencias Sociales y Juridicas de Elche, 1*(4), 216–238.
Conferenza Stato-città ed autonomie locali. (2023). *Rapporto di fine anno 2022.* Retrieved April 20, 2024, from http://www.conferenzastatocitta.it/home/conferenza/attivita/rapporti-annuali/rapporto-di-fine-anno-2022/
Conferenza Stato-città ed autonomie locali. (2024a). *Rapporto di fine anno 2023.* Retrieved April 20, 2024, from http://www.conferenzastatocitta.it/home/conferenza/attivita/rapporti-annuali/rapporto-di-fine-anno-2023/
Conferenza Stato-città ed autonomie locali. (2024b). *Rapporto di fine anno 2014–2023.* Retrieved April 20, 2024, from www.conferenzastatocitta.it
D'Orlando, E., & Grisostolo, F. E. (2018). La disciplina degli enti locali tra uniformità e differenziazione. In F. Palermo & S. Parolari (Eds.), *Le variabili della specialitá* (pp. 99–159). Edizioni scientifiche italiane.
Del Prete, F. (2020). L'attuazione del principio di leale collaborazione nella prassi della Conferenza Stato-Regioni. *Le Istituzioni del Federalismo, 1*, 69–99.
Di Carpegna Brivio, D. E. (2018). Il CAL tra sogno e realtà. Problemi attuali delle istituzioni di raccordo nel sistema regionale delle fonti. *federalismi.it, 5.* Retrieved April 20, 2024, from https://www.federalismi.it/nv14/articolo-documento.cfm?Artid=35863
Klotz, G. (2024). *Interkommunale Zusammenarbeit im Alpenraum: Die lokalen Dienstleistungen in Graubünden, Südtirol und Tirol.* Peter Lang.
Ladner, A., Keuffer, N., Baldersheim, H., Hlepas, N., Swianiewicz, P., Steyvers, K., & Navarro, C. (2019). *Patterns of local autonomy in Europe*. Palgrave Macmillan.
Lippi, A. (2011). Evaluating the "quasi federalist" programme of decentralisation in Italy since the 1990s: A side-effect approach. *Local Government Studies, 37*(5), 495–516.
Palermo, F. (2021). Asymmetries in the Italian regional system and their role model. In E. Arban, G. Martinico, & F. Palermo (Eds.), *Federalism and constitutional law. The Italian contribution to comparative regionalism* (pp. 136–151). Routledge.
Palermo, F., & Kössler, K. (2017). *Comparative federalism: Constitutional arrangements and case law*. Hart Publishing.
Rolla, G. (2003). Il difficile equilibrio tra autonomia e unità nel regionalismo italiano. In G. Rolla (Ed.), *La definizione del principio unitario negli ordinamenti decentrati* (pp. 1–16). Giappichelli.
Valdesalici, A., & Trettel, M. (2023). The system of local government in Italy: A stress-test to traditional paradigms? In M. Nicolini & A. Valdesalici (Eds.), *Local governance in multi-layered systems—A comparative legal study in the federal-local connection* (pp. 261–282). Springer.
Villamena, S. (2013). Italy—Organisation and responsibilities of the local authorities in Italy between unity and autonomy. In C. Panara & M. Varney (Eds.), *Local government in Europe. The "fourth level" in the EU multi-layered system of governance* (pp. 183–230). Routledge.

Woelk, J. (2021). Loyal cooperation. Systemic principle of Italy's regionalism. In E. Arban, G. Martinico, & F. Palermo (Eds.), *Federalism and constitutional law. The Italian contribution to comparative regionalism* (pp. 170–188). Routledge.

Zuddas, P. (2005). *Organi e procedure di consultazione di enti locali e forze sociali, I Consigli delle autonomie locali istituti dai nuovi Statuti regionali.* ISSiRFA, Istituto di Studi sui sistemi regionali federali e sulle autonomie, Rapporto sulla legislazione delle Regioni (2004–2005).

Open Access This chapter is licensed under the terms of the Creative Commons Attribution 4.0 International License (http://creativecommons.org/licenses/by/4.0/), which permits use, sharing, adaptation, distribution and reproduction in any medium or format, as long as you give appropriate credit to the original author(s) and the source, provide a link to the Creative Commons license and indicate if changes were made.

The images or other third party material in this chapter are included in the chapter's Creative Commons license, unless indicated otherwise in a credit line to the material. If material is not included in the chapter's Creative Commons license and your intended use is not permitted by statutory regulation or exceeds the permitted use, you will need to obtain permission directly from the copyright holder.

Chapter 11
The Joint Commission of the Government and Territorial Self-Government in Poland

Andżelika Mirska

Abstract The effectiveness and legitimacy of democratic governance in modern states depend critically on the government's ability to coordinate decision-making processes in the environment of ever-changing urban-rural relations. Moreover, policy-making at national and subnational levels undeniably necessitates both horizontal and vertical coordination. However, the strategies for establishing legal frameworks and practical approaches to coordination across levels of government and across territorial units can vary greatly between countries. The legal solutions that Poland has adopted in this field are quite specific and deserve an in-depth analysis. The Joint Commission of the Government and Territorial Self-Government provides a platform for representing the interests of the three levels of local government towards the central government as well as a forum for articulating the positions, problems and needs of rural, urban and metropolitan local governments. The aim of this analysis is to present the concept and model of intergovernmental coordination in a decentralized unitary state as well as the role of local government organizations for the functioning of the Joint Commission.

Keywords Joint Commission of the Government and Territorial Self-Government · Intergovernmental relations · Horizontal coordination · Vertical coordination · Poland · Umbrella organizations

---

A. Mirska (✉)
Faculty of Political Science and International Studies, University of Warsaw, Warsaw, Poland
e-mail: amirska@uw.edu.pl

© The Author(s) 2026

K. Kössler, E. M. Belser (eds.), *Local Government Structure and Intergovernmental Relations*, Local and Urban Governance,
https://doi.org/10.1007/978-3-031-99820-1_11

11.1 Introduction

One of the hallmarks of Poland's political-administrative system is the institutionalization of intergovernmental relations in the form of a body called the Joint Commission of the Government and Territorial Self-Government[1] (hereinafter: the Joint Commission). One of the elements of a well-functioning state is the coordination of decision-making processes, cooperation, sharing information and ensuring its flow between territorial units, as well as between different levels of government. The establishment of well-functioning coordination mechanisms, both horizontal and vertical, determines the effectiveness and legitimacy of democratic governance. The aim of the Joint Commission is first to provide channels for vertical coordination—to make it possible for local government to influence the actions of the central government (Izdebski, 2013). At the same time, the Joint Commission has become a forum for horizontal coordination, as it brings together all three levels of local government and various categories of local government units: rural, urban-rural, urban and metropolitan municipalities.

In order to show the Joint Commission's role and importance in the political system, it is necessary to first outline the specific nature of the Polish state, that is, the historical, political and administrative context which determined the establishment of this body, its role and position in the political system, its competences, internal organization and operating procedures.

The decision to establish this specific mechanism for the coordination of interests between the central government and the local government was part of the systemic concept of the Polish state, which was shaped by the process of a systemic transformation initiated in 1989. Its central feature was the deep decentralization of the state and the creation of an extensive local government administration (Lipowicz, 2010). Municipal self-government began to function as early as 1990, while county self-government was introduced in 1999 as the second level of local government, along with the voivodeships as institutions of regional self-government. Poland's population is today not very heterogenous in terms of nationality and ethnicity[2] so that one major factor, in many other countries, for establishing autonomous regions has been absent.[3] Thus, Poland is a unitary state with three levels of local government.

The Polish Constitution of 1997 enshrines the principles of subsidiarity and decentralization of the public power and provides legal guarantees for local government as a part of the executive power and an expression of local democracy. Article 16(2) of the Constitution is of crucial importance as it states that "local government shall participate in the exercise of public power. The substantial part of public duties which local government is empowered to discharge by statute shall be done in its

[1] In Polish: *Komisja Wspólna Rządu i Samorządu Terytorialnego*.

[2] The results of the 2021 census indicate that 97.7% of all Polish residents self-identify as Polish. See: National Population and Housing Census 2021, Preliminary results of the National Population Census 2021 in terms of national and ethnic structure as well as language of household contacts.

[3] There was one autonomous region in Poland (the Silesian Voivodeship) in the period 1920–1939.

own name and under its own responsibility." The Constitution enshrines the principle of the general authorization of local government to perform public tasks: "Local government shall perform public tasks not reserved by the Constitution or statutes to the organs of other public authorities" (Article 163). In accordance with the principle of subsidiarity, "the commune shall perform all tasks of local government not reserved to other units of local government" (Article 164(3)).

A characteristic feature of the Polish territorial-administrative system is that the number of levels of local government depends on the number of levels of basic territorial division. This follows from Article 16(1) of the Constitution: "The inhabitants of the units of basic territorial division shall form a self-governing community in accordance with law." In the period from 1990 to 1997, that is until the new Constitution was adopted, the basic territorial division consisted of two tiers, but local government functioned at only one level—the municipalities. There was no local government at the second level—the voivodeships. Currently, pursuant to Article 16(1) of the Constitution, such a situation is not possible. The decision on the number of tiers of the basic territorial division entails the obligation to create local government bodies elected by residents at each level of the basic territorial division. This means that the law which determines the number of tiers of the basic territorial division determines the depth of territorial decentralisation in Poland.

The current three-level basic territorial division of Poland was introduced by an ordinary law on January 1, 1999.[4] The territory of Poland is divided into three basic levels: voivodeships (provinces, Polish: *województwo*); these are divided into counties (*powiat*), and these, in turn, into municipalities (*gmina*). Thus, there is a local government at each level of basic territorial division, namely, municipality self-government, county self-government and voivodeship self-government.

Therefore, Poland has four levels of political representation of government: the central government and three levels of territorial self-government.

1. the central level: the Council of Ministers with the Prime Minister;
2. the voivodeship level (regional level): 16 voivodeships[5];
3. the county level (supra-municipal local level; intermediate level): 380 counties, including 66 cities with county rights;
4. the municipal level (basic local level): 2477 communes.[6]

[4] A three-level territorial division was in place in Poland in 1918–1975 (commune, county, voivodeship), followed in 1975–1999 by a two-level division, i.e. the division of the state into communes and voivodeships. Thus, the country returned to the pre-1975 tradition in 1999.

[5] According to the Eurostat classification, this is the NUTS 2 level. Currently, the number of NUTS 2 territorial units in Poland is 17 because in 2018, the voivodeship where the capital of Poland is located was divided into two separate NUTS 2 units.

[6] According to the Eurostat classification, the municipality level in Poland means local administrative units—LAU.

11.2 The Creation of the Joint Commission

Given the above and the fact that local governments do not have any legally obligatory representation at the central level, establishing the Joint Commission as mechanism for their interaction with the central government, represented by the prime minister as head of the Council of Ministers, was of considerable importance. The Constitution guarantees local governments the right of association but only on a voluntary basis (Article 172). During the process of systemic transformation, there was a proposal for the upper house of the Polish parliament (the Senate) to act as the representation of local government (Osiński, 2010; Radomski, 2019) and the Joint Commission put forward a similar proposal in 2010 during broad consultations on local government reforms. However, no such solution was adopted, and in 1993 the Joint Commission was established as a special subsidiary body of the Council of Ministers to provide a platform for cooperation and discussion between the two segments of public authority. Undoubtedly, Poland's ratification of the European Charter of Local Self-Government in 1993 was an important circumstance that accompanied the decision to establish this body (Gawłowski, 2019b). According to Article 4(6) of the Charter, "local authorities shall be consulted, insofar as possible, in due time and in an appropriate way in the planning and decision-making process of matters which concern them directly."

Between 1993 and 2005, the Joint Commission functioned under an internal order of the prime minister and then regulations by the Council of Ministers. The Joint Commission received a stable legal basis with the enactment of the Act of May 6, 2005, on the Joint Commission of Government and Territorial Self-Government and on Representatives of the Republic of Poland in the Committee of the Regions of the European Union (hereinafter: Act of 2005). This was related to Poland's accession to the European Union, as it became necessary to specify the method of selecting Polish representatives to the Committee of the Regions of the European Union. Therefore, a decision was taken to include these two issues in a single act: to regulate the manner of selecting local government representation in relations with the Polish government and in relations with the European Union.

11.3 The Composition of the Joint Commission

As for the composition of the Joint Commission, the rule is that both sides are represented by the same number of members. Until 2023, the Commission had 24 members: 12 representatives of the central government and 12 representatives of local government. Since the Act of 2005 was amended in 2023, it has had 32 members: 16 representatives of the central government and 16 representatives of local government.

The central government is represented in the Joint Commission by the minister for public administration and 15 government representatives who are appointed and dismissed by the prime minister at this minister's request. These people serve as secretaries and undersecretaries of state in various ministries, so that they are *de facto* deputy ministers.

It was a much more complicated issue to determine how local government representatives should be selected. The Act of 2005 used the term "nationwide organizations of local government units", which have the right to appoint their representatives to the Joint Commission. However, another issue was to specify which "nationwide organizations" would have the right to delegate their representatives. This was resolved in the Act of 2005 by listing the following categories of such organizations:

1. One nationwide organization that represents the voivodeship self-government;
2. One nationwide organization that represents the county self-government;
3. Four nationwide organizations at the municipality level, which reflect four different types of communes in Poland: municipalities with more than 300,000 inhabitants (urban units); municipalities with city status (urban units); municipalities which include both cities within administrative boundaries and areas outside city boundaries (urban-rural units) and municipalities that do not have any city within their boundaries (rural units).

The 2023 amendment to the Act of 2005 added two more categories of local government organizations which have the right to delegate two representatives each to the Joint Commission. These are:

1. A nationwide organization that represents all three levels of local government units (municipalities, counties, voivodeships) and has at least 100 members;
2. A nationwide organization that represents umbrella organisations of self-government units (local and regional), meaning that the members of this organisation are not individual self-government units, but only associations of self-governments of different territorial scopes, e.g. the Silesian Union of Communes and Counties or the Association of Communes of the South-Western Mazovian Region.

Organizations which fulfil these criteria may submit requests to the prime minister to be recognized and entitled to appoint their representatives to the Joint Commission. If more than one organization applies, the law foresees that the one with the largest number of members (local government units affiliated to it) is selected by the Council of Ministers The government's decision takes the form of a regulation.

Currently, the following nationwide local government organizations are members of the Joint Commission with each of them having the right to delegate two representatives:

1. At the voivodeship level, this is the Association of Voivodeships of the Republic of Poland, which brings together all 16 voivodeship self-governments;
2. At the county level: the Association of Polish Counties, which brings together 321 counties (there are 314 counties and 66 cities with county rights in Poland);

3. At the municipal level, Poland has 2477 municipalities, including 302 urban municipalities, 677 urban-rural municipalities and 1498 rural municipalities. The following four organizations have their representatives on the Joint Commission:
   - The Union of Polish Metropolises, which brings together the 12 largest cities in Poland, nine of which have populations over 300,000;
   - The Association of Polish Cities, which brings together 355 urban municipalitities;
   - The Union of Small Polish Towns, with 52 members;
   - The Association of Rural Communes of the Republic of Poland, which includes 644 municipalities;
4. At all three levels of local government: the Association of Polish Local Governments, whose members include 144 municipalities, 24 counties and six voivodeship self-governments;
5. As an umbrella organization: the All-Poland Alliance of Local Government Organizations, which brings together eight self-government organizations.

If we look at Polish local government at the municipal level, it is indeed very diverse. This diversity is reflected in the fact that the Joint Commission includes representatives of four organizations which represent these diverse interests. Both rural and urban municipalities are represented, while the Union of Polish Metropolises shows a high degree of distinctiveness. Three organizations are very active and visible in the public forum (the Union of Polish Metropolises, the Association of Polish Cities and the Union of Rural Communes of Republic of Poland). A fourth organisation, the Union of Small Polish Towns, is slowly beginning to rebuild its position after a certain crisis illustrated by a decline in its membership.

11.4 The Internal Organization of the Commission

An important competence of the Joint Commission that demonstrates its independence from the central government is its power to adopt internal rules of procedure. Currently, it operates under the Resolution of the Joint Commission of the Government and Territorial Self-Government of 2006, on the Rules of Procedure of the Joint Commission of the Government and Territorial Self-Government, as amended in 2012, 2014 and 2022.

Two co-chairs are appointed to maintain the balance of power between the central government and local government in the Joint Commission. On the government side, this is always the minister for public administration. As for the co-chair from local government, the established practice is that this is a rotational post: each successive local government organization designates its representative to act as co-chair for a period of 8 months.[7]

The tasks of the co-chairs include chairing the Joint Commission's meetings, arranging the timetable of its work and determining the composition of the permanent and ad hoc task groups. They can also invite representatives of the government administration, local government and other organizations and institutions to participate in the work of the Joint Commission in an advisory capacity. Practice has shown that the Joint Commission is very keen to invite and cooperate with other entities. The co-chair of the Commission who represents the central government has an additional competence: he/she may, on their own initiative or at the request of the other co-chair, appoint experts and commission them to provide opinions and expert reports to the Joint Commission.

The Joint Commission meets in plenary sessions and task groups. According to Article 14 of the Act of 2005, plenary meetings of the Joint Commission should be held when necessary, but at least once every 2 months. Practice has shown that the Joint Commission meets once a month, usually on the last Wednesday of the month.[8] The task groups may be permanent or *ad hoc*. They play an important role, as this is where the day-to-day, substantive work is carried out, mainly with regard to giving opinions on draft legislation. The task groups convene when necessary.

Eleven permanent task groups currently operate under the Joint Commission. These include the Rural Affairs Group, which demonstrates that the Joint Commission, since its inception, has been aware of the distinctiveness of rural local governments, which constitute the majority in Poland. The intensifying process of urbanization and the need to find solutions to the problems of public governance in functional areas of cities have also been reflected in the Commission's internal structure. In 2012 it established the Group for the System of Local Government, Urban and Metropolitan Areas. The other task groups are:

1. The Group for International Affairs, European Union and Regional Policy;
2. The Group for the Public Finance System;
3. The Group for Education, Culture and Sport;
4. The Group for Health and Social Policy;
5. The Group for Infrastructure, Urban Planning and Transport;
6. The Group for Public Administration and Citizen Security;
7. The Group for Information Society;
8. The Group for Public Statistics.
9. The Group for Energy, Climate and Environment was established in 2022.

Regarding the composition of the task groups on the side of local government, each local government organization has the right to delegate one member to each team. It is standard practice that alternates are also appointed to the task groups. For

[7] Information on the website of the Association of Polish Cities, https://www.miasta.pl/strony/komisja-wspolna-rzadu-i-samorzadu-terytorialnego-kwrist (20.09.2023).

[8] The website with current information on the Joint Commission: https://www.gov.pl/web/kwrist-mswia

example, the Association of Polish Counties has appointed between one and 12 alternates to each task group. Another question is who the people are that are delegated to the Joint Commission and to the individual task groups from the local government side. They are most often from the local government executive (mayor), less often a member of the decision-making body (chairman of the council or council member), and very rarely local government officials.

The Commission may also establish *ad hoc* task groups. Importantly, the Joint Commission may appoint outside members to permanent and *ad hoc* task groups. One example of an ad hoc committee is the Committee on the National Recovery Plan, which was established in 2021. The National Recovery Plan is the basis for tapping into the funds from NextGenerationEU. Each member state had to prepare and submit a document to the European Commission. In Poland, the National Recovery Plan comes in the form of a government resolution, which is not subject to further legislative procedure in parliament.

The Ministry of Public Administration provides organizational, technical as well as clerical and office services for the Joint Commission, its teams, and secretariat. The costs of financing the services are covered by the central government budget (Article 15(3) of the Act of 2005).

11.5 The Tasks of the Commission and Decision-Making Procedure

The tasks of the Joint Commission are defined very broadly. First of all, the Act of 2005 defines the Commission as a "forum for working out common positions of the government and local government" on matters related to the functioning of local government and central government policy towards local authorities, as well as matters concerning local government that fall within the remit of the European Union and international organizations of which Poland is a member.

The scope of the Joint Commission's activities primarily includes analyzing and giving opinions on draft legislation, programs and other government documents that concern local government, especially financial issues. This competence does not only derive from the Act of 2005, but has been included in the rules of procedure of the Polish Parliament—the Sejm. The obligation to consult the Joint Commission has also been included in the rules of procedure of the Council of Ministers. Another very important field of the Commission's activity is reviewing and evaluating the existing law on the functioning of local government. This concerns both Polish and European Union law, in particular provisions on the financing of local government, including additional funding from the European Union. The Joint Commission considers matters submitted by members of the Council of Ministers and other government bodies, the Commission's co-chairs, and standing and ad hoc task groups. The Act of 2005 also contains a general mandate for each party to the Joint Commission (the central government and local government) to "take a position" on any matter relating to local government issues, as well as to request the other party to take up a matter that it considers to be relevant to local government issues.

The Act of 2005 uses the term ‘agree’ to regulate the Commission’s operating and decision-making procedures. Article 7(1) of the Act expressly states that “the Joint Commission expresses an opinion that is agreed by both parties to the Commission.” However, an opinion may contain separate statements on specific issues. Conversely, in the absence of consensus, each party adopts its own statement on the matter under discussion. In cases where separate regulations require the opinion of the Joint Commission or the opinion of the Commission’s local government side on a draft normative act or any other document, the deadline for expressing an opinion on such a draft is 30 days from the date of its delivery. Failure to submit an opinion within this deadline means that the right to express an opinion is waived.

11.6 Conclusions: An Assessment of the Joint Commission’s Importance

The Joint Commission, which has been functioning continuously for 30 years, is a stable and fully accepted element of the Polish political-administrative system (Gawłowski, 2015; Mirska, 2021). This mechanism of dialogue is particularly important for local government, which performs an enormous number of public tasks. However, the Commission’s functioning and, above all, financing are determined by the decisions of the central government. However, the Act of 2005 obliges the ministry of public administration to provide the Joint Commission with organizational and technical support. The costs are covered from the central government budget, from the part managed by the minister responsible for public administration. The very broadly defined field of action of the Joint Commission means that its voice should be present in many thematic areas. The central government’s legal obligation to consult draft normative acts with the Joint Commission makes it an indispensable part of decision-making processes in Poland (Gawłowski, 2019a).

However, it should be noted that the Joint Commission’s opinions are not binding. While a positive opinion adds a sense of agreement in the activities of both segments of the executive power (the central government and local government), a negative opinion, though it sends a clear signal of dissonance in central government-local government relations, may be ignored by the central government. This means that it depends only on the goodwill of the central government whether the positions on central government policy towards local government developed in the Joint Commission will be considered. The Joint Commission has no sovereign powers, it cannot block government action, nor does it have a legislative initiative. It is nevertheless important that the Act of 2005, while imposing an obligation on the central government to consult the local government side, also strongly emphasizes the purpose of this obligation: reaching consensus on proposed legal solutions. However, the nature of cooperation between the central government and local government undoubtedly depends on the political parties that hold power at the central level, its attitude towards the principle of decentralization and ideas about the role of local government in the state (Adamowicz et al., 2009).

Therefore, the Joint Commission's powers mostly fall into the category of consultative and advisory powers, but they also have the qualities of control, evaluation, signalling, warning, and calling for changes. They have the quality of both *ex-ante* and *ex-post* evaluation of the actions of external entities that impact local government. This mainly refers to the actions of the Polish government and the European Union. However, the Joint Commission's main objective is to evaluate *ex-ante* the government's intentions towards the local government—that is, to assess whether the prepared normative acts are consistent with the expectations of local government and do not infringe upon the interests of local government.

In addition, the Joint Commission undoubtedly fulfils an important information function for local government units. The group of entities that have access to information on draft legislation expands thanks to the Joint Commission. It can be said that, on the one hand, the Joint Commission contributes to the dissemination of knowledge about the central government's activities among local government officials and ensures greater transparency in the central government's decision-making processes. The Commission can be regarded as an institution that monitors legislation and thus becomes a body for improving the quality of the legislative process, even if this results in longer legislative procedures.

The Joint Commission's information function is multiplied by the activities of the local government organizations that have their representatives on the Commission (Mirska, 2022, Mirska, 2021a). They provide information to their members and reach a wide audience by publishing reports from the Commission's meetings as well as their own positions, analyses, and comments on their websites.

It should be remembered that the Joint Commission was established in the initial phase of Poland's systemic transformation when the objective of the changes was clearly defined as a decentralized Poland with strong, extensive local government[9] but it was necessary to develop new systemic solutions. The Joint Commission represented a new quality in designing the reforms to decentralize the state, which were discussed with the stakeholders rather than imposed from above. The Joint Commission has been evaluated in a positive light as an example of good practices in a democratic state (Zachariasz, 2015).

However, like any long-standing institution, it is judged differently owing to different experiences, practices, achievements and changing political determinants. On the one hand, it is impossible to not to recognize the enormous contribution and labour input of the members of the Joint Commission (Mirska, 2023). On the other hand, there are certain aspects both in the formal construction of this body and the practice of its operation that may raise doubts regarding the function of this instrument in contemporary, politically polarized Poland (Adamowicz et al., 2009; Sularz, 2017).

[9] It is worth mentioning that already in the 1980s there were political programs prepared by the anti-communism opposition regarding the need to base the Polish political system on strong local government. "Self-Governing Poland" was the name of one of the chapters in the political program adopted on October 7, 1981 at the end of the first National Congress of Delegates of the Independent Self-Governing Trade Union "Solidarity".

Krzysztof Iwańczuk, the chairman of the board of the Association of Rural Communes of the Republic of Poland and a member of the Joint Commission, confirmed that experts representing central government and local self-governments in the Committee must analyze draft legal acts and their possible consequences for the functioning of the local self-government. Iwańczuk noted that there are a lot of legislative projects in Poland. Every month, about 30–60 draft legal acts are submitted to the Commission. These projects are of very different importance, from minor issues to those of fundamental character. There are also issues which remain important for the self-government and, regardless of who exercised central authority, they were and are resolved contrary to the expectations of the self-government. The effectiveness of the Commission is differentiated. There are some problems which have been discussed for a long time, such as the necessary reform of local self-government revenues—but no progress has been made (Mirska, 2023).

Another topic that has been discussed at the Commission for years is the education financing model, which is very negatively assessed by local governments. However, despite the determination of local governments, a new education financing system has not yet been developed, which is the reason for the dissatisfaction of the local governments. This can be seen as an example of the Commission's ineffectiveness in reaching a compromise between the government and local governments.

Recently, the phenomenon of "bypassing" the Commission has intensified, i.e. more and more bills are submitted to the Sejm by groups of deputies, whereas the Commission may only issue opinions on bills proposed by the government (Mirska, 2023). Thus, a certain tendency was indicated, which, according to external observers, is also present in the central government's strategy towards the Joint Commission. Namely, draft laws that the government submits to the parliament must be subjected to broad consultations, including at the Joint Commission. However, a draft law prepared by the central government can also be submitted by a group of Members of Parliament and then does not have to be referred to the Joint Commission for an opinion (Przedańska & Szwast, 2019). Therefore, not only is the nature of these opinions for the central government non-binding but the central government may choose to bypass the Joint Commission, which may lead to a significant diminution of this mechanism, which was designed to achieve consensus. Some analysts believe that this situation has been intensifying in recent years and even leading to the marginalization of the Commission's role (Przedańska, 2021).

Another controversial issue of fundamental importance for the credibility of this institution is the problem of the representativeness of the Joint Commission (Przedańska & Szwast, 2019). Its legal construction assumes that local government is represented in the Joint Commission by nationwide local government organizations. The academic literature raises the issue that not all local government units are members of local government organizations that delegate representatives to the Joint Commission (Sularz, 2017). This means that the Joint Commission does not represent all local government units. It should be emphasized that the Constitution of the Republic of Poland guarantees the right of association, while membership in local government organizations is voluntary rather than compulsory. The problem of establishing a representation for all local government was considered at the beginning of the systemic transformation. During the formulation of a law on local government in 1990, an idea was put forward to establish an obligatory representation of local government under the name of the National Association of Municipalities. However, this did not happen due to opposition from the trade union 'solidarity' and local government politicians and activists (Mirska, 2023).

Obviously, opinions are divided on whether membership in a local government organization is advisable. Local government units not affiliated to any nationwide organization claim that this is not an effective representation of their interests. According to one local politician: "I do not want to pay a membership fee for an organization which does not represent me and does not respond to the problems I report." (Mirska, 2023).

On the other hand, the representative of a municipality that belongs to one of the local government organizations represented on the Joint Commission assessed its activities in a very positive way: "From the point of view of the member commune, the expert knowledge, lobbying activity and representation of the interests of the communes offered by the organization are important. The role of nationwide self-government organizations was especially visible during the pandemic: from lobbying organizations they changed into organizations supporting local self-governments with professional knowledge. Moreover, the more self-government is exposed to the processes of recentralization, the more such self-government organizations are needed. It also shows the currently increasing activity of the association—as a reaction to these processes. However, the question of representativeness of these organizations poses a challenge. Currently, about 50% of local self-government units in Poland do not belong to any local self-government organization. Consequently, the question arises how to achieve a higher level of representativeness" (Mirska, 2023).

In 2023, the number of nationwide organizations representing local government in the Joint Commission increased by two, and their concept of membership is different from the one that was previously defined in the Act of 2005. Namely, organizations that bring together local government units of a specific category could be represented on the Joint Commission. The case of the Association of Polish Local Governments involves an organization that brings together local government units from all three levels of local government. The other organization that joined the Joint Commission is the All-Poland Alliance of Local Government Organizations. This is a completely new addition to the Joint Commission, as it is an umbrella organization that brings together regional government organizations rather than individual local government units.

The organizations that sit on the Joint Commission reacted negatively to the expansion of the Joint Commission's composition to include representatives of these two organizations. In their view, this disrupts the previously clear concept of representation of the local government side in the Joint Commission.[10]

[10] An appeal from the local government to the President of Poland not to sign the amendment to the Joint Commission Act, source: https://samorzad.pap.pl/kategoria/aktualnosci/apel-strony-samorzadowej-do-prezydenta-o-niepodpisywanie-noweli-ustawy-o (20.09.2013).

References

Adamowicz, M., Duklewski, P., Maciej, L., Mazur, J., Mazurek, J., Rosa, A., & Słowikowski, W. (2009). Współpraca administracji rządowej z administracją samorządową na przykładzie funkcjonowania Komisji Wspólnej Rządu i Samorządu Terytorialnego. In S. Mirosław (Ed.), *Współdziałanie administracji rządowej z administracją samorządową* (pp. 14–38). KSAP.

Gawłowski, R. (2015). Komisja Wspólna Rządu i Samorządu Terytorialnego—Od konsultacji do współudziału w rządowym procesie decyzyjnym. *Samorząd Terytorialny, 25*(12), 5–14.

Gawłowski, R. (2019a). *Między współpracą a przetargiem i rywalizacją Relacje rządowo-samorządowe w systemie administracji publicznej*. ASPRA.

Gawłowski, R. (2019b). Relacje rządowo-samorządowe z perspektywy Komisji Wspólnej Rządu i Samorządu Terytorialnego. In K. Karski & I. Wieczorek (Eds.), *Trzy dekady doświadczeń samorządu terytorialnego* (pp. 133–154). Narodowy Instytut Samorządu Terytorialnego.

Izdebski, H. (2013). Pozycja ustrojowa Komisji Wspólnej Rządu i Samorządu Terytorialnego. *Samorząd Terytorialny, 23*(12), 7–20.

Lipowicz, I. (2010). Verfassungsrechtliche Garantie der Selbstständigkeit der kommunalen Selbstverwaltung in Polen. In E. Šileikis (Ed.), *Verfassungsentwicklung in Litauen und Polen im Kontext der Europäisierung* (pp. 89–105). Lietuvos Mokslo Periodikos Asociacija.

Mirska, A. (2021). Institutionalizing intergovernmental relations in Poland. The Joint Commission of the Government and Territorial Self-Government. In A. Mirska (Ed.), *Local government in Poland: Responses to urban-rural challenges* (pp. 85–87). Zenodo. https://doi.org/10.5281/zenodo.5556111

Mirska, A. (2021a). The interface between subnational and national levels of government. The role of national local self-government organizations. In A. Mirska (Ed.), *Local government in Poland: Responses to urban-rural challenges* (pp. 94–100). Zenodo. https://doi.org/10.5281/zenodo.5556128

Mirska, A. (2022). *LoGov Poland Interview Report n°10 [Data set]*. Zenodo. https://doi.org/10.5281/zenodo.6499336

Mirska, A. (2023). *LoGov Poland Workshop Report n°1 [Data set]*. Zenodo. https://doi.org/10.5281/zenodo.10075817

Osiński, J. (2010). Constitution of the Republic of Poland as the Foundation of Democratic. *Society and State Warsaw Forum of Economic Sociology, 2*, 123–142.

Przedańska, J. (2021). Rola Komisji Wspólnej Rządu i Samorządu Terytorialnego w kształtowaniu zasad wsparcia finansowego dla jednostek samorządu terytorialnego w ramach Rządowego Funduszu Inwestycji Lokalnych. *Acta Universitatis Wratislaviensis* No 4058 PRAWO CCCXXXIII (pp. 414–426). https://doi.org/10.19195/0524-4544.333.27

Przedańska, J., & Szwast, M. (2019). Komisja Wspólna Rządu i Samorządu Terytorialnego–w stronę upodmiotowienia samorządu terytorialnego. *Ruch Prawniczy, Ekonomiczny i Socjologiczny, 4*, 165–178.

Radomski, G. (2019). The self-government constitutes an essential element of the civil security in polish political thought after 1989. *Polish Political Science Yearbook, 48*(2), 232–241. https://doi.org/10.15804/ppsy2019203

Sularz, P. (2017). Odrzucenie zasady reprezentatywności w Komisji Wspólnej Rządu i Samorządu Terytorialnego. Dialog rząd—Samorząd czy dialog rząd—Organizacje jednostek samorządu terytorialnego. *Przegląd Prawa Publicznego, 3*, 114–128.

Zachariasz, I. (2015). Geneza Komisji Wspólnej Rządu i Samorządu Terytorialnego. *Samorząd Terytorialny, 25*(12), 15–24.

Open Access This chapter is licensed under the terms of the Creative Commons Attribution 4.0 International License (http://creativecommons.org/licenses/by/4.0/), which permits use, sharing, adaptation, distribution and reproduction in any medium or format, as long as you give appropriate credit to the original author(s) and the source, provide a link to the Creative Commons license and indicate if changes were made.

The images or other third party material in this chapter are included in the chapter's Creative Commons license, unless indicated otherwise in a credit line to the material. If material is not included in the chapter's Creative Commons license and your intended use is not permitted by statutory regulation or exceeds the permitted use, you will need to obtain permission directly from the copyright holder.

Chapter 12
The Role of Local Authorities in Intergovernmental Conferences in South Africa

Nico Steytler

Abstract This role that local government plays in intergovernmental conferences is addressed at the hand of four interrelated questions: First, what is the formal place of local government within the legislative framework of intergovernmental relations? Secondly, how do local governments and organized local government perform their formal role in intergovernmental relations in practice? Thirdly, given the wide diversity of local governments, from very small local municipalities to mega-metropolitan municipalities, does the latter perform a different or separate role in intergovernmental relations? Finally, can local government's role in intergovernmental relations be improved, and if so, how? The chapter argues that the South African Constitution premises devolution upon the principles of sound intergovernmental relations and cooperative government, and that local government is an integral part of that system primarily through organized local government. Despite its strong place in the overall system, various factors hamper the fulfilment of that role. Moreover, organized local government finds it difficult to represent all categories of municipalities, particularly the large metropolitan municipalities. Finally, local government can do better in asserting its own voice in intergovernmental conferences, but that requires some adjustments to its functioning, as well as a change in attitude of provincial and national governments.

Keywords South Africa · Local government · Cooperative government · IGR · SALGA · Metropolitan municipalities

N. Steytler (✉)
Dullah Omar Institute, University of the Western Cape, Bellville, South Africa
e-mail: nsteytler@uwc.ac.za

© The Author(s) 2026

K. Kössler, E. M. Belser (eds.), *Local Government Structure and Intergovernmental Relations*, Local and Urban Governance,
https://doi.org/10.1007/978-3-031-99820-1_12

12.1 Introduction

As part of the constitutional negotiations to establish a non-racial democracy, limited federal arrangements were entrenched in the 1993 Constitution—nine provinces with concurrent powers only were established (Steytler, 2005b). In addition, local government was recognized as a constitutional institution with its own autonomy (*Fedsure Life Assurance Ltd and Others v Greater Johannesburg Transitional Metropolitan Council and Others.* (1) SA 374 (CC)). In the 1996 Constitution, the position of local government was enhanced by its recognition as "a sphere of government" alongside national and provincial governments (Steytler & de Visser, 2007, p. 1–14).

The new constitutional dispensation placed the exercise of devolution firmly within the value framework of cooperative government. The 1996 Constitution, in Chap. 3 on "Co-operative Government", provides that "[i]n the Republic, government is constituted as national, provincial and local spheres of government which are distinctive, interdependent and interrelated" (Section 40(1) of the Constitution). The new position of local government was a radical change from its pre-democratic status when municipalities were mere creatures of provincial or national statutes. Devolution was undergirded by the principles of cooperative government and intergovernmental relations (Sections 40(1) and 41(1) of the Constitution), resulting in a thick web of intergovernmental relations and structures to facilitate such relations.

This chapter focuses on the role that local government plays in intergovernmental conferences, or in the South African parlance, intergovernmental structures or forums. It poses four questions: First, what is the formal place of local government within the legislative framework of intergovernmental relations? This question includes the legislative recognition of the place and role of organized local government in such a framework. Secondly, how do local governments and organized local government perform their formal role in intergovernmental relations in practice? Thirdly, given the wide diversity of local governments, from very small local municipalities to mega-metropolitan municipalities, does the latter perform a different or separate role in intergovernmental relations? Finally, given the state of play, can local government's role in intergovernmental relations be improved, and if so, how?

It is argued that the Constitution premises devolution upon the principles of sound intergovernmental relations and cooperative government, and that local government is part and parcel of that system primarily through organized local government. Although local government has formally a strong place in the overall system, various factors hamper the fulfilment of that role. Moreover, organized local government, although constitutionally recognized, finds it difficult to represent all categories of municipalities, particularly the large metropolitan municipalities. Finally, local government can do better in asserting its own voice in intergovernmental engagements, but that requires some adjustments to its functioning, as well as a change in attitude of provincial and national governments.

The argument is presented in four sections. The first section sketches the broad constitutional architecture of cooperative government and intergovernmental relations, situating local government's place in this context. The second section focuses on the practice of intergovernmental relations and local government's role therein. The third section deals with the position of metropolitan municipalities as a distinct component of local government in intergovernmental relations. In the final section, some reflections are offered on how local government can better fulfil its constitutional role in the system of intergovernmental relations.

12.2 The Intergovernmental Constitutional and Legislative Architecture

As noted above, local government is an integral part of governing South Africa and is thus bound by the constitutional principles of intergovernmental and cooperative government (Section 40(2) of the Constitution). The most relevant principle is that of cooperative government: how the different spheres of government must work together for the greater good of the public as a whole.

12.2.1 Principle of Cooperative Government

Section 41(1)(h) of the Constitution defines the principle of cooperative government and the obligations that go along with it as follows:

> All spheres of government and all organs of state within each sphere must cooperate with one another in mutual trust and good faith by:
> (i) fostering friendly relations;
> (ii) assisting and supporting one another;
> (iii) informing one another of, and consulting one another on, matters of common interest;
> (iv) co-ordinating their actions and legislation with one another;
> (v) adhering to agreed procedures; and
> (vi) avoiding legal proceedings against one another.

In addition to the generic principle, the Constitution contains provisions that elaborate on the duty to assist and consult with local government. Section 154, with the heading "Municipalities in co-operative government", reads as follows:

1. The national government and provincial governments, by legislative and other measures, *must support and strengthen the capacity of municipalities* to manage their own affairs, to exercise their powers and to perform their functions.
2. Draft national or provincial legislation that affects the status, institutions, powers or functions of local government must be published for public comment before it is introduced in Parliament or a provincial legislature, in a manner that *allows*

organised local government, municipalities and other interested persons an opportunity to make representations with regard to the draft legislation. (emphasis added)

The duty to support in terms of cooperative government is very different from the obligation to assist in the context of provincial and national governments' supervisory functions. In the former, the relationship is one of equality, while in the latter it is hierarchical. Supervision comprises monitoring, support where mismanagement is detected, and intervention if the mismanagement continues.

In Section 154(2), the distinction between municipalities and organized local government is clearly drawn; the focus of consultation is first with organized local government—the collective of municipalities—before mentioning municipalities who act individually. The focus on organized local government is also pertinent when parliament seeks to adopt the annual division of revenue bill; it must first consult with the provinces and organized local government (Section 214(2)). Another prescribed consultation process is triggered when the national government seeks to assign functions to municipalities (Section 229(5)).

12.2.2 Organized Local Government

While the place of local government is increasingly recognized in federal constitutions, and references to organized local government are extremely rare,[1] the South African Constitution does so with a measure of detail. The institutionalization of organized local government was inevitable. As a partner in government, local government should have its own voice in the system and, in particular, in the various state institutions that perform an intergovernmental relations function.

Section 63 requires that an Act of Parliament must be enacted, providing "for the recognition of national and provincial organizations representing municipalities". It must also determine the procedures by which local government may "consult with the national or a provincial government". Finally, the Act must also provide how organised local government participates in two important intergovernmental relations structures. First, how should it designate representatives to participate in the National Council of Provinces (the second chamber of parliament) and nominate members to the Finance and Fiscal Commission, the body that advises on intergovernmental financial transfers.

The Organised Local Government Act of 1997, giving effect to Section 163 of the Constitution, requires the national minister responsible for local government to recognize one national association representing the majority of provincial associations, which, ex-ante, requires the recognition of the provincial associations, representing the majority of municipalities in a province, provided, though, that all the

[1] The Constitution of Austria recognizes organized local government as do some of Argentinian provincial constitutions (Steytler, 2023).

categories of municipalities (metropolitan, district, and local) are represented (Section 2(1)(b)). One of the goals of this body is 'to facilitate compliance with the principles of cooperative government and intergovernmental relations' (Section 3(d) Municipal Systems Act of 2000).

12.2.3 National Council of Provinces for Legislative Intergovernmental Relations

As a typical institution of shared rule in a federal system, the National Council of Provinces (NCOP) is the second chamber of parliament and represents the provinces. It has legislative, executive and appointment powers. Where national legislation affects provinces, it co-determines its adoption by a majority vote. Given provinces' supervisory role in respect of local government, legislation affecting local government is perforce also legislation affecting provincial interests. In *SAMWU v Minister of Cooperative Government and Traditional Affairs* 2917 (5) BCLR 641 (CC) the Constitutional Court invalidated the Municipal Structures Amendment Act 7 of 2011 because it was not adopted without following the correct legislative procedure which gives the NCOP a co-determinative role. When a conflict between the National Assembly (NA) (the popular chamber) and NCOP arises, the former can override the NCOP's veto with a two-thirds majority vote (Section 76). It also performs a "peer review" function when the national executive intervenes in a province (Section 100) and in the case of a provincial intervention in a municipality (Section 139(1)(b-c)). In the former case, the NCOP may play a protective role towards one of its own, while in the latter it may set the bar low when one province intervenes in a municipality.

Each provincial legislature sends a delegation of ten members, carrying provincially formulated mandates and each delegation has one vote. In this context, local government is somewhat accommodated. Almost as an afterthought, organized local government may have a delegation of ten non-voting members—a voice but not a vote. The ten members must be elected municipal councillors but may serve only part-time. Their participation is limited to matters "when necessary", which has been broadly interpreted by the NCOP's presiding officers to include any matter affecting local government, including legislation and provincial interventions in municipalities.

12.2.4 Financial and Fiscal Commission (FFC)

An independent finance commission is often seen as an integral component of a federal system, mandated with the task of ensuring the fair division of revenue raised nationally among the different orders of government. In South Africa, the

Finance and Fiscal Commission's (FFC) task is to advise Parliament on the division of revenue raised nationally between the three spheres of government as well as between provinces and municipalities (Section 214(1)(a)). While three members of the nine-person body are appointed by the president from a list prepared by the nine premiers, organized local government nominates two members (Section 221(2)). The local government nominees are not representatives of organized local government but act as independent experts. The FFC is not an ordinary IGR forum where stakeholders bargain and compromise on transfers, but seeks to produce an objective, non-political, set of recommendations. As such the appointees must be experts in the field of intergovernmental finances and should not act as advocates for the interests of their nominators.

12.2.5 Legislated Bodies for Executive Intergovernmental Relations

As noted above, the Constitution envisaged the statutory establishment of "structures and institutions to promote and facilitate intergovernmental relations" (Section 41(2)). After a delay of 8 years since the coming into operation of the 1996 Constitution in 1997, the Intergovernmental Relations Framework Act of 2005 (IGR Framework Act) was eventually included in the statute book. The delay was purposeful; the aim was to assess the practices of intergovernmental relations that had already emerged since the inception of the interim Constitution, before rushing into lawmaking.

The IGR Framework Act created an entire system of interlocking IGR structures and defined ways how IGR at an executive level should be conducted. Local government, in the shape of organized local government, has its ordained place. The Act has, however, been critiqued for displaying a rather a top-down coercive approach (Steytler, 2011). It is evident from the apex IGR body, the President's Coordinated Council, as well as other national platforms.

The President's Coordinating Council (PCC) is composed of:

1. the president;
2. the deputy president;
3. four national ministers;
4. the premiers of the nine provinces; and
5. a municipal councilor designated by organized local government.

The PPC is described as "a consultative forum *for* the president, who is also its chair and determines the agenda. To this purpose, the president may then …

1. raise matters of national interest with provincial governments and organized local government and to hear their views on those matters;
2. consult provincial governments and organized local government on the implementation of national policy and legislation in provinces and municipalities;

3. discuss performance in the provision of services in order to detect failures and to initiate preventive or corrective action when necessary…" (Section 7 of the IGR Framework Act, emphasis added)

The notion that organized local government may also raise matters of local concern—for example, how national regulation overburdens municipalities—is not envisaged, although it may suggest agenda items to the president. Whether such items appear on the agenda is a question of practice in the president's discretion.

The same slant is also present in the sectoral IGR forums when the national ministers meet with their counterparts in the provinces, in so-called MinMECs (a Minister and Members of the [Provincial] Executive Councils). Organized local government becomes part of the structure when local government interests are involved (Section 10). Again, the focus is on the national minister: it is "a consultative forum *for* the minister" (Section 11, emphasis added), who convenes and sets the agenda for the meetings. The MinMECs are the main engine room for cooperative government as they deal with the substantive issues of governance. They are supported by technical support structures composed of officials from the participating parties.

The IGR forums set up by the IGR Framework Act in a particular field become unnecessary when another act creates a similar institution. In the focal area of intergovernmental fiscal relations, the Intergovernmental Fiscal Relations Act of 1997 created two statutory consultative forums—the Budget Council and the Budget Forum—both with the principal task of allowing provinces and local government to participate in the formation of the Division of Revenue Bill. As noted above, the budget process commences with the recommendations of the FFC to the National Treasury, which then prepares the bill. The minister of finance meets first with the nine MECs for finance in the Budget Council. When a councillor, representing organized local government, joins the Council, it becomes the Budget Forum, which is concerned with transfers to municipalities. It is important to note that the forums are not decision-making bodies, but are there for consultation, as is discussed further below.

A second layer of IGR structures is at the provincial level, dedicated to the relationship between a provincial executive, headed by the premier, and the district and metropolitan municipalities in that province. A significant characteristic is that these forums treat the province and municipalities more like equal partners. The objective of the Premier's Coordinating Forum (PCF) is thus to be "a consultative forum for Premier *and* local governments in the province" (Section 18, emphasis added). It is not a forum of consultation only for the benefit of the premier, but also for the mayors.

The PCF's membership is thus the premier, at least the member of the provincial executive council (MEC) responsible for local government, the mayors of district municipalities and, where a province has metropolitan municipalities, them as well, and a municipal councillor designated by organized local government in that province (Section 17(1)). A brief explanation of district municipalities is due: outside metropolitan areas the country is carved up into (currently) 44 district municipalities, each of which include a number of local municipalities. The listed local government powers are divided between the district and the locals, the former focusing on district-wide planning and the provision of bulk services. The mayors of local municipalities have been omitted on the reasoning that the district mayor represents not only the district municipality but all local municipalities falling within the district. The district mayor is thus conceived of as the communication channel between national and provincial governments and local municipalities.

The premier is designated as the chairperson of the forum, convening meetings and determining the agenda. However, the other members may suggest the inclusion of other agenda items (Section 19). The forum also functions as a crypto implementation agency for decisions made higher up the food chain. So, one of the functions is to discuss matters arising in the PCC and MinMECs affecting local government, and the implementation of national policies and legislation (Section 18(a)). To this end, highlighting upward "accountability", the PCF "must report at least annually" to the PCC "on progress with the implementation of national policy and legislation in the province" (Section 20(a)). More fitting functions are the discussion of matters of mutual interest, including "the co-ordination of provincial and municipal development planning to facilitate coherent planning in the province as a whole" (Section 18(a)(vii)) and "any other matters of strategic importance that affect the interests of local governments in the province" (Section 18(a)(ix)).

12.2.6 Nature of IGR Forums

An IGR forum, including those in which local government participates, is described in the IGR Framework Act as "a forum for intergovernmental consultation and discussion" (Section 32(1)). Consequently, such a forum "is not an executive decision-making body", but "may adopt resolutions or make recommendations in terms of agreed procedures" (Section 32(2)). An agreement reached between the executives becomes legally binding only when they adopt it within their own decision-making structures. The executives from the three spheres of government (or municipalities within the local government sphere) may, however, coordinate their actions by entering into an implementation protocol (or agreement) (Section 35(1)). Again, such an agreement is not per se binding, unless approved by each party's internal decision-making body. This places organized local government at a disadvantage; it is merely a representative body of municipal councils and cannot take a decision that binds every member council. It must persuade its members to adopt such an agreement.

12.3 The Impact of Local Government's Participation on Policy Formation Through Intergovernmental Structures

With an elaborate IGR system statutory framework, albeit with a bias towards the national government, the question remains: how has local government exploited the listed intergovernmental platforms to achieve the maximum impact? Measuring impact is, of course, notoriously difficult, and in the absence of independent research, one is bound to rely on the reported experiences of participants. As far as organized local government's participation is concerned, the focus then falls on the South African Local Government Association (SALGA).

12.3.1 South African Local Government Association

SALGA, established in 1996, is a voluntary body representing all nine provincial associations, which in 1997 was recognized by the responsible national minister as the body representing local government. It is funded by its members and a direct grant from the national government. Its relationship with its members is defined in the SALGA Constitution.

The SALGA Constitution was amended in 2002 to reflect a very unitary organization (Steytler, 2005a). In a drive in 2000s by the ANC to minimize the role of provinces (even considering their abolition (Steytler, 2014), SALGA, contrary to the Constitution, sought to sideline provincial control of organised local government. All provincial associations became chapters of SALGA. Each municipality is a member directly, and not through its membership of a provincial association. The elective bodies of SALGA comprise elected councillors; it is thus a political body which, in the IGR context, engages with the elected politicians of the other spheres of government. Mayors and speakers of municipal councils (full-time municipal positions) dominate these bodies, who are then called upon to represent SALGA (not their own municipalities) in various intergovernmental forums. SALGA has two basic mandates: first, to provide assistance to their member municipalities, and second, to engage with provincial and national governments in promoting local government's interests (Steytler, 2005a. Over the years, it has built a formidable infrastructure to execute these mandates.

In perusing SALGA's annual reported IGR activities, several features stand out. First, SALGA is active in a range of strategic areas, taking the initiative in some of them. The areas include the routine topic of financial transfers, but also, in pushing the envelope, new issues such as climate change, the devolution of public transport, the generation of clean energy by municipalities, the provision of municipal health services, and emergency housing.

Secondly, it has numerous engagements with national and provincial legislatures as well as with their executives. In the 2022–2023 financial year, SALGA reported that it had 54 engagements with the national parliament, 74 with provincial legislatures, 59 intergovernmental engagements with the national government, and 117 with provinces (SALGA, 2023, p. 45).

Thirdly, given the width of areas covered, it engages directly with a range of national line departments, such as the National Treasury and the Departments of Cooperative Governance and Traditional Affairs (COGTA), which is responsible for local government, Water and Sanitation, Human Settlements, Environmental Affairs, Transport, Mineral and Energy Affairs, Arts and Culture, and Public Works.

Fourthly, many of these engagements occur outside the formal IGR forums designed for this purpose. By engaging directly with the national departments, provincial governments are effectively side-lined, providing further evidence of South Africa's "hourglass federalism" (Steytler, 2017); the strong national government from above and the emerging strength of local government from below squeeze the provinces in the middle.

Fifthly, some engagements result in joint work with national departments. SALGA collaborated with the Department of Environmental Affairs to implement a waste management system by developing and revising model by-laws for municipalities (SALGA, 2020, p. 36). With the Department of Arts and Culture, SALGA developed a position paper on library management (SALGA, 2019, p. 35). SALGA and the Department of Human Settlement conducted joint research on emergency housing (SALGA, 2019, p. 43).

Finally, SALGA claims that their positive impact on national and provincial governments can be attributed to their skilled interventions. In the 2022–2023 Annual Report it is stated: "SALGA's extensive, well-prepared and well-informed engagements with legislatures and across intergovernmental relations platforms support the significance of its role in shaping local government policies and advocating for the interests of local communities. SALGA's position papers, recommendations and participation in legislative processes contributed to more informed and collaborative decision-making processes that impact local governance." (SALGA, 2023, p. 45–46)

In summary, SALGA's annual reports now and then refer specifically to the statutory IGR forums, but it is the exception; its focus is on its substantive programs that are pursued by the most effective means, mostly through direct engagements with national departments.

12.3.2 Participation in the National Legislative Processes

On the face of it, participation in the NCOP should be an important platform in which local government can make its voice heard. There are, however, a few constraints that hamper SALGA's participation. First, there are structural constraints. SALGA's ten-person delegation can only be part-time (in terms of the Constitution) and the SALGA leadership are also full-time mayors or speakers, mostly hailing from large metropolitan municipalities. The challenge is then to find able and willing councillors to attend, fully prepared sessions and committee meetings of the NCOP when matters pertaining to local government are under discussion. Although SALGA has established a dedicated office in Cape Town to manage and support its activities in the NCOP, SALGA's political participation in the chamber remains weak.

Secondly, the political status of the NCOP in the national legislative process is low. Politically, the National Assembly dominates because the ruling party, the African National Congress (ANC), controls both chambers. Consequently, SALGA prefers to make its submissions directly to the National Assembly, along with members of the public and civil society organizations, where it hopes to make the most impact. For example, in 2019 SALGA lobbied the National Assembly's Portfolio Committee on Transport on the devolution of public transport to local government, while at the same time petitioning the presidency on the same matter (SALGA, 2020, p. 36).

SALGA reported that during the 2022–2023 financial year it had 54 engagements with parliament, not stating, though, what the breakdown is between the National Assembly and the NCOP (SALGA, 2023, p. 45). Outside formal NCOP proceedings, SALGA has, jointly with the NCOP, been hosting a Local Government Week since 2013, a national conference on local government policies (SALGA, 2019). The outcomes of the conference are then the subject of a special sitting of the NCOP (PMG, 2022).

12.3.3 Participation in Executive Statutory Structures

Whether dedicated IGR executive structures allow for meaningful engagement of SALGA is an open question. It depends very much on whether an ethos of cooperation between equals prevails, or whether IGR is a top-down affair where the forums are used as information dissemination opportunities for the top dog in charge.

The PCC usually meets twice a year as part of an extended national cabinet meeting. Reporting on the nature and tone of the meetings, the extent of inputs made by sub-national governments, and the eventual outcomes, is limited and even less commented upon. The role of the PCC came to the fore during the Covid-19 pandemic as countermeasures fell under the jurisdiction of all three spheres of government. From March 2020 to the beginning of 2023, 31 special PCC meetings were held, focussing on the pandemic and the national states of disaster (Presidency, 2023). However, instead of being the center of coordination, the PCC became the implementation instrument for national direction, which was formulated by the National Coronavirus Command Council, comprising at first a few national ministers and later the entire cabinet (Steytler et al., 2022, p. 347). Although municipalities play a pivotal role in combatting the pandemic through grassroots actions, it appears as if they were recipients of instructions rather than co-authors of policy. In the 2 June 2023 meeting, the first ordinary meeting since 2020, the President 'directed the PCC to focus on the acceleration of service delivery improvement', especially local services (Presidency, 2023).

As noted above, it would appear from SALGA's reports that their primary focus was not to work through the MinMECS, where they would be only one voice among the national minister and nine provincial MECs, but to direct their engagements directly with national line departments. There are only a few references to participation in MinMECs. For example, in 2019 SALGA made inputs to the Human Settlement, Water and Sanitation MinMEC (SALGA, 2020, p. 34), of which SALGA was a member given local government's functions relating to the provision of water and sanitation.

While there are rare references to SALGA's participation in the Budget Forum (SALGA, 2019, p. 43), there are ample mentions of it pursuing budgetary issues with national line departments. For example, in 2018 SALGA lobbied COGTA and the Finance and Fiscal Commission on the need for a grant for municipal health services (SALGA, 2019, p. 33). In 2022, SALGA engaged COGTA and the Department of Water Services for the inclusion in the Division of Revenue Act of 2023, a conditional grant for innovative technological solutions to improve basic water services (SALGA, 2023, p. 36). Direct engagements with the National Treasury were also reported; in 2023, SALGA claimed that it successfully lobbied the National Treasury for a 1.4% increase in the fiscal allocations to local government (SALGA, 2023, p. 37).

Engagements with the provinces took place both at an executive and legislative level. As noted above, SALGA reported that it had 74 provincial legislative engagements in the nine provinces and a further 117 with provincial governments (SALGA, 2023, p. 45). Given the fewer numbers, municipalities themselves are directly engaging with the provincial executive through the Premier's Coordinating Council (PCF). The prescribed membership of the PCF—every district and metropolitan mayor has a seat as well as one for SALGA—did not wash in practice. The fundamental problem is that district municipalities are weak institutions with few powers and even less resources (Powell, 2015, p. 326). In contrast, some local municipalities, particularly where secondary cities are located, are significantly more powerful than the district in which they are located. When the PCFs were formed, their membership was immediately expanded to include local municipalities as well (see Fessha, 2006). At PCF meetings, the debate is between the municipalities and the province, with SALGA playing only a supportive role. Whether there is real dialogue seems to depend much on the premiers' attitude towards municipalities.

12.4 The Place and Role of Urban Local Governments (Metropolitan Municipalities) in Intergovernmental Relations

Although metropolitan municipalities must be included in the composition of any local government association to be recognized by the national government, they fit uncomfortably under the umbrella of SALGA. They are very different from the other 249 municipalities: they house a third of the country's population and are the location of two-thirds of economic activities, their budgets constitute over half of all municipal budgets, and some have larger budgets than rural provinces. As engines of economic growth and home of the poor, they face different challenges governing populations ranging from 700,000 (Buffalo City) to six million (City of Johannesburg). Although they are few in number, mayors from the metros have dominated leadership positions since SALGA's inception.

The executive mayor of the eight metros have not formed an association through which to engage the national government. As their number is small, the practice has been for individual metros to directly engage with national departments. This approach is also manifested in the statutory body created to organize infrastructure development in the country. The Infrastructure Development Act of 2014 established the President's Infrastructure Coordinating Commission (PICC), the membership comprising the president, the deputy president, the ministers responsible for infrastructure, the nine provincial premiers, the eight metro executive mayors, and a SALGA representative (Section 3(3)), with a majority vote of those present carrying a decision (Section 3(7)). Unlike all other IGR forums, the Commission is given executive powers over the systematic selection, planning and monitoring of large infrastructure projects (Powell, 2015, p. 328[2]), including the expropriation of land (Section 5). With a sizeable representation of eight commissioners and a SALGA representative, local government equals provincial representation. As to the functioning of this body, little is known, including how the local government component performs. In 2018, the PICC published a Summary of the South African Infrastructure Plan (PICC, 2018), merely roughly outlined the plan, but no further reports of the Commission could be traced.

A non-statutory body focusing on urban governance emerged soon after the inauguration of the new local government dispensation in 2000—the South African CitiesNetwork established in 2002. It is a voluntary, expert-driven association not representing any of the metropolitan councils, and focuses on generating and implementing knowledge about urban governance. Although the chairperson of the board is the current mayor of Buffalo City (a metro), it carries no political clout but nevertheless engages with a number of key national departments concerned with urban development in joint research projects (SACN, 2022). It also partnered with SALGA in 2022 in convening the City Waste Managers' Forum and Water Resilient Cities event (SALGA, 2023, p. 41).

[2] The author incorrectly refers to the body as the *Provincial* Infrastructure Coordinating *Council* (Powell 2015, p. 327).

12.5 Conclusions: Towards Effective Dialogue Between Local, Provincial and National Governments

It is clear that local government is engaged with provincial and national government, and there is evidence to suggest that cooperation is not only a constitutional prescript, but also a lived reality. Given the fact of South Africa's "hourglass federation", local government enjoys direct access to the national legislature and executive; these engagements are not mediated through the provinces. There are sufficient formal structures and institutions in which local government's voice, as mostly articulated by SALGA, can be heard: in the NCOP, the President's Coordinating Council, the MinMECs, and the various Premier's Coordinating Forums. However, the bulk of engagements takes place informally through direct engagements between SALGA and national departments, and, of course, metros in their own capacity. Evidence also suggests that the engagements are not only a one-way traffic; local government has played a role in shaping national and provincial laws and policies.

Although the reported engagements are widespread and their effect felt, the question remains whether the existing structures and platforms can be further enhanced to ensure an effective dialogue and cooperation. In concluding this chapter a few remarks and suggestions are made.

First, intergovernmental relations and cooperative government have been overformalized. Practice has shown that the detailed provisions in the IGR Framework Act could not contain the real politique of intergovernmental relations. Confining local government's participation in the national Parliament to the NCOP did not prevent SALGA from seeking out the most effective national partner—the National Assembly—to engage with. It was not feasible to leave out strong local municipalities from the PCFs; however attractive the communication role of district mayors may appear in theory, it did not resonate with the power dynamics on the ground.

Secondly, more effective engagements—whether formal or informal—would require changes among all the affected parties. For SALGA to play a meaningful representative role it must be organized to be fit for purpose. The SALGA leadership, all full-time councillors at the head of demanding municipalities, may have the political clout, but do not have the time to meet all SALGA's political engagements. National and provincial executives do not want to meet with officials; they want to dialogue with their political peers. It has thus been suggested to nominate councillors doing SALGA work on a full-time basis (Steytler, 2005a p. 516). In any event, SALGA must obviously be well capacitated for the task of leading the dialogue with the relevant knowledge and experience. It could further hone its capacity and skills sets for the tasks at hand. But SALGA is also only as strong as its members are. The current decline of the majority of municipalities through mismanagement, corruption, and bankruptcy undermines their collective voice. Who is going to take seriously a hapless and hopeless government sector? It merely skews the dialogue in favour of national and provincial governments.

Thirdly, it is appropriate for metros to give voice to their concerns both individually and collectively. They operate on par with provinces, and the future stability of

South Africa depends in part on how they facilitate economic growth and ameliorate poverty. This requires political stability and good governance of these institutions, which is often in short supply.

Fourthly, provincial governments have dual but conflicting roles. On the one hand they must supervise municipalities in a hierarchical manner, while on the other they must cooperate with them on the basis of equality. Where municipalities are not a partner of integrity but a basket case of mismanagement and corruption, the first role becomes dominant at the expense of the latter. Furthermore, where provinces themselves are poorly governed, as is the case in some, they cannot and do not perform their supervisory role of monitoring, support and interventions adequately.

Finally, a similar argument applies to local government being a partner for the national government. While a centralizing trend has been an ongoing concern, vibrant and well-governed local governments can claim and fill their rightful place in South Africa's system of intergovernmental relations, as envisaged by the Constitution. The emergence of a politically more diverse landscape may bring much needed competition and good governance to the sector.

References

Fessha, Y. (2006). The practice of premier's intergovernmental forums. *Local Government Bulletin, 8*(5), 4.

Parliamentary Monitoring Group (PMG). (2022). *Parliament's role in local governance 2022*. Retrieved July 10, 2023, from https://pmg.org.za/blog/Parliament%E2%80%99sroleinLocalGovernance2022

Powell, D. (2015). Constructing a developmental state in South Africa: The corporatization of intergovernmental relations. In J. Poirier, C. Saunders, & J. Kincaid (Eds.), *Intergovernmental relations in federal systems: Comparative structures and dynamics* (pp. 305–349). Oxford University Press.

Presidency. (2023). *President Ramaphosa focuses the Presidential Coordinating Council on service delivery*. Retrieved July 14, 2023, from https://www.thepresidency.gov.za/press-statements/president-ramaphosa-focuses-presidential-coordinating-council-service-delivery

Presidential Infrastructure Coordinating Commission (PICC). (2018). *Summary of the South African Infrastructure Plan*. Retrieved July 15, 2023, from https://www.gov.za/sites/default/files/PICC_Final.pdf

South African CitiesNetwork (SACN). (2022). *Integrated Annual Report 2022*. Retrieved July 15, 2023, from https://www.sacities.net/wp-content/uploads/2023/06/SACN-Integrated-Annual-Report-2022_Draft05.pdf

South African Local Government Association (SALGA). (2019). *Annual Report 2018/19*. Retrieved July 15, 2023, from https://www.SALGA.org.za/Documents/Documents%20and%20Publications/Annual%20Reports/SALGA%20AR2019_final.pdf

South African Local Government Association (SALGA). (2020). *Annual Report 2019–2020*. Retrieved July 15, 2023, from https://www.SALGA.org.za/event/nma20/documents/Close%20Session%20Documents/SALGA%20Annual%20Report%202019-20.pdf

South African Local Government Association (SALGA). (2023). *Annual Report 2022–2023*. Retrieved November 1, 2023, from https://www.SALGA.org.za/Documents/Documents%20and%20Publications/Annual%20Reports/SALGA%20Annual%20Report%202022-2023.pdf

Steytler, N. (2005a). The role of organized local government in intergovernmental relations in South Africa. In L. C. Jain (Ed.), *Decentralisation and local governance: Essays for George Matthew* (pp. 495–520). Orient Longman.

Steytler, N. (2005b). Republic of South Africa. In J. Kincaid & A. Tarr (Eds.), *Constitutional origins, structure, and change in federal countries* (pp. 311–346). McGill-Queen's University Press.

Steytler, N. (2011). Cooperative and coercive models of intergovernmental relations: A South African case study. In T. J. Courchene, J. R. Allen, C. Leuprecht, & N. Verrelli (Eds.), *The federal idea: Essays in honour of Ronald L. Watts* (pp. 413–428). McGill-Queen's University Press.

Steytler, N. (2014). The politics of provinces and the provincialisation of politics. In T. Maluwa (Ed.), *Law, politics and rights: Essays in memory of Kader Asmal* (pp. 191–214). Brill/Nijhoff.

Steytler, N. (2017). The Constitutional Court: Reinforcing South Africa's hourglass system of multilevel government. In N. Arony & J. Kincaid (Eds.), *Courts in federal countries: Federalists or unitarists* (pp. 328–366). University of Toronto Press.

Steytler, N. (2023). Comparative conclusions. In N. Steytler (Ed.), *The Forum of Federations handbook on local government in federal systems* (pp. 533–586). Palgrave Macmillan.

Steytler, N., & de Visser, J. (2007). *Local Government Law of South Africa.* Butterworths LexisNexis.

Steytler, N., de Visser, J., & Chigwata, T. (2022). South Africa: Surfing towards centralisation. In N. Steytler (Ed.), *Comparative federalism and Covid-19: Combatting the pandemic* (pp. 336–354). Routledge.

Open Access This chapter is licensed under the terms of the Creative Commons Attribution 4.0 International License (http://creativecommons.org/licenses/by/4.0/), which permits use, sharing, adaptation, distribution and reproduction in any medium or format, as long as you give appropriate credit to the original author(s) and the source, provide a link to the Creative Commons license and indicate if changes were made.

The images or other third party material in this chapter are included in the chapter's Creative Commons license, unless indicated otherwise in a credit line to the material. If material is not included in the chapter's Creative Commons license and your intended use is not permitted by statutory regulation or exceeds the permitted use, you will need to obtain permission directly from the copyright holder.

Chapter 13
A Better Role in the Play? Municipalities in Intergovernmental Relations in Spain

Carmen Navarro

Abstract This chapter takes an in-depth look at the role of local governments in intergovernmental relations (IGR) in Spain, their institutional framework, the representation of local interests and their capacity to respond to crises. It describes the general patterns and dynamics of IGR within the Spanish political system, highlighting the structural characteristics and pointing out the limitations faced by local authorities in fully participating in the formal bodies of central-local government relations (i.e. sectoral conferences). The chapter also examines the role of local government associations in advocating for local interests within formal IGR bodies and through informal mechanisms. The analysis reveals the weakness of the infrastructure of permanent formal representative bodies through which local government demands are channeled. However, it also shows how informal IGR relations and political parties serve as alternative mechanisms, providing avenues for local authorities to influence decision-making.

Keywords Local government · Intergovernmental relations · Multilevel governance · Municipal associations

13.1 Introduction

Most policies are intergovernmental in nature. Sustainability, education, security, mobility, employment, etc., are all areas of public policy in which different governments intervene to various degrees, regardless of the level of decentralization in the country. National governments often set guidelines or the legal framework, or fund policies of regional and local governments in whole or in part in areas where these authorities also have competences. The politically decentralized units also decide over those areas, exercising their own autonomy and powers. This is what

C. Navarro (✉)
Institute of Local Government Law, Autonomous University of Madrid, Madrid, Spain
e-mail: c.navarro@uam.es

© The Author(s) 2026

K. Kössler, E. M. Belser (eds.), *Local Government Structure and Intergovernmental Relations*, Local and Urban Governance,
https://doi.org/10.1007/978-3-031-99820-1_13

decentralization and multi-level governance is about. In addition, decentralization is an unquestionable feature of current political systems. A look at measurements of levels of regional and local autonomy by means of the Regional Authority Index and the Local Autonomy Index confirms that this is an increasing trait of today's democracies (Marks et al., 2008; Ladner et al., 2019). Political devolution is here to stay.

National, regional, and local authorities are structurally placed in a situation of mutual interdependencies. Adopting decisions in these contexts requires coordination among levels of government. Moreover, coordination is channeled through formal and informal mechanisms that enable the necessary cooperation to provide comprehensive responses to policy problems. The intergovernmental relations that result from these interactions allow for the exchange of information, consultation, or decision-making. Against this background, systems of intergovernmental relations (IGR) become key structures of political systems.

However, IGR systems are not always stable or free of tensions. Generally, both coordination and cooperation are subject to constant problems of politics, organization, communication, common identification of goals or difficulties in reaching consensus. Yet, they are essential to the functioning of democracy and to the resolution of complex problems. While academia and political debates have focused much more on IGR between the national and the regional levels of government, there is still much to be known about the position of local governments in the vertical relation systems and about how and in what kind of dynamics they are involved.

Spain is not an exception regarding the lack of studies on IGR and local governments. Research is mainly centered on relations between the central and the regional governments—the autonomous communities—while there are only a few exceptions that analyze the case of local governments' interactions with higher authorities (Agranoff, 2010). Given the well-established position of local authorities in the multi-level governance system, this absence is quite inexplicable. Plausible explanations could be found in the large number of more than 8000 local authorities in the country and their diversity, which increases the difficulty of any kind of empirical research on local government. In addition, the 17 autonomous communities in the country all have their own regional-local IGR systems, which adds challenges for data gathering and in the identification of common patterns. One could be tempted to think that there is not much to research. For central-local intergovernmental relations some authors have stated that they are scarce and sporadic (Colino, 2012). Whether the same applies to relations between regional and local governments is an open question. Given the interdependencies in many policy areas, we would assume that there are more extensive relations. But the research effort has simply been moved somewhere else. Whatever the explanation for this lack of academic interest, the fact is that there are good reasons to look at this dimension of IGR. This because local governments are a key piece in the Spanish multi-level governance system. Their existence and autonomy are guaranteed by the Constitution. Local governments provide many services and intervene in a good set of policy areas. For the provision of many of them, local authorities are in an interdependence relation with other levels of government.

This chapter analyses the position and dynamics of local authorities in intergovernmental relations with a special focus on the formal structures of interaction, such as conferences and councils. It aims at addressing questions such as, what institutionalized bodies exist to bring together actors from two levels (local-subnational and/or local-national) and three levels of government? What is the impact of these conferences on policy-making? What is the role of local government associations within these conferences? Is the local government voice sufficiently heard?

To try to answer these questions, the chapter proceeds in four steps. First, it presents the general patterns and dynamics of IGR in Spain in order to provide the context for a better understanding of the issue. This section notes that the main structural features that characterize IGR in the political system also affect those in which municipalities are involved. The chapter then presents and assesses the architecture of the institutionalized structures of interaction in which local governments are present. In a further step it analyzes the role of associations of municipalities in representing the voice of local governments in the IGR game. Before moving on to the conclusions, it describes how the IGR system dealt with the Covid-19 crisis, in order to show how it reacts when subjected to a stress test, thus revealing its main strengths and weaknesses.

13.2 Intergovernmental Relations in Spain

The Spanish Constitution keeps an eloquent silence when it comes to intergovernmental relations in the political system and the mechanisms to exercise them. It was only after its adoption in 1978 and the implementation of a far-reaching program of decentralization that the need for coordination between levels of governments led to the creation of formal bodies for cooperation in vertical relations. In the Spanish system, these permanent bodies are called sectoral conferences (*Conferencias Sectoriales*) and began to operate in the 1980s when the development of the devolution required constant interaction specially between central and regional authorities. By the beginning of the 1990s, they were regulated by national legislation, which defined their general functions, and composition (Law 30/1992 on the Legal System of Public Administrations and the Administrative Procedure). The adoption by each sectoral conference of its own by-law supplemented the details and particularities for the operation of each of these bodies.

Sectoral conferences are multilateral forums attended mainly by central and regional governments' representatives. Only in a few cases local governments have been given formal representation in sectoral conferences, when the central government has considered that they were particularly affected by the policy area or issue under discussion. Sectoral conferences have a similar operating dynamic. The central government minister responsible for the area convenes the meetings and chairs the conference. The vice-chair is usually held by a representative of an autonomous community, while an administrative unit of the ministry takes minutes, provides administrative support and coordinates technical work. When the sectoral conference includes local authorities as members, the Spanish Association of Municipalities (FEMP) represents the municipalities. Typical tasks of sectoral conferences are to report on preliminary drafts of national legislation, report on initiatives adopted by the European Commission, discuss and adopt criteria for the co-financing of actions in policy areas, adopt joint plans, or establish mechanisms for the exchange of information.

Always set up by the central government, the most active sectoral conferences to date were initiated in the 1980s on key areas of competence of the autonomous communities that needed to be activated in the fields of agriculture and rural development, higher education, regional fiscal and financial policy, education, health, EU affairs, environment, housing and urban planning, consumption, transport, and social services. Others were set up in the 1990s as EU matters became prominent and new issues were included in the agenda (fisheries, tourism, culture, internal trade, infrastructure and town and country planning, agriculture, administration of justice, small and medium-sized enterprises, gambling, maritime rescue, and public administration). In the early 2000s, new areas were added, including a specific Conference on Local Affairs in 2005. More recently, the central government has activated a Sectoral conference with local government representation to coordinate the actions of the Transformation and Resilience Recovery Plan, in which governments cooperate to implement the massive financial package of EU Next Generation Funds. In total, there are 43 sectoral conferences.[1] Of all these formal IGR bodies, local authorities are only represented in two, that is the above-mentioned Conference on Local Affairs and Conference for the Transformation and Resilience Recovery Plan.

The work of the sectoral conferences is supported by a large number of auxiliary bodies, such as commissions and working groups, which bring together representatives below the ministerial level to deal with general or more specialized and technical issues. A problem-solving and consensus-building style almost always prevails in technical bodies. Voting does not usually take place, although the rules of procedure may allow it. In practice, deliberation continues until a consensus is reached (Aja & Colino, 2014).

Not all sectoral conferences have been equally active. Empirical work suggests that only about 20 have operated consistently over the years. The most active (about seven) meet frequently, but most meet no more than once a trimester (Colino, 2012). In terms of the dynamics of interaction, as in other countries, there is a certain degree of partisan politicization, especially in the top-level political meetings where central and regional ministers meet. But empirical studies have not shown a systematic conflict between the national government and the autonomous regions when both levels of government were not politically aligned (Colino, 2012). However, the management of the Covid-19 pandemic affected the functioning dynamics of some salient sectoral conferences (in particular those related to health issues) as partisan

[1] See https://mpt.gob.es/dam/es/portal/politica-territorial/autonomica/coop_autonomica/Conf_Sectoriales/Documentacion/Conf_Sect_exist/parrafo/0/CONFERENCIAS-SECTORIALES_REGIMEN_JURIDICO_ACTUALIZADO

political conflict between some regional authorities and the central government came to the fore (Navarro & Velasco, 2022). Whether this is still the case today is a matter for future empirical research.

The Spanish IGR system did not have a specific forum at the highest political level for the dialogue between the Spanish and regional prime ministers until 2004, when the Conference of Presidents (*Conferencia de Presidentes*) was created. Since 2021, the local voice also began to be heard in these summits, as the president of the Spanish Municipalities Association was invited to participate in this conference. This inclusion was facilitated by the Covid-19 crisis management and the acknowledgement that the needed concerted actions had to include local authorities. The Conference of Presidents is, on paper, the highest body for political cooperation in sectoral and territorial public policies. The Conference of Presidents also draws up joint actions of a strategic nature and on relevant matters that impact of competences of the autonomous communities and that of the central state. In reality, this forum has found it very difficult to fulfil its role because of its poor record. In the first decade and a half of its existence, it met only six times due to a combination of difficulties in getting all the autonomous communities around the table and a lack of interest on the part of national leaders, who are responsible for calling the meetings. Then, during the first phase of the Covid-19 crisis, it met weekly, completing 17 meetings from March to October 2020. The meetings served to exchange information rather than to make decisions (Castellà-Andreu & Kölling, 2022). However, once the crisis had passed, the frequency of meetings reverted to its previous pattern of at most one per year, with some years seeing none at all.

As in many other countries, IGRs are also channelled through bilateral formal bodies and informal relations. Bilateral relations take place between the central government and an individual autonomous community. This is the case of the partnership agreements (*Convenios de colaboración*) that governments from different levels sign to implement policies in areas of shared competence (for example, between a regional and a local government for the implementation of social services). Informal relations occur in the context of simple networks of contacts between officials or politicians, without a clear legal form, for the informal exchange of information or for deliberation and agreements. Informal IGR also takes place in more intangible ways, such as by the representation of local elites in higher institutions. This happens, for instance, in situations of dual mandate, where mayors or councillors are also members of regional or national assemblies, and they can bring the local voice to these institutions acting as local brokers in parliament (Van de Voorde & de Vet, 2020). About one in five national senators and one in ten members of the national lower house are also (mainly) mayors or councillors. At the regional level these figures are even much higher. Although there is no empirical research on the impact of dual mandates on parliamentary activity in Spain, it is clear that it, at least, allows intergovernmental interactions to be established.

The panorama of IGR is rounded off with a reference to political parties. A particular feature of Spanish IGR is the importance of political parties as alternative mechanisms of intergovernmental relations. Party channels are crucial to understanding government-to-government interactions (Agranoff, 2010).

Central-regional-local party interactions to implement projects or investments in the territory are a typical example of this, where contacts at the party-political level function to facilitate processes and overcome obstacles. The political party element can work to exacerbate conflict as well. This happens where political alignment is key for smoothing conflictual relations and could lead to sub-national governments boycotting central policies in areas of shared competence when cabinets at different levels of government belong to opposing political camps.

13.3 Representation of Municipalities in Formal IGR Bodies

The fact that local governments embody autonomy to set goals and make autonomous decisions in large areas of responsibility implies the need for access to other levels of government and the capacity to represent and protect local interests before them in shared areas of competence. The right of local authorities to be consulted by higher levels of government on matters that concern them is a core principle of local democracy, enshrined in the European Charter of Local Self-Government (Council of Europe—Congress f Local and Regional Authorities, 2018). To be effective, it requires a well-defined regulatory framework and appropriate institutions to exercise it. For their part, local authorities need institutions capable of representing and protecting their interests. Associations of local authorities play this role in cooperation and consultation processes.

The constitutional guarantee of local government autonomy implies, among other things, that these authorities are not hierarchically subordinate to either the central or the corresponding autonomous governments. This principle grants the participation of local governments on an equal basis to central-local and regional-local IGR for cooperation and coordination in shared areas of responsibility. Whether inclusive and active multilateral bodies actually exist and meet regularly depends on the will of the higher levels of government responsible for their establishment and operation.

13.3.1 Central-Local IGR Structures

In terms of vertical intergovernmental relations channeled through permanent IGR bodies, we find that local governments are largely excluded from them. Since sectoral conferences are the main bodies for formal IGR and cover areas of local responsibility, one would have expected local authorities to have some form of representation and influence in them. However, they only have formal representation in two of the 43 existing bodies of this type and one of them is completely inactive. Outside of the financial sphere, IGRs would be rare and infrequent (Colino, 2012). Indeed, bilateral interactions end in partnership agreements (*Convenios de colaboración*) for the implementation of conditional transfers that develop services and projects. But the main formal and permanent mechanism that the Spanish system offers for multilateral central-local interaction, i.e. the sectoral conferences, has not reached the municipal sphere.

In total, only three formal bodies define the structure of IGR in which local governments are involved: the Sectoral Conference for Local Affairs (*Conferencia Sectorial para Asuntos Locales*, CSAL), the National Commission for Local Administration (*Comisión Nacional de la Administración Local*, CNAL), and the Sectoral Conference for the Transformation and Resilience Recovery Plan (*Conferencia Sectorial del Plan de Recuperación, Transformación y Resiliencia*). However, the first of them is completely inactive, the second is not a sectoral conference but a body in the internal structure of a central ministry and the third is very issue-specific (EU NextGen Funds) and only met in 2021, during the initial stage of the Recovery Plan 2021.

The Sectoral Conference for Local Affairs (*Conferencia Sectorial para Asuntos Locales*, CSAL) was formally created in 2005 as a coordination platform gathering the three levels of government (central, regional, and local). On paper, it was designed as the highest IGR body for cooperation, meetings, and consultation for the articulation of relations between the national administration, the autonomous communities, and the local governments. In addition, its main objective is to achieve maximum coherence in the definition and application of the policies adopted by the state and the autonomous communities in matters of local government and administration. It was established that it would be chaired by the head of the ministry responsible for local affairs, and its members were the regional ministers responsible for local government in each autonomous community and the municipal representatives appointed by the Spanish Federation of Municipalities and Provinces.

But, unlike other sectoral conferences, the CSAL has not met on a regular basis since 2007 and has not even approved its own by-law establishing its composition, functions, and rules for the adoption of agreements. In fact, there have been only seven meetings of this conference. All of them took place between the years 2005 and 2007, a period of ambitious plans for a local government reforme that never took place. Since then, no activity has been reported, although the conference has not been formally eliminated. When it was active, its meetings served to discuss a draft reform of the Local Government Act, an ambitious project that the national government launched at that time to deepen local government and change the legislation on local finances and competences (Navarro & Velasco, 2016). However, this draft reform did not pass by parliament and, after its abandonment in 2006, the CSAL prolonged its existence with two more meetings on technical issues in 2007, before ceasing its activities altogether. There are no empirical works measuring the influence of this body in policy-making, but a look at the reduced number of meetings and issues treated and the inexistent operability held since 2007 point to an almost nonexistent impact.

The Sectoral Conference on the Transformation and Resilience Recovery Plan is the body for cooperation between the central government and the autonomous communities to coordinate the EU's Resilience and Recovery Mechanism (RRM). The EU approved the RRM in 2020 and Spain was entitled to 70 billion EUR from this fund, provided that it proceeds with some structural reforms and investments. The conference brings together mainly central and regional government ministers responsible for the implementation of EU funds. The President of the Spanish Association of Municipalities (FEMP) has been invited to the three meetings held so far, all in 2021. The fact that municipalities are very much involved in the implementation of projects using these funds and that the FEMP was active in claiming a seat at the IGR table during the management of the Covid-19 pandemic (and was successful in being invited to the Conference of Presidents) explain the participation of the representatives of the local level.

In order to find a permanent and really active body that has channeled the relationships between local governments at the central administration for the last four decades, we have to turn to a commission whose existence is provided for in the Local Government Act, the National Commission of Local Administration (CNAL). But the CNAL is not a proper sectoral conference for IGR relations but rather an organ within the structure of the Ministry of Territorial Policy and Public Administration. This means that, in contrast to the equal relationship established with the autonomous communities through the sectoral conferences, the central government has created a more top-down-approach body for local authorities, with a rather informative role.

CNAL's competences include (1) the preparation of reports on preliminary drafts of laws and regulations concerning the powers of the central state in matters relating to local government (e.g. organizational and operational regime, the regime of functions and services, the status of local civil servants, administrative procedures, contracts, concessions and other forms of public service provision, expropriation and patrimonial jurisdiction; the regime of its assets and local treasuries), and (2) to make proposals and suggestions to the central government on matters relating to local government, and in particular on the allocation and delegation of powers in favor of local authorities, the distribution of subsidies, credits and transfers from the state to local government, and local government's share of state taxes and provisions of the general state budget affecting local authorities.

It is chaired by the minister responsible for territorial administration issues and composed of 13 representatives appointed by the central government and 13 representatives of the local authorities. Representatives of autonomous communities can be called to sessions as well. An analysis of their meetings' agenda reveals the overall informative character of its contents. The central government representatives tend to inform local representatives about their projects and plans, and only rarely the agenda includes a point for agreement. Therefore, this body is not an instrument for the expression of local interests but rather serves to ensure political cooperation with the central state.

The aforementioned Conference of Presidents, as the highest-level intergovernmental institution, completes the map of the central-local IGR. It was initially designed to bring together only national and regional prime ministers. However, its recently modified rules of procedure allow representatives of associations and institutions affected by an item on the agenda to attend as guests. Since then, this rule has been applied to allow the participation of the president of the Spanish Association of Municipalities (FEMP) in its meetings not as member but as a guest, who has been representing the local level of government in all conferences from 2021 to date.

13.3.2 Regional-Local IGR Structures

In terms of regional-local relations, the fact that the autonomous communities exercise powers in matters of local concerns has led them to create institutional structures for articulating relations as well. These structures are relatively new, having been established after the autonomous communities reformed their constitutional charters (*estatutos*) in the 2000s to include explicit powers to regulate local government. In general, they have tended to create structures similar to the sectoral conferences described above. This is the case of the autonomous communities such as Castilla-La Mancha, Castilla-León, Basque Country, Andalusia, and Catalonia, among others, that have created permanent bodies of consultation composed of representatives of local entities and the regional government. Other autonomous communities (e.g. Aragón, Madrid, and Murcia) reduce intergovernmental relationships to the interadministrative cooperation required for the exercise of each administration's competences. In the latter case, there is no permanent body that brings together regional and local governments but there are various forms of cooperation (e.g. exchange of information, development of policy programs, creation of ad hoc commissions, among others) (de Haro et al., 2022).

The lack of empirical studies on the impact and functioning of these permanent structures complicates their assessment at a comprehensive level. A look at some general information published on websites describes different degrees of activity. In the case of Catalonia, the Council of Local Governments (*Consell de Governs Locals*) is the interlocutor of the demands of the municipalities with the Catalan Government and Parliament and was constituted for the first time on October 27, 2011, but it remained inactive between 2013 and 2022. The Andalucian Council for Local Concertation (*Consejo Andaluz de Concertación Local*) is presented as the highest body for cooperation and agreement between the regional government of Andalusia and the local governments. It is permanent, advisory, and consultative in nature and reports more activity than its Catalan counterpart. Since its creation in 2007, it has met regularly on an annual basis.

One of the newest formal regional-local IGR bodies is the Basque Council for Local Public Policies (*Consejo Vasco de Políticas Públicas Locales*), created in 2016 as a permanent institution with the task of ensuring effective institutional cooperation between local and regional governments and guaranteeing the recognition of municipal interests in the processes of planning, implementing, and evaluating public policies. It is also responsible for requiring the Basque Government Council to lodge a complaint of alleged unconstitutionality if it detects a violation of local autonomy. The Basque Council guarantees the diversity of municipalities in its composition. It is made up of 18 members: six members representing the regional government, two members from each of the three provincial councils and six members representing the municipalities, with at least one third of municipal representatives coming from municipalities with a population of less than 5000. The interesting element in this body is that it guarantees the representation of both rural and urban local interests in a way that other councils of this type do not explicitly recognize.

13.4 The Role of Municipal Associations in Local-Central Intergovernmental Relations

Municipal associations have an undeniable role in intergovernmental relations, in particular, in the way in which they promote their interests vis-à-vis other levels of government (regional and national). They are organizations within a geographical area that share common interests and engage in collective action to meet some of their goals. They provide services for their members and establish horizontal networks among them. But they also participate in vertical IGR in their advocacy role towards regional and national governments. Advocacy consists of the promotion of common objectives with the aim of influencing the policy decisions of higher levels of government. This advocacy role can be exerted through formal and informal mechanisms. Their participation in conferences would be an example of formal relations, and lobbying would be the illustration of informal IGR.

In the Spanish case, most municipal and provincial governments are integrated into associations. At the national level, there is only one national association which includes more than 90% of all municipalities, the Spanish National Federation of Municipalities and Provinces (FEMP). At the regional level, we find one association of municipalities in each autonomous community, which is not organically linked to the national one. However, these regional associations (*e.g. FAMP—Federación Andaluza de Municipios y Provincias, FMC—Federación de Municipios de Cataluña*) establish relationships for collaboration with the FEMP and they tend to involve most municipalities in their territory. In addition, there is a plethora of single-issue associations of municipalities that focus on specific issues or problems affecting their communities, such as the Spanish Association against Depopulation, the Spanish Network for Rural Development, or the Association of Municipalities in Mountain Areas. They have tended to emerge when and where problems have arisen. For instance, in 2013, a group of mountain mayors and senators decided to join forces to defend the specific needs of mountain communities. Thus, the Spanish Association of Mountain Municipalities (*ESMontañas*) was born with the aim of promoting legislative improvements and actions that contribute to improving the lives of their inhabitants, halting the depopulation of these areas and generating economic and social development in these municipalities. It currently comprises 239 municipalities. Other associations follow similar patterns.

Due to the relevance and broad scope of the FEMP, it is worth have a closer look at its structure, dynamics, and challenges in representing its members. The FEMP is responsible for representing the local voice in the permanent bodies of central-local IGR relations, i.e. the Sectoral Conference for the Transformation and Resilience Recovery Plan, the Commission of Local Public Administration and the Conference of Presidents. This system of representation promotes the role of associations as mediators of local interests. However, the process of aggregating interests is particularly difficult for a large association like this one. The heterogeneity of local interests because of differences in size, territory, and socio-economic conditions poses a challenge in terms of prioritizing issues on the agenda and agreeing on a common position.

This is why the work for setting the organization's political agenda is a crucial yet controversial stage. This phase of agenda setting allows for the identification of common concerns and conflicting issues. However, the process of shaping the public agenda on local issues is not straightforward. Sometimes the orientation of the institutional agenda is explained solely in terms of majorities in the FEMP governing bodies and are related to the party ideology. The governing bodies (presidency, executive board, and territorial council) reflect the power of political parties in the local arena and are assigned after each local electoral process depending on the political representation that each party obtains. But, depending on the issues at stake, partisan dynamics can give way to transversal territorial interests that disregard some relevant local government interests.

The identification of issues and the association's position on them also comes from the work of all sectoral commissions and working groups within the institutional structure of FEMP. This way of working makes it possible to coordinate local interests in different policy areas. In commissions and working groups, the association not only deals with the main traditional areas of local action, but also produces work on other areas where local responsibility is more blurred or shared with other levels of government (e.g. employment, health services, international relations), and also tackles pressing challenges that are beginning to feature on the political agenda (e.g. depopulation, the digital agenda). Monitoring and addressing a wide range of issues on an ongoing basis enhances its ability to develop common positions and to represent local interests in national discussions.

But local interests are not only activated in the national arena. Regional associations do exist and operate within varied institutional frameworks established by regional laws. In the existent 17 regional associations of municipalities (1 per Autonomous Community), local authorities channel their interests towards the regional governments sometimes in slightly different directions from the positions taken in the FEMP. Consequently, the intergovernmental relations exercised through the associations of municipalities are characterized by a certain degree of fragmentation resulting from the coexistence of regional and national platforms. Despite this fragmentation, the FEMP's main strength lies in its role as the sole interlocutor of the central government. This strong position is facilitated through various mechanisms, including the official recognition of FEMP representatives in central government consultative bodies and agreements with central government institutions.

However, FEMP is also subjected to various challenges (de Haro et al., 2022). In the first place, the consolidation of local interests by a national association can limit the agenda to issues that avoid internal conflict or are promoted by the most influential units or regional associations. This approach achieves consensus on proposals, but at the cost of not defining concrete measures for implementation. As a result, the programmatic action plans adopted by the FEMP tend to focus more on setting priorities and objectives than on detailing the means to achieve them. Secondly, the FEMP's position as the sole representative of local interests cannot be taken for granted. The FEMP does not interfere with the powers and responsibilities of its members individually or of the regional associations between which there is no organic relationship of dependence. Thirdly, the partisan logic of its functioning can lead to prioritize the interests of the dominant party over genuinely local interests, making it difficult to achieve a balanced representation of all local entities.

Finally, its role as a platform for coordinating and representing local interests on the international stage is also one of its functions, particularly at the European level. An example of this is the Council of European Municipalities and Regions (CEMR), the largest European association of local and regional authorities. Founded in 1951, it has 60 member associations from 40 countries. The FEMP appoints a Spanish National Section, and its delegates work in the Steering Committee to define the working lines of the European association. Because of its size, the FEMP is guaranteed a presence on the CEMR's executive committee. However, despite its institutionalization since the 1950s, it has not acquired the status of an institution or interlocutor recognized by the EU system, although it is often consulted when the European institutions need to hear the views of local governments (Pazos Vidal, 2023).

13.5 The IGR Stress Test During the Covid-19 Crisis

The above lines have analyzed the state of IGRs in normal times. But the picture is not complete until we consider how IGRs behave in times of crisis. Intergovernmental relations are particularly challenged when it comes to dealing with particularly complex issues or crises (Paquet & Schertzer, 2020). The dynamics that characterize them also describe the strengths and weaknesses of the system, in the sense of how much or how little the elements that make up the IGR resist or change during these periods. The recent experience of countries in managing the early stages of the Covid-19 pandemic provides a good example of how IGRs can be subjected to such a stress test (Bergström et al., 2022). The Spanish experience tells us a lot about the weaknesses of the position of local governments in the system but also about their resilience (Navarro & Velasco, 2022).

In times of serious crisis, political decision-making tends to move to central governments in order to unify a position and make decision-making processes faster and more effective (Peters, 2011). This is exactly what happened in Spain during the first weeks of the pandemic, when the key strategy to deal with it was to centralize power completely in the hands of the national government through the exceptional prerogative of declaring an unprecedented state of alarm. This type of centralization strategy was more or less evident in other countries (Bergström et al., 2022), but what characterizes the Spanish case is the complete lack of involvement of autonomous communities or local governments in IGR coordination structures.

The Conference of Presidents (which brings together national and regional prime ministers) was the most active institution during the first three and a half months of the pandemic. The Spanish Prime Minister convened it weekly during this period, whereas it had met only six times in the previous 14 years of its existence. But it served more as a tool for top-down communication from central to regional governments than as a method for real coordination. Due to its poor track record in its trajectory until the arrival of the pandemic, both as an effective IGR body for vertical coordination and as a decision-making mechanism, it did not manage to play a more relevant role in the IGR to mitigate the centralizing effects of the state of alert. This lack of experience in working together also prevented the central authorities from considering the inclusion of the municipal voice, as they did in the post-Covid meetings, once it was seen that they too had a legitimate interest.

Local governments engaged in interactions with the central government in different ways and with different purposes. Firstly, as loyal partners of the national government in implementing and supervising the enforcement of the lockdown with their local police in cooperation with the Ministry of Interior. Secondly, to lobby the central government to get permission to use their budgets' surplus. The crisis arrived when municipal treasuries amounted substantial surpluses, but the austerity reforms adopted during the Great Recession had imposed strict financial rules preventing them from using these surpluses. The Spanish Association of Municipalities and Provinces (FEMP) successfully exerted pressure on the central government, bringing the local demand to the Ministry of Finance. Finally, in mid-September, the central government responded to municipal demands by lifting the restriction on the use of municipal surpluses, and local governments were able to add more resources to fund the many social and economic strategies they had been implementing since the crisis broke out (Navarro & Velasco, 2022).

After the first months of the crisis, the Spanish IGR system underwent a process of adaptation, moving towards a more inclusive system. The central authorities put in place better and more collaborative multi-level structures and ended up with a model of a certain co-governance in which the municipalities were invited to participate in the renovated mechanisms that emerged from the crisis: the Conference of Presidents and the Sectoral Conference for the Recovery and Resilience Transformation Plan. Ultimately, the crisis has shown that the system can suspend established subnational powers and that the quasi-federal elements of the Spanish political system have not resisted the centralizing turn that was implemented at the beginning (Navarro & Velasco, 2022). Interestingly, when it comes to local governments, the crisis has also shown the active and complementary role that municipalities have played in responding to citizens' demands, even if they are not included in effective formal structures where they can make their voices heard. In this way, they have once again demonstrated their unyielding resilience.

13.6 Conclusions

This chapter has analyzed the position of municipalities in intergovernmental relations in Spain by identifying the main traits of the IGR system, the participation of local entities in permanent bodies of interaction at the national and regional levels and the role of associations in bringing the local voice to other levels of government.

The analysis has revealed several weaknesses in the infrastructure of permanent bodies of formal representation through which the demands of local governments can be channeled. There are few bodies, and their activities are limited. At the national level, only three formal bodies define the structure of the IGR in which local governments are involved: one is well designed for the goal but completely inactive; another is very thematic (EU NextGen Funds) and only met during 2021; and the remaining one is not a sectoral conference but a body within the internal structure of a central ministry. At the regional level, the governments of the autonomous communities have tended to create their own permanent bodies for cooperation. However, a brief overview of some of them shows that it does not seem to be a priority in the regional agendas. They could play a role in the future, but nowadays they have limited activity or have just been created. This assessment has painted a picture in which the central state seems to favor formal cooperation with the autonomous communities, neglecting local interests.

These findings should not be taken as an indication of a lack of necessary interaction and coordination between local authorities and higher levels of government. As we know from the literature, in Spain there is a large space for informal IGR relations, and political parties are alternative mechanisms of IGR and crucial for understanding government interactions (Agranoff, 2010). Against this background, it is to be expected that large cities have more influence in central decision-making processes than small local authorities. But small municipalities have also learned to activate collective action and form associations to channel their interests to other levels of government, as the case of the *Association of Municipalities in Mountain Areas* shows.

However, formal representation cannot be neglected when assessing the impact of local governments action in IGRs. The extent to which local authorities have actual channels to influence the higher-level governments' policy-making through formal representation structures ensures access when other mechanisms fail. However, it is not clear whether Spain's intergovernmental infrastructure could be reformed to be more inclusive regarding municipalities and grant them a better seat at the table. As the analysis has shown, the mere existence of IGR permanent bodies does not guarantee their effectiveness.

References

Agranoff, R. (2010). *Local governments and their intergovernmental networks in federalizing Spain*. McGill-Queen's Press-MQUP.

Aja, E., & César, C. (2014). Multilevel structures, coordination and partisan politics in Spanish intergovernmental relations. *Comparative European Politics* 12.4, 444–467.

Castellà-Andreu, J. M., & Kölling, M. (2022). Intergovernmental relations and communal tensions in Spain. In *Intergovernmental relations in divided societies* (pp. 159–182). Springer.

Bergström, T., Kuhlmann, S., Laffin, M., & Wayenberg, E. (2022). Special issue on comparative intergovernmental relations and the pandemic: How European devolved governments responded to a public health crisis. *Local Government Studies, 48*(2), 179–190.

Colino, C. (2012). Las relaciones intergubernamentales en España y su práctica: Un estado de la cuestión y algunas consideraciones en perspectiva comparada. In C. Colino, S. León, M. Ferri, & M. Salvador (Eds.), *La práctica de la cooperación intergubernamental en España*. CEPC.

Council of Europe—Congress f Local and Regional Authorities. (2018). *The consultation of local authorities by higher levels of government*. Report CG35(2018)20final. Retrieved October 11, 2023, from https://rm.coe.int/the-consultation-of-local-authorities-by-higher-levels-of-government-g/16808d3c72

de Haro, A. E., Navarro, C., de Santiago, J. M. R., & Sastre, S. D. (2022). The coordinating role of local government associations in intergovernmental relations: The case of FEMP. In F. V. Caballero, S. D. Sastre, E. M. Peñas, M. D. Martín, A. E. de Haro, & C. N. Gómez (Eds.), *Local government in Spain: Responses to urban-rural challenges* (pp. 51–57). Zenodo. https://doi.org/10.5281/zenodo.5734299

Ladner, A., Keuffer, N., Baldersheim, H., Hlepas, N., Swianiewicz, P., Steyvers, K., & Navarro, C. (2019). *Patterns of local autonomy in Europe*. Palgrave Macmillan.

Marks, G., Hooghe, L., & Schakel, A. H. (2008). Patterns of regional authority. *Regional and Federal Studies, 18*(2–3), 167–181.

Navarro, C., & Velasco, F. (2016). 'In wealth and in poverty?' The changing role of Spanish municipalities in implementing childcare policies. *International Review of Administrative Sciences, 82*(2), 315–334.

Navarro, C., & Velasco, F. (2022). From centralization to new ways of multi-level coordination: Spain's intergovernmental response to the COVID-19 pandemic. *Local Government Studies, 48*(2), 191–210.

Paquet, M., & Schertzer, R. (2020). COVID-19 as a complex intergovernmental problem. *Canadian Journal of Political Science/Revue Canadienne de Science Politique, 53*, 343–347.

Pazos Vidal, S. (2023). Las ciudades como actores institucionales en el contexto global y europeo: En especial, las redes de ciudades. *Anuario de Gobierno Local 2022*.

Peters, B. G. (2011). Governance responses to the fiscal crisis—Comparative perspectives. *Public Money & Management, 31*(1), 75–80.

Van de Voorde, N., & de Vet, B. (2020). Is all politics indeed local? A comparative study of dual mandate-holders' role attitudes and behaviours in parliament. *Swiss Political Science Review, 26*(1), 51–72.

Open Access This chapter is licensed under the terms of the Creative Commons Attribution 4.0 International License (http://creativecommons.org/licenses/by/4.0/), which permits use, sharing, adaptation, distribution and reproduction in any medium or format, as long as you give appropriate credit to the original author(s) and the source, provide a link to the Creative Commons license and indicate if changes were made.

The images or other third party material in this chapter are included in the chapter's Creative Commons license, unless indicated otherwise in a credit line to the material. If material is not included in the chapter's Creative Commons license and your intended use is not permitted by statutory regulation or exceeds the permitted use, you will need to obtain permission directly from the copyright holder.

Part IV
Local Government Associations and the Representation of Urban and Rural Interests

Chapter 14
Local Government Associations and Urban and Rural Interests in Austria

Sofia Calzola and Thomas Prorok

Abstract Urban local governments (ULGs) and rural local governments (RLGs) face different challenges and have unique needs that require representation and tailor-made solutions. This chapter aims to provide a comprehensive analysis of the role of the Austrian Association of Cities and Towns (AACT) and the Austrian Association of Municipalities (AAM) as representative entities of local government interests. The objectives of the chapter are the following: first, to determine the placement of local government associations within the Austrian legal framework and assess the extent to which these local government associations are integrated into intergovernmental dialogue and the legislative process; secondly, to find out whether urban and rural interests are considered and represented in advocacy efforts; thirdly, to explore whether and to what extent Austrian local government associations cooperate and on what issues they differ due to urban-rural representation. The chapter also delves into the representation of Austrian local government associations at the EU level. The analysis aims to improve the understanding of the articulation of local government interests in Austria by highlighting the role, challenges and opportunities faced by local government associations.

For the development of the chapter, interviews were conducted with two representatives of the Austrian Association of Cities and Towns and the Austrian Association of Municipalities. In this regard, we extend our gratitude to Alexander Lesigang from the Austrian Association of Cities and Towns (AACT) and Kathrin Wildpert from the Austrian Association of Municipalities (AAM) for their generous collaboration. Their willingness to share their knowledge was instrumental, particularly given the fragmented and limited literature available on Austrian local government associations. Special appreciation is also extended to Simona Wolesa, Head of the Brussels office of the Austrian Association of Towns and Municipalities, and our esteemed colleague Alexandra Schantl, for her unwavering support and the valuable knowledge she shared throughout the process. Their contributions greatly enriched the content of this work. In cases where direct quotations are unavailable, information was obtained from the interviews.

S. Calzola · T. Prorok (✉)
KDZ Centre for Public Administration Research, Vienna, Austria
e-mail: calzola@kdz.or.at; prorok@kdz.or.at

© The Author(s) 2026

K. Kössler, E. M. Belser (eds.), *Local Government Structure and Intergovernmental Relations*, Local and Urban Governance,
https://doi.org/10.1007/978-3-031-99820-1_14

Keywords Local government associations · EU representation · Urban-rural representation · ÖROK · Austria · Municipalities

14.1 Introduction

Austria is a federal state composed of three tiers of government: the central government, the states (*Länder*) and the municipalities (*Gemeinden*). Specifically, Article 116(1) of the Constitution outlines that "[e]very Land is divided into Municipalities". Currently, there are nine states (Burgenland, Carinthia, Lower Austria, Upper Austria, Salzburg, Styria, Tyrol, Vorarlberg, Vienna) and 2093 municipalities.

Aligned with the principles of the European Charter of Local-Self Government,[1] ratified by Austria in 1987, both federal and state constitutions recognize municipalities as legal entities endowed with self-governing authority. Article 116 explicitly defines municipalities as both local administrative units and institutions of self-government. Emphasizing their economic independence, Articles 116(1) and 116(2) assert the municipalities' entitlement, within the boundaries set by federal and state laws, to own, acquire, dispose of assets, operate economic enterprises, manage budgets independently within the financial constitution, and levy taxes.

The organizational structure, powers, and intergovernmental relations of municipalities are pre-determined by Articles 115–120 of the Constitution. According to these provisions, municipalities are mandated to fulfil both their own tasks and those delegated by the states and the federal level (Pernthaler & Gamper, 2005). Key functions assigned to municipalities encompass the management of traffic and urban transports, water resources, waste collection, sewage disposal, kindergartens, aspects of education, elderly care, as well as cultural and sports facilities.

As far as the size of municipalities in Austria is concerned, the data reveals that out of 2093 municipalities, only 87 have a population exceeding 10,000 inhabitants. This constitutes approximately 4% of the total municipalities. In contrast, the majority of municipalities, numbering 2006, have populations below 10,000, making up about 96% of the total (see Table 14.1). These statistics highlight Austria as a country predominantly comprised of small rural municipalities, with larger urban municipalities constituting only a minor portion of the overall municipal landscape.

In this light, the chapter is divided into four main sections. The first section provides an overview of the legal and historical background of Austrian local government associations. The second one presents the Austrian Association of Towns and Municipalities (AACT) and the Austrian Association of Municipalities (AAM). Their structure, membership, roles and tasks are described with a focus on potential differences in representation between urban and rural areas. The third section delves into the legal framework concerning the institutional guarantees of associations,

[1] The charter commits the parties to applying basic rules guaranteeing the political, administrative and financial independence of local authorities. See https://www.coe.int/en/web/impact-convention-human-rights/european-charter-of-local-self-government#/

Table 14.1 Population structure of Austrian municipalities

Population-size groups	Number of municipalities
0–500 EW	108
501–1.000 EW	298
1.001–2.500 EW	947
2.501–5.000 EW	466
5.001–10.000 EW	187
10.001–20.000 EW	60
20.001–50.000 EW	17
50.001–500.000 EW	9
Over 500.000 EW	1
Austria	**2093**

Source: Statistik Austria: Statistik des Bevölkerungsstandes 2023, aggregated and edited by KDZ

focusing on the importance of constitutional recognition for intergovernmental dialogue, fiscal relations and representation at the European level. The last section is devoted to the Austrian Conference on Spatial Planning (ÖROK) and the role of AACT and AAM regarding this conference.

14.2 Local Government Associations in Austria: Legal and Historical Context

The right of local authorities to associate stands as a fundamental pillar, recognized in Article 10 of the European Charter of Local Self-Government. This recognition aims to ensure autonomy, protection, and representation for localities. National local government associations exist in every European country with local administrative units and institutions of self-government. They are organizations that unite municipalities and advocate for their interests in dealings with central governments. They can perform a number of different activities and roles, such as contributing to the legislative process by providing opinions on draft legislation, negotiating and meeting with parliament and government, participating in national and international forums, etc. (Kołsut, 2018).

In Austria, there is a longstanding tradition of accommodating diverse interests through extensive multilateral dialogue and social partnership agreements between associations of employers and employees. This practice was initiated in the aftermath of the Second World War, given the variety of actors present in the national context, including the Austrian Chamber of Commerce (WKÖ), the Austrian Chamber of Agriculture (LKÖ), the Federal Chamber of Labor (BAK), the Austrian Trade Union Confederation (ÖGB), and more. The local government associations have operated within this context which led as early as in the 1950s to a practice of informal consultation (Kiefer & Schausberger, 2009, p. 57). Peculiarly, Austria has two local government associations of a long-standing tradition: the Austrian Association of Cities and Towns (AACT or *Städtebund*), existing since 1915, and the Austrian Association of Municipalities (AAM or *Gemeindebund*), established in 1947. These associations defend and represent the interests of local governments vis-à-vis the federal and state governments and at the European level. The legislative framework in which the associations are embedded enables them to play a significant role on the national scene and to fulfil their responsibilities effectively. In this regard, the constitutional recognition of the associations marked a crucial milestone by definitively enshrining their role in the national context and in intergovernmental relations and giving them the legitimacy to carry out their responsibilities effectively.

The Austrian political landscape has historically been shaped by two major parties: the conservative Austrian People's Party and the Social Democratic Party of Austria. These parties have traditionally held the parliamentary majority, leading to the presence of two local government associations in a relatively small country. At the local level, the influence of the People's Party and the Social Democrats extends to the local government associations. The AAM is often associated with the Conservative Party and represents smaller rural municipalities. In contrast, the Austrian Association of Towns is closer to the Social Democrats and targets larger cities. However, it is crucial to note that, nowadays, many municipalities and cities are members of both associations, which indicates that membership goes beyond narrow party affiliations (Weninger, 2015).

14.3 The Austrian Association of Cities and Towns and the Austrian Association of Municipalities

The AAM and AACT are both constitutionally recognized in Article 115(3) which states that "[t]he Austrian Association of Municipalities and the Austrian Federation of Cities and Towns are competent to represent the interests of the municipalities". Thus, they have a legal mandate to promote local interests in dealings with the federal government, states, and at the European level.

Regarding their function and structure, the AACT is centrally organized. It has direct membership and directly gathers cities and towns, including Vienna and the capitals of the states, all municipalities with more than 10,000 inhabitants and those with special statutes.[2] The smallest member, Rust (Burgenland), has less than 2000 inhabitants. In total, the AACT has 258 members. Although smaller municipalities

[2] Article 116(3) of the Austrian Constitution grants municipalities with at least 20,000 inhabitants the right to have their own statute (*Statut*), becoming a statutory city, which in addition to municipal administrative functions also includes those of the district administration. Currently in Austria there are 15 Statutory Cities. See https://www.ris.bka.gv.at/Dokumente/Erv/ERV_1930_1/ERV_1930_1.html

are also affiliated with AACT, the association focuses mainly on representing large cities. Besides that, the association also maintains regional offices and contact persons in the capital cities of the states. They offer support to their members and have approximately 40 technical committees which review innovative measures and programs adopted by cities and communities, draft statements on new legislation, and discuss the implementation of new policies. It also invests significantly in research on local government, finances projects and publications, and closely cooperates with KDZ, a competence center and knowledge platform for public management consulting, urban policies, public finances and federalism, which has been offering expertise since 1969.[3] An example is "Österreichs Städte in Zahlen",[4] which is published every 2 years and analyzes the status quo of the cities in Austria. Furthermore, the AACT has a long history of collaboration with neighboring countries. In this context, since 2015 it has been the lead partner in the BACID[5] Project, which supports local governments in Western Balkans and Moldova on their path to EU integration, thus closely cooperating with the Network of Associations of Local Authorities of South-East Europe (NALAS),[6] based in Skopje (North Macedonia), which is the umbrella association of local governments in South-East Europe.

Conversely, the AAM has a decentralized organization. The municipalities are not their direct members, it consists of 10 regional organizations: except for Vienna, each state has its own association, apart from Lower Austria and Burgenland, which, for the historical reasons mentioned above, have two: one associated with the conservative Austrian People's Party and the other associated with the Social Democratic Party. The municipalities are more in contact with these regional associations, which have their own structure, offer their members direct support (e.g. for legal issues and financial advice) and represent their interests. Overall, the AAM has 2082 members and mainly gathers and represents small rural municipalities. Its headquarters in Vienna act as an umbrella organization for all these regional branches which collects data and information coming from the regional associations and reports on all interests, and problems at the federal and European level. The AAM also funds research and is active in international exchange.

As proficient advocates for municipal interests, the tasks and duties of the AACT and AAM consist in participating in the preparation of legislation, commenting on federal regulations from the point of view of local government, and lobbying for policies that enhance local autonomy. Acting as intermediaries between local governments and higher echelons of government, they play a pivotal role in ensuring that the concerns of municipalities are not only heard but also given due consideration in the policymaking process. Foremost among their responsibilities is the crucial task of representing the interests of local governments in negotiations concerning

[3] https://www.kdz.eu/en

[4] https://www.staedtebund.gv.at/services/publikationen/staedte-in-zahlen-oestiz/

[5] See https://www.bacid.eu/About_BACID_III

[6] NALAS is a network of associations of local authorities of South-East Europe and brings together 13 associations which represent roughly 9000 local authorities. See http://www.nalas.eu/about-us/

the allocation of budgetary funds and taxation rights between the federal government, states, and local authorities, which is an area where differences in perspectives often emerge. In adherence to the constitutional framework, government proposals for federal laws must be communicated to the states, the AACT and AAM. Similarly, the states are obligated to inform the two associations about their legislative proposals. In a concrete procedural approach, the AACT and the AAM receive draft federal and state laws, subject to a 4-week scrutiny period, during which they evaluate the legislative proposal and subsequently submit their view on the matter. In addition to this, the advantages that municipalities gain from being members of the associations are not limited to representation. They also encompass constant information, as associations proactively update their members on relevant issues. This communication flow operates bidirectionally, not only from municipalities upward to the highest tiers of government but also vice versa. Another advantage is being in a network that fosters interaction among local units through meetings, conferences, and networking events, local government associations provide a platform for the exchange of ideas, best practices, and knowledge sharing.

For both associations, membership is not compulsory and no minimum number of inhabitants is required. Municipalities join on a voluntary basis. Notably, some municipalities opt for dual membership. Only nine members of the AACT are not affiliated with the AAM, while the remaining 249 municipalities hold dual membership. Dual affiliation provides a broader network and a stronger negotiating position, allowing representation by both associations.

In summary, there are two nationwide associations which cooperate on a daily basis to carry out their tasks and duties: to safeguard and represent the interests of municipalities. This cooperation is regular but not institutionalized. It mainly takes place informally at the level of the employees and the general secretaries. There are no institutionalized bodies with set procedure. The main differences between the two associations are four. First, the AACT is centrally organized, whereas the AAM has a regional structure. Secondly, the AACT represents mainly urban local governments (larger municipalities), whereas the AAM mainly focuses on the representation of small rural local governments because they represent the majority of its members. Thirdly, the topics which they address reflect the diverse needs and interests of urban and rural areas, respectively (e.g. EU structural funds for rural development may have limited relevance for the AACT, whereas the issue of "heat islands" in densely populated urban areas due to the high concentration of buildings might receive less attention in the AAM). Fourthly, they have different views regarding some areas of legislation.

These result from the different needs of urban and rural local governments. The challenges and priorities faced by these two types of municipalities necessarily require different solutions, reflecting the associations' commitment to respond to the needs of their members. In summary, their common goal unites them in advocacy, but their approaches change and may differ according to the specific needs and dynamics of urban and rural contexts. For instance, with regard to land use in spatial planning, different positions emerge between the AACT and AAM. The former leans towards advocating for stricter regulations for municipalities, potentially involving a shift of competencies to higher political levels. In contrast, the latter does not see any necessity for changes to the existing legal provisions. Another example are financial matters. On the premise that the first priority is the financial stability and security of cities and municipalities, they tend to diverge on the allocation of financial resources. According to current fiscal equalization mechanisms, funds are redistributed based on a tiered population scheme. According to the scheme, more money is made available per resident for larger communities, resulting in a larger share of revenues being allocated to urban municipalities with larger populations. The AACT supports this mechanism, emphasizing that larger urban local governments also perform tasks for the surrounding smaller ones. Conversely, the Austrian Association of Municipalities opposes this mechanism, advocating for the idea that every resident should have the same value, irrespective of their population. However, there are many areas where the two associations typically present a unified front on major legislative proposals. For example, public procurement law is a field in which they share aligned interests and closely coordinate. This cooperative approach extends to various other legislative projects as well.

Additionally, the AACT and the AAM are members of the Public Accounting Committee. The committee coordinates the standards for the accounting of the states, and municipalities based on an accrual system. It consists of representatives from the Ministry of Finance, the states and the two associations. While the requirements for accounting are generally similar in rural and urban local governments, different interests can occur in questions of the valuation of roads and assets as well as the depreciation of pensions.

14.4 The Legal Framework Regarding the Associations' Institutional Guarantee, Financial Mechanisms and Representation at the EU Level

The legal framework holds paramount importance for Austrian associations of local authorities, and four key aspects will be explored in this context.

Firstly, the above-mentioned official recognition of the Austrian Association of Cities and Towns and the Austrian Association of Municipalities in Article 115(3) of the Constitution is pivotal. Anchored in constitutional law, this recognition as organizations representing local governments is crucial, as the Constitution evidently represents the highest legislative level and cannot be superseded or derogated by any lower law. This provides the two associations with a strong institutional guarantee which protects them from being easily abolished. It is important to note that the strengthening of the AACT and AAM has been an incremental process for which their official constitutional recognition with an amendment in 1988 was a major milestone.

The second point pertains to the Fiscal Equalization Act, a central instrument regulating fiscal relations among Austria's three tiers of government. This act is revised every 3–6 years and involves negotiations between the federal government, the states, and the AACT and AAM on behalf of local governments. Although the federal government plays an important role, it provides the two associations with an additional tool to directly influence and negotiate fiscal equalization mechanisms. In this context, the federal government holds the final authority and the legislation does not require the consent of the states or municipalities when the Fiscal Equalization Act is passed; however, the enactment is preceded by three-level negotiations in which the two local government associations are involved. During the negotiation phase, the associations have the opportunity to directly intervene and discuss the fund distribution mechanisms. Participation in the negotiations on intergovernmental fiscal relations provides the AACT and AAM with an additional and key instrument to represent and advocate the interests and needs of municipalities.

The third key aspect of the legal framework concerns two constitutional concordats focusing on financial matters which were established between the federal government, the states, and the municipalities.[7] A 1999 agreement introduced a Consultation Mechanism that can be called upon if one of the contracting parties intends to adopt legislation that imposes financial obligations on the others. Under this mechanism, the federal and state governments are required to provide information regarding the administrative and financial impacts of the proposed laws or statutes on other government levels. A Consultation Committee, consisting of representatives from all tiers of government, may be convened. If no agreement is reached, the party that intends to adopt the legislation in question will be responsible for financing its own legislation. (Gamper, 2008; Kössler, 2024). The Consultation Mechanism represents a powerful tool for associations since it allows them to scrutinize proposed legislation and engage in direct dialogue with other tiers of government. This capability empowers associations to potentially impede or block the legislative process and exert influence. In addition, it formalizes the opportunity for associations to fulfil their duty towards their members by ensuring their perspectives and concerns are considered in the decision-making process which also enables associations to raise awareness of possible financial burdens on municipalities. The second agreement is the 2012 Austrian Stability Pact, which outlines the coordination of the national budget among the federal government, states, and municipalities. In accordance with this pact, two committees were formed: the Austrian Coordination Committee and the State Coordination Committee. The former facilitates budget coordination between the federal government, states, and municipalities, while the latter oversees budget coordination between the states and municipalities. The Coordination Committees are convened at the request of a contracting party by the Federal Minister of Finance or the respective state, with the Austrian Coordination Committee meeting at least once a year. This ensures that

[7] As a rule, pursuant to Article 15a B-VG, constitutional concordats are only concluded between the Federation and the Länder. The municipalities, represented by the Austrian Association of Cities and Towns and the Austrian Association of Municipalities, were specifically authorized to participate in these two concordats through a special Federal Constitutional Act, which empowered the AACT and the AAM to conclude such concordats.

Austrian local government associations are actively engaged in the entire national budget coordination process, not only in the ratification of the pact.

In this context, it is also worth mentioning that the Fiscal Advisory Council (*Fiskalrat*) is an independent body responsible for monitoring the fiscal discipline of Austria's public entities. It consists of 15 members, experts in public finances, nominated by the federal government, the Austrian Economic Chambers in agreement with the Austrian Chamber of Agriculture, the Federal Chamber of Labour, the AACT, the AAM and the Conference of Provincial Governors. The Fiscal Advisory Council assesses the fiscal situation in Austria, contributes to the public debate, provides recommendations, and reports its analyses and findings to the Austrian parliament on an annual basis. If necessary, it also indicates adjustment paths. The Fiscal Advisory Council plays an essential role because it strengthens the budgetary discipline of the federal government, the states and the local governments (Federal Ministry of Finance, 2021).

A fourth key aspect of the legal framework concerns the representation of local interests at the EU level. Indeed, the Austrian local government associations have established a robust and longstanding presence in Brussels. It has been emphasized that their overall role received a boost during the late 1980s, since the national government enlisted them as allies in the process of Austria's accession to the EU (Fallend et al., 2001, p. 57). Both the AACT and AAM have maintained offices at the Austrian Permanent Representation (PermRep) to the EU since the 1990s. The AACT officially initiated its work in 1994, followed by the AAM in 1996, delegating one staff member each to Brussels. In 1995, the introduction of Article 23(c-d) of the Constitution granted the states and local governments the right to participate in decision-making regarding European integration issues which directly affect them, marking a significant stride forward. According to that provision, the AACT and the AAM must be informed and have the right to comment on any issues within the European Union framework concerning local governments. Information is channelled through the Federal Chancellery, the Federal Ministry of Foreign Affairs, and other federal ministries. In this way the associations receive a wide variety of documents and participate in the internal preliminary discussions of the ministries. In addition, pursuant to Article 23c(4) of the Federal Constitution, both the states and the two associations (AACT and AAM) have the authority to jointly propose three delegates to the government to be nominated to the Committee of the Regions of the European Union.

Nowadays, staff members are fully integrated into PermRep. This integration ensures swift information exchange with representatives of federal ministries and establishes direct communication channels with various Austrian representative bodies within PermRep. These bodies include Länder representatives, the Chamber of Commerce, the Chamber of Labour, the Federation of Industry, the National Bank, and the Association of Farmers, among others. This interconnected network facilitates direct engagement, allowing for the prompt exchange of information and, consequently, for the effective representation of Austrian local government interests at the EU level. Furthermore, as staff members of the official Austrian delegation to the EU, AACT and AAM staff can actively participate in working groups of the

Council of the European Union addressing specific local government issues, such as public procurement, urban mobility, and digital policy. This represents a unique opportunity in the EU since they can discuss relevant topics, exchange experiences and practices on addressing common challenges and influence discussions in these specialized forums.

The Brussels Office of the AACT and AAM functions as the main point of contact for Members of the European Parliament (MEPs), EU institutions, and inquiries from non-Austrian local authorities. It operates as a multilingual hub and guides the main office in Vienna regarding EU issues through various channels, including the AACT monthly magazine ÖGZ (*Österreichische Gemeindezeitung*), contributions to AACT committees, and responses to direct inquiries. Additionally, the office actively engages in speaking engagements, contributes to publications, and works to influence decision-makers by maintaining established contacts with key policymakers. Besides that, the primary role of Austrian local government offices in Brussels is to monitor and support the legislative process, network, promote the interests of local governments at the EU level and lobby. Lobbying is of course a central focus for the Brussels Office: annual priorities aligned with AACT's goals are formulated, analyses on the European Commission's work program are conducted, and a strategy is developed to influence decisions during proposal drafting. This underscores the importance of establishing and maintaining contacts with Commission officials, which usually prefer to receive representative groups covering several member states, underscoring the significance of being members of the Council of European Municipalities and Regions (CEMR) as a representative body.[8] Following the publication of a Commission proposal, it advances into a political decision-making phase involving the European Parliament (EP) and the Council. The EP stands out as the most effective channel for influencing decisions, and effective collaboration with its members and their staff supporting local government interests is crucial. During this phase, domestic decisions are made concerning the implementation of new policies and associated funding responsibilities, namely, who will be responsible for implementing new policies and paying for them. This stage is crucial for local governments, prompting the AACT Office in Vienna to closely monitor the domestic implementation of EU legislation to prevent any unjustified additional financial burdens. In the event of such burdens, both local government associations have the right to invoke the Consultation Mechanism mentioned above (Wolesa, 2022).

Notably, while urban-rural differences sometimes do play a role for the associations at the national level, they speak with one voice at the European level, representing the Austrian local governments as a whole. This unified approach at the European level reflects the understanding that representing different national

[8] Both the AACT and the AAM are members of the Council of European Municipalities and Regions (CEMR), which is the European association for local and regional governments and gathers about 60 member associations whose main tasks are influencing European policy and legislation and providing a forum for debates. For more info see https://www.ccre.org/en/article/introducing_cemr

subdivisions is of little significance in the EU context and might even be counterproductive regarding the achievement of common goals.

14.5 Austrian Local Government Associations and the Austrian Conference on Spatial Planning (ÖROK)

"Spatial planning and spatial development are defined as the joint responsibility of the federal government, the nine federal states (*Länder*), the cities, and the municipalities. The Austrian Conference on Spatial Planning (ÖROK) and the Austrian Spatial Development Concept (ÖREK) are an expression of this understanding of shared responsibility" (Austrian Conference on Spatial Planning, 2021). As a consequence, the planning system in Austria involves various authorities across the three tiers of government. Local governments hold a significant role in this area, as they are responsible for local development planning within their competences. However, other spatial planning tasks are often shared among different tiers of government, necessitating intergovernmental communication, coordination, and cooperation.

For this purpose, the Austrian Conference on Spatial Planning (*Österreichische Raumordnungskonferenz*—ÖROK) was established in 1971 as a political body by the federal government, the states and the municipalities. It is an organization that serves as the central intergovernmental communication and coordination platform for spatial planning. It operates as an instrument of cooperation and partnership across sectors and tiers of government, playing a crucial role in fostering collaboration and addressing the complexities of spatial planning in Austria. Its members include representatives of the federal government, the governors of the nine states, both the AACT and the AAM, which are equal and full members of the ÖROK's political decision-making body, and the economic and social partners, in advisory capacity.[9] Within ÖROK's bodies, voting rights are weighted according to the amount of financial contributions. The federal government and the states hold a significant share, each having 48% of the total voting rights, while AACT and AAM, representing the smaller contributors, hold 2% each, thus having a relatively low weight. Despite their smaller share of voting rights, the statutes afford AACT and AAM certain minority rights to ensure their participation in the governance process. Among these, the AACT and AAM have the prerogative to request meetings and propose agenda items. As an institutional platform ÖROK represents a valuable resource, as it brings together all actors, creating a common ground for intergovernmental dialogue, cooperation, and coordination. It plays a crucial role for Austrian local government associations, providing them with continuous opportunities to be

[9] See https://www.oerok.gv.at/

present and actively involved in the national scene and intergovernmental relations, bringing forth the voices and perspectives of the municipalities.

One of the central tasks of the ÖROK is the formulation of the Austrian Spatial Development Concept (ÖREK), a set of guidelines outlining priority themes to be implemented within a 10-year timeframe. ÖREK is not legally binding, but it provides a nationwide strategy by defining guiding principles and priorities for spatial development without imposing legal obligations on the authorities involved. The formulation of the ÖREK relies on a consensual agreement among all partners, and its development involves an extensive dialogue among members and various relevant actors, including the participation of process experts, planners, and decision-makers, engaging in conferences and think tanks to contribute to the development of the ÖREK.

Within the framework of the previous concept, ÖREK 2011, significant initiatives which are still of high importance were introduced: ÖREK partnerships were launched as an instrument to further enhance the effectiveness and the implementation of the guidelines. They involve collaboration among members of the ÖROK and other stakeholders in various thematic working groups, each focusing on one or more task areas. The core concerns of the ÖREK are thus addressed step by step.

Under the ÖREK partnership "Cooperation Platform City Regions", the Austrian City Regions Agenda (*Agenda Stadtregionen*), the City Regions platform (*Stadtregionen Platform*)[10] and the City Region Day (*Österreichische Stadtregionentag*) were established. It is worth mentioning that the AACT plays a highly active role, as it took the lead regarding the Austrian City Regions Agenda. It has developed, in cooperation with the KDZ—Centre for Public Administration Research, the City Regions platform, where up-to-date data and facts on urban regions can be found. In addition, in cooperation with the KDZ, the AACT organizes the City Region Day, a permanent exchange that takes place once a year and brings together all parties and stakeholders with the aim of exchanging information, results, and examples of good practice.

The present concept, ÖREK 2030, was published in 2021 and contains priority themes to be implemented within 2030. Climate change and its impacts is the key topic of the current concept. ÖREK 2030 identifies several megatrends, defined as "global developments with a long-term impact", which affect the country as a whole but have different impacts depending on the characteristics of the spatial type, to be understood as spaces with common characteristics (e.g. larger urban regions, smaller urban regions, rural centres, etc.), presenting specific and differentiated challenges. Digitization, demographic change, rising demand for energy, urbanization and suburbanization are some of the identified trends that are reshaping the landscape and presenting challenges that Austrian governments must tackle.

Regarding demographic changes and urbanization, Austria is experiencing a division into growth regions and declining regions. The country's population is growing, primarily fuelled by immigration. Simultaneously, there is a shift in the

[10] See https://www.stadtregionen.at/

age structure, with an increase in the number of elderly people across Austria. In contrast, the number of children and young people is rising in the capital cities and surrounding areas. Urban regions, especially cities with more than 50,000 inhabitants, are expected to continue growing, with a projected 20% increase in population by 2050 (Austrian Conference on Spatial Planning, 2021).

In the context of larger urban regions, where business, employment, cultural and educational activities are concentrated and characterized by continuous population growth, there is a necessity for strategic interventions concerning housing, efficient and eco-friendly mobility, high-quality open spaces and sustainable resource utilisation. As pointed out in ÖREK 2030, some of the key challenges identified for these territorial spaces include:

1. Ensuring an appealing living and working environment, also to prevent internal migration to peripheral areas.
2. Managing growth without significant spikes in housing costs, overcrowding and social dislocation.
3. Making locations favorable for international service sector companies.
4. Implementing sustainable management of higher traffic volumes within and between cities, their surroundings and wider catchment areas.
5. Making essential investments to ensure basic services for a growing population.

On the other hand, in rural areas with low population density, the population tends to decrease, and the challenges that need to be tackled are different. Among these, one can mention:

1. Motivating young adults who have left for education purposes and other target groups, such as senior citizens and young families, to move to rural areas by highlighting the high quality of the landscape, low environmental pollution, and an intact social fabric.
2. Addressing the loss of basic services and lack of capacities for elderly care and healthcare.
3. Dealing with the loss of revenues and difficulties in maintaining transport, technical, social, and cultural infrastructure.
4. Managing the expansions of high-voltage power lines for energy transmission.
5. Providing basic services through the use of digital services.

Through the analysis of territorial areas, identification of trends, needs and highlighting challenges, the Austrian Conference on Spatial Planning is an important actor in addressing the challenges associated with disparities and interactions between urban and rural areas, fostering awareness, cooperation and proposing solutions.

Furthermore, ÖROK conducts analyses and studies, producing essential planning materials for Austria's spatial development policy, such as the ÖROK Forecasts, the results of which can be presented in the form of ÖROK Recommendations, which are also accepted at the political level. There is also the ÖROK Publication Series. Every 3 years, the Spatial Planning Report is published, which includes analyses of relevant spatial developments and reports on the activities of its members. As part of the Regional Monitoring System, it offers the ÖROK Atlas, a web tool that provides different materials and indicators for spatial planning analysis in Austria.

The various initiatives undertaken by ÖROK serve to empower municipalities, both urban and rural, by actively involving them, through their representative associations, in the development and implementation of the Austrian planning strategy. Through ongoing intergovernmental dialogue and collaborative efforts, ÖROK contributes to addressing the specific needs of municipalities and advancing cooperative governance, ultimately fostering stronger linkages between urban and rural areas (Hochholdinger, 2021).

14.6 Conclusions

In Austria, the presence of two local government associations is a distinctive characteristic which is influenced by historical factors. Following a longstanding tradition of balancing interests, the AACT and AAM are very well embedded in the constitutional framework of the country, which allows them to be recognized as legitimate and relevant actors. As such they actively participate in intergovernmental dialogue and influence the legislative process, with the above-mentioned Consultation Mechanism being a key tool.

Also, both associations are represented at the European level, holding Offices in Brussels since 1994 (AACT) and 1996 (AAM), respectively, and representing Austrian local government on this bigger stage. In terms of urban-rural interplay, AACT mainly represents urban local governments, including all municipalities with more than 10,000 inhabitants and statutory cities, while AAM predominantly represents the interests of rural local governments, which form the majority in Austria. However, many municipalities hold double membership in both associations for better representation and networking.

The associations generally cooperate on various issues, advocating for the interests of municipalities and coordinating the urban-rural interplay in relation to the federal government and the states. However, given the different needs of their members, different approaches may arise when it comes to specific issues such as the allocation of funds through the fiscal equalization mechanism. In contrast, at the European level, the divergences stemming from the urban-rural divisions are not evident. The two associations rather speak with one voice, representing Austrian local government as a whole.

The Austrian Conference for Spatial Planning (ÖROK), in which both the AACT and the AAM are members, represents again an important tool for local government representation, since the platform gathers all tiers of government and relevant stakeholders, fostering multi-level dialogue and cooperation. The various activities carried out by the institution also cover the urban-rural linkage, pointing out current challenges for the single spatial types (larger urban regions, smaller urban regions, rural areas with low population density etc.), fostering collaborative approaches and implementation actions, empowering local governments and addressing the challenges that affect urban and rural areas.

The Austrian case is interesting due to the presence of two local government associations in a relatively small country. While this offers advantages, such as an extensive network and comprehensive representation of municipalities covering both rural and urban contexts, the existence of two associations with distinct voices could also pose challenges. As mentioned above, one can cite financial matters and the reallocation of funds through the fiscal equalization mechanism. While larger municipalities receive a higher amount per capita to meet their different responsibilities, rural municipalities are allocated a smaller amount. When discussing the Fiscal Equalization Act, the different perspectives of the AACT and the AAM emerge, making careful negotiations necessary to find compromises or agreements that balance interests without jeopardising the overall position of urban and rural local governments. Despite the significant and relevant position that Austrian local government associations generally hold in the country, fulfilling their roles and responsibilities, there is always potential for enhancements in fostering stronger cooperation and collaboration between the two entities.

References

Austrian Conference on Spatial Planning. (2021). *Austrian Spatial Development Concept ÖREK 2030*. Retrieved October 12, 2023, from https://www.oerok.gv.at/fileadmin/user_upload/OEREK_2030-in_brief.pdf

Fallend, F., Mühlböck, A., & Wolfgruber, E. (2001). Die österreichische Gemeinde: Fundament oder "Restgröße" im Mehrebenensystem von Kommunen, Ländern, Bund und Europäischer Union? In Forum Politische Bildung (Ed.), *Regionalismus, Föderalismus, Supranationalismus* (Vienna and Innsbruck) (pp. 45–61).

Federal Ministry of Finance. (2021). *Austrian Stability Programme (update for the period 2020 to 2024)*. https://commission.europa.eu/system/files/2021-05/2021-austria-stability-programme_en.pdf

Gamper, A. (2008). The third tier in Austria: Legal profiles and trends of local government. *Hrvatska I komparativna javna uprava—Croatian and Comparative Public Administration, 8*(1), 71–94.

Hochholdinger, N. (2021). Austrian conference of spatial planning: ÖROK. In A. Schantl, D. Pichler, & T. Prorok (Eds.), *Local government in Austria: Responses to urban–rural challenges* (pp. 80–84). Zenodo. https://doi.org/10.5281/zenodo.5711411

Karl, K. (2024). Austria. In N. Steytler (Ed.), *The Forum of Federations handbook on local government in federal systems* (pp. 83–114). Palgrave Macmillan.

Kiefer, A., & Schausberger, F. (2009). Republic of Austria. In N. Steytler (Ed.), *Local government and metropolitan regions in federal systems* (pp. 38–74). McGill-Queen's University Press.

Kołsut, B. (2018). National associations of municipalities in Europe—Different models of institutionalized political cooperation. *Geography, Environment, Sustainability, 11*(4), 39–55. https://doi.org/10.24057/2071-9388-2018-11-4-39-55

Pernthaler, P., & Gamper, A. (2005). Local government in Austria. In N. Steytler (Ed.), *The place and role of local government in federal systems* (pp. 65–81). Konrad-Adenauer-Stiftung.
Weninger, T. (2015). *100 Jahre kommunale Interessenvertretung—Österreichischer Städtebund 1915–2015*. Österreichischer Städtebund.
Wolesa, S. (2022). *Austrian local government interest representation at EU level*. Retrieved October 20, 2023, from https://www.igadi.gal/wp-content/uploads/tempoexterior_44_web-75-84_en_0.pdf

Open Access This chapter is licensed under the terms of the Creative Commons Attribution 4.0 International License (http://creativecommons.org/licenses/by/4.0/), which permits use, sharing, adaptation, distribution and reproduction in any medium or format, as long as you give appropriate credit to the original author(s) and the source, provide a link to the Creative Commons license and indicate if changes were made.

The images or other third party material in this chapter are included in the chapter's Creative Commons license, unless indicated otherwise in a credit line to the material. If material is not included in the chapter's Creative Commons license and your intended use is not permitted by statutory regulation or exceeds the permitted use, you will need to obtain permission directly from the copyright holder.

Chapter 15
Participation Rights and Channels of Influence of Local Government Associations in the Policy-Making Processes of the German Federation

Annegret Eppler

Abstract The chapter examines how the local government associations (LGAs) carry their interests into the policy-making process of the German Federation. It is shown that the organization and the work of LGAs is strongly influenced by the federal character of Germany. Formally, the local level is part of the *Länder* and their administrations, and the character, rights and structure of the local municipalities and counties is dependent on the rules of the respective *Land*. At the same time, the local level has the right of local self-government and assumes important tasks for the overall system. Local interests are formally and informally represented by the LGAs at *Länder* and federal level. Competition between the LGAs is less due to the urban-rural divide and more due overlapping membership structures (for reasons of history and also German federalism), party-politics and questions of prestige. The cooperative character of the German political system plays a key role in overcoming the different interests. With a few exceptions, the local government associations are organized under private law, and the chapter discusses whether a more formal organization would be more in line with the character of self-governing bodies of the municipalities and counties.

Keywords German federation · Cooperative federalism · Multi-level governance · Association under private law · Path dependency

A. Eppler (✉)
University of Applied Sciences for Public Administration, Kehl, Germany
e-mail: eppler@hs-kehl.de

© The Author(s) 2026

K. Kössler, E. M. Belser (eds.), *Local Government Structure and Intergovernmental Relations*, Local and Urban Governance,
https://doi.org/10.1007/978-3-031-99820-1_15

15.1 Introduction: Local Government Associations in Germany

There are three local government associations (LGAs) in the Federal Republic of Germany: the *Deutscher Städtetag* (DST, German Association of Cities), the *Deutscher Landkreistag* (DLT, the German Association of Counties) and the *Deutscher Städte- und Gemeindebund* (DStGB, German Association of Towns and Municipalities). The DST represents the larger cities, the DLT the counties (*Landkreise*) and the DStGB the medium-sized and smaller towns and villages. All three associations see themselves as information networks for their members and as frameworks for the exchange of experiences. Furthermore, they all focus on representing local interests in the political decision-making process. As classic associations, they do not participate in political elections (Reutter, 2001, p. 135–143; Brüsewitz, 2017, p. 15–17). In contrast to other political associations, the municipalities and counties represented by the LGAs are corporations under public law (*Körperschaften des öffentlichen Rechts*) which perform public tasks, enjoy the right of self-government and must have a democratic legitimacy according to Article 28(1–2) Basic Law (German Constitution, *Grundgesetz*, GG). Like other associations, the LGAs are organized under civil law (*Vereinsrecht*). The DST is an unregistered association, the other two are registered associations. They see the private form of organization as a reaction to their enforced conformity during the Nazi era, in which they were forced to integrate in the *Deutscher Gemeindetag* (background conversation II, Reutter, 2001, p. 140–142; Henneke, 2005, p. 701–702). As organizations under private law, they are not subject to legal supervision by state authorities. Only the LGAs in Bavaria (i.e. the associations at *Länder* level in Bavaria) are organized as corporations under public law.

Germany's federal structure shapes the membership structure of LGAs. In each of the 16 German *Länder* (states, i.e. the subnational units of the German Federation) there are LGAs of the respective *Land* (state). At federal level, the members of the DLT and the DStGB are the respective LGAs at *Länder* level. The DST is made up of associations at *Länder* level (Baden-Württemberg, Bavaria, North Rhine-Westphalia) as well as direct members (direct members are about 200 cities, some of them part of a county, others not, plus the city states of Berlin, Hamburg and Bremen, which have the same legal position as the other 13 *Länder*). The DLT and the DST also have other members which deal with local issues (the DST, e.g. a pension fund and a transport association; the DLT e.g. supra-local child, youth and social welfare organizations; some are members of both LGAs, the DLT and the DST, e.g. the Hesse Welfare Association at *Land* level (*Landeswohlfahrtsverband* Hessen) (Bernard & Klausch, 2023, p. 484–486).

The membership structure of the LGAs is also characterized by a partial overlap of their core clientele. While the DLT represents all of the 294 German counties, the

DST and the DStGB compete for members. The tripartite division of the LGAs has historical roots: after the end of the Nazi regime and the Second World War, LGAs were re-established bottom-up in the mid and late 1940s. They differed not only between the partly newly formed German *Länder*, but also between the then existing Allied occupation zones. In addition to the DST (which emerged partly from a "Mayors' Conference") and the DLT, two other associations initially began their work: the *Deutsche Städtebund* (Association of Cities) and *Deutsche Gemeindetag* (Association of Municipalities). It was not until 1973 that the latter two merged to form the DStGB, which primarily represents the towns and villages belonging to a county (Henneke, 2012, p. 117–126). Since then, medium-sized towns and cities can be represented by both, the DST and the DStGB. In the course of German unification at the beginning of the 1990s, five Eastern German *Länder* were created on the territory of the former German Democratic Republic. Subsequently, LGAs developed at the level of the five Eastern *Länder*, representing both larger and smaller cities, towns and villages (unified associations, Bernard & Klausch, 2023, p. 487–488). At federal level, all of these unified associations are members of both the DST and the DStGB. In each of the Eastern *Länder*, there are therefore only two local government associations, one representing counties and one unified association representing municipalities of any size. In some Western German *Länder*, too, there is only either an association of cities or an association of towns and villages (*Städtetag Rheinland-Pfalz*, *Hessischer Städtetag*, *Städtetag Niedersachsen*, *Städteverband Schleswig-Holstein*, *Saarländischer Städte- und Gemeindetag*), all of which are dual members of the DST and the DStGB) (Bernard & Klausch, 2023, p. 484–486 and appendix: 2).

This chapter examines how the LGAs in Germany carry their interests into the policy-making process at *Länder* level and at federal level. The analysis is carried out on the basis of predefined guiding questions in order to enable an international comparison in conjunction with the other chapters of the edited volume. The literature on the LGAs in Germany is not extensive. The majority of the older contributions were written by then acting or former officials of the associations. For this chapter, therefore, in addition to laws, the existing literature and internet sources, three expert interviews and some background conversations were conducted. Where the rules differ between the German *Länder*, reference is made to Baden-Württemberg law. In the following, the relations between the local level, *Länder* level and federal level is illustrated and participation rights and channels of influence of LGAs at both the *Länder* and the federal level are discussed. Subsequently, differences between the three LGAs are analyzed. In particular, the question of whether the representation of rural areas differs from that of urban areas is examined. In a next step, the structures and mechanisms that help to bridge the differences will be examined. Finally, the LGAs are classified in terms of their future development potential.

15.2 Legal Relations Between the Local, *Länder* and Federal Level

According to Article 20(1) Basic Law, the Federal Republic of Germany is a democratic and social federal state. There are 16 *Länder* of which each has a fully developed political system with its own *Land* constitution. Three *Länder* consist of large cities (city states): Berlin, Bremen and Hamburg. The local level comprises municipalities (cities, towns, villages of different sizes) and counties and is not formally considered a third level in the multi-level system of the German Federation, but is assigned to the *Länder*. Within the scope of their competences, the *Länder* decide on their *Gemeindeordnungen* (municipal codes, in some *Länder*, they are called *Gemeindeverfassung,* "municipal constitutions") and *Landkreisordnungen* (county codes). At the same time, the right of local self-government is guaranteed according to Article 28(2) Basic Law, i.e. there is a local area in which the state (i.e. the federal and the *Länder* level) may not intervene.

Within Germany, the responsibility for the "exercise of state powers" and the "fulfilment of state tasks" lies with the *Länder* (Article 30 Basic Law). The federal level is only allowed to act in those fields that are explicitly written down in the Basic Law. Over the decades, amendments to the Basic Law have increasingly transferred legislative competences from the *Länder* to the federal level, including policy fields that affect citizens locally. At the same time, legislative competences have also remained with the *Länder* (which continue to adopt rules, in some cases within the same policy areas as the federal level). In contrast to legislative competences, administrative competences have largely remained at the *Länder* level. The administration of the law enacted at the *Länder*, federal and EU level is therefore primarily a matter for the *Länder* and occupies a large space in the range of tasks of the *Länder*. The *Länder* implement federal laws as their own affairs (Article 84 Basic Law) or act on behalf of the Federation (Article 85 Basic Law). However, the law of the implementing *Land* and not, federal law transfers tasks to the local level. Exceptions are possible within which the local level has to perform certain administrative tasks on behalf of the federal government (Article 85 Basic Law, e.g. disaster control). The principle of connexity (*Konnexitätsprinzip*) applies between the local level and the *Länder*, i.e. financial compensation must be given when new mandatory tasks are transferred to the local level.

As far as the organization of the *Länder* administrations and the position of the local level are concerned, the highest *Land* authority are the *Land* governments, i.e. the prime minister *(Ministerpräsident)* and their ministers. In most *Länder* with a large territory, intermediate authorities between the *Land* and the local level are set up (*Regierungspräsidien*, *Bezirksregierungen*) for the general administration. The lower administrative authorities are subordinate to them. Most of the tasks of the lower administrative authorities are covered by the local level. For instance, in Baden-Württemberg, the structure of the state administration is regulated in the *Landesverwaltungsgesetz* (LVG, Land Administration Act). Here, the *Land* ministries are set up as "supreme state authorities" according to §§ 7–9 LVG and the

Regierungspräsidien as intermediate authorities according to §§ 11–14 LVG. The counties and the bigger municipalities perform tasks of the lower administrative authorities (*Untere Verwaltungsbehörde*, §§ 15–22 LVG).

The *Länder* decide on their municipal codes or municipal constitutions which are both simple laws. As far as the three city states are concerned, in Berlin and Hamburg, the municipal constitutions are superimposed by the respective *Land* constitutions. In Bremen the two municipalities of Bremen and Bremerhaven have independent municipal constitutions. The German municipal codes or constitutions have long historical roots (such as the *Ordnung für sämtliche Städte der preußischen Monarchie* (Order for all Cities of the Prussian Monarchy) of 1808 developed by Freiherr vom Stein). However, after the Second World War, the municipal codes were also significantly shaped by the Allies in their respective occupation zones, where the local level was initially rebuilt. Therefore, different types of municipal codes exist in Germany. The most common one has its roots in Southern Germany (*Bürgermeisterverfassung*). There, both the mayor and a representative body (council) are directly elected and the mayors have their own area of responsibility as heads of the municipal administration. In the municipal code which in the beginning used to prevail in Northern Germany (*Ratsverfassung*), the council elects the mayor, who primarily acts as (honorary) council chairperson. The actual business of the municipal administration is carried out by an official also elected by the council (that was the case in North Rhine-Westphalia and Lower Saxony until the late 1990s). The third model (*Magistratsverfassung*) provides for a strict separation of powers between a magistrate (mayor and aldermen as the head of the administration) and a city council (people's representation) (only in Hesse and Bremerhaven, repealed in Schleswig-Holstein at the end of the 1990s). To this day, the different models shape the nuances of municipal organization in the different *Länder* (Ipsen, 2007).

The local authorities, i.e. counties and municipalities, of all German *Länder* are subject to the guarantee of local self-government under Article 28(2) Basic Law, which is also enshrined in most *Land* constitutions (e.g. Article 71(1) Constitution of Baden-Württemberg). There are municipalities of different sizes (in Baden-Württemberg: *Große Kreisstädte* (larger towns with more than 20,000 inhabitants that are part of a county), *Stadtkreise* (large cities that are not part of a county and fulfill the same tasks as a county, in some *Länder* they are called *kreisfreie Stadt*) and "*sonstige Gemeinden*" (small municipalities and villages that are part of a county)). All municipalities are subject to the principle of universality, i.e. they are responsible for all public tasks in their respective municipal area, and they have a right to determine their tasks. This is linked to the expectation that the municipality promotes the common welfare of its inhabitants in civic self-government (cf. §§ 1, 2 Municipal Code Baden-Württemberg). In contrast, counties do not have such a comprehensive responsibility. Their responsibility begins where the municipalities being part of the county reach the limits of their capacity ("subsidiary universality"). There is also a difference between municipalities and counties when it comes to the distinction from the *Land*. When the municipalities perform tasks of the "lower administrative authority", they do so as indirect *Land* authorities (*mittelbare*

Landesbehörde), quasi on behalf of the *Land*, being a self-governing authority, not identic with the *Land*. In contrast, the counties have a double function: they are both, self-governing authorities and lower *Land* authorities ("Janus-facedness") (Plate et al., 2018; Fleckenstein, 2024).

In summary, first and foremost, the local level in Germany enjoys local self-government. This puts both municipalities and counties in a tense relationship with the respective *Land*. At the same time, the local level is not considered a third level in German federalism, but is clearly assigned to the German *Länder*, which decide on their classification, supervision, municipal constitution, organs and bodies as well as on their responsibilities as (in the case of municipalities: indirect) lower administrative authorities. The relationship between the federal level and the local level is mediated by the *Länder*. Apart from exceptions, the federal level is not allowed to assign tasks to the municipalities. Nevertheless, the vast majority of all federal laws (and also all *Länder* laws and EU legislative acts) concern the local level. This raises the question of the extent to which municipalities and counties can influence federal and *Land* laws.

15.3 Rights and Opportunities of LGAs to Participate

As "lower administrative authorities", municipalities act on behalf of the *Land* and counties act in their capacity as *Land* authorities. In doing so, they are part of a hierarchy of administrative authorities that culminates in the *Land* government with its ministries and finally the prime ministers as the highest authority of the *Land* administration. The governments of the *Länder* have clearly set up possibilities of influencing the policy-making process at the federal level: depending on the size of the *Land*, they have different numbers of votes in the Bundesrat (Article 51 Basic Law, a special kind of second parliamentary chamber at federal level). The *Bundesrat* has a suspensive veto right in the legislative processes at the federal level, which is staggered depending on the extent to which the *Länder* level is affected. However, when the municipalities or counties act in the broad range of self-governing tasks, they face a kind of "glass ceiling". There are no formally predetermined channels of influence or "chains of legitimacy" from the local level to the *Land* and federal level in order to carry the local interests, political assessments or experiences upwards. This gap is only bridged by the LGAs (Reutter, 2002, p. 1573–74).

15.3.1 Formal Participation Rights at Länder *Level*

First of all, the municipalities and counties can influence the LGA at *Land* level. Organized according to private association law (except in Bavaria, as mentioned above), the LGAs have statutes (*Satzungen*) which settle the preconditions of membership, i.e. the types of municipalities and counties to which the association is open

(Henneke, 2005, p. 702). A municipality or county can decide through its elected representative body to join a LGA (the procedure is written down in the municipal and county codes). According to the statutes of the LGA, the member municipalities or counties send a certain number of representatives to the general assembly. In most cases, the representatives are elected chief administrative officials and members of the local representative bodies (Henneke, 2005, p. 702). Association law links the general assembly to the association bodies, and the executive board *(Präsidium)* represents the association externally (Henneke, 2005, p. 702).

Since the 1970s, the then 11 Western German *Länder* gave more and more rights to participate in legislative procedures to the LGAs at *Land* level (Henneke, 2012, p. 205). Many *Länder* constitutions contain respective rules. The constitution of Baden-Württemberg states in Article 71(4) that the municipalities and counties or their associations must be heard early enough before general questions affecting them are regulated by law or regulation ("Verordnung", general-abstract legislative act by the government). The respective rules in the other *Länder* constitutions are almost identical in their wording (cf. the overviews of Riederle, 1995, p. 13–28; Brüsewitz, 2017, p. 75–110 and 140–164; Henneke, 2012, p. 205–226) (Table 15.1).

Most other *Länder* write down the participation rights of the *Land* LGAs by simple law. Some of these are more detailed than the rules in the *Länder* constitutions. For example, the municipal constitution of Mecklenburg-Vorpommern (although called "constitution", it is a simple law) states in § 6 first the right to form LGAs, then the duty of the *Land* government to maintain contact with them and to cooperate with them in the preparation of the rules that affect them. In Rhineland-Palatinate, the municipal code stipulates in § 129 that drafts of legal provisions and general administrative regulations that affect local self-government must be discussed with the LGAs in an appropriate form and in good time (Table 15.2).

In Hesse, there is a specific simple law on the safeguarding of local self-government in legislation (*Gesetz über die Sicherung der kommunalen Selbstverwaltung bei der Gesetzgebung*, *Beteiligungsgesetz*, KomBetG) since 1999. It concerns the participation of LGAs in draft laws and draft regulations as well as in drafts of administrative regulations in §§ 2–4 and goes into more detail about the processes and deadlines of the participation procedure. In North Rhine-Westphalia, there is neither a constitutional nor a non-constitutional regulation that addresses

Table 15.1 Participation rights regulated in German *Länder* constitutions

Land	Article of *Land* constitution
Baden-Württemberg	Article 71(4)
Bavaria	Article 83 (7) sentence 1
Brandenburg	Article 97(4)
Lower Saxony	Article 57(6)
Saarland	Article 124
Saxony	Article 84(2)
Thuringia	Article 91(4)

Source: Own illustration

Table 15.2 Participation rights regulated in simple laws of the *Länder*

Land	Municipal constitution/municipal or county code
Mecklenburg-Vorpommern	§ 6 (Municipalities), § 93 (Counties) Municipal Constitution (*Kommunalverfassung*)
Rhineland-Palatinate	§ 129 Municipal Code (*Gemeindeordnung*), § 72 County Code (*Landkreisordnung*)
Saxony-Anhalt	§ 160 Municipal Constitution Act (*Kommunalverfassungsgesetz*), § 73a County Code (*Landkreisordnung*)
Schleswig-Holstein	§ 132 Municipal Code (*Gemeindeordnung*), § 17 County Code (*Kreisordnung*)

Source: Own illustration

Table 15.3 Participation rights regulated in the rules of procedure of the German *Länder* parliaments

Land	Paragraph rules of procedure of *Land* parliament
Baden-Württemberg	§ 31b(3) and (6); § 50a(6)
Bavaria	§ 174
Brandenburg	§ 81(2) sentence 1
Hesse	§ 93(4)
Mecklenburg-Vorpommern	§ 23(4)
North Rhine-Westphalia	§ 58
Rhineland-Palatinate	§ 53(3) and § 81(4)
Saxony	§ 36
Saxony-Anhalt	§ 86a
Schleswig-Holstein	§ 25(3)
Thuringia	§ 79(2)

Source: Own illustration

cooperation between the *Land* government and LGAs (but there is a provision in the rules of procedure of the *Land* parliament).

All 16 *Länder* have *Länder* parliaments with their own legislative powers (most of them are called *Landtage*). In the rules of procedure of many *Länder* parliaments, participation rights of the LGAs at *Länder* level can be found. For instance, in Baden-Württemberg the LGAs have access to the meetings of the committees of the *Landtag* and are heard there insofar as their consultation is required by any law, even if a written statement has already been made (§ 31b, 50a (6) rules of procedure of the Baden-Württemberg *Landtag*) (Table 15.3).

§§ 17 and 18 of the rules of procedure of the *Landtag* of the Saarland settle the hearing of experts and associations, but do not make any special provisions for LGAs. § 94(6) of the rules of procedure of the *Landtag* of Lower Saxony writes down the hearing of "interest representatives, experts and other persons providing information" (translation by the author), also without mentioning the LGAs separately. In the rules of procedure of other *Land* parliaments, there are corresponding provisions of hearings without special rights for the LGAs (Bremen: § 75(3); Berlin: § 28; Hamburg § 59).

There are further consultation rights of the LGAs at *Länder* level on certain, particularly financial, issues (Henneke, 2012, p. 211–214). Special rules to ensure compliance with the above-mentioned principle of connexity (*Konnexitätsprinzip*) have been established in the constitutions of Bavaria (Article 83(7)) and North Rhine-Westphalia (Article 78), both accompanied by single laws. In Rhineland-Palatinate there is a single law to safeguard the principle of connexity. These laws implement procedures for consultations between the *Land* government and the *Land* LGAs (cf. Henneke, 2012, p. 207–209). In some *Länder*, special rights of participation also exist in matters of financial distribution to preserve the constitutional guarantee of self-government in financial matters (Henneke, 2012, p. 211–215). To this end, special processes have been established, e.g. commissions on the financial distribution between the *Land* and the local level in Hesse and Baden-Württemberg (in Baden-Württemberg, this commission consists of three members of the *Land* government and three members of the *Land* LGAs). In Brandenburg, Saarland and Saxony advisory boards have been set up (Henneke, 2012, p. 211–215).

In Rhineland-Palatinate, a *Kommunaler Rat* ("local council")—an institution in which the local level is represented at *Land* level with the aim to further develop local self-government—has been established in 1995 by simple law (Landesgesetz über den Kommunalen Rat vom 22. Dezember 1995). It advises the *Land* government, can make recommendations to the *Land* parliament at any time and receives draft legislation at the same time as the LGAs (§ 1 Landesgesetz über den Kommunalen Rat). Initial fears on the part of the LGAs that such an institution could impair their function were counteracted by its composition (Henneke, 2012, p. 210). It has 28 members, including nine members from each of the three LGAs at *Land* level and one representative of the Ministry of the Interior who is the chairperson and has no voting rights. More than half of the members should be elected, i.e. belong to a municipal representative body or be an honorary municipal civil servant (Landesverordnung zur Ausführung des Landesgesetzes über den Kommunalen Rat vom 18. Juni 1996). In practice, the chairpersons of the LGAs and their deputies have always been members of the *Kommunaler Rat* (Henneke, 2012, p. 210).

15.3.2 Formal Participation Rights at Federal Level

The three LGAs at federal level, DST, DLT and DStGB, represent the interests of the local level in the policy-making process at the federal level. The respective LGAs at *Länder* level are members of the DLT and the DStGB and send delegates to their general committees (*Hauptausschuss*). The DST not only has such a general committee consisting of the delegates of the member associations. The supreme organ of the DST is the general meeting (*Hauptversammlung*), which includes not only the member associations at *Länder* level but also the direct member cities and other direct members (Henneke, 2005, p. 702; Henneke, 2012, p. 96–99, 112–114, 122–125). However, the German *Länder* see the local level as part of themselves and have the constitutional right to represent the *Länder* level via the *Bundesrat* (Jaedicke & Wollmann, 1999, p. 318). Therefore, the *Länder* interpret the representation of local interests as their task and in some situations, there may be competition between LGAs and *Länder at the federal level*.

The participation rights of the LGAs vis-à-vis the federal government are laid down in the Joint Rules of Procedure of the Federal Government (*Gemeinsame Geschäftsordnung der Bundesregierung*, GGO; Henneke, 2012, p. 216–218; cf. Riederle, 1995, p. 28–29). According to § 41 GGO, the opinion of the *Länder* and the LGAs is to be obtained before drafting legislative acts that affect the interests of the *Länder* or the local level. At the stage at which the draft law is on the table, it must be forwarded to the *Länder*, the LGAs and the representations of the *Länder* to the Federation as early as possible. Therefore, the LGAs are consulted on the drafts, and their hearings take place before the other associations and interest groups are heard. The provisions also apply to regulations ("*Verordnungen*", i.e. legislative acts of the government, § 62(2) GGO) and administrative regulations (§ 70 GGO). However, in these cases, an opinion is not obtained before the draft is completed. Before the reform of the GGO in 2000, the LGAs did not have to be informed and heard until the first draft had been completed, even in the case of legislative proposals, i.e., their participation rights have been strengthened since then (Riederle, 1995, p. 28–29; Henneke, 2012, p. 216).

As part of the explanatory memorandum to the envisaged law, the federal ministries must submit an impact assessment including an estimate of the impact on revenue and expenditure of public budgets (§ 44 GGO). The estimated effects on the budgets of the *Länder* and the local level have to be listed separately, which often means that figures have to be obtained from them (Henneke, 2012, p. 216–217). In addition, the result of the association's participation, in particular the presentation of essential suggestions that have not been complied with in the draft law, have to be mentioned in the cover letter to the cabinet (i.e. the collegium of Federal Ministers and the Federal Chancellor). There are additional participation rights of the LGAs when it comes to EU policy (§ 74 GGO).

The participation rights of the LGAs vis-à-vis the German *Bundestag* (the German federal parliament) are laid down in the Rules of Procedure of the *Bundestag* (*Geschäftsordnung des Deutschen Bundestags*, GO-BT, Henneke, 2012, p. 218–220; cf. Riederle, 1995, p. 30). The lead committee on a draft of a legislative act must give the LGAs the opportunity to comment before the committee adopts a resolution if the essential interests of the local level are affected, § 69a Rules of Procedure of the Bundestag (cf. § 70 for non-public hearings). Essential interests of the local level are affected by laws which are to be implemented in whole or in part by the local level, which directly affect their public finances or which affect their administrative organization. The hearings may be waived for the drafts of the government if the views of the LGAs are evident from the explanatory memorandum. Committee reports must reproduce the statements of the LGAs in their essential points (§§ 66, 69a(5), 70 GO-BT).

At present, there is no institutional connection between the LGAs or other local actors and the Federal Government or the *Bundestag*. In the 1950s, two departments for local affairs were founded in the Federal Ministry of the Interior, but they no longer exist. In 1951, a *Bundestag* committee for local affairs was set up, which was dissolved in 1969; in the 17th and 18th legislative periods (2009–2017) a subcommittee for local affairs was set up as part of the Committee on Internal Affairs (Henneke, 2012, p. 215–216, cf. also 183–187).

The LGAs have participation rights in special policies. They are involved in EU affairs (see the Act on Cooperation between the Federal Government and the Bundesrat in European Union Matters (*Gesetz über die Zusammenarbeit von Bund und Ländern in Angelegenheiten der Europäischen Union,* EUZBLG)). Moreover, they are represented in the Economic Council for the Public Sector (*Konjunkturrat für die öffentliche Hand*). The task of this institution is to coordinate and give advice on major economic questions. It is made up of representatives of the federal and *Länder* ministries and the LGAs. The involvement of the local level in overall economic planning is considered important (Henneke, 2012, p. 222–224), as other associations are not invited, and the local level is equally represented. This was also the case in the Financial Planning Council (*Finanzplanungsrat*) since 1969. However, since its reform and renaming to "Stability Council" (*Stabilitätsrat*) in 2010, the LGAs are only invited as guests. The LGAs are also represented in the administrative board of the Federal Employment Agency (*Bundesagentur für Arbeit*) (Henneke, 2012, p. 205) and in the boards of organizations such as the German Hospital Association (*Deutsche Krankenhaus-Gesellschaft*), the German Association for Public and Private Welfare (*Deutscher Verein für öffentliche und private Fürsorge*), the German Association for Housing (*Deutscher Verband für Wohnungswesen*), the German Tourism Association (*Deutscher Tourismusverband*) and the National Committee for the Protection of Monuments (*Nationalkomitee für Denkmalschutz*) (Bernard & Klausch, 2023, p. 486, Henneke, 2012, p. 226–229).

Moreover, the LGAs participated in reform commissions at federal level, e.g. in the so-called Federalism Commission I (*Kommission zur Modernisierung der bundesstaatlichen Ordnung* 2003–2004), in the Federalism Commission II (*Kommission zur Modernisierung der Bund-Länder-Finanzbeziehungen* 2007–2009) and the Commission on the Reform of local finances (K*ommunalfinanzreformkommission* 2010–2011) (Henneke, 2012, p. 187–205).

15.3.3 Assessments of the Actual Influence

The LGAs themselves consider their participation rights to be insufficient (Interview I; Deutscher Städtetag, 2020; Bernard & Klausch, 2023, p. 485). They note that at the federal level, participation rights are only enshrined in the rules of procedure of the government and the parliament and that these rules are only binding internally (Henneke, 2012, p. 218; Meyer, 1994). They also note that the provisions are largely formulated as "should" provisions and a failure would therefore have no consequences (Henneke, 2012, p. 218). Furthermore, they complain that the federal ministries usually do not adhere to § 41 GGO, i.e. their inclusion in the stage before the first draft is prepared (Henneke, 2012, p. 216). All in all, they state that their rights are often not recognized (Ruge, 2022, p. 549–551), applied inadequately or not at all (Henneke, 2012, p. 218). The LGAs also state that the various federal ministries act differently. Moreover, they complain that deadlines for comments are often too short (Schrader, 2004, p. 218). While all this speaks in favor of a further formalizing and strengthening of their rights, others even see the danger of a too close cooperation with the federal and *Länder* governments that could be directed against the interests of the local level (Interview I). When it comes to the participation rights vis-à-vis the *Bundestag*, the LGAs argue that the right to be heard is treated differently in the various parliamentary committees (Henneke, 2012, p. 219). They complain, that in many cases there are de facto no privileged hearings compared to other associations. Many hearings also took place very late (Henneke, 2012, p. 219 lists specific cases).

A scientific analysis from 2023 deals with all laws promulgated in the 19th legislative period (2017–2021) and shows that participation in the *Bundestag* committees is documented in only 62% of all legislative procedures which are relevant for the local level (Bernhard & Klausch 2023). Compared to the parliament, the participation of LGAs by the federal ministries was higher overall. Nevertheless, there are differences from one ministry to the other and also between the different parliamentary committees. The explanatory approaches of the authors of the study search in the political significance of projects as well as in their complexity and thus the need for practical knowledge (Bernard & Klausch, 2023).

Despite various attempts, for example in the Commission on the Reform of Local Finances (*Kommunalfinanzreformkommission* 2010–2011), there has not yet been a far-reaching reform of the participation rights of the LGAs. The extension of their rights in the rules of procedure of federal government and federal parliament are rather path-dependent developments. However, there is no shortage of proposals for reform (cf. Henneke, 2012, p. 231–241). The most important proposal is to supplement Article 28(2) Basic Law with a constitutionally guaranteed right of the LGAs to be heard when the local level is affected by legislative projects. This idea was repeatedly rejected in several constitutional reform commissions since the 1970s (Henneke, 2012, p. 231–234 gives an overview). It was feared that the Basic Law would be overloaded, and the LGAs were accused of overvaluing their right to be heard. Other proposals focused on the rules of procedure of the *Bundesrat* (i.e. the representation of the *Länder* governments in the federal policy making, cf. Henneke, 2012, p. 234) or the committee which mediates, if the *Bundestag* and the *Bundesrat* are not of the same opinion (*Vermittlungsausschuss,* cf. Henneke, 2012, p. 234–235). However, participation in the phase in which a law is already in the *Bundesrat* is very late, and moreover, the *Bundesrat*, composed of *Länder* representatives, sees itself as a representant of the local level (Jaedicke & Wollmann, 1999, p. 317–318).

At the level of the *Länder*, it was discussed whether (advisory) chambers for local affairs could be introduced in the *Länder* parliaments in order to make relations between the local level and the *Länder* more formal and transparent. An attempt to do so failed in Lower Saxony in 1995. Arguments against local chambers are that the decision-making sovereignty and effectiveness of the already relatively weak *Länder* parliaments could be restricted (Henneke, 2012, p. 241–242).

15.3.4 Informal Channels of Influence

In addition to their formal rights of participation, the LGAs use all possible informal channels at *Länder* and federal level to bring their interests into the policy-making process in the sense of multi-level governance (Marks et al., 1996).

The informal channels at the federal level include talks with the Federal Chancellor (*Bundeskanzler*), the Federal Ministers and staff of the ministries, especially, the Federal Minister of the Interior, but also with other ministers and ministries (Henneke, 2012, p. 226–227). When it comes to the *Bundestag*, connections with the political groups and their chairpersons are maintained. Many parliamentary groups in the *Länder* and the federal parliaments have spokespersons for and working groups on local affairs. There is also an ongoing exchange with the political parties and their experts and working groups. The frequency of discussions, especially with the highest-level discussion partners, increases when special reform projects affecting the local level are pending (Henneke, 2012, p. 226–229).

The DST, DLT and DStGB hold regular talks with the Conference of the Prime Ministers, i.e. the meeting of the heads of government of the *Länder* (*Ministerpräsidentenkonferenz*), and, in some cases, also with conferences of ministers of the *Länder* on specific policies (Jaedicke & Wollmann, 1999, p. 318; Henneke, 2012, p. 227). In the course of reform processes, e.g. the reform commissions concerning the German Federation, these contacts intensified. Although the *Länder* politicians then act in their function at federal level, some LGAs at *Länder* level saw themselves partly in competition with their own federal associations (Henneke, 2012, p. 227).

The informal channels of influence also extend to the Members of the *Bundestag* and the *Länder* parliaments (Henneke, 2012, p. 228). Members of parliament who performed local functions before being elected to parliament can feed the local perspective into the political groups, committee meetings and the plenary. In the *Bundestag* and in most *Länder* parliaments, it is not permitted to be a member of parliament and a full-time representative at local level at the same time. In the past, in some *Länder* honorary mayors were elected according to the municipal code, especially in Northern Germany (*Ratsverfassung*, as explained above), who could then hold a parliamentary mandate at the same time. However, it is discussed how far their influence actually reached, as they also had to act in line with their political groups (Dieckmann, 1999, p. 303).

15.4 Differences and Competition Between the Local Government Associations

The formal participation rights of the LGAs at *Länder* and at federal level, and also the proposals discussed to strengthen them, affect all associations. Differences between the LGAs occur due to the tasks of municipalities and counties, due to the urban-rural divide, due to the path dependent membership structure of the LGAs, due to party politics and questions of prestige.

The responsibilities and competences of the larger and smaller municipalities as well as the counties influence the thematic priorities of the LGAs. The various tasks of municipalities are shown here on the basis of the Baden-Württemberg municipal code (Plate et al., 2018; Fleckenstein, 2024). There are three different types of tasks of municipalities: (1) Self-governing tasks, in which the municipality itself determines whether and how it acts. This is accompanied by the principle of financial responsibility and, in particular, the rule that there must be a representation of the people in the municipalities. These tasks are voluntary and include for instance public swimming pools, town twinning, assisted living, hiking trails, local public transport, economic development, museums and theatres. The financial possibilities and thus also the size of a municipality play a role in their realization. (2) Compulsory tasks which the municipality must fulfill according to the legislator but are not subject to instructions, i.e. the municipality decides on how it acts. These tasks include, for example, the establishment of schools, kindergartens, cemeteries and fire departments. As a rule, tasks are transferred by *Länder* laws and not by federal laws. In the event of the transfer of new mandatory tasks, financial compensation must be given ("principle of connexity") and legal supervision is effective. (3) Instruction tasks in which the municipality cannot decide on the "whether" and the "how". The municipalities perform these public tasks on their own responsibility, on behalf of the *Land* administration. Instruction tasks include duties assigned to the lower administrative authority. A comprehensive right of instruction of the higher authorities as well as legal and technical supervision applies. In addition to police and public order law (*Polizeirecht*), instruction tasks are, for example, the civil status system (registry office), the passport and registration system, the organization of elections for the federal, *Länder* and EU level (Plate et al., 2018; Fleckenstein, 2024). Many policy fields are spread across the different types of tasks.

Regardless of the size of a municipality, it is responsible for all tasks that have their roots in the local community (principle of universality). In this field of local self-government, the size of the municipality plays a role when it comes to the financial viability of the tasks. However, a legal distinction between different types of municipalities has to be made with regard to the activity as a lower administrative authority. Large cities not being part of a county (in Baden-Württemberg: *Stadtkreise*) take over all the tasks of the lower administrative authority. Such big cities are represented in the DST and, respectively, in the correspondent association at *Land* level. Medium sized towns (in Baden-Württemberg: *Große Kreisstadt*, with more than 20,000 inhabitants) have limited jurisdiction as a lower administrative authority, as certain areas are excluded. These towns can be a member in the DST and in the DStGB and, respectively, in their corresponding *Länder* associations. Small municipalities only act as lower administrative authorities in exceptional cases (e.g. passports, police public order law, restaurants, water issues, Fleckenstein, 2024). They are represented by the DStGB respectively its *Länder* associations. The tasks of the lower administrative authority not fulfilled by the medium sized towns and by the small municipalities are fulfilled by their county.

The counties in Baden-Württemberg—unlike municipalities—have no universal responsibility but may only act where the municipalities reach the limits of their capacity (subsidiary universality). As mentioned already above, counties perform a double function: they are both self-governing and *Länder* authorities. In the case of voluntary tasks, the county decides on the "whether" and the "how", taking into account its subsidiary universality. Counties are mainly active in the cultural sector, in economic development and in the area of public transport. In the case of compulsory tasks that are not subject to instructions, the legislature decides the "whether", while the "how" remains the responsibility of the county (e.g. waste disposal, vocational schools, social and youth welfare, Plate et al., 2018, Fleckenstein, 2024). In the case of instructional tasks, the county office acts as a *Land* authority (e.g. in the case of housing benefit or educational support). Counties are represented in the DLT and, respectively, in its correspondent associations at *Länder* level.

In many places, however, there are also different interests between urban and rural areas. Examples can be found in the maintenance and expansion of infrastructure (road construction, broadband development, health care), in the concern for and connection with nature and landscape (agriculture, animal welfare, nature protection, soil and water protection, emission control), in the effects of demographic change, urbanization versus rural exodus, as well as in the labor shortage versus shortage of workforce. The DLT and the DStGB tend to represent rural areas, while the DST represents urban areas (Interview II). An example of differing interests is the electrification of local public transport, where the DST is clearly in favor of electric buses, while the DLT is against electric buses because of their still short range (background conversation II; Henneke, 2012, p. 147–148 mentions also issues relating to financial equalization and the allocation of tasks).

The special feature for medium-sized towns is that they can join both the LGAs of cities and those for smaller municipalities at *Länder* level (the precondition for membership is determined by the statutes of the LGAs). These towns then decide in which association they want to be involved on which issues (e.g. in working groups, Interview III). This makes it difficult to clearly allocate rural and urban issues. As mentioned above, for historical reasons, in some German *Länder*, there are only two LGAs, a county association and an association representing the interests of cities, towns and villages. In other *Länder*, there is, next to an association representing the counties, both a LGA representing bigger cities and one representing small and medium-sized municipalities. A dual affiliation can also be found in the membership of the *Länder* associations in the federal associations. If there are only two LGAs in a *Land*, it is common to belong to both the DST and the DStGB at the federal level (Bernard & Klausch, 2023, p. 487–488 and appendix: 2; cf. also Henneke, 2012, p. 154–159) (Table 15.4).

The academic literature attests to a competitive relationship between the three LGAs that is not only based on different interests but has also historical roots and is driven by prestige issues (Jaedicke & Wollmann, 1999, p. 308). It is stated that the DST took a dominant position, which it still holds today. Shortly after the Second World War, the DST claimed to represent not only the large cities, but also the small towns and villages, and thus gained more influence because it also represented the municipalities being part of a county (Jaedicke & Wollmann, 1999, p. 308). Because of this, the DST entered into competition with two predecessor institutions of the DStGB mentioned above. There is also competition between the DLT and the DStGB because they cover almost the same geographical (rural) areas. There was disagreement among them about how to define the supra-local (county) and local (municipal) functions and whether to use the formal allocation of competences

Table 15.4 Membership structure of the local government associations

	DLT		DST		DStGB
Federal level	Exclusive membership	Dual membership	Exclusive membership	Dual membership	Exclusive membership
Länder level	LKT Baden-Württemberg, LKT Bavaria, LKT Brandenburg, LKT Hesse, LKT Mecklenburg-Vorpommern, LKT Lower Saxony, LKT North Rhine-Westphalia, LKT Rhineland-Palatinate, LKT Saarland, LKT Saxony, LKT Saxony-Anhalt, LKT Schleswig-Holstein, LKT Thuringia	None	ST Baden-Württemberg, ST Bavaria, ST North Rhine-Westphalia Berlin, Bremen, Hamburg Ca. 200 direct members (big cities)	ST Rhineland-Palatinate, ST Hesse, ST Lower Saxony, Städteverb. Schleswig-Holstein, StGt Saarland, StGT Saxony, StGB Brandenburg, StGT Mecklenburg-Vorpommern, StGB Saxony-Anhalt, GStB Thuringia	Gemeindetag Baden-Württemberg, Gemeindetag Bavaria, StGB North Rhine-Westphalia, StGB Rhineland-Palatinate, StGB Hesse, StGB Lower Saxony, Gemeindetag Schleswig-Holstein

Source: This table can be found in Bernhard & Klausch 2023, appendix: 2, first half of the chart, translation and small changes by the author. A similar diagram can be found in Schwarting, 2008, p. 470

(e.g., the municipal code and the laws that assign powers to the municipalities and counties) for this purpose. In the course of municipal reforms (in the Western German *Länder* in the 1960s and 1970s, in the Eastern German *Länder* basically up to the present day), independent cities (which until then had performed the same tasks as counties) were incorporated in counties. Because of this, the conflict zones between the tasks of counties and those of cities being part of cities enlarged (Jaedicke & Wollmann, 1999, p. 308).

Differences between the LGAs with regard to thematic priorities and interests also correspond to the party-political majority within the associations. The major political parties, especially the Social Democrats (SPD) and the Christian Democrats (CDU/CSU), organize themselves in groups (similar to parliamentary groups in parliaments) in the presidiums and main committees of the DST and the DStGB. The political parties have units that specialize in local politics (e.g. *Kommunalpolitische Vereinigung der CDU und CSU* (KPV), *Sozialdemokratische Gemeinschaft für Kommunalpolitik* (SGK)). These units support the functionaries in the LGAs (Jaedicke & Wollmann, 1999, p. 312). The party-political orientation of the LGAs is based on the political majorities of their members, i.e. in the case of the DLT and the DStGB on the majorities in the *Länder* associations, in the case of the DST on the party-political majorities of its direct members (large cities and city-states) and their respective associations at *Länder* level. Especially in the early years of the Federal Republic, the SPD had a majority in the big cities and thus in the DST, while rural areas and thus especially the DLT were dominated by the CDU.

15.5 Institutional and Procedural Balancing Mechanisms

The LGAs have institutional and procedural compensation mechanisms at their disposal in order to manage the competitions just described. As far as party-political imbalances are concerned, the LGAs have adopted internal statutory regulations to compensate for them. As early as in the 1960s, the DST, on request from the CDU/CSU, introduced a two-year rotation of the presidency between the SPD and the CDU. Since 1982, the DLT has elected some additional SPD politicians to its presidium (but the chairperson of the DLT has always been a CDU member). In the DST and the DStGB, the leadership positions in the *Länder* offices are held equally by different political parties (Jaedicke & Wollmann, 1999, p. 312).

In matters of policy and the associated financial issues, the associations aim at achieving a balance between their different members. The DST requires a ¾ majority for resolutions. However, open conflicts are avoided from the outset. There are de facto no combat votes (Jaedicke & Wollmann, 1999, p. 313). Regardless of the specific statutory provisions, the principle of consensus is established in all of the LGAs. Extreme positions and minority positions are subordinated to the clout of the association and the communication of the association's positions (Henneke, 2005, p. 702). The offices of the LGAs prepare proposals for resolutions for the meetings in a way that a balance of interests is achieved between all members (Jaedicke &

Wollmann, 1999, p. 313). If opposing positions emerge in the run-up to committee meetings and package deals fail, agreements are reached on the lowest common denominator or decisions are postponed (Henneke, 2005, p. 703). Henneke states that meetings of LGAs therefore serve "less as a decision-making level, but primarily as an identification-creating event" (Henneke, 2005, p. 703, translation by the author). Tradition plays a major role, the work is characterized by "less polarization and pressure" and more "cooperation and commonality" (Henneke, 2005, p. 703, translation by the author). Individuals who repeatedly behave uncooperatively risk their reputation as cooperation partners within the association (ibid).

Coordination between the three LGAs at federal level is carried out by an umbrella organization founded in 1953 (*Bundesvereinigung der kommunalen Spitzenverbände*). This framework association has its roots in an agreement concluded in 1947 between the Association of Cities and the Association of Counties on the territory of the US and British Allies. Even before the associations were brought into line by National Socialism, there had been institutionalized cooperation between the LGAs since 1927. The *Bundesvereinigung der kommunalen Spitzenverbände* mainly appears when a particularly large amount of unity is to be demonstrated or when forces and channels of influence are otherwise to be bundled. In the *Bundesvereinigung*, the DST is in charge formally, but there is a full board consisting of the responsibles of the three LGAs (Jaedicke & Wollmann, 1999, p. 308; Weinberger, 1982; Henneke, 2012, p. 132–136).

On the one hand, the consensus orientation of the LGAs is due to the need for their assertiveness. On the other hand, the cooperative nature of the German government system is also noticeable here. The LGAs work together on many technical issues via their working groups, also on a division of labor basis (Background conversation I). In the field of European politics, the LGAs cooperate at *Länder* and federal level to such an extent that the offices of all three LGAs are located in the same building in Brussels (Background conversation I). The office of the Baden-Württemberg municipalities and counties is jointly financed and maintained by the three *Land* LGAs (Background conversation I). At least at *Länder* level, the presidents and chief executives of the associations within a *Land* work closely together, so that weekly or even daily telephone calls for coordination are normalcy (Interview II).

15.6 Conclusions: Classification and Development Potential

As a lower administrative authority, municipalities and counties are in the chain of legitimacy via the *Länder*. In this function, they have a direct, albeit long, line to the *Bundesrat* and thus to the policy-making process at the federal level (and via the *Bundesrat* and Article 23 Basic Law also to the EU level). In the field of local self-government, the LGAs are the only direct bottom-up link between the local level and the *Länder* and the federal level in Germany. The formal participation rights of the LGAs are laid down in the constitutions of the *Länder*, in simple laws of the

Länder and in the rules of procedure of the *Länder* parliaments, the joint rules of procedure of the federal ministries (GGO) and in the rules of procedure of the *Bundestag* (GO-BT). In addition to these formal opportunities—often criticized by the LGAs as being too weak—there are many informal channels of influence. Hooghe and Marks examined the activities of local actors in the EU since the early 1990s and established their "multi-level governance" approach (Marks et al., 1996). According to their findings, the actors maintain formal and informal relationships with state and non-state actors, even across political levels. In this light, the LGAs in Germany are ideal-typical actors in the German multi-level system. Despite all the bottom-up organization and representation, it can be discussed whether their focus is more on further input legitimization of the multi-level political system or on the output-side, i.e. their influence.

The LGAs, their membership structure and also their competition are strongly characterized by historical path dependencies and German federalism. This is particularly evident in the overlapping membership structure of the DST and DStGB. However, the methods of conflict resolution are also subject to path dependencies and correspond to the cooperative German system of government. Conflicts within LGAs are rarely dealt with openly and consensual decisions predominate.

In their organization, the LGAs are very similar to other associations which do not represent local authorities. The LGAs in Germany emphasize that their private-law organization corresponds with local self-government and is due to the demarcation from the state. From a normative and theoretical point of view, the question arises as to whether, in their capacity as local self-governing authorities, municipalities and counties should be dependent on organizations under private law for their relations to other political levels. Recent empirical developments suggest a more formal involvement of municipalities and counties in their capacity of strengthening the input legitimacy of the system as a whole. Firstly, municipalities are playing an increasingly important role in the EU's supranational multi-level system. This role goes far beyond the administrative implementation of EU law. Secondly, especially the municipalities are called upon in times of increasing societal cleavages and emerging "constraining dissensus" (Hooghe & Marks, 2009). The latter calls into question the functioning of our political systems. The municipalities have the potential to become a legitimizing actor, being "closest to the citizens". This is a public task that they perform for the entire multi-level system, not only the municipal level. A path-dependent development that has grown over about 150 years, as shown by the German LGAs, can hardly be interrupted by theoretically justified reforms of a large scale. To give the municipalities and counties as self-governing authorities their own formal connection to the other levels of the political system, the introduction of *Kommunale Räte* ("local councils") as prevalent in Rhineland-Palatinate could be discussed, i.e. a formal institution in which the local level is represented at *Land* level and which opens the opportunity to discuss transparently local issues and formally bring local positions in the policy making process. Even if the LGAs play a significant role in the composition of the *Kommunaler Rat in Rhineland-Palatinate*, this institution has a formal, institutional and legally guaranteed existence.

References

Bernard, J., & Klausch, M. (2023). Beteiligung der kommunalen Spitzenverbände an der Bundesgesetzgebung: Eine Analyse der Anhörungspraxis in den Bundesministerien und den Ausschüssen des Deutschen Bundestages (2017–2021). *DMS—Der Moderne Staat, 16*, 484–506.

Brüsewitz, L. (2017). *Interessenvertretung im föderalen System: Kommunale Spitzenverbände in Hessen und Niedersachsen*. Dissertation.

Deutscher Städtetag. (2020). *Angemessene Beteiligung der kommunalen Spitzenverbände im Gesetzgebungsverfahren*. Beschluss des Hauptausschusses des Deutschen Städtetages.

Dieckmann, J. (1999). Die Städte im Bundesstaat. In H. Wollmann & R. Roth (Eds.), *Kommunalpolitik* (pp. 292–305). Springer Fachmedien.

Fleckenstein, J. (2024). *Skript Kommunalrecht*. Kehl.

Henneke, H.-G. (2005). Zum Binnenleben der kommunalen Spitzenverbände. *Der Landkreis, 12*(2005), 701–707.

Henneke, H.-G. (2012). *Die kommunalen Spitzenverbände* (2nd ed.). Kommunal- und Schulverlag.

Hooghe, L., & Marks, G. (2009). A postfunctionalist theory of European integration: From permissive consensus to constraining dissensus. *British Journal of Political Science, 39*(1), 1–23.

Ipsen, J. (2007). Die Entwicklung der Kommunalverfassung in Deutschland. In T. Mann & G. Püttner (Eds.), *Handbuch der kommunalen Wissenschaft und Praxis* (pp. 565–660). Springer.

Jaedicke, W., & Wollmann, H. (1999). Kommunale Spitzenverbände. In H. Wollmann & R. Roth (Eds.), *Kommunalpolitik* (pp. 306–322). Springer Fachmedien.

Marks, G., Hooghe, L., & Blank, K. (1996). European integration since the 1980s: State-centric vs. multi-level governance. *Journal of Common Market Studies (JCMS), 3*(1996), 341–378.

Meyer, H. (1994). Beteiligung der Kommunen an kommunalrelevanten Rechtsetzungsakten von Bund und Ländern. *Zeitschrift für Gesetzgebung, 9*, 262.

Plate, K., Schulze, C., & Fleckenstein, J. (2018). *Kommunalrecht Baden-Württemberg* (8th ed.). Kohlhammer.

Reutter, W. (2001). Kommunale Spitzenverbände und Demokratie. In A. Zimmer & B. Weßels (Eds.), *Verbände und Demokratie in Deutschland* (pp. 135–157). Springer Fachmedien.

Reutter, W. (2002). Kommunale Interessen im kooperativen Föderalismus. *Zeitschrift für Politikwissenschaft, 12*(4), 1573–1599.

Riederle, M. (1995). *Kommunale Spitzenverbände im Gesetzgebungsverfahren: Ihre rechtliche Stellung am Beispiel des Freistaats Bayern*. Juristischer Verlag Müller.

Ruge, K. (2022). Aktuelle Situation und Perspektiven der kommunalen Spitzenverbände auf Bundesebene. In M. Burgi & C. Waldhoff (Eds.), *Kommunale Selbstverwaltung im Bundes- und Finanzstaat* (pp. 545–559). Carl Heymanns Verlag.

Schrader, C. (2004). *Die kommunalen Spitzenverbände und der Schutz der kommunalen Selbstverwaltungsgarantie durch Verfahren und Verfahrensgestaltung*. Nomos.

Schwarting, G. (2008). Kommunale Spitzenverbände in Deutschland. Geschichte, Stellung, Funktion. In S. Magiera, K.-P. Sommermann, & J. Ziller (Eds.), *Verwaltungswissenschaft und Verwaltungspraxis in nationaler und transnationaler Perspektive* (pp. 465–483). Duncker & Humblot.

Weinberger, B. (1982). Die Bundesvereinigung der kommunalen Spitzenverbände. In G. Püttner et al. (Eds.), *Handbuch der kommunalen Wissenschaft und Praxis*. Springer.

Interviews and Background Conversation

Interview I. (2023, December 6). *Senior political advisor at federal level.*

Interview II. (2023, December 13). *President of a local government association at Land level representing towns and municipalities.*

Interview III. (2023, December 8). *Member of a working group of a local government association at Land and federal level.*

Background Conversation I. (2022, December). *Member of EU office of a local government association in Brussels.*

Background Conversation II. (2024, September 17). *President of a local government association at Land level representing counties.*

Open Access This chapter is licensed under the terms of the Creative Commons Attribution 4.0 International License (http://creativecommons.org/licenses/by/4.0/), which permits use, sharing, adaptation, distribution and reproduction in any medium or format, as long as you give appropriate credit to the original author(s) and the source, provide a link to the Creative Commons license and indicate if changes were made.

The images or other third party material in this chapter are included in the chapter's Creative Commons license, unless indicated otherwise in a credit line to the material. If material is not included in the chapter's Creative Commons license and your intended use is not permitted by statutory regulation or exceeds the permitted use, you will need to obtain permission directly from the copyright holder.

Chapter 16
Swiss Local Government Associations and the Representation of Urban and Rural Interests

Claire Kaiser, Jana Machljankin, and Reto Steiner

Abstract This chapter examines the role of Swiss local governments in intergovernmental relations as well as the role of the local government associations (LGAs). It combines different methodological approaches including a survey of all Swiss LGAs at the national and subnational level. The results show that the LGAs' role lies in the representation of local interests while preserving municipal autonomy, but also in acting as a partner to the respective canton, that is the subnational level above the local government, in matters affecting municipalities. Differences between LGAs in different cantons occur concerning their political influence, as well as their organizational and financial resources. Success factors of LGAs in intergovernmental relations may be divided into different aspects, ranging from internal to external factors such as positioning of the LGA, communication towards superordinate government levels, internal factors at the LGA level and cooperation/networking within and between LGAs.

Keywords Local government associations · Representation of interests · Local government · Switzerland · Associations · LGA

16.1 Introduction

The purpose of this chapter is to examine the role of Swiss local governments in intergovernmental relations as well as the role of the local government associations (LGAs)[1] and what differences there may be between urban local governments

[1] In this chapter, "local government associations (LGAs)", refers to the interest group/association of municipalities and/or cities. This is not to be confused with functionally oriented intermunicipal organisations that are established for intermunicipal cooperation (so-called "Zweckverbände" or

C. Kaiser · J. Machljankin · R. Steiner (✉)
School of Management and Law, ZHAW, Winterthur, Switzerland
e-mail: claire.kaiser@zhaw.ch; jana.machljankin@zhaw.ch; reto.steiner@zhaw.ch

© The Author(s) 2026

K. Kössler, E. M. Belser (eds.), *Local Government Structure and Intergovernmental Relations*, Local and Urban Governance,
https://doi.org/10.1007/978-3-031-99820-1_16

(ULGs) and rural local governments (RLGs). A further topic of interest in this regard is how urban and rural interests are represented in these associations. In particular, the role of municipal associations and, connected to this, differences in addressing urban and rural interests have thus far been under-scrutinised in the Swiss context. To shed some light on this, we address the following research questions in this chapter: (1) What is the role and impact of local government associations in intergovernmental relations? What are the differences between LGAs in different Swiss cantons? (2) Can local government associations represent the differing interests of ULGs and RLGs? How do they manage to do this? (3) What factors make LGAs successful in intergovernmental relations?

For a better understanding of the context of this chapter, the position of local government within the Swiss political system is presented in brief. Twenty-six cantons form the Swiss federal state, and the municipalities are part of the internal organisation of the cantons. The canton supervises its municipalities and organises and determines their tasks (Friederich et al., 1998, p. 11). Within cantonal law, municipalities can choose their political structure and administrative organisation, raise taxes, and independently fulfil those tasks that are not part of the jurisdiction of the cantons or the federal government (Linder, 2010). The degree of autonomy is relatively large for Swiss local authorities, although this varies depending on the legislation of the respective canton (Friederich et al., 1998; Steiner, 2003). Furthermore, municipalities with larger populations and cities have more room for manoeuvre than small municipalities, which may only be able to finance and implement specific local tasks (Ladner & Haus, 2021, p. 65). Because of these differences, interests between smaller and larger municipalities may vary, thereby influencing the representation of interests by local government associations. On an international scale, Switzerland has small local authorities (Council of Europe, 2001). With 2131 local governments (as of 1 January 2024), the municipal structure in Switzerland is highly fragmented, and the median municipal population size is only 1615 inhabitants (as of 31 December 2021; Federal Statistical Office (FSO), 2024).

Concerning the methodology for this chapter, we first conducted a literature, document, and website analysis to gain general information about intergovernmental relations in Switzerland and local government associations. For more in-depth knowledge and to answer the main research questions addressed in this chapter, we also surveyed local government associations at the national and subnational level concerning the tasks, influence, organisation, and success factors used by LGAs to fulfil their mandate (see, for example, Rhodes, 1986). A written survey was sent out by email to two associations at the national level, namely, the Swiss Association of Municipalities and the Swiss Association of Cities, as well as 24 municipal associations at the cantonal level (for a complete list, see the appendix). Depending on the

"Gemeindeverbände"), which are sometimes referred to in their English translation as 'municipal associations' but are not the object of our research here. The terms "local government associations (LGAs)" and "municipal associations" are used as synonyms in this chapter.

canton, these are associations of the municipalities, conferences of mayors,[2] or similar. Two of the 26 Swiss cantons, that is Basel-City and Graubünden, do not have a municipal association at the cantonal level. In the case of Basel-City, there are only three municipalities. An attempt to establish a municipal organization failed in the canton of Graubünden in 2020. The reasons for this were the different interests of the municipalities (diversity in terms of size, economic focus, perspectives, local needs) and the estimated costs for the administration of the association.[3] The survey was distributed in autumn 2023, and we received responses from 19 of the 24 cantonal LGAs, achieving a remarkable response rate of 80%.

This chapter is structured as follows: First, in Sect. 16.2, we examine intergovernmental relations between the local level and the national and subnational levels of government in Switzerland. The results of the analysis of the Swiss local government associations are presented at the national level (Sect. 16.3) and at the subnational levels (Sect. 16.4). In Sect. 16.5, we draw our conclusions.

16.2 Intergovernmental Relations Between the Local Level and National and Sub-national Levels of Government in Switzerland

Intergovernmental relations (IGRs) may be defined as "activities and interactions occurring between governmental units of all types and levels within the federal system" (Anderson, 1960, p. 3). They "denote a negotiated, nonhierarchic exchange, not only between institutions on different governmental levels but also between different substates" (Bolleyer, 2006, p. 472; see also Peters & Pierre, 2001, p. 131 and Agranoff, 2004). In Western federal systems, these exchanges have increased (Bolleyer, 2006). IGRs imply coordination among governments without transferring competencies to other state levels (Arens, 2020). This chapter focuses on vertical intergovernmental relations, which also concern urban and rural municipalities.

Switzerland is one of the classical federal states (similar to the United States of America and Canada) with three state levels: the Confederation at the national level, the 26 cantons at the subnational level, and the 2131 municipalities at the local level. Vertical and horizontal relationships exist between the different government levels or entities of the same government level, respectively. Switzerland is a decentralised country where cantons and municipalities are essential for implementing federal programmes (Vatter, 2004).

[2] The conferences of mayors (*Gemeindepräsidentenkonferenzen*) are composed of the mayors/presidents of the municipality.

[3] By contrast, there are separate municipal interest groups for various sectoral policies, such as the Association of Graubünden Municipal Tax Offices, the Association of Graubünden Municipal Employees, or, at a political level, a rather loose grouping of municipal representatives in the Grand Council.

Switzerland is characterised by what is known as "cooperative federalism". This means that legislative power lies with the Confederation in many policy areas, and the cantons and municipalities are responsible for implementing these policies (Vatter, 2004). Thus, a close collaboration between the Confederation, the cantons and the municipalities is necessary. The three government levels are highly interdependent and rely on each other. The Confederation needs the subnational levels to implement federal policies, and the cantons and municipalities need the Confederation because of its financial and organisational resources (Bächtiger & Hitz, 2007, p. 89).

According to Linder, historically, Swiss federalism can be seen as a case of non-centralisation (Linder, 2010) because the cantons and, to some extent, the municipalities have retained important areas of state autonomy, such as constitutional and fiscal sovereignty. According to Article 3 of the Swiss Federal Constitution, tasks which are not expressly a federal matter become the responsibility of the cantons and their municipalities. Constitutionally, the position of the Swiss municipalities is regulated by cantonal law (Article 50). Swiss local governments have a significant degree of autonomy, despite some differences between cantons (see also the Local Autonomy Index by Ladner et al., 2023) and depending on their size (Ladner & Haus, 2021).

In Switzerland, urban and rural municipalities are firmly embedded within their cantons, and for a long time, there was relatively little direct interaction between the federal and the local level (Bächtiger & Hitz, 2007; Kübler et al., 2003, p. 271), as planning programmes and activities for urban and rural municipalities at the federal level have been absent. Hence, the urban and rural municipalities have organised themselves into associations, such as the Swiss Association of Municipalities (founded in 1897) and the Swiss Association of Cities (founded in 1953), with the purpose of "voicing their interests at the federal level and influencing federal policies" (Bächtiger & Hitz, 2007, p. 81). Accordingly, the influence of these associations at the federal level depends on the issue and the federal department involved. From the 1990s, the local level gained strength vis-à-vis the subordinate state levels, e.g. through Article 50 of the Swiss Constitution of 1999 or the TAK (which will be explained below). The interaction between the federal and local levels increased. In fact, the federal government has no direct means to implement its policies but is reliant on the cantons and the municipalities (Bächtiger & Hitz, 2007, p. 81–85).

There are different possibilities for the local level to voice its interests at the federal level. In the pre-parliamentary consultation procedure, bills are submitted by the Confederation to various actors in the political system and society, among them the cantons and the municipal associations at the national levels (Bächtiger & Hitz, 2007, p. 82). In this way, the federal administration receives a range of opinions, and the actors can evaluate the bill and express their interests. At the national level, a specific parliamentary group deals with communal affairs, called *Kommunalpolitik* (that is, "local politics"), which was constituted in 1987 with the objectives of drafting joint statements, consulting on topics of the council agenda and representing local political concerns vis-à-vis the federal government and the public. It comprises 39 members of the national parliament and meets twice a year

(Swiss Parliament, 2023). Municipalities and municipal associations can also address individual members of the national parliament (Bächtiger & Hitz, 2007, p. 83). As multiple mandates are allowed in many cantons, national or cantonal parliament members may also be members of municipal authorities, representing municipal and urban interests in the national or cantonal parliament.

One vessel for exchange between the three levels of government and the voicing of the interests of the local level is the Tripartite Conference (*Tripartite Konferenz* (TK)). It is a platform to improve the vertical cooperation between the Confederation, cantons and municipalities, and between urban and rural areas. It was established in 2001 as the Tripartite Agglomeration Conference (*Tripartite Agglomerationskonferenz* (TAK)), where a joint agglomeration policy was created focusing on metropolitan or urban regions. Although 74% of the Swiss population lives in one of the 52 agglomerations, "there is no level of government designed for addressing agglomeration interests and effects" (Debela, 2020). Therefore, the cities lack planning tools and options as they cannot reach the neighbouring municipalities (Linder, 2010). The TAK became the *Tripartite Konferenz* in 2016 to consider the close interdependence between urban and rural areas. As such, it deals with spatially relevant topics of interest to the whole of Switzerland that affect all three levels of government. Representing the municipal level, the Swiss Association of Cities and the Swiss Association of Municipalities participate in the TK (Federal Council, 2016).

Swiss municipalities have different intergovernmental associations or forums in which they can participate and reflect their interests. In the next two sections, based on the survey as well as on document and website analysis, we present the local government associations (LGAs) at the national and sub-national level, as well as some means of differentiation, including organisational resources (such as internal structure) and political resources (e.g. type of decision-making) (see, for example, Rhodes, 1986).

16.3 Swiss LGAs at the National Level

At the national level, there is the Swiss Association of Municipalities and the Swiss Association of Towns/Cities.

The Swiss Association of Municipalities *(Schweizerischer Gemeindeverband (SGV))* represents the various interests of the municipalities in the heterogeneous Swiss municipal landscape. It has been the political representative of the municipalities at the federal level since 1953, and 71% of all Swiss municipalities are members (1506 from a total of 2131 municipalities as of 1 January 2024). As a recognised partner, it represents the joint positions of the municipalities to the federal authorities. It is managed by a board of 16 members, who are also members of municipal executives and federal parliament, that is the National Council or the Council of States, with experience in local politics. There is also a close collaboration with cantonal and municipal organisations. For the municipalities to benefit mutually from specialist knowledge and experience, the Swiss Association of

Municipalities provides information at conferences and on its website, and it publishes practice-oriented and scientific articles in the magazine *Schweizer Gemeinde*. Furthermore, the Swiss Association of Municipalities is committed to a comprehensive and exemplary public service because all municipalities have a constitutional right to it (Schweizerischer Gemeindeverband, 2023).

The Swiss Association of Cities (*Schweizerischer Städteverband* (SSV)) represents the interests of urban areas in the political sphere. It was founded in 1897 and today has 131 members. Compared to the Swiss Association of Municipalities, the Swiss Association of Cities has many members with dual memberships of both organisations. The SSV offers its members a platform for exchanging experiences and networking and informs the public about urban Switzerland. It participates in federal consultation procedures as a permanent partner, works on federal expert commissions and maintains regular contact with the federal administration, parliament, and its commissions. This political work of the Association of Cities is based on Article 50 of the Federal Constitution, which obliges the Confederation to take account of the interests of the cities and urban areas (Schweizerischer Städteverband, 2023) (as well as the mountain regions).

The SSV board comprises 16 members, who are executive members of a city or a town, and any Swiss municipality with an urban character owing to its tradition or development may become a member of the Swiss Association of Cities (Article 4 of the SSV Statutes). The board of directors decides upon the admission of a member. If an application is rejected, a final decision may be requested at the next ordinary delegates' meeting (Article 7 of the SSV Statutes). The association's members are large, medium-sized, or small towns, core towns, agglomeration municipalities, and municipalities in all regions. Currently, 131 towns are members, equating to around three-quarters of all Swiss cities. Of the cities with over 15,000 inhabitants, over 90% are members.

The Association of Cities has a dual mandate to represent the interests of cities and agglomerations vis-à-vis the federal government and cantonal conferences and to offer services to its members. In general, the Association of Cities can have a constructive influence on the Confederation if it succeeds in convincing parliamentarians or federal agencies with sound arguments or if it can voice its concerns together with other interest groups (e.g. sections of the Association, Swiss Association of Municipalities, or cantonal conferences). However, during the most recent crises, this was felt to be inadequate. According to the SSV, "[d]uring events such as the coronavirus, the war in Ukraine and associated reception of refugees, and the energy shortage, the Association of Cities was not sufficiently involved at the federal level (too little and too late)" (authors' translation; survey answer by SSV, 2023). Therefore, the topic of crisis management will continue to be important in the future, as the SSV is committed to the appropriate involvement at the municipal level, which should contribute to better consideration of the concerns of cities and municipalities in crisis situations.

16.4 Swiss LGAs at the Sub-national Level

With the exception of Basel-Stadt and Graubünden, all cantons have municipal organisations in the form of associations or conferences of mayors. As a rule, these LGAs at the cantonal level are an umbrella organisation of the political municipalities, which disposes of general competence in municipal affairs (as opposed to single-task communes, e.g., school municipalities or church municipalities) in the respective canton. They are often non-partisan advocates of the political municipalities vis-à-vis the canton and Confederation, as well as further associations and partners, in preserving municipal autonomy.

Some local government associations recognise particular principles of association policy, such as partisan attitude, relationship with the canton, and communication. Using the *Vereinigung der Gemeindepräsidentinnen und Gemeindepräsidenten des Kantons Schaffhausen* (VGGSH) as an example, possible principles of association policy can be shown here. They state that the association views its relationship with the canton as a reliable partnership, while in terms of party politics, they position themselves as politically neutral. They do not comment on socio-political matters or interfere in conflicts regarding the distribution of funding, which they consider the responsibility of politicians. In the event of differing interests among the municipalities, the association seeks a balance, while in the case of deviating attitudes, a legitimate authority (e.g. government, parliament, or those entitled to vote) must make a decision. In addition, the association pursues a policy of open communication with its members (VGGSH, 2023).

16.4.1 Formal Role and Tasks Vis-à-Vis the Confederation, the Canton, and the Municipalities

Vis-à-vis the *Confederation*, there are, as a rule, no legal foundations, and there are no direct roles and tasks because the canton is the usual point of contact with the federal government. More than 90% of the local government associations rate their influence as low or non-existent vis-à-vis the Confederation. One way in which local government associations can strengthen their influence and implement their decisions effectively is by lobbying cantonal representatives in the National Council and the Council of States. LGAs that feel they have greater influence reported maintaining close personal or political contacts with the members of the federal parliament. For example, the Executive Director of the *Verband Solothurner Einwohnergemeinden* (VSEG) makes himself available as a representative of the Swiss Association of Municipalities in federal working groups. The *Verband Thurgauer Gemeinden* (VTG) also mentioned communication via the Swiss Association of Municipalities. However, the *Verband der Gemeindepräsidien des Kantons Zürich* (GPVZH) sees the role and task of the local government association in safeguarding, promoting, and representing the common interests of the municipalities. In practice, this means supporting the Swiss Association of Municipalities and Cities in their lobbying activities.

Vis-à-vis the *canton*, the formal roles and tasks are more pronounced. In some cantons, the law even stipulates that municipalities or LGAs must be consulted (e.g. *Vereinigung St. Galler Gemeindepräsidentinnen und Gemeindepräsidenten* (VSGP) and *Verband Luzerner Gemeinden* (VLG)). As a rule, the local government association at the cantonal level represents the political municipalities vis-à-vis the canton. They are the central point of contact with the canton concerning cantonal matters or issues that affect all or several municipalities, as cited by the *Gemeindepräsidentenkonferenz des Kantons Appenzell Ausserrhoden*, who coordinate, mediate, take a stand, and become involved. Organized in a municipal association, the municipalities are perceived by cantonal administrations and cantonal government councils as considerably more potent than when acting in isolation (see, for example, *Gemeinde Glarus Nord*). Political lobbying vis-à-vis the cantonal government and cantonal council includes drafting statements and representation/deputations in relevant cantonal committees (*Verband der Gemeindepräsidien des Kantons Zürich* (GPVZH)). As stated in the case of the *Gemeindepräsidenten-Konferenz der zugerischen Gemeinden*, when laws are changed and the canton takes a decision that affects municipalities financially or practically, the LGA advocates for the municipalities. Furthermore, local government associations see their role as defending the interests of the municipalities and acting as partners of the canton in matters affecting the municipalities. For example, the *Verband Solothurner Einwohnergemeinde* (VSEG) actively deals with the various issues affecting the municipalities and is a reliable partner for the canton in drafting legislation, revision projects and consultation procedures. Its network also enables the canton and its offices to provide targeted information to the municipalities. In so doing, cantonal municipal associations are interested in tackling business "on an equal footing" with the canton.

The influence vis-à-vis the canton is clearly higher than vis-à-vis the Confederation and is estimated to range between medium and high. As multiple mandates are allowed in most cantons (except Geneva and Neuchâtel), members of municipal authorities also represent municipal and urban interests in the national or cantonal parliament. This is also in line with the feedback from the survey where, for example, the *Union des Communes Vaudoises* (UCV), when asked about the interconnection between the LGA tasks vis-à-vis the canton, indicated that one-third of deputies in the cantonal parliament also have an executive function in their municipality. According to the results of a Swiss survey of elected executives at the local level, 4.7% of the respondents indicate also to be member of the cantonal parliament. However, significant differences exist when analyzing individual cantons; these range from 0% in the cantons of Geneva and Neuchâtel (obviously, as role combinations are not permitted) up to 36.4% in the canton of Glarus. According to the results of the Swiss wide survey of elected executives at the local level, in 18 cantons, the share of local executives as members of the cantonal parliament is below 10%, in four cantons between 10 and 20% (Appenzell Ausserrhoden, Zug, Obwalden, Nidwalden) and only in two cantons above 20% (28.6% in Appenzell Innerrhoden and 36.4% in Glarus). Even if the results of the survey do not provide a complete picture, they do serve as an approximation of the reality. Overall, the survey results indicate that smaller, often more rural cantons tend to assume they have less influence at the cantonal level. At the same time, the proportion of executive members who are also members of a cantonal parliament is higher in these cantons.

LGAs are usually invited to participate in consultations on laws and ordinances (see, for example, the statement by the *Vereinigung St. Galler Gemeindepräsidentinnen und Gemeindepräsidenten* (VSGP)). Regular collaboration between the LGA and the canton means that communal interests are better considered, although the balance is fragile, and tensions are inevitable (*Association des communes neuchâteloises* (ACN)). As the primary point of contact, the influence is relatively significant, LGAs are heard, and their voice carries weight (*Federation des Communes Valaisannes* (FCV)/*Verband Walliser Gemeinden* (VWG)). As the *Verband Solothurner Einwohnergemeinden* (VSEG) states, municipalities are involved in most cantonal business through the LGA. Even if the canton does not always share the opinion of the municipalities, it has been shown that the LGA can support or even overturn cantonal plans. The association fulfils its role as a partner and, in return, demands to be consulted on relevant business. Hardly any other interest organisation has the same influence at the cantonal level. As shown in the case of the *Association des communes neuchâteloises* (ACN), however, there may also be some barriers from the point of view of the LGA. As mandates are no longer allowed to be held concurrently (since 2021), the absence of members of communal executives in the Grand Council has led to a loss of links between the LGA and the cantonal parliament. However, a possible reintroduction of multiple mandates is currently being discussed in the respective cantons, as municipalities are no longer sufficiently represented at the cantonal level (RTN, 2024).

Concerning the *municipalities,* the formal roles and tasks were reported in the survey as follows: For the municipalities, the local government association is a forum for the mutual exchange of information and opinions and mutual support (e.g, *Gemeindepräsidentenkonferenz des Kantons Appenzell Ausserrhoden*). The cantonal municipal associations enable the harmonisation of municipal projects and the use of synergies, they offer further training, and the municipalities are members of the association (see, for example, statements by the *Verband Thurgauer Gemeinden* (VTG) and *Gemeinde Glarus Nord*). Some LGAs mention the promotion of training opportunities for members of municipal authorities and commissions as well as employees of the municipalities and their organisations as one of the formal tasks of the LGAs. Regardless of whether they are urban or rural (*Urner Gemeindeverband, Union des Communes Vaudoises* (UCV)), they also provide certain services to their members, including legal advice (*Verband Bernischer Gemeinden* (VBG)).

Regarding their influence vis-à-vis the municipalities, perceptions vary considerably between different LGAs. While some associations classify their influence on the municipalities to be factually very high since this is the central task of the association according to the statutes (e.g. *Vereinigung St. Galler Gemeindepräsidentinnen und Gemeindepräsidenten* (VSGP)), other associations explicitly state that they do not exert any influence whatsoever on the municipalities because they are not allowed to interfere with municipal autonomy (e.g. cantons of Neuchâtel and Jura). It is interesting to note that associations with no or little indication of influence on municipalities are mostly associations from French-speaking Switzerland, where local autonomy is supposedly lower than in the rest of the country (Steiner et al., 2021, p. 9). LGAs may also be necessary for coordination between the municipalities (see *Gemeinde Glarus Nord*). The *Verband Solothurner Einwohnergemeinden* (VSEG) stated that municipalities value the services provided and feel well represented.

16.4.2 Statutory and Factual Differences Between Urban and Rural Municipalities Regarding Services and Commitments

As our survey shows, most LGAs are the same for urban and rural local governments in terms of services and commitment. However, since members' needs vary, factual differences between urban and rural municipalities may exist, although they are often relatively small. For example, while larger municipalities or cities are actively involved in cantonal legislation processes, smaller rural municipalities depend on consultations by the LGAs during these political processes. For this reason, some LGAs have a so-called 'balancing mechanism' between those different interests, which is also part of the LGA statutes (e.g. Article 4 of the Statute of the *Verband Luzerner Gemeinden*). Accordingly, it must be remembered that some Swiss cantons are very rural with no or only a few small towns, while others are more heterogeneous regarding their municipal structure, with cities and small municipalities alike.

An organisation that gave one-sided favour to cities or rural municipalities risks, in the medium term, that some municipalities feel underrepresented and that parts of the association could break away. This would result in the association losing its role as the sole point of contact with the canton, as stated by the *Verband Solothurner Einwohnergemeinden* (VSEG). According to the *Gemeindepräsidentenkonferenz des Kantons Appenzell Ausserrhoden*, when forming opinions, care is taken to ensure that at least one large (more urban) and one small (more rural) municipality is represented and that equal regional representation is guaranteed. For example, information events may be held in cities to enable greater accessibility, but general meetings may take place in a different municipality every year so that no jurisdiction is completely neglected. The *Association jurassienne des communes* (AJC) states that its main objective is to pool what unites municipalities rather than what divides them. In the *Association des communes neuchateloises* (ACN), each municipality is treated equally at the general assembly, with one vote apiece. However, while seats at the conference of municipal directors are guaranteed for municipalities with a professional executive, smaller municipalities also retain the option of being represented. Here, the LGA points out that this "difference in treatment" is mainly due to the greater availability of professionals and does not generate tension with the other municipalities, as some of the available seats remain vacant. Although, in general, almost all LGAs stress that no distinction is made in what is offered to urban or rural local governments, cities (which sometimes make up most of a canton's population) may carry a different weight from rural municipalities (e.g. *Vereinigung der Gemeindepräsidentinnen und Gemeindepräsidenten des Kantons Schaffhausen* (VGGSH) or *Gemeindepräsidenten-Konferenz der zugerischen Gemeinden*). The *Union des Communes Vaudoises* (UCV) statutes stipulate that voting rights are determined according to the size of the municipality, meaning the bigger the municipality, the louder its voice.

16.4.3 Membership Base and Representation of Types of Municipalities

According to our survey, in most cantonal LGAs, all the municipalities in the canton are association members. Sixteen of all the organisations surveyed have a 100% membership base. In the remaining cantons, it is still a significant proportion, meaning that the interests of all municipalities in the canton are represented. In most cases, the membership fee is determined depending on the size of the municipality's population. As the case of the *Verband Schwyzer Gemeinden und Bezirke* (VSZGB) shows, cantonal districts can also be members. Indeed, care is taken to ensure that cities and medium-sized and smaller municipalities from all districts can participate. In the canton of Jura, all the municipalities are members of the *Association jurassienne des communes* (AJC), but so may neighbouring municipalities, provided they share the objectives set out in the AJC's articles of association. For example, this is currently the case with the town of Moutier, whose electorate voted in 2021 to switch cantons from Bern to Jura. Ultimately, the only weighting between municipalities relates to their membership fees, which are determined based on their population. In the canton of St. Gallen, all 75 municipalities are members of the *Vereinigung St. Galler Gemeindepräsidentinnen und Gemeindepräsidenten* (VSGP), the VSGP member being the mayor of the municipal/town council. In fact, however, there are 79 members since the city of St. Gallen has four additional councillors who also have a vote. The votes cannot be delegated but are personal to the elected representatives. The board is made up of representatives from all regions. The *Verband Solothurner Einwohnergemeinden* (VSEG) has devised a constellation in which the different types of municipalities are represented in the leading roles of the association since the differences and their resulting needs must be considered. If this were not the case, some municipalities would feel unrepresented. In the canton of Zurich, all municipalities and municipal councils are members of the association *Verband der Gemeindepräsidien des Kantons Zürich* (GPVZH), ensuring that both urban and rural interests are considered. If their positions differ on individual issues, attempts are made to find a compromise or at least to harmonize the positions. Concerning organisational structure, a special case can be found in the canton of Glarus, where the conference of mayors is not a formal organisation. As of 2010 and after a major reform of the municipal structure, there are only three municipalities in the canton and their political weight is balanced.

16.4.4 Institutional Structure, Organs, and Decision-Making

Regarding the structure of local government associations, we need to examine their institutional structure, bodies and working groups, and the associations' decision-making. Local government associations may be organized, in the legal sense, as an association (*Verein*) within the meaning of Articles 60–79 of the Swiss Civil Code (for example, the *Association jurassienne des communes* (AJC)). Its central bodies are the general meeting and a committee of nine members, including representatives from the three cantonal districts and large and small municipalities. An exception is the canton of Glarus, where there is no formal local governmental organisation and, thus, no rules. Instead, it functions as an informal forum to exchange ideas.

The organs of the municipal associations often consist of a delegate assembly as well as a board of directors and, in many cases, other organs such as an executive committee, an office, auditors, and special commissions and working groups. The *delegate assembly* is the association's supreme body and is usually convened once a year. Statutes determine who is entitled to vote at the delegate assembly, for example, delegates of member municipalities and board members. Its primary responsibilities may include approving the annual report and accounts, determining the membership fee, passing resolutions on the budget, and electing the presidium, board and auditors. A *board of directors* manages the business of the cantonal association. For example, they constitute the association, elect the office head and others entrusted with special tasks, and determine remuneration. They can also decide to join other organizations and convene a general meeting. The *auditors*' duties include examining the annual accounts and reporting to the delegate assembly, including proposing whether the accounts should be approved. The responsibilities of the *office*, elected by the board of directors, include administrative support in the association's day-to-day business. The structures and tasks may differ between the various cantonal associations; for more information, also see their statutes.

As a rule, in most municipal associations, each member has one vote, and the decision is made by majority vote. Overall, cantonal associations that are smaller in size aim at unanimity (e.g. *Vereinigung der Gemeindepräsidentinnen und Gemeindepräsidenten des Kantons Schaffhausen* (VGGSH)). In the canton of Glarus, which has no formal LGA, they can only be active together if there is unanimity, which, according to the *Gemeinde Glarus Nord*, is feasible with only three mayors. Important distinctions are included in the institutional structure of some LGAs (e.g. *Vereinigung der Gemeindepräsidentinnen und Gemeindepräsidenten des Kantons Schaffhausen* (VGGSH), *Verband Schwyzer Gemeinden und Bezirke* (vszgb), *Verband Solothurner Einwohnergemeinden* (VSEG)), which point to the aim of balancing interests between different types of municipalities, such as the composition of the board of directors which must take into account the diversity of the municipalities in the canton (Article 14 of the Statute of the *Vereinigung der Gemeindepräsidentinnen und Gemeindepräsidenten des Kantons Schaffhausen* (VGGSH)). In the *Verband Solothurner Einwohnergemeinden* (VSEG), each district provides two board members who then form the board of directors, pointing to the balancing of interests at the local level. Another example of the inclusion of different interests at the local level is the composition and representation of members at the general meeting of the *Verband Schwyzer Gemeinden und Bezirke* (vszgb), *Verband Thurgauer Gemeinden*, or *Federation des Communes Valaisannes* (FCV)/*Verband Walliser Gemeinden* (VWG). At the *Verband Schwyzer Gemeinden und Bezirke* (vszgb), the general meeting is attended by equal numbers of representatives of the political executives as well as the administrators of the members involved.

In addition, the number of representatives is in some cantons adapted to the size of the member municipality: two representatives per member with 1–4999 inhabitants, including one member from the administration, and four representatives per member with 5000 inhabitants or more, including two members from the administration (Article 6 of the Statute of the *Verband Schwyzer Gemeinden und Bezirke* (vszgb).

16.4.5 Success Factors of the Associations in Their Relationship with the Confederation and the Canton

Several success factors of LGAs in their relationship with the Confederation and the canton can be identified. From the survey of the LGAs, as well as from additional desk research and website analysis, we can list the following:

1. Positioning of the LGA:
   - Unity in the behaviour towards the canton and a clear positioning of the LGA makes it a reliable partner.
   - Mutual recognition of function and interests.
   - Neutral position in terms of party politics.
2. Communication towards superordinate government levels:
   - Open communication, transparency, and fairness.
   - Objective and technically sound argumentation.
   - Joint dialogue where everyone can contribute their opinions.
   - Direct, regular, informal, and unbureaucratic exchanges and contact with the cantonal government; straightforward and uncomplicated channels to the cantonal administration and their heads of service.

3. Internal factors at the LGA level:
    - Lean but professional organisation of the LGA.
    - High level of commitment from the members of its bodies.
    - Establishing a good climate of dialogue and exchange between municipalities despite the sometimes different contexts.
4. Cooperation/networking within and between LGAs:
    - Networking and the exchange of best practices.
    - Constructive cooperation creates the necessary trust to guarantee the basis for finding a pragmatic and objective solution, even in the event of sensitive issues and conflicts of interest.

16.5 Conclusions

When analysing the role and impact of local government associations in intergovernmental relations, the representation of local interests plays a central role, while preserving municipal autonomy is of utmost importance to all the LGAs surveyed. LGAs see their role not only as defending the interests of the local governments but also in acting as a partner to the canton in matters affecting municipalities. Thus, the LGA's role is also to support the political process of drafting legislation related to issues of local relevance. Close relations and a degree of political influence by LGAs on the higher levels of government can be observed in most of the cases surveyed. In a few cases, the relationship is even institutionalised, e.g. in the case of the *Urner Gemeindeverband*, where a representative of the canton supplements the board of directors. However, there appears to be an opposing development in the French-speaking cantons at the sub-national level, especially considering the possibility of multiple mandates. Success factors of the associations in intergovernmental relations include different aspects, ranging from positioning and communication towards superordinate state levels to internal factors of the LGA and cooperation and networking activities within and between the different LGAs, including the national LGAs, which, according to some of the LGAs at the cantonal level could be further strengthened between the two LGAs at the national level.

Overall, there are differences in how local government associations ensure the representation of different interests of their members and how they are organised to influence legislation and lobby on behalf of their members. Differences can be observed regarding:

- Political influence, for example, through maintaining close personal or political contacts to the federal or cantonal parliament members.
- Organisational resources by securing a broad membership base and special regulations in the institutional structure, e.g. concerning the composition of the board of directors or the regulation concerning representation at the general meetings as well as the decision-taking and voting rights.
- Financial resources by granting specific rights and obligations to its members.

Those LGAs that represent the different types of local government generally state that they manage to balance the sometimes varying interests of urban and rural local governments well. Among the LGAs that responded to our survey, most LGAs are the same for urban and rural local governments regarding their services and commitments. All the respondents indicated their ability to represent different interests, although they acknowledged differing interests between rural and urban local governments. In most cases, there are no statutory differences in the representation of the two types of local governments, so the LGAs recognize the somewhat divergent wishes and interests of the municipality types that exist and try to serve these. Factors which indicate a successful balance of differing interests include the large membership base across all organisations, as well as the regulation of voting rights and membership fees. In most organizations, all members are treated equally, which positively affects the perception of the representation of interests. However, some cantonal LGAs do distinguish according to size regarding voting rights or the payment of membership fees (this tendency can be observed in French-speaking cantons).

To communicate with members, provide relevant services, and ensure transparency, the associations often use websites and the support of general secretariats. Thus, one of the strategies for mastering the challenge of representing the potentially different interests of ULGs and RLGs is also based on professionalisation, of which permanent offices and staff are indicators. Although requiring more financial resources, they improve the administrative capacity of the associations. In addition, differentiation in terms of specific working groups and committees can be interpreted as steps towards differentiation and professionalisation, as they pool specific expertise. Based on their expertise, committee members can more easily develop shared policy perspectives and overcome potential conflicts of interest between association members. In addition, special working groups and committees represent a vital link to the members, as they are themselves representatives of the local authorities and have a direct and significant influence on the work and direction of an association. Many of those success factors are also partly consistent with those cited by the LGAs when asked about the factors that contribute to their relationship within the IGR at the cantonal and national levels.

As for future developments regarding the representation of interests at the local level, the survey indicates that various developments are likely to make the work of the Swiss LGAs at the cantonal and national levels more difficult. These include the continued strong growth of cities, which increases the imbalances within institutions (e.g. Council of States), as well as the increasing polarization of society and the segregation of the population along formative values and lifestyles, reducing mutual understanding between urban and rural populations. Based on our analysis of the Swiss landscape at the municipal level, the steady merging of urban and rural areas increases the importance of agglomerations (almost three-quarters of the Swiss population live in such areas). Therefore, the distinction between urban and rural interests might decrease while the importance of representing the interests of the agglomeration increases.

Regarding the future development of the representation of interests at the municipal level, we observe an increase in the diversity and often the complexity of increasingly specialized issues (e.g. digitalization). As digitalization and developments in digital transformation proceed, processes are becoming increasingly interconnected between different government levels. However, the corresponding (procedural and technical) implementation is extremely challenging and requires attentive support from the municipalities and their interest groups. To tackle such future challenges more effectively and to coordinate better with individual interest organizations, greater coordination, and closer cooperation between the different LGAs are necessary. In addition to foreseeable developments such as digitalization, non-foreseeable events such as pandemics highlight the need for better coordination between the various levels (vertical IGR), primarily through cooperation with national LGAs, which have a vital interface function.

Appendix

List of the associations surveyed

Cantonal level	Canton	Participated
Gemeindeammänner Vereinigung des Kantons Aargau	AG	/
Hauptleutekonferenz des Kantons Appenzell Innerrhoden	AI	/
Gemeindepräsidentenkonferenz des Kantons Appenzell Ausserrhoden	AR	X
Verband Bernischer Gemeinden (VBG)	BE	X
Verband Basellandschaftlicher Gemeinden (VBLG)	BL	X
Association des communes fribourgeois (ACF)/Freiburger Gemeindeverband (FGV)	FR	X
Association des communes Genevoises (ACG)	GE	/
Gemeinde Glarus Nord	GL	X
Association jurassienne des communes (AJC)	JU	X
Verband Luzerner Gemeinden (VLG)	LU	X
Association des communes neuchateloises (ACN)	NE	X
Gemeindepräsidentenkonferenz des Kantons Nidwalden	NW	/
Gemeindepräsidentenkonferenz des Kantons Obwalden	OW	/
Vereinigung St. Galler Gemeindepräsidentinnen und Gemeindepräsidenten (VSGP)	SG	X
Vereinigung der Gemeindepräsidentinnen und Gemeindepräsidenten des Kantons Schaffhausen (VGGSH)	SH	X
Verband Solothurner Einwohnergemeinden (VSEG)	SO	X
Verband Schwyzer Gemeinden und Bezirke (vszgb)	SZ	X
Verband Thurgauer Gemeinden (VTG)	TG	X
Associazione dei Comuni Ticinesi (ACT)	TI	X
Urner Gemeindeverband	UR	X
Union des Communes Vaudoises (UCV)	VD	X

Cantonal level	Canton	Participated
Federation des Communes Valaisannes (FCV)/Verband Walliser Gemeinden (VWG)	VS	X
Verband der Gemeindepräsidien des Kantons Zürich (GPVZH)	ZH	X
Gemeindepräsidenten-Konferenz der zugerischen Gemeinden	ZG	X
National Level		
Schweizerischer Gemeindeverband		X
Schweizerischer Städteverband		X

References

Agranoff, R. (2004). Autonomy, devolution, and intergovernmental relations. *Regional and Federal Studies, 14*, 26–65.

Anderson, W. (1960). *Intergovernmental relations in review*. University of Minnesota Press.

Arens, A. U. (2020). *Federal reform and intergovernmental relations in Switzerland: An analysis of intercantonal agreements and parliamentary scrutiny in the wake of the NFA*. Inaugural dissertation, Bern.

Bächtiger, A., & Hitz, A. (2007). The matrix extended: federal-municipal relations in Switzerland. In H. Lazar & C. Leuprecht (Eds.), *Spheres of governance—Comparative studies of cities in multilevel governance systems*.

Bolleyer, N. (2006). Federal dynamics in Canada, the United States, and Switzerland: How substates' internal organization affects intergovernmental relations. *The Journal of Federalism, 36*(4), 471–502. https://doi.org/10.1093/publius/pjl003

Council of Europe. (2001). *Relationship between the size of local and regional authorities and their effectiveness and economy of their action*. CDLR.

Debela K.W. (2020). Local governance in Switzerland: Adequate municipal autonomy cumintergovernmental cooperation?. *Cogent Social Sciences*, 6(1), 1763889, https://doi.org/10.1080/23311886.2020.1763889.

Federal Council. (2016). *Bund, Kantone, Städte und Gemeinden dehnen Zusammenarbeit auf ländliche Räume aus*. Retrieved August 27, 2025, from news.admin.ch/de/nsb?id=65045

Federal Statistical Office (FSO). (2024). *Bevölkerungsstatistik*. The Statistical Encyclopedia.

Friederich, U., Arn, D., & Wichtermann, J. (1998). Neubildung Politischer Gemeinden im Kanton Schaffhausen. In *Überlegungen zu einer Optimalen Gemeindegrösse und zu Vor- und Nachteilen von Gemeindefusionen*. Mimeo.

Kübler, D., Schenkel, W., & Leresche, J.-P. (2003). Bright lights, big cities? Metropolisation, intergovernmental relations, and the new Federal urban policy in Switzerland. *Swiss Political Science Review, 9*(1), 261–282.

Ladner, A., & Haus, A. (2021). *Aufgabenerbringung der Gemeinden in der Schweiz: Organisation, Zuständigkeiten und Auswirkungen*. Cahier de l'IDHEAP319/2021.

Ladner, A., Keuffer, N., & Bastianen, A. (2023). Local autonomy around the world: The updated and extended Local Autonomy Index (LAI 2.0). *Regional and Federal Studies, 35*, 163–185. https://doi.org/10.1080/13597566.2023.2267990

Linder, W. (2010). *Schweizerische Demokratie. Institutionen, Prozesse, Perspektiven, Bern*. Haupt.

Peters, B. G., & Pierre, J. (2001). Developments in intergovernmental relations: Towards multilevel governance. *Policy and Politics, 29*, 131–135.

Rhodes, R. A. W. (1986). *The national world of local government*. Allen & Unwin.

RTN. (2024). *Cumul de mandats: "On ne peut pas changer une loi à toutes les législatures"*. Retrieved August 27, 2025, from https://www.rtn.ch/rtn/Actualite/Region/20240708-Cumul-de-mandats-On-ne-peut-pas-changer-uneloi-a-toutes-les-legislatures.html

Schweizerischer Gemeindeverband. (2023). Retrieved August 8, 2023, from https://www.chgemeinden.ch/de/ueber-uns/gemeindeverband/

Schweizerischer Städteverband. (2023). Retrieved August 24, 2023, from https://staedteverband.ch/de/Info/stadteverband

Steiner, R. (2003). The causes, spread and effects of intermunicipal cooperation and municipal mergers in Switzerland. *Public Management Review, 5*(4), 551–571. https://doi.org/10.1080/1471903032000178581

Swiss Parliament. (2023). Retrieved October 19, 2023, from https://www.parlament.ch/centers/documents/de/gruppen-der-bundesversammlung.pdf

Steiner, R., Ladner, A., Kaiser, C., Haus, A., Amsellem, A., & Keuffer, N. (2021). *Zustand und Entwicklung der Schweizer Gemeinden—Ergebnisse des nationalen Gemeindemonitorings* 2017. Glarus/Chur. Somedia.

Vatter, A. (2004). Challenges to intergovernmental relations in Switzerland and Japan. *Swiss Political Science Review, 10*(3), 77–102.

VGGSH (Verband der Gemeindepräsidentinnen und Gemeindepräsidenten des Kantons Schaffhausen). (2023). *Leitgedanken zur Verbandspolitik*. Retrieved October 19, 2023, from https://www.gemeinden.sh/vggsh/organisation

Open Access This chapter is licensed under the terms of the Creative Commons Attribution 4.0 International License (http://creativecommons.org/licenses/by/4.0/), which permits use, sharing, adaptation, distribution and reproduction in any medium or format, as long as you give appropriate credit to the original author(s) and the source, provide a link to the Creative Commons license and indicate if changes were made.

The images or other third party material in this chapter are included in the chapter's Creative Commons license, unless indicated otherwise in a credit line to the material. If material is not included in the chapter's Creative Commons license and your intended use is not permitted by statutory regulation or exceeds the permitted use, you will need to obtain permission directly from the copyright holder.

Chapter 17
Comparative Conclusions

Karl Kössler and Eva Maria Belser

As urbanization has become an important phenomenon in many countries around the world, both the structure of local government and the relations of local authorities with other government levels need a rethink. Urbanization sparked the emergence of huge metropolitan cities, on the one hand, and the depopulation of rural areas, on the other, which requires strategies for structural reforms and for the effective representation of both urban and rural interests in intergovernmental relations.

The case studies presented in this book have brought to light an impressive *variety* of local government structures. It is well known that local governments and their structures regularly form, change, and evolve under the radar of vertical power struggles and deals fought and made between regions and centers, and that the relative lack of attention is conducive to unconventional developments and innovations. For these as well as historic, geographic, and demographic reasons, institutional experimentation at the local level is considerable. Local government structures and relations tend to be more unique, idiosyncratic, and tentative then the structures and relations of regional and central governments which are usually more directly associated with a country's political and economic power, and which are more exposed to mediatic attention and academic scrutiny.

This edited volume has also covered a broad range of forms of how local authorities are involved in intergovernmental relations. The chapters mostly confirm that the respective subnational government remains typically the primary reference point for municipalities, even if direct relations with the national government are on the rise. While local interests may be effectively represented through informal

K. Kössler (✉)
Institute for Comparative Federalism, Eurac Research, Bolzano, Italy
e-mail: karl.koessler@eurac.edu

E. M. Belser
Institute for Federalism, University of Fribourg, Fribourg, Switzerland
e-mail: evamaria.belser@unifr.ch

© The Author(s) 2026

K. Kössler, E. M. Belser (eds.), *Local Government Structure and Intergovernmental Relations*, Local and Urban Governance,
https://doi.org/10.1007/978-3-031-99820-1_17

interactions, especially urban interests of more powerful cities, formal interactions remain a necessary complement. This holds true, in particular, for smaller rural municipalities which usually do not have enough political clout to get direct access to subnational and national governments. Although traditions vary when it comes to the formalization of intergovernmental relations, vertical conference that bring together actors (mostly from the executive branches) from three government levels (local, subnational and national) or at least two of them are widespread. While local government associations (LGAs) commonly play a key role in these conferences, their functions go far beyond just that. In all their work, however, they face the challenge of representing the often-divergent interests of urban and rural municipalities. Thus, LGAs do not only have to ensure that they are generally effective associations vis-à-vis other government levels. They also have to achieve this for all their members and concerning increasingly different realities of local authorities.

In this light, the chapters in this book centered on four particularly salient issues: (1) decentralization within metropolitan areas, (2) mergers and inter-municipal cooperation in rural areas, (3) the role of local authorities in intergovernmental conferences and (4) the representation of urban and rural interests[1] through local government associations.

17.1 Decentralized Governance Within Metropolitan Areas

The diversity of local governance structures and their highly evolutive nature become particularly apparent when the question of institutional arrangements within particularly large local units or cooperation between particularly small units are examined. How can large metropolitan areas avoid being too large and too far away from the various and diverging needs of different urban dwellers and their neighborhoods? How can decentralization—or other forms of bringing (urban) government closer to the people—work within one vibrant and interconnected metropolitan space? The different case studies present surprisingly different approaches to dealing with such metropolitan governance challenges. Most systems struggle finding an appropriate trade-off between democratic access, participation, and responsiveness of metropolitan sections with an identity to preserve or an agenda to promote, and frictions among different districts, self-interested neighborhood politics, and lack of coordination and solidarity ("not in my backyard"). Convergence on a single model is unlikely to occur, not even within the different metropolitan areas of a single country.

[1] This dualism is, of course, as simplification. Instead of a binary distinction implied by the thinking of an urban-rural divide, our point of departure is the recognition that it is more appropriate to speak of an urban-rural continuum and that local governments are located at different points of this continuum.

17.1.1 Coordinating Metropolitan Local Governments

Most metropolitan areas are composed of different local governments which must coordinate their actions to ensure a coherent planning and development of the area. Strategies and mechanisms to achieve such coordination goals differ tremendously between the case studies and their regional jurisdictions. While some federal systems opt for (repeated) amalgamation processes to achieve the greatest possible alignment between legal-political governance and rapidly evolving everyday urban life, others rely on inter-municipal cooperation or other formal or informal mechanisms to provide for coherent metropolitan governance. In a striking number of case studies, different models are experimented with—one after the other, or simultaneously—producing variations in space and time. This wealth of approaches is, firstly, due to the fact that sprawling urban areas require local governance innovation to deal with rapid urbanization and the manifold policy challenges that come in its towline. Secondly, vertical power-sharing systems, providing only loose national framework legislation or (fully) empowering the regions to deal with cities, are conducive to a diversity of governance strategies and tactics. Thirdly, metropolitan areas cannot (permanently) be captured by one simple model of governance as they are confronted with numerous intricate and interdependent tasks and develop dynamically, politically, economically, socially, and territorially. In most cases, idiosyncratic processes and power relations of various sorts have created path dependent and often highly complex *artefacts* of governance structures which sometimes focus more on enabling a lively local democracy and policy innovation, and sometimes more on coherent urban planning and efficient development. Frequently, they more or less successfully navigate between the two objectives.

It does not come as a surprise that many states and regions have pursued—or are still pursuing—the strategy of integrating neighboring municipalities that have become functionally dependent agglomerations of an urban center through amalgamations. However, whenever urban governance structures stop being "too small" to deal with city development challenges, they risk being "too big" to respond to the diverse needs of city dwellers. It is interesting to note that larger structures which have been made in the interest of efficiency, are sometimes later reversed. Urban de-amalgamation or other (re)decentralization processes seem to be almost as common as amalgamation processes.

In India, for example, the Municipal Corporation of Delhi was trifurcated into the North, the South, and the East in 2012, only to be re-amalgamated into a single entity 2022. In Montreal, the 28 municipalities on Montreal Island were also first amalgamated, but the forced merger proved to be so controversial, especially in suburbs with English-speaking majorities fearing domination by the francophone majority city, that in 2006 15 municipalities were re-created on the Island and four demerged in the suburbs. City-wide coordination is now achieved by agglomeration councils, created by the provincial government, and creating a complex "administrative archipelago". In contrast, the provincial government of Ontario opted for far-reaching amalgamation processes to govern Toronto.

In Mexico, the different municipalities of Mexico City were originally transformed into mere delegations of a new amalgamated local government. During the 2016 reform, their de-amalgamation was considered, but not accepted; instead, the delegations were upgraded into 16 boroughs. Mexico City and its 16 subdivisions are the center of a large metropolitan area, a "administrative valley", which is just as complex as the archipelago of Montreal. In addition to Mexico City, the Valley of Mexico is composed of 59 municipalities of the State of Mexico and one of the State of Hidalgo. According to the 2016 reform, a Metropolitan Development Council oversees the planning and coordinating of urban settlements, transport as well as other services. However, the federal state establishing the Council is yet to be enacted.

In Spain, amalgamations have rarely been used to match daily urban life with political-administrative borders. It was only during the authoritarian Franco regime that surrounding towns and villages were merged with Madrid and other urban centers. Ever since, the Spanish legal framework has refrained from amalgamations and, instead, provides for the possibility of creating metropolitan areas. However, only the autonomous communities of Catalonia and Valencia have made use of this option. Other regions have abstained from creating entities capable of coherently governing a metropolitan region (and of competing with regional power) and rather opted for sectoral metropolitan agencies, inter-municipal cooperation agreements, consortia, as well as public and mixed enterprises to deal with metropolitan challenges. Barcelona which has institutionalized a Metropolitan Area constitutes an outlier. However, even the Metropolitan Area of Barcelona is not governed by directly elected actors and operates more like an inter-municipal coordination body with no fora for public participation. As in other areas, the City of Barcelona tends to dominate the supra-municipal institution. Its consensual structure, however, prevents the making of urban strategies and decision which do not have the support of other municipalities. In Madrid, where the territory of the region and the metropolitan area broadly match, it is *de facto* the government of the Autonomous Community of Madrid which governs the metropolitan area. Such regional-urban government offers great advantages in efficiency but comes at the price of diminishing local government and participation.

17.1.2 Decentralizing Metropolitan Local Governments

Some metropolitan local governments are divided into districts, wards, or boroughs, but even when such subdivisions exist, their relevance and salience vary considerably between countries but often also within countries. Urban subdivisions can, first, be relevant for local representative institutions. In Canada, where most large or urban municipalities are divided into wards, provincial laws leave it to the discretion of urban municipalities to determine their importance. In particular, they decide whether or not urban councils are elected from one urban-wide electorate, or whether the wards operate as electoral districts creating different urban constituencies and guaranteeing territorial representation in municipal councils. Ward elections, meant to facilitate the representation of geographically concentrated urban groups, are the typical choice. Political representation, however, can vary significantly between different Canadian metropolitan areas, within metropolitan areas, and even within the suburban zones of metropolitan areas. When the City of Montreal was divided into boroughs, these entities mostly corresponded to formerly independent local units. Importantly, the City of Montréal was also subdivided into boroughs which created new venues for district-based representation. The 19 boroughs of Montreal, which all have a directly elected mayor and elect the borough councils as well as their representatives in the city council, assume power over local planning, roads, culture and recreation, and have become a crucial element of the political life in Montréal. This important role contrasts with the 44 wards in Toronto, which have been created in 2000 (out of the previous 28 wards, mirroring pre-existing local governments) to increase public participation and neighborhood influence. However, and in sharp contrast to the strongly decentralized system of Montreal, the wards in Toronto are little more than subordinate city council committees handling minor planning matters.

In India, the 74th Constitutional Amendment Act of 1992 empowered urban local bodies all over the country and created ward committees as sub-city entities. According to the spirit of the amendment, ward committees at the zone level are to be enabled, administratively and financially, to design and implement decentralized urban policies. As they can provide local solutions to local concerns of fragmented urban areas, such as Delhi, ward committees are seen as crucial actors for helping citizens to improve the quality of their lives. However, not all urban governance structures live up to these ideas, and in Delhi, the powers and functions of municipal councilor are greatly undermined. Just as in Montréal, Delhi suffers from service delivery overlaps and sub-city rivalry.

Since the constitutional reform of 2016, Mexico City is also divided into 16 urban subdivisions, the so called *alcaldias*, which have their origin in the colonial municipal governance structure. Other, more equal territorial entities were discussed, but vested interests prevented the process from being taken forward. Just like other subdivisions, the historic *alcaldias* have been formed or rather brought back to life to better deal with population growth and to organize service delivery more effectively. They are political-administrative bodies which are governed by a mayor and a council which are both directly elected by the *alcadia*. Otherwise, *alcadias*, which enjoy broad competencies in fields such as services, transport, public space, safety, development, education, culture, and sport, are autonomous in their internal structure. Despite their institutional autonomy and their considerable competences, *alcadias* remain institutionally subordinate and do not enjoy the autonomy of a Mexican municipality, especially in the financial sphere. The tutelage of the central government of Mexico City weighs heavily on the city's neighborhoods. The local councils thus struggle to deliver on the promise of improving citizen participation as the councils lack normative power. The mayors, not the representative councils, are the crucial actors in the neighborhoods and in the city. The Council of the City of Mexico is composed of the mayors of the 16 *alcadias* and the

Chief of Government of Mexico City. The supra-district Council, however, struggles to fulfil its mandate of planning and coordinating. As its decisions are made by consensus, confrontations as well as stalemates frequently prevent meaningful coordination.

In Spain as well, most large cities are decentralized into districts to bring local government closer to the people and to accommodate the diversity within urban governments. The reform of 2003, mandating urban decentralization, accelerated and generalized this process to increase local participation and to improve service delivery. However, as the regulation of the districts remains in the competence not of the regions but of each city, which determines the territorial delineation, the political structure, the functions and the funding of its districts, there is a considerable variety of urban decentralization. As a matter of fact, most cities have been reluctant to share functions, funds and functionaries with their subunits; as a result, the potential of district-based self-governance has not yet been fully explored in Spain. The districts, 21 in Madrid and 10 in Barcelona, rely on mere deconcentration, remain part of the operational structure of the city government and enjoy little room for maneuver when it comes to planning and improving district-based city life.

17.2 Mergers and Inter-municipal Cooperation in Rural Areas

The highly idiosyncratic and evolutive nature of local government structures can also be seen when examining territorial and cooperative dynamics in rural areas. There is an impressive wealth of means and methods small rural governments use to deal with the fact that they are unlikely to deliver services reliably if they fail to merge or cooperate. A number of questions were worth investigating from a comparative perspective: How can states impose or incentivize amalgamations without betraying the promises of decentralization and disregarding local identities, needs and aspirations? How can inter-municipal cooperation prevent or complement amalgamation without impacting negatively on local ownership and accountability? The answers that emerge from the case studies are, in this field too, much more diverse than in usual comparative studies of federalism. Few case studies offer clear and unambiguous answers, as structures and relations typically are not governed or implemented nationwide but develop regionally or even locally of their own accord, and often change dramatically over time, triggered by top-down as well as bottom-up strategies and initiatives.

17.2.1 Structuring the Rural Space

In most countries, rapid urbanization corresponds to a depopulation of rural and remote areas. Rural local governments thus are confronted with multiple challenges: to provide services to a sparse and often relatively aged population, to respond to local expectations of development or the avoidance of regression, and to deal with often severe financial constraints as well as the difficulty to attract and hold trained personnel. Amalgamations and inter-municipal cooperation for service delivery and other local tasks constitute the two most common answers to the multiple and complex challenges of the rural space. However, as the case studies show, the strategies and tactics as well as their implementation on the ground differ greatly between states and the various regions of states.

While some countries have adopted a uniform approach to dealing with (rural) local government, others accept or even encourage diversity and leave it to the regions or provinces to organize their local governments. In the former case, rural local governments have uniformly either been reorganized to form reasonable sized entities or left unchanged throughout the country; in the latter case, developments have been very different from one region to the next. In Canada, for instance, some provinces, like New Brunswick, Nova Scotia, Ontario, and Québec, have used their constitutional powers to amalgamate unreasonable small municipalities into larger ones, other provinces have, in contrast, opted for leaving the historical organization intact. In Australia and New Zealand, subnational respectively national governments originally opted for top-down amalgamation processes as the preferred strategy to uphold high quality service delivery in rural areas. Despite of century-long processes of amalgamations in Australia, which were designed to increase local government efficiency and have affected all the states and territories, the difference in size and capacity of local governments remain immense. The same is true for New Zealand with its uniform but highly fluctuating approach to local government. In addition, the top-down approaches of imposed mergers have more and more frequently been met with robust local opposition. Local councils and residents regularly fear a loss of influence, representation, local development and identity. While such opposition has not prevented amalgamation processes from being taken forward in the 1990s and early 2000s, local protests since have increased to the point that numerous actors have recently committed to no longer impose mergers. In both countries, amalgamation projects have become a political minefield. As not all of the merged municipalities have been able to reap the financial gains of scale, some areas even considered demerging. The focus of provincial and national strategies has shifted to incentivizing voluntary amalgamations and promoting combined councils which leave the territorial structure intact but allow for the use of economies of scale in specific areas.

In Italy, a country with numerous unfinished (territorial) reforms, only special, but not normal regions, have been able to use their mandate to deal with local governments effectively. Since the 1990s, their merger has been encouraged by the national government, although with limited success. Regions have also offered financial and technical support to amalgamation processes. When willing to merge local units, regions must consult the population and may approve the establishment of a new municipality if the consultation is positive. However, considerable differences exist in the organization of the consultation and the interpretation of its result. Where the regions have offered significant incentives, some mergers have occurred. However, the interest in amalgamations, complicated to plan and difficult to implement, waned in recent years.

In Mexico, most subnational constitutions provide that the state congresses may modify and merge municipalities; however, amalgamation of municipalities only rarely occur, and the creation of new municipalities constitutes the more likely use of congressional powers. Similarly, amalgamations are hardly possible in Spain. The last rural territorial reform occurred during the Franco regime and merged small and depopulated municipalities into new politically and administrative viable entities. Poland as well has refrained from making comprehensive top-down changes to the country's territorial structure at the local level. Consequently, the number of local governments in Poland remained relatively stable over time; if changes occurred, they also rather increased the number of municipalities (despite of overall population decline). Over time, the government has offered different, increasingly attractive, financial packages to incentivize municipalities to voluntarily amalgamate—with little to no effect. In 2015, measures were taken to prevent at least the further fragmentation of (rural) communities into even smaller units. New municipalities must since fulfill economic and demographic thresholds. Poland's politicians, conscience of the attachment of people to their "small homeland" and the considerable political costs of amalgamations, show no appetite for large territorial reform, and rather opt for the financial support of (too) small local governments. A major and unresolved concern of rural municipalities in Poland is the tendency of the central government to adjust the borders of cities expanding into their rural surroundings. Despite manifest opposition, the central government has allowed spreading cities to take over part of the neighboring rural municipality leaving the latter deprived of its (sub-)urbanizing territory. Such risk of territorial dismemberment creates an instability for rural areas which are in close contact with neighboring cities and hinders long-term (development) planning.

In Ethiopia, where local governments were empowered during the second decentralization phase of the early 2000s, the strengthening of the third tier included a process of dividing and merging existing local units. Just as in Mexico and Poland, divisions are more frequent than amalgamations in the Ethiopian context. States, in charge of dealing with local government, but constrained by national (development) strategies, distinguish between regular and ethnic local governments. Both types of local governments are in charge of local service delivery, ethnic ones, in addition, deal with cultural matters. Amalgamations of ethnic local governments raise ethnic self-determination issues; more generally, they are not a priority, even in regular local governments. A major challenge rather stems from the fact that boundaries are endlessly revised and units frequently divided. Neither the autonomy nor the integrity of local governments is guaranteed, and the territorial reorganization is not constrained by substantive and/or procedural rules. The few states which have adopted legal frameworks for local government allow the state executives to design and implement territorial changes as they please. Consequently, states can amend local units arbitrarily and often do so for political reasons.

17.2.2 Cooperating in the Rural Space

Where amalgamations are legally banned or politically unpractical, the key strategy to strengthen service delivery in the rural space and to decrease financial and personal stress consists in inter-municipal cooperation. Just as in the field of territorial reorganization, approaches to inter-governmental cooperation between local governments differ tremendously from one case study to the next—and often within one and the same country as well. In Australia and New Zealand, combined councils, which do not replace but complement local councils are promoted to coordinate actions and use economies of scope and scale. In some areas, more structured Joint Organizations have become popular alternatives to amalgamations. Joint Organizations, establishing purpose-specific partnerships between municipalities, are voluntary, underpinned by legislation, and financially supported.

In Italy, inter-municipal cooperation is used as a complement or alternative to (controversial) amalgamations. Conventions are widely used, sometimes even across regions. Such agreements between two or more municipalities allow for the joint delivery of a service or the joint fulfillment of a local task. Consortia for the joint management of one or public service, establishing a new local entity with an assembly, a president and a management board, are rarely used. Instead, municipalities opt for Unions of Municipalities as instruments to jointly exercise an array of functions. For smaller municipalities, establishing such a Union is mandatory. Until recently, such voluntary or mandatory Unions have been seen as precursors of amalgamations; nowadays, they are considered sustainable instruments of rural service delivery in their own right. In parallel, the regional prerogative to regulate such Unions has been limited, not least by the Constitutional Court, and yielded to national approaches of inter-municipal cooperation. Only special regions still provide for their own models and incentives of horizontal cooperation between their municipalities. As the case of Italy also illustrates, for inter-municipal cooperation to flourish in under-resourced rural areas, national and regional financial support packages incentivizing and funding autonomous and collective initiatives are necessary, in addition to a legislative framework guaranteeing local ownership and public participation.

In Poland, the right of municipalities to voluntarily cooperate is guaranteed, not only by the European Charter of Local Self-Government, but also by the Polish constitution. Seen the unwillingness of municipalities to merge and the reluctance of the government to impose a territorial reform, inter-municipal cooperation offers crucial mechanisms to allow (small) municipalities to fulfill their tasks. Municipalities can, and often do, establish Unions of local governments, i.e. new legal entities with assemblies and managements boards to which they delegate the delivery of one or several services or the fulfillment of certain tasks, such as education, transport, or other infrastructure. Municipalities can also enter into agreements and, without creating a new institutional structure, delegate the performance of a local tasks to a (neighboring) municipality. Finally, municipalities may establish or join associations supporting them in the fulfillment of their tasks and defending their interests. Just as in other countries, municipalities can, in addition to these instruments, create joint foundations or enterprises, or use other private or informal forms of cooperation. Most of these cooperations are incentivized and financially supported by the financial means of the government and, more importantly, EU funds.

When Ethiopia entered the second phase of decentralization, restructuring and empowering local governments, little to no attention was given to inter-municipal cooperation. Seen the absence of amalgamations, such cooperation would be crucial to administer and finance public services in rural areas. Instead of horizontal cooperation between woredas, zones, comprising numerous local units, often play the role of planning and coordinating across local boundaries. Zones are, however, deconcentrated actors of the state government and use top-down approaches to coordinate the action of woredas. Some states have called for the establishment of associations of woredas, which would allow for bottom-up coordination and for peer-to-peer learning, or foresee the establishment of joint committees, but no such association or committee has yet come into being. As a result, inter-municipal cooperation is virtually inexistent.

17.3 The Role of Local Authorities in Intergovernmental Conferences

17.3.1 Intergovernmental Conferences Involving Local Governments

As for institutions with participation of local authorities, insights from the chapters in this book require us to make a basic distinction between bodies that bring together two or more levels of government.

As for *two-level* bodies, a Premier's Coordinating Forum brings together in each South African province the provincial executive and municipalities. Spain is similar insofar, as its two-level bodies of intergovernmental relations (IGR) are focused on cooperation between the autonomous communities as regional governments, on the one hand, and the municipalities, on the other. Direct formal relations between the national government and municipalities are virtually non-existent in the Spanish case. This contrasts sharply with Italy where the State, Cities and Local Autonomies Conference provides a direct central-local link bypassing the regions as intermediary level of government. No two-level conferences at all, whether central-local or regional-local, exist in Poland. This seems hardly surprising given the country's lack of a strong subnational government between local and national authorities.

What further distinguishes the countries analyzed, is the degree to which municipalities are involved in *multi-level* institutions together with the national and subnational government levels. This degree is quite high in the case of South Africa. The Budget Forum and the President's Coordinating Council, the apex body of IGR, are cases in point. Moreover, municipalities are involved in the National Council of Provinces (NCOP) which is not technically a multi-level institution as defined above (because the *national* government is not part of it) but still has de facto multi-level aspects through its function represent provincial and local interests in the *national* legislative process. The South African Local Government Association (SALGA) appoints ten elected municipal councilors as representatives who may participate in the debates on matters affecting local government but may not vote. The extent to which local authorities are included in multi-level institutions is much lower in the Spanish case. As the chapter in this book points out, local government participation is foreseen in merely two out of the 43 sectoral conferences which are at the core of the IGR system. In the Italian case, such participation is foreseen in one central institution, i.e. the so-called Unified Conference including national, regional and local representatives. Compared to the Italian IGR system which also includes, as mentioned above, also two-level conferences, the Polish one is even more concentrated. Everything revolves around the Joint Commission which brings together representatives from the central government, voivodeships, counties and municipalities.

Another interesting aspect is how the creation of intergovernmental conferences with participation of local governments has been embedded in specific historical contexts. In both South Africa and Poland, these new institutions were linked to systemic transformation. In South Africa, the above-mentioned emphasis on cooperative government was necessitated by the complex distribution of functions which was in turn the result of negotiations between the apartheid regime and opposition forces during the transition period. An interesting feature was then that parliament only enacted the seminal legislation to establish cooperation mechanisms including local governments with a deliberate delay in 2005, since the aim was to have time for evaluating the practices that emerged in a "natural" manner. Poland's Joint Commission is similar insofar as its creation must be seen in the transformative context of post-communism, especially the reestablishment of municipal self-government in 1990, and equally took place as a gradual process. In this regard, the country's European integration played a role. It is no coincidence that the commission was only entrenched in an ordinary law in 2005, year after EU accession, and that the same piece of legislation also regulated local government representation in relations with Brussels. The contexts in which conferences were put in place in the Spanish and Italian cases have less to do with such wholesale systematic transformations but are still closely linked with decentralization. While the development of autonomous communities in Spain based on the 1978 Constitution soon demonstrated the need for formal IGR, these did not initially include local governments at all. It was only in 2005 that they were included for the first time through the creation of a Sectoral Conference on Local Affairs. While the Italian case shows a similar link to decentralization, the involvement of Italian municipalities, by means of the State, Cities and Local Autonomies Conference, was more systematic. After the constitutional reform on decentralization in 2001 other government levels felt the need for that to ensure two-way communication on respective responsibilities, finances, etc. in light of a changed distribution of powers.

Of course, the mere existence of conferences with participation of local governments does not in itself guarantee that actors from various government levels are really brought together. Indeed, the chapters in this book reveal enormous variety in terms of how often the members of these institutions actually meet. In South Africa, the frequency of the sessions of the broad range of IGR bodies depends on their internal regulation. But all of them meet very regularly. Italy's State, Cities and Local Autonomies Conference and Poland's Joint Commission also meet on a fairly regular basis with sessions taking place at least once a month and every 2 months, respectively. The one country which really stands out in comparison is Spain. Its Sectoral Conference for Local Affairs was only convened seven times during the almost 20 years of its existence, with all these meetings taking place in 2005–2007 to debate a proposed reform of the Local Government Act. This and the conference's failure so far to adopt its own statute about composition, functions and decision-making procedures adds to the impression that has been for all intents and purposes a single-issue body.

17.3.2 The Impact of Intergovernmental Conferences on Policymaking

Regarding the impact of intergovernmental conferences that involve local governments, one obvious key issue is the weight that their decisions carry in both legal and political terms. What these institutions have in common is the typically non-binding nature of their opinions. Admittedly, the latter are sometimes mandatory in the sense that hearing the advice is a procedural requirement. A case in point is the Italy where both regional and local governments must be heard through the so-called Unified Conference when draft legislation concerns their affairs, even if the views expressed are not legally binding. The country's State, Cities and Local Autonomies Conference does have stronger instruments like agreements at its disposal but mostly uses, as the empirical analysis of the case study in this volume shows, the weaker tool of opinions. The latter only require the consent of a majority of the members and are non-binding in nature. The same holds true for opinions of Poland's Joint Commission. As the author of the case study puts it, the body's consent benefits the national government by adding a sense of broad consensus, while its opposition is easily (and often) ignored.

Besides the largely non-binding nature of the views expressed by the conferences compared, another interesting point revealed by the four case studies is the often-differentiated impact, depending on the subject at stake. Even if the topics are usually defined very broadly, as in the Polish case, as all matters related to local government, some of them clearly play a more prominent role in practice than others. Research conducted for the chapter on Italy demonstrates that the by far most frequent subjects debated by the State, Cities and Local Autonomies Conference are the economic and financial challenges of municipalities such as their human resources, budget and, importantly from an urban-rural perspective, special investments in small municipalities. One topic that has particularly facilitated the role of intergovernmental conferences and of local government within them was Covid-19. In Spain, for instance, the realization that local authorities are key actors in fighting the pandemic contributed to the inclusion in 2021 of the chairperson of the Spanish Association of Municipalities (FEMP) in the Conference of Presidents which had until then only involved the national and regional premiers. Furthermore, FEMP has also been part of the Sectoral Conference on the Transformation and Resilience Recovery Plan which deals with projects sponsored by the large EU funds provided in the wake of the pandemic.

Having established that intergovernmental conferences often have limited impact, albeit a differentiated one according to the topic concerned, one must wonder about possible alternative channels for local governments to wield influence. In this regard, an interesting observation emerged from the chapter about the role played by SALGA. As revealed by an analysis of its annual reports, the organization relies much more on direct engagements with the National Assembly or cabinet members. This is because formal institutions such as the above-mentioned Budget Forum and NCOP play rather weak roles, respectively, as consultative body for financial relations and as institution to represent provincial and local interests in the national legislative process. Therefore, following what might be called the "iron law of lobbying", SALGA simply turns—like citizens and civil society organizations—to the places where real power lies and where local influence can be wielded most effectively. Another factor is obviously the dominance until the 2024 elections by the African National Congress (ANC) in both the first chamber of parliament and the cabinet so that intra-party dealings substituted formal intergovernmental relations. This latter phenomenon is widespread and is also reported in the other chapters. In Italy, close informal intergovernmental relations through party affiliations are reinforced by the phenomenon that mayors of major Italian cities have recently become more and more visible in public and then decided to end their local career in favor of running in national elections. In Spain, informal influence-seeking through party channels is even facilitated by the same people having at the same time political roles at different government levels. In the not uncommon case of dual mandates, mayors or local councillors are simultaneously members of the regional or national legislatures so that intra-party relations are seen as an alternative to formal intergovernmental mechanisms. While this can sometimes facilitate relations, it can also exacerbate conflict. The latter is reflected in Spain in regional governments boycotting central government policies in areas of shared responsibility and in Poland in the phenomenon of "bypassing" the Joint Commission. This means that in recent times of mounting political polarization more and more bills have been submitted to parliament by groups of MPs which are—unlike government bills—not subject to the consultation procedure involving the commission. Generally, the predominance of informal intra-party collaboration across levels of government risks that large cities have (even) more influence than small rural municipalities than they do in formal settings. Yet, there is also a different, potentially more positive link between formal and informal IGR, as the chapter on Italy highlights. Apparently, the country's conference system has also allowed for the creation of networks between those represented which then might facilitate informal relations. Overall, intergovernmental conferences that include local governments seem to be of limited importance. The clearest example is the near irrelevance of Spain's Sectoral Conference for Local Affairs which had been designed as highest body for cooperation with local authorities.

17.3.3 The Role of Local Government Associations Within Intergovernmental Conferences

Due to their high number, local authorities are typically represented collectively in intergovernmental conferences through local government associations (LGAs). A first key question is then which LGAs are admitted to these formal institutions which makes this representation more or less fragmented. In the South African case, legislation clearly states how members are nominated to the primary bodies of IGR such as the National Council of Provinces and the Finance and Fiscal Commission, and thereby affords a quasi-monopoly to SALGA. Fragmented representation is similarly absent in Spain where FEMP is the association that represents municipalities in (few) sectoral conferences and since 2021 also in the Conference of Presidents. Regarding the Italian conference system, representation is not as monopolized as in the Spanish case, even though the National Association of Municipalities (ANCI) is certainly dominant. However, the conferences also include other LGAs such as National Union of Mountain Towns and Municipalities (UNCEM), while the National Association of Small Municipalities (ANPCI) is not given a seat at the table. As the chapter in this book explains, this reflects differences between associations in terms of their political clout. While there is in Italy with the involvement of UNCEM at least a nod to the special interests of smaller rural municipalities, the aim to ensure the inclusion of the interests of various categories of local government has led in Poland to fragmented representation. The country's crucial IGR body, i.e. the Joint Commission, features members from the Association of Polish Local Governments, which represents municipal and supra-municipal governments (counties and voivodeship), and nationwide LGAs of four categories of municipalities: the country's 12 metropolises, Polish cities, towns and rural communes.

Besides the issue of how many LGAs are allowed to participate in relevant intergovernmental conferences, there remains the question to what extent these can first speak for *all* local authorities and then, once a decision is made in these institutions, also nudge their or even oblige their members to implement them. In the South African case, it is the constitutional recognition of SALGA as *the* voice of organized local government and IGR involving them rather than with single municipalities. This was further reinforced with the integration of all provincial associations as chapters of SALGA with the result that there is a direct membership of individual municipalities in this now unitary association. While FEMP in Spain is almost as broadly representative, being the only nationwide association and covering over 90% of all municipalities, it has this central status despite the fact that lobbying for local interests by regional LGAs or even single municipalities is not precluded. Speaking for all local governments obviously becomes difficult when too many of them remain outside LGAs. Although Poland's Joint Commission includes, as mentioned above, several associations, they still do not cover all municipalities which the chapter in this book also attributes to the fact that membership is entirely voluntary. As for the eventual implementation of what is decided at intergovernmental conferences, LGAs may be disadvantaged compared to other participants. As they represent a large number of local authorities, sometimes several thousands, they cannot always ensure that their members fall in line and simply accept the decisions made. In the South African case, for instance, SALGA cannot make decisions in intergovernmental bodies that are binding for its members. Instead, the association's representatives must persuade them to comply with implementation protocol which usually outline how agreements are put into practice.

If we then have a closer look at who actually represents LGAs in intergovernmental conferences, chapters in this volume show considerable diversity. To be sure, most local government members of these bodies are, as expected, from the executive branch, primarily mayors themselves, which is characteristic of Italy and Spain, in particular. While this also holds true for Poland, although the country's Joint Commission sometimes also features local councilors or civil servants as members. South Africa is quite an outlier insofar, as SALGA "only" nominates independent experts to the important Finance and Fiscal Commission and in other instances mostly sends councillors to represent local interests. In the latter case, there is, as the chapter in this volume reports, the dilemma that councillors from big municipalities may have more political but less time to effectively engage in intergovernmental conferences.

17.3.4 The Relative Importance of Urban and Rural Local Governments Within Intergovernmental Conferences

As for the respective roles that urban and rural local government play in intergovernmental conferences, the fact that they are indirectly represented by LGAs is of course crucial. Special-purpose LGAs focusing exclusively on the need of rural municipalities do exist in Spain (e.g. the Spanish Association against Depopulation and the Association of Municipalities in Mountain Areas) but are not admitted to the sectoral conferences, while they are completely absent in South Africa. This means that the representation of rural interests must rely in both cases on the general-purpose associations, i.e. FEMP and regional LGAs in Spain and SALGA in South Africa, which notoriously find it hard to give sufficient space to the manifold and often divergent interests of their members. Indeed, the South African chapter emphasizes that the country's eight metropolitan municipalities have always dominated SALGA's leadership positions so that they have two options to pursue their interests, i.e. individually or through the association. In one specific case, these local governments are even formally recognized as a particular category. The important President's Infrastructure Coordinating Commission, which is responsible for the selection and implementation of big projects, includes beyond one SALGA member the executive mayors of the eight metropolitan municipalities.

As explained above, IGR institutions of Italy and Poland foresee the formal membership of delegates from associations of rural municipalities. However, this does not necessarily mean, of course, that they wield much power. This may be due to explicit rules that give particular weight to the voices of city mayors and/or to the fact that they are more influential than their counterparts from rural municipalities in the LGAs that nominate the members of intergovernmental conferences. While the latter scenario provides for a more indirect political influence of urban local governments, the former directly entrenches their position within the intergovernmental body. The rules regarding the composition of Italy's State-Cities and Local Autonomies Conference, for instance, foresee that 14 mayors shall be appointed by ANCI. But they go beyond just that by requiring that five of them shall come from the nine major Italian cities. Currently, six members are from cities with at least 70,000 inhabitants, whereas only one is the mayor of a municipality with less than 5000 citizens which make up more than 70% of all Italian municipalities. Rural local governments are similarly outnumbered in Poland's Joint Commission with them and Polish metropolises, cities and towns each appointing two representatives. Yet, it should be mentioned that the commission has demonstrated awareness of rural distinctiveness by including among their permanent task forces from the outset a Rural Affairs Group, whereas a Group for the System of Local Government, Urban and Metropolitan Areas was only set up much later in 2012.

17.3.5 Cooperation or Non-cooperation Within Intergovernmental Conferences

A final question is then, provided that local governments are adequately represented in intergovernmental conferences, whether actual practice in these bodies reflect cooperative relations. Unsurprisingly, there is sometimes a considerable gap between ambition and reality.

This is particularly evident in South Africa. The country's constitution dedicates its entire Chap. 3 to co-operative governance. However, as the chapter in this volume points out, the relevant ordinary legislation established an IGR system characterized by a top-down coercive approach which is clearly reflected, for instance, in the workings of the President's Coordinating Council as apex body of IGR. Even during the Covid-19 pandemic, when this body met much more frequently, it remained an instrument for the implementation of national directives. Interestingly, the situation is different at the provincial level where the executive of a province and municipalities are in the Premier's Coordinating Forum more like equal partners in a cooperative relationship. Still, the provincial government does find itself in the odd situation that they shall collaborate with the municipalities based on equality, whereas they have at the same time a constitutional obligation to supervise them.

There is a similar difference between constitutional concepts and practice in the Italian case where the mid-1990s witnessed the legal regulation of a conference system, which had developed informally roughly one decade earlier. Once entrenched, this system came soon to be seen as a symbol of a move from dual to cooperative regionalism and as an expression of the constitutional principle of loyal cooperation between government levels. Yet, the dynamics within the conferences have been very much top-down with Italy's Prime Minister (or a delegated minister) convening the sessions, setting the agenda and acting as chairperson.

This is very similar in the case of Spain's sectoral conferences where the national minister responsible for the policy field concerned is clearly the person in charge. Yet, regardless of the evidently top-down dynamics in these conferences, the Spanish chapter in this book espouses a considerable degree of scepticism when it comes to the prospects of institutional reforms towards a more cooperative relationship. Instead, it is suggested that a better representation of local interests is rather ensured by IGR learning processes such as the one during the Covid-19 pandemic. At that time, the national government simply realized that a more cooperative relationship with local governments is needed, at least concerning some governance challenges.

In the Polish case, such a more balanced relationship seems to be foreshadowed by several rules of formal parity. For instance, the central government and local government send 12 members each to the Joint Commission and one member from each side is then appointed to act as co-chairs. Another indication of a collaborative relationship might be seen in the use of the notion "agree" when the relevant ordinary legislation describes the commission's decision-making procedures. However, the fact that opinions shall be agreed by both parties to the commission does not ensure that a consensus is found. One issue that has been particularly emblematic for this institution's inability to forge a compromise is the financing of education. Despite local government's often-voiced discontent with the current funding model, a new one is still not on the horizon. Thus, there is in Poland, as in other countries a substantial gap between a formally cooperative relationship and actual practice which clearly reveals an imbalance in terms of power between government levels.

17.4 Local Government Associations and the Representation of Urban and Rural Interests

17.4.1 The Formal Position of LGAs in Intergovernmental Relations

While the preceding section examined the role of local authorities in intergovernmental conferences, of course often mediated by LGAs,[2] this section is about the latter's function to represent urban and rural municipalities more generally. One first issue in this regard concerns the legal position that LGAs have in relations to other levels of government. The Article 50(2–3) of the Swiss Constitution oblige the national government since 1999 to "take account in its activities of the possible consequences for the communes" and "of the special position of the cities and urban areas as well as the mountain regions" and thus provide a certain basis for the work of the country's LGAs. However, Article 115(3) of the Austrian Constitution stands out in international comparison insofar, as it explicitly empowers the Austrian Association of Municipalities and the Austrian Association of Cities and Towns "to represent the interests of the municipalities" which evidently gives these organizations and their activities an exceptionally strong institutional guarantee. Yet, being legally enshrined is not the only basis for the legitimacy of LGAs. Even though the German Association of Cities and the German Association of Towns and Municipalities are not recognized constitutionally in a comparable manner, they derive a lot of legitimacy from their longevity. The former was founded as early as in 1905, and the latter's roots go back to the early aftermath of World War II.

An important context factor for the position of the LGAs is their embeddedness in a federal system which has several implications. First, it means that there is, albeit to different extents, a multilevel structure of associations. While the Austrian Association of Cities and Towns is more centralized with mere offices in the *Länder*, the Austrian Association of Municipalities has a decentralized organization, as its members are actually not the municipalities themselves but their LGAs in the *Länder*. The German Association of Towns and Municipalities characterized by a similar model of indirect representation. The cantonal LGAs in Switzerland are particularly autonomous, even though a regular exchange of information with the national associations takes place. Secondly, a federal system may provide space for organizational autonomy of subnational entities to such a degree that some may choose to not even establish LGAs, as in the case of two Swiss cantons. Thirdly, federalism implies that associations will be in most cases key actors in complex interactions with the subnational and national levels, even though the relations with one level may be stronger than with the other. A case in point is Switzerland where LGAs are more firmly embedded within their cantons, with relatively little federal-local interaction until the 1990s. Fourthly, local governments have fewer formal

[2] See Sect. 17.3.3 above.

procedures at their disposal for influencing federal decision-making than subnational governments. This is particularly evident in the German case where the *Länder* are co-legislators through their representation in the *Bundesrat*, while the municipalities are not involved at the federal level in any comparable way. This "glass ceiling", as the chapter on Germany puts it, implies that the role of LGAs as promotors of local interests regarding national policies is even more important.

17.4.2 *Matters Covered by LGAs in Intergovernmental Relations*

As for the subjects that LGAs deal with in their relations with higher government levels, their mandate is mostly a very broad one. As much of subnational and national legislation affects municipalities directly or indirectly, their input and influence are crucial in many different policy fields. Importantly, LGAs are not only key regarding the formulation of policies but also concerning their implementation so that intergovernmental communication occurs bidirectionally, both upwards and downwards. In fact, the services that associations provide to their members (e.g. training events, reports and advice) are often related to policies decided at higher levels of government which then, however, need to be implemented at the local level. Such a role of LGAs with regard to implementation evidently presupposes that they have effective influence vis-à-vis their member municipalities. As the Swiss chapter points out, perceptions of cantonal LGAs about such influence varies considerably, with some seeing it as a core task and other as interference with municipal autonomy.

Concerning certain matters of local relevance LGAs are in some countries involved in specific intergovernmental mechanisms. A particularly interesting example is spatial planning in Austria which is perceived as shared responsibility with municipalities being in charge of local development planning. Consequently, both the Austrian Association of Cities and Towns and Austrian Association of Municipalities are full members of the political decision-making body of the Austrian Conference on Spatial Planning (ÖROK). A transversal issue that is obviously key for the implementation of any legislation at the local level is finances so that LGAs are sometimes also involved in specific formal procedures in this area. For instance, the two associations represent the local level in the three-level talks that precede the adoption of the Financial Equalization Act which determines for each tax the respective revenue portions and thus regulates 84% of the total fiscal revenue. On the other hand, this example also demonstrates the limits of LGAs in such intergovernmental mechanisms because the federal government clearly dominates these negotiations. In contrast to this three-level mechanism in Austria, several German *Länder* such as Bavaria and North Rhine-Westphalia have established consultation procedures which bring together only them and the LGAs regarding financial issues (e.g. a distribution of funds that ensures the constitutional guarantee of financial self-government). Yet, another matter which often foresees particular involvement of LGAs is economic development which evidently needs an integrated strategy across government levels. In Germany, for instance, such overall economic planning is the aim of the Economic Council for the Public Sector, an intergovernmental body composed of federal and *Länder* ministries, as well as the LGAs. In addition, the latter are represented in a multitude of other, more specialized institutions with relevance for economic development. Cases in point are the administrative board of the Federal Employment Agency, the German Association for Public and Private Welfare, the German Association for Housing and the German Tourism Association.

17.4.3 Representation of Local Interests Through LGAs with Broad and Special Membership Base

The chapters in this volume confirm that different categories of local governments indeed have different interests in many areas. An example cited in the chapter on Germany is the country's debate about the electrification of local public transport. While cities are clearly in favor of electric buses, rural municipalities are against them because of their still short range. The introduction to this book emphasized that such divergence of urban and rural interests may make it very difficult for LGAs to speak with one voice. Indeed, there is a risk that such divergence leads them to either being muted in case of a failure to find a consensus or to a cacophony. Both these scenarios are obviously detrimental to an effective representation of local interests. Instead, a successful reconciliation of different interests can basically be achieved in two ways. Specialized LGAs can be created which represent either urban or rural interests so that a balance between them must be found *between* these associations. An alternative strategy is to have an LGA with a broad membership base that includes both urban and rural municipalities so that compromises must be reached *within* the association.

A preliminary question therefore concerns the membership of the LGAs compared in this volume. While Switzerland features at the national level the Swiss Association of Municipalities with a rather broad base, representing 71% of all municipalities, there is also the Swiss Association of Cities with a focus on urban interests. It is important to note that the two associations cannot be neatly separated, as many cities actually have dual membership. Among the cantonal LGAs surveyed for the chapter on Switzerland, the vast majority has a 100% membership base so that they can claim to speak with a strong voice for all municipalities. In Austria, dual membership is also the norm, as only nine out of the 258 cities united in the Austrian Association of Cities and Towns are not at the same time affiliated with the Austrian Association of Municipalities. The fact that the latter counts a considerable number of cities among its members entails, similar to the Swiss Association of Municipalities, that the organization cannot be seen as representing *exclusively* rural interests. Still, as both associations are the only LGAs for the many small rural municipalities in these two countries, the latter's interests are represented to some extent. It is clear from these examples and from the German case that dual membership favors urban municipalities. In Germany, many medium-sized cities, not the large ones, are affiliated with both the German Association of Cities and the German Association of Towns and Municipalities and this gives them the advantage of that they can decide in which association they want to pursue which of their interests. Moreover, urban local governments are sometimes also favored by the demographic circumstances. As the Swiss chapter highlights, there is, especially in LGAs of small cantons, often a considerable asymmetry in political power which results from the cantonal capital being much larger in population size than the other members. If the City of Schaffhausen accounts for 44% of the total population of the homonymous canton, it is easy to comprehend that its voice is more important than those of smaller rural municipalities.

As for the balancing of different interests and asymmetrical power of urban and rural local governments *within* an LGA, one formal mechanism is to adjust decision-making procedures. In fact, the majority of Swiss cantonal LGAs operates based on the principle "one member, one vote" and decisions being taken by majority vote. Only some of them, like the LGA of the Canton of Schwyz, grant bigger municipalities more votes than smaller ones. In Germany, a way to avoid the predominance of few local governments is to adhere to the principle of consensus in all of the LGAs. A downside is then sometimes that this results in agreement being reached on the lowest common denominator or decisions being postponed. Other mechanisms employed by cantonal LGAs in Switzerland to balance divergent interests are having different types of municipalities represented in leading positions (e.g. in Solothurn) and ensuring the involvement of at least one large (more urban) and one small (more rural) municipality when formal decisions are made (e.g. in Appenzell Ausserrhoden). All these efforts to balance different urban and rural interests are arguably made out of conviction that a lopsided LGA considering the needs of only some of its members will sooner or later have to face the discontent (or even exit) of other members which would in turn weaken its position as single and unified interlocutor for higher levels of government.

When it comes to balancing divergent urban and rural interests *between* LGAs, the chapters in this book reveal the relevance of several factors. First, personal links are key for effective coordination and eventually reaching compromises. This holds true, in particular, for informal contacts like the weekly or even daily calls between the presidents and chief executives of LGAs in the German *Länder*. Secondly, the balancing of interests may be facilitated by overarching institutions. In the early post-war era, the German Association of Cities had acquired a dominant position, since it claimed to speak not only for large cities but also for other municipalities, and it remains powerful today. But coordination with the other LGAs at the national level was ensured by the establishment of an umbrella organization (*Bundesvereinigung der kommunalen Spitzenverbände*) in 1953. Thirdly, the EU context may have a unifying effect on a country's LGAs. This is a lesson from the Austrian example. The offices that the Austrian Association of Cities and Towns and

Austrian Association of Municipalities have maintained at the Austrian Permanent Representation to the EU since the 1990s have closely cooperated, as both associations have the right to be informed about and comment on any issues that concern local governments. Thus, while urban-rural differences are sometimes visible at the national level, for instance in negotiations regarding the above-mentioned Financial Equalization Act, the two LGAs typically speak with one voice in Brussels and represent Austrian local government as a whole.

17.4.4 Factors of LGAs' Success in Intergovernmental Relations

There are certainly a number of political and legal factors which are conducive or detrimental to the effectiveness of LGAs in their relations with other government levels. The chapters in this book highlighted three factors: a political culture of dialogue, gaining influence through partnership and an adequate mix of formal and informal relations as complementary channels for wielding influence.

A tradition of dialogue as strategy to accommodate political differences is of course not something that can be easily achieved. It is rather a positive context factor which facilitates the work of LGAs and their impact. For instance, the chapter on the Austrian case emphasizes that the country's two nation-wide associations became quickly embedded in a post-war era culture aimed at societal and political consensus. This gave rise already in the 1950s to informal practices of consultation, even without the national and *Länder* governments being obliged to hear the LGAs. A culture of dialogue may also permeate relations within an association. As the German chapter points out, LGAs are characterized by a climate of "cooperation and commonality" rather than polarization. Indeed, this serves not only as basis for being effective in dealings with other government levels but also reinforces the cohesion and identity of local government actors.

A second important political factor concerns the self-understanding of LGAs. It is particularly evident from the examples of cantonal associations in Switzerland that they see themselves not only as staunch defenders of local interests but also as cooperation-minded partners of the respective canton in matters affecting municipalities. Close relations have arguably led to a considerable degree of political influence of the LGAs, as they are regularly consulted in exchange for their constructive role as partners. Sometimes cantonal-local relations are so close that there are people playing roles on both sides. For instance, some LGAs are obliged to have a representative of the canton in their board of directors and around 5% of local officeholders have a double mandate, being at the same time members of the cantonal parliament. While this is often seen as conducive to a strong representation of local interests, such multiple roles and loyalties may also be a double-edged sword. While in Germany, for example, many call for a further formalization of LGAs' participation in decision-making of the federal and *Länder* governments, there is also the counterargument that being too close might actually go against the interests of local governments. This concern is perhaps understandable in the German context the *Länder* sometimes tend to see "their" municipalities as an integral part of themselves and the representation of local interests as their task.

A third factor for LGAs to be effective in relations with subnational and national governments is an appropriate mix between formal and informal channel. What is appropriate certainly varies from country to country and depends on the political culture which may rely to quite different degrees on legal proceduralization as an instrument to foster intergovernmental relations.

As for formal mechanisms, those linking LGAs with the national level generally seem to be weaker than those with subnational one. In Austria, the two nation-wide associations are not formally involved in the legislative process of the federal parliament, even though they are consulted. Similarly, there is in Switzerland a pre-parliamentary consultation procedure through which federal bills are submitted to relevant political actors, among them the nationwide LGAs. In Germany, draft legislative acts tabled by a ministry which affect local governments must even be presented in a hearing to the associations before that is done with other interest groups. Yet, LGAs often regard the effectiveness of these formal procedures as insufficient. They lament, in the German case, that these procedures are largely formulated as "should" provisions and only laid down in the rules of procedure of the federal government and parliament which probably contributes to the fact that the procedures are sometimes ignored. The LGAs surveyed for the chapter on Switzerland, seem to feel equally powerless vis-à-vis the federal government, as over 90% of them rate their influence as low or non-existent. Overall, the situation is arguably better regarding LGAs' formal relations with the subnational level of government. A requirement to consult them is in some Swiss cantons entrenched in ordinary legislation and Germany also has witnessed since the 1970s a trend of formalizing more and more LGA rights to participate in the legislative process of the *Länder*. This has mostly been done through provisions in ordinary laws but sometimes also in the constitutions of the *Länder* (e.g. Baden-Württemberg).

Despite these formal mechanisms, informal channels for LGAs to represent and promote local interests to other government levels remain an important complement. This holds true not only but in particular for cases in which formal procedures are inexistent or ineffective, as often seems to be the case for local-national relations. In this light, it is hardly surprising that Swiss LGAs consider informal relations very important. They can lobby (cantonal) members of the two chambers of the federal parliament individually or target the parliamentary group *Kommunalpolitik* which deals with local politics. For similar reasons, the German LGAs focus significantly on informal contacts with the spokespersons of the parliamentary groups in charge of local affairs, as well as with the Federal Ministry of the Interior, other ministries and the conference of the heads of government of the *Länder*. These contacts appear to be intensified, upon initiative of the national and/or subnational governments, especially in times of major reforms and crises. In Germany, this was the case, for instance, in the context of the reforms of the Germany federal system in the 2000s. Informal relations typically also intensify in emergencies because local governments are often the first responders. Yet, this very much depends on the nature of the concrete emergency. Regarding the Ukraine and energy crises, for instance, the Swiss Association of Cities lamented that they were not involved enough. It seems important that LGAs have continued strong relations with both subnational and national governments. This applies to formal mechanisms and informal contacts alike.

This edited book has assembled chapters dealing with several crucial issues regarding the structure of local government and the role played by municipalities in intergovernmental relations. The different chapters have focused on particularly noteworthy and under-researched aspects of local government, decentralization within metropolitan areas, mergers and inter-municipal cooperation as tools to tackle structural challenges in rural areas, the role of local authorities in vertical intergovernmental conferences, and the representation of urban and rural interests through local government associations. All these topics are of crucial relevance for local ownership, inclusive governance, democratic legitimacy, human rights protection and service delivery. Even though most good governance indices focus on central governments, good local governance is just as decisive for the wellbeing of people and for the protection of their—rural or urban—environment. It thus seems important to build on the research results presented in this book, to broaden the geographic scope of the investigation, and to continue researching the great varieties of governance tools which large metropolitan areas, small rural villages, and the numerous areas in between constantly develop and improve to better serve their population. Their efforts seem particularly worthy of the attention of scholars and practitioners as they often continue and still thrive when national institutions are being captured by self-serving elites, undergo authoritarian turns, or are otherwise preoccupied with themselves or with matters that do not correspond to their mission to legitimately and reliably provide services to their citizens.

Open Access This chapter is licensed under the terms of the Creative Commons Attribution 4.0 International License (http://creativecommons.org/licenses/by/4.0/), which permits use, sharing, adaptation, distribution and reproduction in any medium or format, as long as you give appropriate credit to the original author(s) and the source, provide a link to the Creative Commons license and indicate if changes were made.

The images or other third party material in this chapter are included in the chapter's Creative Commons license, unless indicated otherwise in a credit line to the material. If material is not included in the chapter's Creative Commons license and your intended use is not permitted by statutory regulation or exceeds the permitted use, you will need to obtain permission directly from the copyright holder.

Index

© The Editor(s) (if applicable) and The Author(s) 2026

K. Kössler, E. M. Belser (eds.), *Local Government Structure and Intergovernmental Relations*, Local and Urban Governance,
https://doi.org/10.1007/978-3-031-99820-1

MIX
Papier aus verantwortungsvollen Quellen
Paper from responsible sources
FSC® C105338

If you have any concerns about our products,
you can contact us on
ProductSafety@springernature.com

In case Publisher is established outside the EU,
the EU authorized representative is:
Springer Nature Customer Service Center GmbH
Europaplatz 3, 69115 Heidelberg, Germany

Printed by Libri Plureos GmbH
in Hamburg, Germany